W9-BCS-939

RACISM

An American Cauldron

Third Edition

Christopher Bates Doob

Southern Connecticut State University

LONGMAN

An imprint of Addison Wesley Longman, Inc.

New York • Reading, Massachusetts • Menlo Park, California • Harlow, England
Don Mills, Ontario • Sydney • Mexico City • Madrid • Amsterdam

Editor-in-Chief: Priscilla McGeehon
Marketing Manager: Megan Galvin
Project Coordination and Text Design: Elm Street Publishing Services, Inc.
Cover Designer/Manager: Nancy Danahy
Full Service Production Manager: Valerie Zaborski
Print Buyer: Denise Sandler
Electronic Page Makeup: Elm Street Publishing Services, Inc.
Printer and Binder: The Maple-Vail Book Manufacturing Group
Cover Printer: Phoenix Color Corp.

Library of Congress Cataloging-in-Publication Data
Doob, Christopher Bates.
    Racism: an American cauldron/Christopher Bates Doob.—3rd ed.
      p.   cm.
    Includes bibliographical references and index.
    ISBN 0-321-02369-2
    1. United States—Race Relations.   2. Racism—United States.
  I. Title.
  E184.A1D66 1999
  305.8'00973—dc21   98-36707
                                                                      CIP

Copyright © 1999 by Addison Wesley Longman, Inc.

Please visit our website at http://longman.awl.com

ISBN 0-321-02369-2

12345678910—MA—01009998

Brief Contents

Detailed Contents

Preface

In the three years since the second edition of this book was published, race and racism seem to have moved more centrally into the American consciousness. Discussion has been widespread, with the president calling for a national conversation about race and analysis, and debate on this issue increasingly prominent in the mass media. It seems, however, that Americans' struggle with racism has not eased.

The tumultuous nature of the problem is apparent in the book's title. The cauldron imagery is also consistent with the conflict perspective provided by the internal colonialist theory introduced in the opening chapter and used throughout the text.

The central issue here is racism as suffered by large racial minorities in this society—African Americans, Mexican Americans, Puerto Ricans, Native Americans, Japanese Americans, and Chinese Americans—as well as by the majority group it also ensnares. The book avoids lengthy, discursive material about individual minority groups. In particular, I have provided studies and illustrations that demonstrate why institutional racism persists and how it affects people's lives. The use of internal colonialism helps keep students focused, guiding their analysis of material. I use this theory because its application can make students keenly aware of the nature of racism and, in particular, of its economic and political sources.

The opening chapter presents basic concepts and analyzes the significance of racism in American society. Chapter 2 examines theories of racism; Chapter 3 provides historical information about the largest American racial minorities. Chapters 4 through 8 explore minorities' exposure to racism in politics, the criminal justice system, violent situations, work, housing, education, the family, and the mass media. Chapter 9 analyzes racism in South Africa and Brazil, and the final chapter suggests possible solutions to racism.

I sought to create a readable book. Vignettes introduce each chapter, and narratives of specific incidents or experiences help to keep the presentation interesting and informative. The book also provides a substantial body of factual information, including historical sources, recent studies, and up-to-date statistical information.

Certain changes stand out in this edition. Readers will find more discussion about white racism, with the introduction of the concept of "the cultural camouflage for modern racism" and the analysis of white women in extremist groups serving as prominent examples. Furthermore, in an effort to emphasize that people can often effectively alleviate racist situations, I have offered more illustrations of solutions, such as procedures for preventing police violence against minorities, successful efforts to rejuvenate inner-city schools, and contributions colleges and universities can make toward eliminating or curtailing the major problems suffered by poor minority group members. This revision features about 220 new sources.

Acknowledgments

A number of individuals have played critical roles in this book's development. Several colleagues in sociology have provided invaluable commentary on the manuscript, indicating how this edition should reflect recent developments involving race and racism. The list of reviewers of this edition follows.

> Melissa Latimer, *West Virginia University*
> Joane Nagel, *University of Kansas*
> Ron Stewart, *SUNY–College at Buffalo*
> Christian Ukaegbu, *University of Wyoming*

As acquisitions editor at Longman, Alan McClare has continued to offer very effective guidance throughout the process. For this edition Cathy Wacaser of Elm Street Publishing Services did a fine job as project editor.

Once again I thank Teresa Carballal for her unwavering support and wise commentary.

Recognizing how interesting and valuable readers' input can be, I encourage any instructor or student with a comment or question about this book to write me at one of the following addresses. I promise to answer all letters or e-mail messages.

Chris Doob

CHAPTER 1

Significance of Race and Racism

■ Analysis of Racism
   Majority Group, Minority Group, Prejudice, and Discrimination
   Ethnicity, Race, Racism, and Related Concepts
■ Significance of Racism in the United States
■ Internal Colonialism
   Control over a Minority Group's Governance
   Restriction of a Racial Minority's Freedom of Movement
   The Colonial Labor Principle
   Belief in the Inferiority of a Minority Group's Culture and Social Organization
   Three Types of White Racism
   A Ku Klux Klan Member's Rejection of Racism

In 1951 Oliver L. Brown and 12 other black parents in Topeka, Kansas, went to court, contending that their children's school was inferior to those nearby attended by whites. In 1954 the U.S. Supreme Court concurred, declaring that segregating children on the basis of race deprived the children in the minority group of equal opportunity.

It was a momentous decision, producing sweeping if sometimes tumultuous change in many states. Obviously the racial picture of American education was drastically changing . . . or was it?

Forty-five years after the *Brown* case, the level of school integration has barely been altered. In 1968, the first year such national data were available, 78 percent of black students attended predominantly minority schools; that figure had barely declined, to 70 percent, by 1994. Eleven of Topeka's 26 elementary schools, a middle school, and a high school remain largely segregated (Celis, 1996). Furthermore, in many inner city areas, schools are often no less segregated today than in the middle 1950s.

In modern times the culprit is no longer laws supporting school segregation: It's century-old discriminatory housing patterns locking minority groups, most notably African Americans, into restricted residential areas. Where a person or family lives strongly affects many opportunities, including the availability of schools. Not surprisingly, the students attending segregated schools tend to be the poorest in the country.

Over recent years the proportion of American minority citizens suffering inferior education, housing, income, and other significant liabilities has remained fairly stable. In addition, public and private initiatives to confront these problems have been in decline.

Meanwhile the national sensitivity to the appearance of racism has become acute, penetrating all major institutional areas. Consider, for instance, the furor created when, following black golfer Tiger Woods's victory at the 1997 Masters, Fuzzy Zoeller, a white golfer, referred to Woods as "a little boy." Zoeller further urged that when Woods exercised the winner's privilege to choose the main course at the next Champions' Dinner, he not opt for fried chicken and collard greens. Although Zoeller soon apologized for what admittedly was an insensitive remark, he was quickly fired as Kmart's golf spokesman and felt compelled to drop out of the upcoming Greater Greensboro Classic (Sandomir, 1997). This was only one of many recent cases where a sports personality found that sporting officials, business personnel, reporters, and the public had become increasingly antagonistic toward racist statements.

Perhaps the above events represent our society's current attitudes about race and racism: There is considerable heated discussion about the topics but little effective drive to resolve the most virulent problems. To do so would require a commitment that both wealthy and powerful groups and the public at large currently appear unprepared to make.

This book focuses on racism among large American racial minorities—African Americans, Mexican Americans, Puerto Ricans, Chinese Americans, Japanese Americans, and Native Americans.[*] By 1990 nearly one in four Americans had African, Hispanic, Asian, or Native American ancestry, a sharp increase from 1980 when the proportion was about one in five (Barringer, 1991). By 2010 about 38 percent of children under 18—nearly two in five—will belong to racial minorities (Schwartz and Exter, 1993: 101).

Throughout the book I provide ideas, concepts, theories, and information that will help readers understand why and how racism has developed in our society. Once understood, this deadly disease becomes vulnerable to attack and defeat.

The upcoming discussion about concepts focuses primarily on action, for what people think and feel is important largely to the extent that it affects what they do. Since this book ultimately aims to help lessen the impact of racism, the focus on action seems expedient and will persist throughout all chapters.

---

[*]Currently several racial groups are referred to by more than a single term. My response to this ambiguity is to interchange the terms "Chicanos" and "Mexican Americans," "Indians" and "Native Americans," and "blacks" and "African Americans." A national survey of black respondents found that 17 percent preferred "African American," 17 percent "black," and 58 percent showed no preference; a similar pattern appeared in three surveys done earlier in the 1990s. Slightly more men opted for "African American" while slightly more women chose "black" (Moore, 1995).

Analysis of Racism

Studying a sociological topic like racism requires an approach similar to building or bridge construction; in both cases, tools are necessary. As befits an intellectual exercise, the tools used here are not material but analytic, sociological concepts that define certain key issues that will frequently arise throughout this work. In the pages ahead, we examine two sets of concepts—first, majority group, minority group, prejudice, and discrimination, and second, race, racism, and related concepts.

Majority Group, Minority Group, Prejudice, and Discrimination

A **majority group** is a category of people within a society who possess distinct physical or cultural characteristics and maintain superior power and resources. In contrast, a **minority group** is any category of people with recognizable racial or ethnic traits that place it in a position of restricted power and inferior status so that its members suffer limited opportunities and rewards. Minority group members are inevitably aware of their common oppression, and this awareness helps create a sense of belonging to the group. It is important to understand that majority or minority status has no intrinsic relationship to group size. For instance, sometimes a minority group has been many times larger than the dominant group in the society. Such a situation existed when the European countries established colonies in Africa, Asia, and the Americas. In other cases—African Americans in the United States, for example—the minority group is smaller in numbers than the dominant group. Minority status is the result of a subordinate position in society, not of group size.

Prejudice is a highly negative judgment toward a minority group, focusing on one or more characteristics that are supposedly uniformly shared by all group members. If a person rigidly believes that everyone within a racial or ethnic group is innately lazy, stupid, stubborn, or violent, then that person is prejudiced toward the group in question. Racial, ethnic, and religious prejudice are the most prominently discussed types. In general, prejudice is not easily reversible. This fact distinguishes it from a "misconception," in which someone supports an incorrect conclusion about a group but is willing, when confronted with facts, to change his or her opinion.

When one group of people is prejudiced toward another, stereotypes are inevitably used. A **stereotype** is an exaggerated, oversimplified image, maintained by prejudiced people, of the characteristics of the group members against whom they are prejudiced. In an early study of stereotypes, blacks were considered superstitious, lazy, happy-go-lucky, ignorant, and musical while Jews were designated shrewd, industrious, grasping, mercenary, intelligent, and ambitious (Katz and Braly, 1933). A recent study of stereotyping found that "there is a clear, consistent contemporary stereotype of blacks and that this stereotype is highly negative in nature" (Devine and Elliott, 1995: 1146). A second study corroborated this conclusion but found that the use of stereotypes declined with increased education (Plous and Williams, 1995).

Individuals maintaining stereotypes often find that their oversimplified conclusions offer a more orderly, straightforward analysis of a minority group than a non-stereotyped evaluation would provide. Furthermore, stereotypes help to either confirm that a downtrodden group should remain in its lowly position or encourage members of the dominant group to push down minority group individuals who are starting to achieve some economic and political success (Simpson and Yinger, 1985: 100–101; van den Berghe, 1997). Recent research has shown that whites who perceived members of their racial group as more hard-working, intelligent, and peaceful than minority groups were less positive about issues involving equal opportunity and multiculturalism (Link and Oldendick, 1996). The presence of stereotypes, in short, can affect people's policy positions.

One of the disturbing, potentially tragic qualities of stereotypes is their self-fulfilling nature. A **self-fulfilling prophecy** is an incorrect definition of a situation that comes to pass because people accept the incorrect definition and act on it to make it become true. For instance, if white teachers believe that minority children are superstitious, lazy, happy-go-lucky, and ignorant, then they are unlikely to make a serious effort to help them learn. The students, in turn, will recognize the teachers' disinterest or contempt and will probably exert little effort in school. The teachers see "confirmation" of what they already "know"—that their minority students are inferior. This concept vividly illustrates how prejudice serves as a rationalization for discriminatory behavior.

One more issue to consider is whether minority group members' stereotyping can be considered racist. To begin, minority group members sometimes develop stereotypes that assert their own superiority. For instance, Leonard Jeffries, a political scientist at the City University of New York, described whites as "ice people," who are materialistic, greedy, and driven to domination while characterizing blacks as "sun people," who are kind, caring, and communally oriented (Hacker, 1992: 28–29). These descriptions qualify as stereotypes, but it is debatable that they are racist. Many analysts of race and racism believe that behavior only qualifies as racist if it has the capacity to hurt the members of another racial group, and minority group members' stereotypes generally lack the power to inflict such damage.

While prejudice and the use of stereotypes involve negative judgments toward a minority group, discrimination imposes limitations on a group. **Discrimination** is the behavior by which one group prevents or restricts a minority group's access to scarce resources. Addressing its clear presence in American society, sociologist Peter Rose indicated that even a Martian sociologist on a first visit to the United States would realize that with much of the power held by white males, "the status hierarchy of American society is keyed to color—and to gender as well." He added, "The double traits are related to perceptions deeply rooted in this culture" (Rose, 1997: 9).

The basic position throughout this book is that while discrimination and prejudice influence each other, discrimination has had a greater impact in the social world. Historically the majority group has discriminated against racial minorities for its own political, economic, and social advantage. Prejudice has been a rationalization for this exploitation. In fact, researchers have found that discrimination can occur without prejudice (Campbell and Pettigrew, 1959), and prejudice is neither necessary nor sufficient to produce discrimination (Kutner, Wilkins, and Yarrow, 1952; L. G. Warner and DeFleur, 1969).

Racism involves both discrimination and prejudice, as the following analysis indicates.

Ethnicity, Race, Racism, and Related Concepts

In many people's minds, ethnicity is confused with race. While race usually focuses on physical characteristics, ethnicity concerns cultural traits. Thus **ethnicity** is a classification of people into a particular category with distinct cultural or national qualities. Ethnic groups differ on such issues as values, language, religion, food habits, sexual behavior, recreational patterns, and outlook on work, and the culture of an ethnic group creates a sense of identity among its members.

In U.S. society ethnicity is often synonymous with national group membership. There are Chinese Americans, Irish Americans, Italian Americans, Mexican Americans, Polish Americans, and many other groups. The white ethnic groups are not subjects for this book since they share the same race as the majority group and thus cannot be the victims of racism and, in fact, would widely be considered members of the majority group.

We can begin the discussion of race with the distinction between social and biological definitions. Social races are categories of people that the majority group designates as sharing membership that endures throughout the life span and conveys certain rights and obligations. At first glance this might seem like a straightforward description, but it involves practical difficulties. While members of a given social race sometimes appear racially similar, in other cases they do not. So how is membership in a social race established? Generally there has been one way—descent: Regardless of racial appearance, individuals belong to a social race if they are at least partially descended from individuals who are confirmed members. But what if the particular society, as in Brazil, does not use descent as a basis for establishing membership in a social group, or what if an individual comes from mixed parentage? Then social-group membership is difficult or impossible to establish convincingly (Harris, 1968).

Biological definitions of race have been equally confusing. While many criteria, including skin color, hair and eye color, hair texture, nasal index (the relationship between the nose's length and width), lip form, head shape, and genetic distribution, have been used to distinguish racial types, none of the criteria taken singly has been able to establish distinct racial groups. For instance, skin color, widely considered the most obvious criterion for distinguishing races, is not an obvious indicator when analyzed thoroughly: There are wide variations within what are designated the major racial divisions of human beings, and considerable overlap among these racial divisions also exists (Molnar, 1975; Montagu, 1974).

Over the past several centuries, however, the danger of imprecision did not discourage efforts to develop racial classifications. In 1735 Carl von Linne produced an analysis of human varieties in which American Indians (Native Americans) were summarized as reddish in color, with thick black hair and a personality that was considered "persevering, content, free"; Europeans were described as "light, active, ingenious" and "covered with tailored clothes"; Asians were labeled "severe, miserly, haughty"; and Africans as "crafty, lazy, negligent, anointed with oil" and "governed by whim" (Count, 1950: 359).

This scheme was influential, and yet a rival outlook also developed during that era. The eighteenth century was a period in which leading scholars believed that the influence of education and the natural environment could exert a powerful impact on human beings. A prominent European belief held that the great apes were actually human beings whose progress had been blocked by an unfavorable environment. In the United States, Samuel Stanhope Smith argued that dark skin color was a physical phenomenon like freckles and that with sufficient exposure to the sun, whites could become blacks. Smith contended that the reverse process occurred in the celebrated case of Henry Moss, a Virginia slave who appeared to have lost skin pigmentation after moving from the South to the North.

By the early nineteenth century, however, leading thinkers rejected the conclusion that short-term environmental factors affected people's racial type. Because of a growing knowledge of geology, scholars began to realize that the human species had evolved over a much vaster length of time than previously recognized. Thus, while scientists still accepted the idea that savages could become English gentry, whites or Caucasoids were considered thousands of years more advanced than the other races (Harris, 1968). By the middle and late nineteenth century, prominent leaders supported social Darwinism, which, as we will see in Chapter 3, claimed that a white elite's uncompromising pursuit of its self-interest would promote the most universally beneficial social evolution.

Recent genetic findings have indicated that all members of modern humanity are descendants of Africans, only differentiating into racial groups 50,000 years ago—not a million years ago as once believed. A pair of experts on human evolution concluded that "Homo sapiens must be a startlingly homogenous species. We simply have not had time to diverge genetically in any meaningful manner" (Stringer and McKie, 1997: 15).

Such evidence leads many anthropologists, whose research is often concerned with race, to reject the concept as a biological category. A number cite genetic evidence, indicating that some tests suggest greater variety within any of the so-called races than between one given race and another. In addition, while claims have been made that races have distinct traits, such as shovel-shaped incisors, epicanthic folds over part of the eye, or certain blood types, sorting people according to such traits produces unexpected results—creating, for instance, a "race" combining Swedes and Native Americans with many Asian groups if shovel-shaped incisors are singled out as a trait. Finally, if the division of races into three broad categories truly has a biological basis, then any observer should be readily able to place people into the three groups. The reality, however, is that cultural standards intervene, meaning that the racial group into which a given individual is placed is often not firmly established and can vary from one culture to another (Begley, 1996).

Clearly the designation of racial membership is an imprecise process. Most frequently **race** refers to a classification of people into categories falsely claimed to be derived from a distinct set of biological traits. Racial classification proves useful to the majority group, which is able to use its power both to subordinate minority groups and to establish claims of their inferiority.

On the other hand, the traditional classification of racial groups can prove beneficial to minority groups. Some minority organizations have opposed the Census Bureau establishing a new "multiracial" category, arguing that its inclusion could detract from their group's current numbers and thereby make it more difficult to win job discrimination cases based on claims that the racial group is underrepresented in a particular job area compared to its availability in the relevant labor pool. In July 1997 a federal task force also opposed the idea of a multiracial category, declaring that it would create confusion by lumping together individuals who are the products of different racial combinations—for instance, placing in the same category offspring of a black and white relationship and the children of Asian and white parents. Various surveys have found that between 1 and 2 percent of Americans would place themselves in the multiracial category. While that percentage is small, it has been increasing in the past two decades (Holmes, 1997a, 1997b).

The American tradition has supported a sharp division of racial categories, particularly between whites and blacks. The so-called "one-drop rule," which has prevailed since the days of slavery, states that a person with any black ancestry is considered black. This rule, which was upheld as recently as 1986 in a case that was appealed to the U.S. Supreme Court, once helped legitimate slavery and afterwards promoted a racial caste system. A writer noted, "Most Americans seem unaware that this definition of blacks is extremely unusual in other countries, perhaps even unique to the United States, and that Americans define no other minority in a similar way" (Davis, 1996: 42). Such a harsh standard for distinguishing blacks and whites in American society aptly illustrates that the classification of people into different races promotes racism.

Racism is the belief that actual or alleged differences between racial groups assert the superiority of one racial group. A racist outlook opposes a belief in racial equality, which contends that if the members of different racial groups are given equal opportunity to develop their talents, a similar distribution of talent will appear in each group (Hacker, 1992: 24–25).

Two types of racism exist: individual racism and institutionalized racism. **Individual racism** is an action performed by one person or group that produces racial abuse—for example, verbal or physical mistreatment. Frequently this type of racism is intentional, but it need not be. One might argue, for instance, that individual racism occurs when a white customer seeking information approaches a group of five store employees and addresses the only white member, assuming that this individual is better informed than the others.

Currently individual racism remains fairly common. In lengthy interviews with 37 middle-class blacks, 24 respondents reported incidents in the previous two years concerning individual racism in workplaces, schools, restaurants, and retail stores, and 15 research subjects revealed incidents of street discrimination (Feagin, 1991). Analysis of and research on the topic continue (Gibson, 1996; Jackman, 1996; Tuch and Hughes, 1996a, 1996b).

While individual racism is surely less common than in the past, the impact of particular incidents can be shocking. Consider this response to a questionnaire item in which a student asked her respondents whether they had ever been the victims of racism. A 24-year-old black woman replied:

> I was at the corner of a street getting ready to cross when about five white males ran the red light, drove as close to the curb as possible, and screamed in my face, "Run the nigger over!" I jumped back to avoid getting hit and looked in bewilderment searching for this "nigger." That was my first racist experience, and the first time I had ever been called a "nigger." I became overwhelmed with hate, anger, and fear. (Cloud, 1994)

While undoubtedly less common than in the past, cases of individual racism continue to receive public attention. At this writing recent examples include Fuzzy Zoeller's statement about Tiger Woods, Abner Louima's torture by New York City policemen (examined in Chapter 4), and Texaco executives' racist statements and actions (described in Chapter 5). Unfortunately, by the time the third edition of this text appears, other notable, ugly, and brutal examples will be in the public eye. Furthermore, as analysts of every new prominent illustration of individual racism point out, countless other cases similar to the publicized event have occurred and will occur. Toward the end of the chapter, we discuss another issue involving individual racism.

Institutional racism, unlike individual racism, is not an immediate action but the legacy of a past racist behavioral pattern. Specifically **institutional racism** refers to the discriminatory racial practices built into such prominent structures as the political, economic, and education systems. The idea of institutional racism is distinctly sociological, emphasizing that social structures establish norms guiding people's behavior. By accepting the norms maintained in racist structures, individuals invariably perpetuate discriminatory conditions.

It seems useful to examine institutional racism in detail since many people find this important concept difficult to grasp, not appreciating that within many structures of American society—for instance, communities, schools, work organizations, the criminal justice system, and government agencies—the impact of institutional racism has dramatically limited many citizens' chances for success.

Perhaps the most destructive type of institutional racism involves housing. Systematic patterns of housing discrimination that began at the turn of the twentieth century and received support from journalists, politicians, business people, and most citizens forced African Americans to reside in restricted areas. By about 1940 the boundaries of modern inner-city ghettoes were established in northern and midwestern cities (Massey and Denton, 1993). Living in such areas places residents at an enormous disadvantage concerning schooling, jobs, health, mental health, safety, and life satisfaction.

Housing segregation demonstrates how institutional racism can promote individual racism: Once segregated living areas were established, realtors, bankers, and politicians conspired to maintain the status quo, engaging in individual racism. Charles Bromley, a specialist on housing segregation, indicated that sometimes realtors "will rely on code words, telling a white person 'you wouldn't feel comfortable here,' while a black person will be told 'there's nothing in your price range here.'" A report issued by the Department of Housing and Urban Development estimated that each year there are about two million cases of housing discrimination against African Americans and other minority groups (Minerbrook, 1996: 173).

While individual racism is often formidable, it can be attacked and subdued more easily than institutional racism. Whether a case of individual racism involves housing discrimination, racist comments about public figures, or some other act, authoritative figures can usually do two things: first, identify the racist action; and, second, devise an appropriate response, censuring or punishing the racist behavior.

But institutional racism is another story. With public support and funding distinctly limited, what practical policies can one devise to make racially integrated housing available to the many millions of African American and Latino citizens living in ghettoized inner-city areas or to equalize the quality of education for American children of all racial groups? There are no immediate culprits at whom one can point and certainly no easy solutions.

Finally, in this introduction to concepts related to racism, we need to consider sexism, which all too often accompanies racism. **Sexism** is a set of beliefs that actual or alleged differences between women and men establish the superiority of men. Like racism, sexism is a rationalization for political, economic, and social discriminations—in this case against women. As we proceed through the book, we encounter a variety of situations where women are the simultaneous victims of both sexism and racism.

Significance of Racism in the United States

Although such prominent social theorists as Émile Durkheim, Karl Marx, and Max Weber differed on many issues, they agreed that ethnicity and race were relatively unimportant concepts. Analyzing the development of industrialization, they felt that both the social bonds and conflicts created by people's ethnic or racial status were characteristics of preindustrial times and would disappear in the industrial world. They believed the discriminatory tendencies associated with those narrow, prejudice-laden ties would give way to more rational relationships that would transcend ethnicity and race and help accomplish the practical goals of modern life (Bell-Fialkoff, 1994; Blauner, 1972: 3–4).

The tendency to dismiss or de-emphasize the importance of race and racism is not limited to the past. In *The Declining Significance of Race*, William Julius Wilson (1978) concluded that while modern American capitalism has maintained an under-class of poor people, many of whom are black, the process producing that result has been largely color-blind (Wilson, 1978, 1987).

According to Wilson, there have been three stages of American race relations between blacks and whites. The first stage was blatantly racist, with African Americans exploited as slave workers on plantations and farms. The second stage began with the emancipation of slaves; during the next half-century, industrial expansion was accompanied by both class conflict and racial oppression. The third and current stage involves the transition from racial inequalities to class inequalities.

Wilson concluded that for modern African Americans legalized racial inequality is no longer a barrier. The passage of equal employment and affirmative action legislation has made it possible for blacks with appropriate educational credentials and training to get good jobs and move comfortably into the middle class. In contrast, African Americans, other racial minorities, and even whites who do not have these credentials find job possibilities increasingly limited. Wilson contended that affirmative action programs, set up with the best of intentions, have increased opportunities for privileged African Americans but have not improved chances for poor blacks, thus producing growing economic class divisions among blacks (Wilson, 1978: 19).

While Wilson did not dismiss racism or absolve society of responsibility for people's poverty, many felt that by subordinating race to class, he was misrepresenting black Americans' lives and also undercutting their role in the struggle for equality. One sociologist indicated that Wilson would have saved himself a lot of trouble if he had called the book *The Rising Significance of Class* (Remnick, 1996: 100).

Wilson's critics have emphasized two limitations to his central conclusion about the declining significance of race—one involving the continuing objective significance of racism and the other, its current subjective importance.

First, evidence indicates the extensive persistence of racism in both individual and institutional form. In the chapters on politics and the criminal justice system, work and housing, education, the family, and mass media that follow, we will discuss studies showing that while racism might often be more subtle than in the past, it remains alive and healthy. Particularly significant is the continuation of institutional racism. Racist policies established in the past produce increasingly destructive impacts for minority group members even though government officials and business leaders are no longer openly promoting those policies. For instance, once ghettoes inhabited by racial minorities are established, they continue to grow in size, providing highly restrictive educational and occupational opportunities for the steadily expanding residential body (Rusk, 1993: 47).

Second, there is the subjective dimension of racism. Political scientist Andrew Hacker suggested the significance of this issue while discussing blacks' representation in the mass media. He wrote, "When black Americans go to movies, turn on television, or simply scan the comic strips, it seems as if their nation hardly knows or cares they exist" (Hacker, 1992: 22). A recent study found that blacks are more inclined than whites to see black-white relations as problematic. Compared to whites, blacks perceive both more widespread black hostility toward whites and more white hostility toward blacks (Sigelman and Welch, 1993). Another investigation focused on reports of blacks and whites of similar socioeconomic status, of blacks and whites describing their psychological well-being and quality of life over the 14-year time span from 1972 to 1985. Differences between whites and blacks on these reported feelings remained stable for the time period. The overall result was that blacks had lower life satisfaction, less general happiness, less trust in people, less marital happiness, and lower self-rated physical health than whites. The researchers concluded that being black means "a less positive life experience than being white" (Thomas and Hughes, 1986: 839).

Consider a personal testimony. In *Makes Me Wanna Holler,* journalist Nathan McCall (1994) indicated that growing up black in American society, he felt devalued. Like Andrew Hacker, McCall referred to blacks' representation in the mass media. Sitting spellbound in front of the television, he would drink in the beauty of whites' "ivory skin, which seemed purer, cleaner than my own." At the age of 7 or 8, McCall saw a Clairol hair-color commercial featuring a close-up on a pretty white woman "who sensually tossed her blond mane backward and forward all over her face. Near the end of the commercial, a throaty voice chimed in and asked, 'Is it true blondes have more fun?'" The image stuck with McCall. A group of whites riding in a convertible with their long hair blowing in the breeze reminded him of the blonde's flowing hair. Yes, he decided, whites have more fun (McCall, 1994: 11–12).

As a journalist at the *Atlanta Journal-Constitution,* McCall continued to confront the issue of race. He met blacks who denied that race remained a significant factor— who felt that it was time for African Americans to stop using racism as an excuse for their own shortcomings. Such people, McCall indicated, promoted a detached attitude toward racial issues. He wrote: "The suggestion was that, somehow, if you had allowed racism to make you mad, then you were defeated. I felt the opposite. I felt that any black person who had no anger was defeated" (McCall, 1994: 292).

Let me make a final comment on Wilson's thesis. His assertion of the declining significance of race raises a useful point: that modern conditions limiting minorities' opportunities extend beyond the issue of race. While acknowledging that point, I believe that ample evidence indicates that in the modern world, racism remains a powerful, destructive reality.

In a provocative article, Troy Duster (1987) suggested that when two distinctive social groups, such as whites and African Americans, are in contact, and the members of one group plan to study the other, the most fundamental issue involves what questions are posed and answered. For instance, whites, who have supplied the majority of race-relations researchers, have often begun an investigation of blacks focusing on a question similar to this one: Which group is more likely to have members living in poverty? The answer, Duster indicated, is that African Americans are about three times more likely than whites to be living in poverty. From this information researchers are likely to pursue studies of welfare and its apparently debilitating effect on black communities as well as the absence of a strong work ethic. Recommendations emerging from such research will emphasize the necessity of work-fare programs that force "the lazy parasites" to support themselves and to stop living off productive taxpayers.

On the other hand, Duster indicated, researchers studying black citizens might begin with this question: Between blacks and whites in America, which group is more likely to earn its income by working? The answer is that while blacks obtain 80 percent of their total income from wages and salaries, whites receive only 75 percent of their total income from that source. While blacks receive about $1.2 billion from private property or investment sources, whites obtain $87 billion. From this perspective it seems that whites, not blacks, are more inclined to live off "the fat of the land." Investigators primed with the answer to this second question are then likely to initiate a distinctly different investigation from the first one. They might be particularly interested in discovering why the once highly regarded American work ethic seems less apparent among whites than among blacks.

Thus the questions asked are fundamental, structuring the substance of research, its results, and the recommendations investigators make. Coming back to the present work, we need to find a question broad and incisive enough to guide our inquiry. Duster suggested the following question: "How and why has race been the persistent category of advantage throughout every generation of the nation's history?" (Duster, 1987: 12).

Starting with Duster's question, analysts recognize that American society has consistently practiced racism, with racial minorities invariably losing out in the process. One possible reservation about Duster's question involves the *the* in the phrase "the persistent category of advantage." Many sociologists would argue that social class has been equally persistent, and it seems impossible to determine whether race or social class wins the persistence contest.

Duster's question indicates the importance of historical analysis. To understand why racism has been so persistent in American society, investigators must dig into history. Not only academic specialists but activists recognize the importance of this point.

In this book the importance of historical discussion is apparent not only in Chapter 3, which is devoted to history, but also in major sections focused on historical analysis in various other chapters.

Duster's question also suggests a conflict-theory approach. **Conflict theory** contends that the struggle for power and wealth in society should be the central concern for sociology. Over the past half-century, this perspective has been widely applied to racism. For instance, John Dollard (1937) and W. Lloyd Warner and Leo Srole (1945) indicated that when slavery was abolished, white Southerners established a caste system maintaining segregation in all private and public facilities and ensuring blacks' economic, political, and social disadvantage.

More recently such conflict theorists as Mario Barrera (1979) and Robert Blauner (1972) have described **internal colonialism**, where the control imposed on indigenous racial minorities passes from whites in the home country to whites living within a newly independent nation. This approach appears in the next section and throughout the book.

Why use this theory? Internal colonialism addresses what Bill Lawson (1992) has called "the moral discourse" of discrimination against minorities. While whites often acknowledge the historical inequities imposed on minorities, the discussion and analysis of those issues emanate from their—the oppressors'—cultural tradition. Thus they fail to appreciate the concrete realities of racism for current minority groups. The tenets of internal colonialism are different: They address, or at least attempt to address, such realities, thereby seeking to show how racism impacts its victims' daily lives.

Internal Colonialism

The ideas of control and exploitation are central to internal colonialist theory. Like colonial subjects, members of American racial minorities have been subjected to a battery of extreme political, economic, and social discrimination. They receive limited representation in the political process, and where they live and work is restricted. They labor long and hard for low wages, and they receive inferior food, housing, education, and medical care.

Four conditions of internal colonialism, all of which have been present in American society, are (1) control over a minority group's governance, (2) restriction of its freedom of movement, (3) the colonial labor principle, and (4) belief in the inferiority of racial minorities' culture and social organization (Blauner, 1972: 53–70). Each point is briefly discussed and at least one modern illustration is included in the analysis.

Some of the upcoming examples suggest that when minorities can locate the sources of oppression described by internal colonialism, they are positioned to attack that oppression.

Control over a Minority Group's Governance

Historically, whites imposed government control on racial minorities, making the decisions that determine major outcomes in their lives. One study found that on the Fort Yuma Reservation in California, where Quechan tribespeople are permitted to elect their leaders, government officials still impose a great deal of control—for instance, not providing federal funding for business development unless their favored governing style is maintained. Quechan leaders indicated that while their approach supports more argument and leadership turnover than officials wanted, the Quechan style represents a modern application of their traditional approach—improving people and practices by a process of continuous criticism. Government officials were unimpressed and threatened to cut funding (Bee, 1990).

Sometimes minorities combat an oppressive power structure. In 1987 in Providence, Rhode Island, the multiracial (African American, Latino, Asian American, and white) families in a poor section of the city recognized that unless pushed, city officials would do little or nothing for poor groups. So push they did, forming a group called DARE (Direct Action for Rights and Equality) and demanding the renovation of a deteriorated playground in their neighborhood. At the high point of the protest, 75 parents and children carrying signs and accompanied by members of the media marched into the private office of the parks commissioner, chanting, "We want a tot lot. We want a tot lot." Faced with this pressure, the commissioner agreed to have the playground cleared, new play equipment installed, and the area fenced in. DARE implemented a similar strategy in other poor sections of the city, eventually persuading the city to renovate 10 playgrounds and clean up over 200 vacant lots (Toney, 1996: 17–18).

Restriction of a Racial Minority's Freedom of Movement

Whites stringently limited Indians' and blacks' freedom of movement. Indians had their territory invaded, and for over 400 years, they were systematically deprived of their land and freedom and eventually forced to settle on reservations. Blacks, on the other hand, were transported against their will from Africa to the United States, where they were enslaved until the end of the Civil War. Then, while technically freed, they continued to encounter limitations on their physical freedom. In modern times such limitations still persist. A half-dozen studies conducted in England and the United States indicated that police were more likely to stop, search, and interrogate blacks than whites (Norris, Fielding, Kemp, and Fielding, 1992).

The Colonial Labor Principle

The colonial labor principle indicates that racial minorities must serve white controllers' interests and needs. While capitalist theory emphasizes a free market and free labor, these privileges have primarily been restricted to whites. Historically, racial minorities have been required to serve at the pleasure of those who owned or employed them. They have been expected to "know their place," to be resigned to less-than-full participation in society and denied the rights and privileges reserved for whites. This limitation applies even to occupational areas where minorities have been very active. In April 1994 Nolan Richardson, the coach of the Arkansas men's championship basketball team, remarked that whites retain narrow perceptions of blacks' role in sport, including the coach's role. Whites, Richardson said, recognize that black coaches can be good recruiters and effective motivators. He added, "But we're never great coaches" (Rhoden, 1994: 4). Whether the reference is to coaching or some other occupation, whites have generally believed that the top thinkers, the master strategists, are invariably like them—white.

The reality described by the colonial labor principle is widely under attack. One writer noted that for two decades in California and southwestern states, immigrant workers have been "the backbone of nearly every strike in some of the hardest-fought labor struggles since the farm workers' battles of the late 1960s." Factories and work-places, he observed, "have become pressure cookers, waiting for something to blow" (Bacon, 1996: 98) because such workers as drywallers, framers, janitors, grape pickers, electronic assemblers, and foundry and metal laborers are increasingly willing to strike for better wages and working conditions.

Belief in the Inferiority of a Minority Group's Culture and Social Organization

Finally, a basic tenet in the internal colonialist scheme has been the prejudiced position that racial minorities' culture and social organization are inferior to whites' and that, therefore, these groups should readily discard their traditional culture and embrace that of the dominant culture. Thus traditional cultures have been under-mined or destroyed, and racial minorities wishing to obtain at least some of the privileges of the dominant culture have had to focus on mastering its knowledge and skills. From the seventeenth century to the present, Europeans and, later, white Americans have issued claims about cultural superiority, often making distorted observations about the content of other racial groups' cultural patterns. While historically such claims have tended to go unchallenged, this is no longer the case. In December 1993 Senator Ernest Hollings of South Carolina commented on African diplomats visiting Switzerland for international trade agreement talks, saying that "rather than eating each other, they'd just come up to get a good square meal in Geneva" (*New York Times*, 1993: B16). When the remark drew angry criticism, a Hollings aide defended his boss by saying that Hollings had just made a harmless joke. In an era when cultural putdowns are no longer publicly acceptable, that response drew little support.

One prominent means of stressing the Eurocentric nature of U.S. culture has been the widespread villification of languages other than English. Often the ability to speak another language has been "more generally regarded as a liability than a refinement, a curse of ethnicity and a ban to advancement rather than an economic or educational advantage" (Baron, 1996: 289). In New Mexico the negative attitude toward Spanish delayed statehood for over 60 years. In 1902, in one of the many unsuccessful tries for statehood, witness after witness testified to a congressional subcommittee that ballots and political speeches were either bilingual or entirely in Spanish; that courts required translators so that judges and lawyers could understand the many Spanish-speaking witnesses; and that children who were learning English in school "relapsed" into Spanish on the playground, at home, and after graduation (Baron, 1996: 288).

Table 1.1 demonstrates the interplay among some issues we have analyzed in this chapter.

Some observers of American racism would conclude that while internal colonialism is applicable to our racist past, the theory no longer proves explanatory in today's much more racially equitable society. I disagree, believing that the issues it analyzes are central in grasping the third type of racism examined in the following section.

Table 1.1   Discrimination, Prejudice, and Related Issues

Discrimination ⟵⟶ Prejudice	

Racism: a form of discrimination
  a. Individual racism
  b. Institutional racism
Internal colonialism: a theory analyzing the oppression
  of American racism, with more emphasis on
  discrimination than prejudice
	Stereotype: image maintained by prejudiced
	  people; can support self-fulfilling prophecy

Three Types of White Racism

Let us return to the concept of individual racism, clarifying three types of white racism—old-fashioned racism, symbolic racism, and the cultural camouflage for modern racism. Historically, researchers have focused on what David O. Sears and Tom Jessor designated "old-fashioned racism"—the clear belief in whites' racial superiority (Sears and Jessor, 1996: 752). A body of research has analyzed the characteristics of individuals who become racist in this traditional sense (Allport, 1954; Farley, 1995: 22–24; Merton, 1995).

In the 1960s and 1970s, civil rights legislation began to attack the traditional limitations imposed on minorities in jobs, schooling, housing, and other areas. In the wake of these policies, whites sometimes characterized blacks and other minorities as too demanding, claimed that minorities were receiving special favors, and denied that discrimination was still occurring. At the time David O. Sears and Donald R. Kinder (1971) developed the concept of "symbolic racism"—an emotionally negative response toward minorities, particularly blacks, represented as their transgressions against traditional values (Sears, 1988: 56). For instance, a white person might argue that blacks are too inclined to seek money from welfare programs or special treatment from affirmative action initiatives, legitimating the criticism by noting such actions run counter to our culture's strong support for the work ethic and self-reliance.

In conclusion, symbolic racism focuses on racial groups' purported behavioral deficiencies, not claims of biological inferiority. Other social researchers have reached similar conclusions, describing their own versions of a link between an anti-minority position and a minority group's supposed failure to promote certain cherished values (Bobo and Smith, 1996; Gaertner and Dovidio, 1986; Hass et al., 1991; Jackman, 1996; McConahay, 1986; Tuch and Hughes, 1996a; Tuch and Hughes, 1996b).

Symbolic racism continues to be relevant today, particularly when majority group members face policy decisions on such issues as affirmative action or public assistance. One limitation to the concept is that many situations involving racism extend beyond rational decision making into highly emotional areas. Another, perhaps more significant limitation is that symbolic racism focuses on *the individual's* racism. Consider an additional concept, which requires historical background before its meaning becomes clear.

Recent decades have featured progressive developments in race relations. For instance, the Civil Rights Act of 1964 has been the broadest American legislative effort against racism, covering employment practices of all businesses with over 25 employees, access to all public accommodations, and such federally funded organizations as colleges and hospitals. In 1986 the nation began to celebrate Martin Luther King Jr., Day, acknowledging the notable achievements of a prominent African American and also promoting an esteemed role for blacks in American culture. In the 1997 commemoration of the 50-year anniversary of Jackie Robinson's integration of major league baseball, there was a much publicized ceremony with top political officials and a host of dignitaries, including many African Americans.

Survey data have also indicated a softening racial climate, with a steadily increasing percentage of whites noting that blacks live in their neighborhoods, are friends of theirs, have been dinner guests in their house, and have their approval both to date and marry whites (Thernstrom and Thernstrom, 1997: 521–525).

The current public message, in short, is to emphasize racial equality and condemn racism. One clear manifestation of the message has been the treatment of transgressors. Over the past decade, Fuzzy Zoeller was only one of a number of public figures who have been criticized and then punished for making racist public statements. Not just celebrities are on the line. Occasionally students come to me troubled about whether their outlooks are racist or can be so perceived. More than ever before, it is now un-American to be racist.

Or is it? In contrast to the new public consciousness emphasizing racial equality and condemning racism, the American racist tradition persists. As Sears and Jessor indicated, racism is "a set of core attitudes to which naive children are socialized early in life" (Sears and Jessor, 1996: 755). Andrew Hacker suggested that those core attitudes are particularly virulent in the case of African Americans, where "there remains an unarticulated suspicion: might there be something about the black race that suited them for slavery?" (Hacker, 1992: 14).

Presently majority group members live in a society where the public message stresses racial equality, but they have also been products of the American racist tradition, which has supported majority group privileges. A threat to those privileges elicits racism—when in their eyes an uncomfortable number of African Americans move into their neighborhoods, seemingly bringing crime, violence, and disorder; when excessive minority competition for jobs develops; when an unwanted push to promote school integration occurs; when an apparently unjustified insult or verbal or physical attack comes from a minority group member.

In light of this contrasting pair of approaches to race relations, consider a concept which I designate the **cultural camouflage for modern racism**: that currently many majority group members' racist outlooks and behavior are hidden behind public actions favoring racial equality and are revealed only if race-related fear or opportunity arises. "Camouflage" seems an apt reference, because it leaves open the question of whether or not the act of obscuring is consciously conceived (as by soldiers or hunters) or presumably unconscious (as by animals instinctively hiding from predators).

So circumstances tapping into their race-related fears and tensions can propel people to engage in racist acts. Far from rejecting the relevance of internal colonialism to modern settings, I would argue for its continuing use: Focusing on what can provoke racism in majority group members, internal colonialism alerts analysts to the existence of modern racism, which the current public emphasis on its condemnation is likely to camouflage.

The Gallup Poll offered supportive evidence in a 1997 national survey reviewing black/white relations in the United States. To begin, only about 5.5 percent of whites placed themselves toward the prejudiced end (7 to 10 on a 10-point scale) when asked if they were prejudiced toward members of other racial groups. However, racist behavior seems to have been frequent. When blacks were asked whether they had encountered discrimination over the past 30 days before the interview in five areas—shopping, dining out, at work, with police, and in public transportation—about half replied affirmatively for at least one area (Gallup Organization, June 1997). A discrepancy appears to exist between this information and the preceding finding that 5.5 percent of whites designated themselves prejudiced. It seems extremely unlikely that such a small percentage of whites could be responsible for the widespread discrimination blacks say they have recently encountered.

Discrepancies are apparent: That is a central reality the cultural camouflage for modern racism addresses. In record numbers whites indicate they are not racist, but evidence like that presented here suggests that (a) they are much less inclined than blacks to consider that African Americans are subjected to discrimination and (b) in some instances they are quite possibly overlooking or denying their own racist behavior.

Data on housing suggest that many whites fall far short of the current racism-free ideal. In *American Apartheid: Segregation and the Making of the Underclass*, Douglas S. Massey and Nancy A. Denton indicated that "although whites now accept open housing in principle, they have not yet come to terms with its implications in practice" (Massey and Denton, 1993: 109). They cite a study of suburban working-class whites, which concluded that the respondents:

> express a profound distaste for blacks, a sentiment that pervades almost everything they think about government and politics. . . . Blacks constitute the explanation for their vulnerability and almost everything that has gone wrong in their lives; not being black is what constitutes being middle class; not living with blacks is what makes a neighborhood a decent place to live. (quoted in Massey and Denton, 1993: 94)

This quotation captures the deep-seated fear, repugnance, and desire for separation many whites feel toward blacks. It describes a white racist outlook that is sharply opposed to the now widely supported public position toward blacks.

Not surprisingly given the contradictions just discussed, survey respondents have not been sanguine about future race relations. Among both blacks and whites, 54 percent believed that relations between the two races will always be a problem (Gallup Organization, June 1997). Local events can further exacerbate race relations. Five years after the Los Angeles riots, two-thirds of a randomly selected sample of local residents felt that race relations in the city were poor (*Los Angeles Times*, April 11, 1997).

One way to highlight the special features of the cultural camouflage for modern racism is to compare it to the previously discussed concept—symbolic racism. First, while symbolic racism suggests continuity between traditional and current stances about race issues, the cultural camouflage for modern racism describes a collision between an individual's support for the public rejection of racism and the traditional racist outlooks and pressures to which he or she is exposed. Second, while the individual engaging in symbolic racism is likely to be fairly comfortable with its impact, that is decisively not the case with the cultural camouflage for modern racism, where

Table 1.2   A Comparison between Symbolic Racism and the Cultural Camouflage for Modern Racism

	Symbolic Racism	Cultural Camouflage for Modern Racism
1. *Basic characteristic*	A *continuity* between racist outlooks and traditional values	A *collision* between an individual's support for the public rejection of racism and pressures encouraging him or her to engage in racist acts
2. *Impact on majority group member*	Fairly relaxed acceptance of one's own symbolic racism	Frequent pessimism, confusion, frustration, or guilt

the person in question often feels pessimistic, confused, guilty, or frustrated. In short for many contemporary Americans, the practice of racism has become increasingly emotion-laden and confusing. Table 1.2 summarizes the differences in the two concepts.

The cultural camouflage for modern racism implies that in one sense racism is like an addiction: Until people face the reality of their racism, they will be unable to take the steps to eradicate it. While I would like to believe that racism is dying today, that does not seem to be the case: Often it lies dormant in a subtle, modern form—the hidden monster that circumstances can too readily arouse. Although there is not a great deal of available evidence related to the cultural camouflage for modern racism, we encounter occasional references to the concept at various points throughout the book.

We have been analyzing concepts and a theory. Now, for the first time, we examine a concrete situation demonstrating the occurrence of racism in people's lives. These sections, which occur in most chapters, represent good opportunities to see how cases involving racism develop at the **micro level**: that is, in situations involving the structure and activities of small groups.

A Ku Klux Klan Member's Rejection of Racism

An additional concept supplies the starting point of this discussion. **Social distance** is the feeling of separation between individuals and groups. In the 1920s psychologist Emory Bogardus developed a scale to measure social distance. The scale asks people to indicate their willingness to interact with various racial and ethnic groups in certain social situations, which represent seven degrees of social distance. As one moves down the list, the seven items involve an increasing social distance. The first item is kinship by marriage, followed by regular friendship, and the last item involves exclusion from the country (Marger, 1997: 79–81).

As a result of racist practice, blacks and whites often perceive a great social distance between each other. However, while suspicion and uneasiness are widespread, the gulf between members of the two groups would seldom be as great as between a Ku Klux Klan member and a black activist.

C. P. Ellis is a white man who has spent his entire life in Durham, North Carolina. When he was in the eighth grade, his father died, and he had to quit school and start supporting the family. It was a constant struggle, with over half of his wages going just to pay rent. As time passed, Ellis became more and more bitter, feeling that there was something seriously wrong with the country and that he needed to find someone to blame. He explained, "The natural person for me to hate would be black people, because my father before me was a member of the Klan. . . . It was the only organization that would take care of the white people. So I began to admire the Klan" (Terkel, 1992: 272).

Initiation into the Ku Klux Klan was a momentous event. Suddenly, for the first time, this man who had struggled all his life felt he had achieved something meaningful. Ellis was led into a large meeting room that contained at least 400 people. The lights were dim, and in front of him was an illuminated cross. He knelt before the cross, vowing to uphold the purity of the white race, fight communism, and protect white womanhood. At the end of the oath, the Klan members applauded loudly. Ellis was thrilled.

He became a prominent organizer for the Klan, recruiting young, poor white men who like him had felt deprived of full membership in society and were thrilled at the opportunity to have a chance to belong to an organization where they were valued. Ellis rose to the position of Exalted Cyclops of the Klan's Durham chapter. He visited city leaders in their homes and sometimes received calls from them to attend city council meetings to represent white interests against the growing number of activist blacks.

Ellis explained:

> We'd load up our cars and we'd fill up half the council chambers, and the blacks the other half. During these times, I carried weapons, outside my belt. We would wind up just hollerin' and fussin' at each other. As a result of our fightin' one another, the city council still had their way. They didn't want to give up control to the blacks *nor* the Klan. They were usin' us. (Terkel, 1992: 273)

At first, however, Ellis didn't realize this. He simply focused on the black protesters, whose picketings and demonstrations infuriated him. In particular, he had "a purple passion" about one protest leader—a woman named Ann Atwater, who led a series of demonstrations. Several times the two of them had furious shouting matches.

Then one day Ellis was walking downtown, and he saw a city council member whom he knew well approaching from the other direction. Ellis expected to shake hands with the man and have a friendly chat since he had often spoken to the man on the phone and visited him at home. However, the city council member crossed the street and ignored him. For Ellis, the incident was a painful revelation. He spent many sleepless nights struggling with the humiliating conclusion that the political leaders were using him and other Klan members. He brought the issue up at a Klan meeting, saying he did not like being used. The others were unimpressed and simply declared that they should just "keep fightin' them niggers" (Terkel, 1992: 274).

The situation wore on Ellis. While he still did not like or trust African Americans, he would see a poor black man with ragged shoes and clothes walking down the street and dimly begin to feel a kinship with him. Eventually Ellis wanted to leave the Klan, but he felt unable to take the step.

A turning point occurred when a meeting was convened to figure out how to spend a federal government grant of $78,000 provided to help solve racial problems in the local schools. A variety of groups were asked to participate, including Klansmen and black activists—too many blacks for Ellis to feel comfortable, he told a friend. But the friend persuaded him to go. It was hardly reassuring to walk in the door and immediately see Ann Atwater.

The meeting, Ellis noted, was run "by a great big black guy, but he was very nice." The moderator explained that all participants should feel free to say whatever they wanted. Several blacks indicated that white racism was the source of racial problems in the schools. Ellis listened for a while, but when he could stand listening no longer, he asked for the floor. The reason for these problems, he declared, was "black racism. If we didn't have niggers in the schools, we wouldn't have the problems we got today" (Terkel, 1992: 274). What happened next amazed Ellis. Howard Clement, a black man, stood up and indicated that Ellis was the most honest person at the meeting and that it was a good thing he had shown up. As the meeting broke up, a number of blacks tried to shake hands with Ellis, but he refused and walked away.

Nonetheless, the following evening Ellis was back for another meeting. He had gotten his feelings off his chest and felt more relaxed. Still he was surprised and distinctly uneasy when a black man proposed that he and Ann Atwater be the co-chairs of a committee that would work out the guidelines for how the government money would be spent. Ellis wondered what to do. It seemed impossible to work with Ann Atwater, and yet from the beginning, he felt pride in being asked to co-chair the committee: Here for the second time in his life was a meaningful opportunity for him, a low-income white person, to do something that would produce personal recognition.

One night he telephoned Atwater, saying that while the two of them had had their differences, there was a chance for them to do something important. Would she be willing to put aside their past disputes? Atwater said that she was willing if he was. So they agreed to meet for dinner, along with Bill Rigg, the black man who had been moderating the meetings. Atwater explained that at the cafeteria "C. P. kept pacing up and down the floor." With other whites in the room he "didn't want to be seen sitting at the same table with two blacks" (Terkel, 1992: 280).

It was hardly an easy experience for Ellis. He was struggling to confront his racist past, to work on a project that involved drastically shortening the social distance with black people, whom he had always feared and hated. At night his old friends would sometimes telephone, asking why in the hell was he spending time with black people. Was he selling out the white race? Some support came from Duke University, where he had been doing maintenance work. In recognition of the importance of the biracial effort to relieve racial tension in the schools, the president of Duke gave C. P. Ellis ten days off with full pay.

Atwater and Ellis forged ahead. Seeking support for their program, they went knocking on doors, but this odd couple was too much for most people, whether black or white, to accept. One day, taking a few minutes' break from their arduous effort, the two of them started what at first seemed an idle conversation. Atwater indicated that life had become real tough. Not only was she poor, supporting her family as a domestic, but this committee work was starting to have an impact on her children. Recently her daughter had come home crying because the teacher had made fun of what her mother was doing. Ellis was startled. The same thing had happened to his son, who had come home crying when the teacher had joked about his father. As Ellis explained what happened, he paused, swallowed hard, and stifled a sob.

> I begin to see, here we are, two people from the far ends of the fence, havin' identical problems, except her bein' black and me bein' white. From that moment on, I tell ya, that gal and I worked good together. (Terkel, 1992: 275–276)

Recalling that special moment, Ellis broke into tears.

Twelve years later many changes had occurred. On the job Ellis was elected business manager of the local labor union, which had a two-thirds black membership. Ellis's conception of social distance had changed dramatically. Now he felt comfortable with most black people and estranged from his former Klan friends. His current friends were people who shared his progressive goals emphasizing the importance of working toward a better life for all poor people. Ellis noted, however, that "[t]heir station in life is higher than mine. I don't feel comfortable in their homes. Sometimes I find myself standing in the corner in a social gathering and that ought not to be" (Terkel, 1992: 279). The reader comes away with the feeling that C. P. Ellis feels good about himself and what he is doing but that he also feels somewhat uprooted, separated from the intense support and camaraderie the Klan had provided.

The last point is instructive and sobering, emphasizing a basic sociological reality: that people are strongly influenced by the social world in which they live. If a Klansman stops hating blacks and pursuing the organization's racist activities, he loses his fellow members' friendship and support. At that juncture the friendship such a group provides will disappear, and it can be difficult to replace. Thus an important conclusion that emerges from Ellis's experience is that while individuals' struggles against racism can be uplifting, even inspiring, such personal victories can promote other difficulties in their lives.

In the next chapter, we pursue the task of understanding racism by examining theories addressing the topic.

Discussion Questions

1. Are you comfortable with the terms "majority group" and "minority group"? Explain your position, considering the possibility of alternative terms.
2. Discuss the relationship among the concepts—prejudice, discrimination, and stereotype—providing illustrations. Can prejudice exist without discrimination, or vice versa? Give examples.

3. Convey the idea of institutional racism, clearly distinguishing it from individual racism. Give an example other than the one provided in the text. Do majority group members who belong to institutionally racist structures invariably engage in individual racism? Explain.

4. Evaluate Wilson's thesis about the declining significance race, indicating support for and criticisms of the thesis. What is your opinion?

5. Evaluate internal colonialism, analyzing the theory's apparent strengths and weaknesses. How does the concept of the cultural camouflage for modern racism relate to this theory? Give an illustration of the concept.

6. In 20 years, will racism in the United States differ from how it is today? Discuss.

Sources

Allport, Gordon W. 1954. *The Nature of Prejudice.* Cambridge, MA: Addison-Wesley.

Bacon, David. 1996. "Contesting the Price of Mexican Labor," pp. 97–116 in John Anner (ed.), *Beyond Identity Politics.* Boston: South End Press.

Baron, Dennis. 1996. "English in a Multicultural America," pp. 286–292 in Karen E. Rosenblum and Toni-Michelle C. Travis (eds.), *The Meaning of Difference: American Constructions of Race, Sex and Gender, Social Class, and Sexual Orientation.* New York: McGraw-Hill.

Barrera, Mario. 1979. *Race and Class in the Southwest.* Notre Dame, IN: University of Notre Dame Press.

Barringer, Felicity. 1991. "Census Shows Profound Change in Racial Makeup of the Nation." *New York Times* (March 11): A1+.

Bee, Robert L. 1990. "The Predicament of the Native American Leader: A Second Look." *Human Organization* 49 (Spring): 56–63.

Begley, Sharon. 1996. "Three Is Not Enough," pp. 253–255 in John A. Kromkowski (ed.), *Race and Ethnic Relations 96/97,* 6th ed. Guilford, CT: Dushkin Publishing Group.

Bell-Fialkoff, Andrew. 1994. "Ethnic Conflict," pp. 198–204 in John A. Kromkowski (ed.), *Race and Ethnic Relations 94/95,* 4th ed. Guilford, CT: Dushkin Publishing Group.

Blauner, Robert. 1972. *Racial Oppression in America.* New York: Harper & Row.

Bobo, Lawrence, and Ryan A. Smith. 1996. "From Jim Crow Racism to Laissez-Faire Racism." In Wendy Katkin and Andrea Tyree (eds.), *Beyond Pluralism: Essays on the Conceptions of Groups and Identities in America.* Urbana, IL: University of Illinois Press.

Campbell, Ernest Q., and Thomas Pettigrew. 1959. *Christians in Racial Crisis.* Washington, DC: Public Affairs Press.

Celis, William, III. 1996. "40 Years after *Brown,* Segregation Persists," pp. 164–167 in John A. Kromkowski (ed.), *Race and Ethnic Relations 96/97,* 6th ed. Guilford, CT: Dushkin Publishing Group.

Cloud, Alaina. 1994. "African-Americans' Responses to Racism." Student project, Southern Connecticut State University.

Count, Earl W. (ed.). 1950. *This Is Race: An Anthology Selected from the International Literature on the Races of Man.* New York: Schuman.

Davis, F. James. 1996. "Who Is Black? One Nation's Definition," pp. 35–42 in Karen E. Rosenblum and Toni-Michelle C. Travis (eds.), *The Meaning of Difference: American Constructions of Race, Sex and Gender, Social Class, and Sexual Orientation.* New York: McGraw-Hill.

Devine, Patricia G., and Andrew J. Elliot. 1995. "Are Racial Stereotypes *Really* Fading? The Princeton Trilogy Revisited." *Personality and Social Psychology Bulletin* 21 (November): 1139–1150.

Dollard, John. 1937. *Caste and Class in a Southern Town.* New Haven, CT: Yale University Press.

Duster, Troy. 1987. "Purpose and Bias." *Society* 24 (January/February): 8–12.

Farley, John E. 1995. *Majority-Minority Relations.* Englewood Cliffs, NJ: Prentice Hall.

Feagin, Joe R. 1991. "The Continuing Significance of Race: Antiblack Discrimination in Public Places." *American Sociological Review* 56 (February): 101–116.

Gaertner, Samuel L., and John F. Dovidio. 1986. "The Aversive Form of Racism," pp. 61–89 in John F. Dovidio and Samuel L. Gaertner (eds.), *Prejudice, Discrimination, and Racism.* Orlando, FL: Academic Press.

Gallup Organization. June 1997. "Black/White Relations in the U.S." *Gallup Poll.*

Gibson, Jane W. 1996. "The Social Construction of Whiteness in Shellcracker Haven, Florida." *Human Organization* 55 (Winter): 379–389.

Hacker, Andrew. 1992. *Two Nations: Black and White, Separate, Hostile, Unequal.* New York: Charles Scribner's Sons.

Harris, Marvin. 1968. "Race." *International Encyclopedia of the Social Sciences* 13: 263–269.

Hass, R. Glen, et al. 1991. "Cross-Racial Appraisal as Related to Attitude Ambivalence and Cognitive Complexity." *Personality and Social Psychology Bulletin* 17 (February): 83–92.

Holmes, Steven A. 1997a. "Poll Finds Few Support Label of Multiracial." *New York Times* (May 16): A20.

Holmes, Steven A. 1997b. "Panel Balks at Multiracial Census Category." *New York Times* (July 9): A12.

Jackman, Mary R. 1996. "Individualism, Self-Interest, and White Racism." *Social Science Quarterly* 77 (December): 760–767.

Katz, David, and Kenneth Braly. 1933. "Racial Stereotypes of One Hundred College Students." *Journal of Abnormal and Social Psychology* 28 (October): 280–290.

Kutner, Bernard, Carol Wilkins, and P. R. Yarrow. 1952. "Verbal Attitudes and Overt Behavior Involving Racial Prejudice." *Journal of Abnormal and Social Psychology* 47 (July): 649–652.

Lawson, Bill. 1992. "Nobody Knows Our Plight: Moral Discourse, Slavery, and Social Progress." *Social Theory and Practice* 18 (Spring): 1–20.

Link, Michael W., and Robert W. Oldendick. 1996. "Social Construction and White Attitudes toward Equal Opportunity and Multiculturalism." *Journal of Politics* 58 (February): 149–168.

Los Angeles Times. April 11, 1997. "City Still Viewed as Racially Split." *Los Angeles Times Poll.*

Marger, Martin N. 1997. *Race and Ethnic Relations: American and Global Perspectives.* Belmont, CA: Wadsworth.

Massey, Douglas S., and Nancy A. Denton. 1993. *American Apartheid: Segregation and the Making of the Underclass.* Cambridge, MA: Harvard University Press.

McCall, Nathan. 1994. *Makes Me Wanna Holler: A Young Black Man in America.* New York: Random House.

McConahay, John B. 1986. "Modern Racism, Ambivalence, and the Modern Racism Scale," pp. 91–126 in John F. Dovidio and Samuel Gaertner (eds.), *Prejudice, Discrimination, and Racism.* Orlando, FL: Academic Press.

Merton, Robert K. 1995. "Discrimination and the American Creed," pp. 33–44 in Adalberto Aguirre, Jr., and David V. Baker, *Sources: Notable Sources in Race and Ethnicity.* Guilford, CT: Dushkin Publishing Group.

Minerbrook, Scott. 1996. "Home Ownership Anchors the Middle Class," pp. 171–175 in John A. Kromkowski (ed.), *Race and Ethnic Relations 96/97, 6th ed.* Guilford, CT: Dushkin Publishing Group.

Molnar, Stephen. 1975. *Races, Types, and Ethnic Groups.* Englewood Cliffs, NJ: Prentice-Hall.

Montagu, Ashley. 1974. *Man's Most Dangerous Myth: The Fallacy of Race,* 5th ed. New York: Oxford University Press.

Moore, David W. 1995. " 'Black' or 'African-American' "? *Gallup Poll Monthly* (August): 18–20.

New York Times. 1993. "A Senator's Cannibal 'Joke' Angers Blacks." (December 16): B16.

Norris, Clive, Nigel Fielding, Charles Kemp, and Jane Fielding. 1992. "Black and Blue: An Analysis of the Influence of Race on Being Stopped by the Police." *British Journal of Sociology* 43 (June): 207–24.

Plous, S., and Tyrone Williams. 1995. "Racial Stereotypes from the Days of American Slavery: A Continuing Legacy." *Journal of Applied Social Psychology* 25 (May): 795–817.

Remnick, David. 1996. "Dr. Wilson's Neighborhood." *New Yorker* 72 (April 29/May 6): 96–102.

Rhoden, William C. 1994. "Arkansas's Richardson Delivering a Message." *New York Times* (April 3): Sec. 8, 4.

Rose, Peter I. 1997. *They and We: Racial and Ethnic Relations in the United States,* 5th ed. New York: McGraw-Hill.

Rusk, David. 1993. *Cities without Suburbs.* Washington, DC: Woodrow Wilson Center Press.

Sandomir, Richard. 1997. "Zoeller Learns Race Remarks Carry a Price." *New York Times* (April 24): B9+.

Schwartz, Joe, and Thomas Exter. 1993. "All Our Children," pp. 101–103 in John A. Kromkowski (ed.), *Race and Ethnic Relations 93/94, 3rd ed.* Guilford, CT: Dushkin Publishing Company.

Sears, David O. 1988. "Symbolic Racism," pp. 53–84 in Phyllis A. Katz and Dalmas A. Taylor (eds.), *Eliminating Racism: Profiles in Controversy.* New York: Plenum.

Sears, David O., and Tom Jessor. 1996. "Whites' Racial Policy Attitudes: The Role of White Racism." *Social Science Quarterly* 77 (December): 751–759.

Sears, David O., and Donald R. Kinder. 1971. "Racial Tensions and Voting in Los Angeles," pp. 51–88 in Werner Z. Hirsch (ed.), *Los Angeles: Viability and Prospects for Metropolitan Leadership.* New York: Praeger.

Sigelman, Lee, and Susan Welch. 1993. "The Contact Hypothesis Revisited: Black-White Interaction and Positive Attitudes." *Social Forces* 71 (March): 781–795.

Simpson, George E., and J. Milton Yinger. 1985. *Racial and Cultural Minorities,* 5th ed. New York: Plenum Press.

Stringer, Chris, and Robin McKie. 1997. "Neanderthals on the Run." *New York Times* (July 27): Sec. 4, 15.

Terkel, Studs. 1992. *Race: How Blacks & Whites Think & Feel about the American Obsession.* New York: New Press.

Thernstrom, Stephan, and Abigail Thernstrom. 1997. *America in Black and White: One Nation, Indivisible.* New York: Simon & Schuster.

Thomas, Melvin E., and Michael Hughes. 1986. "The Continuing Significance of Race: A Study of Race, Class, and Quality of Life in America, 1972–1985." *American Sociological Review* 51 (December): 830–841.

Toney, Mark. 1996. "Power Concedes Nothing Without a Demand," pp. 17–28 in John Anner (ed.), *Beyond Identity Politics.* Boston: South End Press.

Tuch, Steven A., and Michael Hughes. 1996a. "Whites' Racial Policy Attitudes." *Social Science Quarterly* 77 (December): 723–745.

Tuch, Steven A., and Michael Hughes. 1996b. "Whites' Opposition to Race-Targeted Policies: One Cause or Many?" *Social Science Quarterly* 77 (December): 778–788.

van den Berghe, Pierre L. 1997. "Rehabilitating Stereotypes." *Ethnic and Racial Studies* 20 (January): 1–16.

Warner, Lyle G., and Melvin L. DeFleur. 1969. "Attitudes as an Interactional Concept." *American Sociological Review* 34 (April): 153–169.

Warner, W. Lloyd, and Leo Srole. 1945. *The Social Systems of American Ethnic Groups.* New Haven: Yale University Press.

Wilson, William Julius. 1978. *The Declining Significance of Race: Blacks and Changing American Institutions.* Chicago: University of Chicago Press.

Wilson, William Julius. 1987. *The Truly Disadvantaged: The Inner City, the Underclass, and Public Policy.* Chicago: University of Chicago Press.

CHAPTER 2

Racism Theories: Perspectives on Intergroup Oppression

■ Macro-Level Theories of Racism
   Structural-Functional Theories of Race Relations
   Conflict Theories of Racism
■ Micro-Level Theories of Racism
   Ishi, the Last Surviving Yahi

A t the age of 13, I was living with my family in Durban, on the east coast of the Union of South Africa. One morning we were at the docks, watching the unloading of a fishing boat.

I left the spot where I'd been standing and walked over to speak to one of my brothers. Suddenly a voice behind me said, "So you're moving because it sickens you to stand next to a dirty Indian." Surprised, I turned around to see a young Indian man, probably in his middle twenties, frowning at me intently.

I started walking away but then stopped and moved back toward him. "I didn't even see you there," I said.

Instantly the frown was gone. "You're an American!" he shouted. "I've never met an American! Tell me," he continued, signaling to come closer, "have you ever been to Chicago?" I shook my head. "No matter. Perhaps just living in the states, you'll know enough. I've got an absolute obsession about Chicago, especially Chicago of the Prohibition era. Tell me. Do shoot-outs between crime families still take place on the streets there?"

We talked for 10 or 15 minutes, and then it was time for my family to leave. The rest of the day and for many days to come, I thought about the encounter. I was old enough to have a general sense of the virulent racism that dominated South Africa. But this encounter had been personal, graphically demonstrating the potent impact of racially linked symbols: A white skin could instantly create anger and frustration for a minority group member, and yet when it became apparent that the white skin covered an American, the sense of oppression could be immediately washed away. Following that incident I was left with the shadowy outlines of questions which I have pon-

---

Table 2.1   Theories Included in Chapter 2

Macro-Level Theories

A. *Structural-Functional Theories of Race Relations*
   1. Park's assimilation theory
   2. Gordon's seven-level assimilation theory
   3. Glazer and Moynihan's pluralism theory
B. *Conflict Theories of Racism*
   1. Davis, Gardner, and Gardner's caste theory
   2. Dollard's caste theory
   3. Cox's theory of racism
   4. Wilhelm's theory of racism
   5. Collins's theory
   6. Internal colonialist theory

Micro-Level Theories

1. Allport's social psychological theory of prejudice
2. Frustration-aggression theory

---

dered ever since: Why does racism develop? Who benefits from it and how? Just what damage does racism produce for the members of both the minority and majority groups? And, above all, how can racism be eliminated?

In the intervening years, I've found that while sociological theories analyzing racism have not provided complete answers to these questions, they do address them. To combat and ultimately eliminate racism, we must first understand it. Theories are a major source of understanding. Theories, in short, are not simply abstract, formal statements: They can provide practical steps toward comprehension and change.

Many theories analyze either macro-level or micro-level issues. **Macro-level** topics involve the large-scale structures and activities that exist within societies and even between one society and another. As we noted in Chapter 1, **micro-level** subjects concern the structure and activities of small groups. Table 2.1 lists the theories included in this chapter.

Macro-Level Theories of Racism

As we observed in the opening chapter, conflict theory contends that the struggle for power and wealth in society should be the central concern for sociology. Many people are restricted or controlled by limits powerful members of society impose, and such restrictions create or at least encourage conflict. According to the proponents of this theory, conflict inevitably produces change.

Structural-functional theory is less concerned with conflict and change. **Structural-functional theory** suggests that groups in interaction tend to influence and adjust to each other in a fairly stable, conflict-free pattern. According to this theory, these groups are mutually supportive and interdependent, and each group contributes to the overall stability of the society. Since World War II, most advocates of structural-functional theory, notably Robert Merton (1968), have acknowledged that conflict and change play roles in social relations, but in this theory those factors are less prominent than in conflict theory. In this section we see that a distinct difference remains between structural-functional theory and conflict theory when applied to the conflict-laden issue of race. One might argue that the structural-functional theories center on race relations, which tend to be stable and lacking in conflict, and that the conflict theories focus on racism.

In this discussion we examine prominent examples of both types of theories.

Structural-Functional Theories of Race Relations

In the opening decades of the twentieth century, one of the most prominent American sociologists was Robert Ezra Park. Park recognized the existence of racism, but based in part on his positive experience serving as secretary to the moderate black leader Booker T. Washington, he remained optimistic that it would eventually be eliminated (Bulmer, 1993: 354). Park wrote: "The race relations cycle, which takes the form . . . of contacts, competition, accommodation and eventual assimilation, is apparently progressive and irreversible" (Park, 1950: 150). Let us consider Park's four steps.

Park indicated that *contacts* between different racial groups occur when explorers from one group discover new areas that can serve as sites for economic gain. Then, according to Park, *competition* develops. But it is not uncontrolled competition; rather, members of the different racial groups must act within established customs and laws. They adapt to the new environment, finding work that, while not necessarily what they would choose to do, contributes to the emerging economy. Eventually a new division of labor forms, incorporating the different racial groups.

With the division of labor in place, *accommodation* begins. Park asserted that within any established economic system, even one as oppressive as slavery, intimate and personal relations among members of different racial groups develop, undermining the more sinister elements within the system. According to Park, one sign of such accomodation during American slavery was that in spite of legislation and custom strongly supporting the system, the number of slaves given freedom by their masters steadily increased (Park, 1950: 150).

Assimilation —the elimination of separate racial interests and the development of a common identity involving all racial groups within a society—is the final step. Park suggested that invariably some racial groups would assimilate more rapidly than others and, writing in the 1930s, he conceded that African Americans had still not fully assimilated—that "though the white man and the Negro have lived and worked together in the United States for three hundred years and more, the two races are still in a certain sense strangers to one another" (Park, 1950: 76).

Park was vague in analyzing the precise nature of African Americans' incomplete assimilation, indicating that while they were not fully assimilated "in just what sense this is true is difficult to say" (Park, 1950: 77).

Milton M. Gordon (1964) sought to be more precise than Park, developing a seven-level framework for analyzing different types of assimilation. To illustrate his scheme, he suggested the existence of two hypothetical ethnic groups—the Sylvanians and the Mundovians. Originally they had separate homelands, but at one point

Mundovians started moving to Sylvania. By the second generation, the Mundovians were completely assimilated. What precisely did this mean?

First, it meant cultural assimilation, by which Mundovians adopted all the patterns of the host culture—the language, education system, religion, beliefs, values, and norms—and put aside their own previous cultural standards.

Second, the second generation Mundovians achieved structural assimilation, making friends by joining cliques, clubs, and other Sylvanian organizations and thereby receiving full acceptance in their residential communities.

Third, the new arrivals obtained marital assimilation, intermarrying in large numbers with native Sylvanians.

Fourth, second-generation Mundovians had developed identificational assimilation, meaning that their sense of themselves as a people was linked to the host culture; in short, they now considered themselves Sylvanians, not Mundovians.

Fifth, the second-generation Mundovians enjoyed a prejudice-free assimilation; the Sylvanians did not feel and thus did not convey a sense of inherent superiority.

Sixth, the Mundovians also benefitted from a discrimination-free assimilation; in no manner were they treated as second class citizens by the Sylvanians.

The seventh, and final step is civic assimilation, in which the group seeking assimilation—in this case the Mundovians—did not make any significant demands on the host culture requiring a change in its established ways of thinking and acting.

Gordon seemed to be less confident than Park about complete assimilation in the United States. When he examined Americans' friendship patterns and club memberships, it was readily apparent that most preferred to associate with their fellow racial and ethnic group members. On the other hand, Gordon noted that by choice some people reached out beyond their own groups and sought the friendship and stimulation of those with diverse racial and ethnic backgrounds. Furthermore, contacts among Americans of varied heritages occurred because of the racial and ethnic mixing produced in the industrial work world and in higher education systems. Gordon wrote:

> Ethnic communality will not disappear in the foreseeable future and its legitimacy and rationale should be recognized and respected. By the same token, the bonds that bind human beings together across the lines of ethnicity and the pathways on which people of diverse ethnic origin meet and mingle should be cherished and strengthened. (Gordon, 1964: 265)

In later years Gordon acknowledged conflict theory's perspective, admitting that groups with greater wealth and power are able to use those scarce resources to exploit groups that are less well situated. His use of conflict theory, however, was brief and unsystematic, failing to analyze in detail the sources and effects of the unequal distribution of wealth and power (Gordon, 1978).

Pluralism is another structural-functional theory concerned with race and ethnicity. **Pluralism** emphasizes that a dispersion of power exists in government or other structures within American society. Unlike assimilation theory, pluralism does not contend that all cultural differences will ultimately fade away. Instead, different racial and ethnic groups will retain some of their own cultural traditions and activities. In fact, a proponent of the theory has argued that in modern times racial and ethnic identities have become stronger than in the past (Scott, 1990).

Nathan Glazer and Daniel Patrick Moynihan (1963), supporters of pluralism, produced a well-known book with a decidedly nonassimilationist title. *Beyond the Melting Pot* was a clear statement that the nineteenth-century idea that all ethnic and racial groups would simply disappear in the great "American melting pot" has been proved inaccurate. Analyzing the major ethnic and racial groups in New York City, Glazer and Moynihan concluded that common history, community ties, organizational linkages, and often religion and language have united members of a given racial or ethnic group, making it likely that the group will serve as an interest group and provide the most efficient means for members to achieve full participatory rights in political and economic systems.

When a racial or ethnic group lacked those rights, members of the group needed to be mobilized to function as an interest group. For example, Glazer and Moynihan contended that in order for blacks to achieve equitable participation in modern society, new, effective African American leaders capable of demanding full rights for their people had to emerge. Writing in 1963, Glazer and Moynihan suggested that while there had been some promising signs of the emergence of such a leadership over the past quarter-century, black leaders had recently proved ineffective. This failure, the authors argued, was significant, because only African Americans could lead their own people in certain problem areas. They wrote:

> It is probable that no investment of public and private agencies on delinquency and crime-prevention programs will equal the return from an investment by Negro-led and Negro-financed agencies. It is probable that no offensive on the public school system to improve the educational results among Negroes will equal what may be gained from an equivalent investment by Negro-led and Negro-financed groups. . . . (Glazer and Moynihan, 1963: 84)

I am convinced that solutions to such pervasive problems will prove formidable and expensive. To expect the emerging leadership of any minority group, in fact the leadership of any single ethnic or racial group, to play a major role in their solution is unfair and unrealistic, particularly in the financial area.

A decade later Glazer and Moynihan reasserted the earlier thesis, emphasizing two points: first, that by the middle 1970s, there were more interracial struggles for prestige, respect, political power, and access to economic opportunity than in the past; second, the use of ethnic groups as interest groups had become a more persistent trend in recent years (Glazer and Moynihan, 1975: 5–7).

Once more, in 1990, Glazer and Moynihan reevaluated their thesis during a panel discussion that occurred at the time of the trials for two white men accused of participating in the killing of a black man in the Bensonhurst section of Queens, New York. They suggested that the racial unrest and hatred the killing had produced underlined the relevance of their thesis and invalidated an assimilationist perspective—that, as a reporter tersely phrased it, "the melting pot metaphor was a crock" (Roberts, 1990: B1). Mr. Moynihan, now Senator Moynihan, took the opportunity to criticize Marxist thought, suggesting that the beyond-the-melting-pot thesis, which emphasizes the prominent role of race and ethnicity, has refuted Marx's claim that industrial forces would annihilate the significance of race and ethnicity and create a unified working force whose only interests were those shared by an oppressed, exploited class. Giving his colleague major credit, Moynihan said, "What Karl Marx proposed in the British Museum, Nat Glazer disproved in the New York Public Library" (Roberts, 1990: B1).

As we noted in the first chapter, it is true that Marx was one of several prominent social scientists—Durkheim and Weber were others—who discounted the significance of race and ethnicity as major forces in the industrial world. In that regard Moynihan was correct: Undeniably, ethnicity and race play important roles in affecting political, economic, and social events in modern society.

On the other hand, the Moynihan and Glazer thesis, which emphasizes that racial and ethnic groups serve as effective interest groups for their members, has often proved inaccurate. For instance, Glazer, who wrote the original chapter on African Americans in *Beyond the Melting Pot,* conceded that his claim that blacks would manage to be as economically and politically mobile as white groups proved to be naive (Roberts, 1990: B1). Naive it might have been, but it was consistent with a theme expressed by pluralist theorists: that in the United States, minority groups have increasing access to power, wealth, and social position.

In contrast, pluralist analyses of such countries as South Africa (van den Berge, 1978) and the British West Indies (Smith, 1965) indicated that while a pluralist model in which different racial groups maintained separate cultural traditions did apply, the lion's share of power and wealth stayed in the dominant white groups' hands (Marger, 1997: 128–130).

Whether assimilationist or pluralist, structural-functional theories fail to address harsh realities of wealth and power inequalities. They simply assume that different racial and ethnic groups have essentially equal access to these scarce commodities and that therefore they will have similar opportunities to receive the prized benefits of society. If, as in the case of African Americans in the early 1960s, many group members have not been successful economically and politically, then, according to Glazer and Moynihan, responsibility rests with the group's leaders, who largely on their own must learn to resolve their group's enormous difficulties. Since such structural-functional theorists never directly analyze issues of unequal distribution of wealth and power, it is hardly surprising that they do not realistically assess the massive mobilization of funds and personnel needed to resolve such problems.

In contrast, conflict theories focus on issues of wealth and power and racial minorities' historically unequal access to these prized commodities.

Conflict Theories of Racism

One of the prominent conflict theories of racism is the caste analysis. A **caste system** is a socially legitimated arrangement of groups in which the ranking of the different groups is clearly designated, members' expected behavior is specified, and the movement of individuals from one group to another is prohibited. In the 1930s and 1940s, social scientists first applied the concept to American race relations, and in recent years researchers have continued to analyze the idea of caste (Forbes, 1990; May, 1992; Oommen, 1994).

In *Deep South,* Allison Davis, Burleigh B. Gardner, and Mary R. Gardner (1941), studied the caste system of a small southern city with nearly 10,000 inhabitants, about half of whom were black. One feature of the caste system was the established set of beliefs subordinating blacks. Whites generally felt that African Americans were inherently inferior—that they were a lower form of organism that was mentally deficient and emotionally underdeveloped. Whites believed that in some general sense, blacks were "unclean," and thus it was not fitting for whites to eat from dishes or wear clothes that African Americans had used. The researchers also found that local whites felt that the caste system was the "will of God." A physician explained:

> The way I look at it is this way: God didn't put the different races here to mix and mingle so you wouldn't know them apart. He put them here as separate races and He meant for them to stay that way. . . . I don't think God meant for a superior race like the whites to blend with an inferior race and become mediocre. I think God put all the different races here for a purpose, and He didn't mean for them to mix. I think I am right in saying that, and my attitude is Christian-like. (Davis, Gardner, and Gardner, 1941: 17)

In addition, whites contended that blacks were "childlike" and would never grow up, living entirely in the present with neither regrets about the past nor fears about the future. Finally, since southern whites believed that blacks were childlike and thus irresponsible, they were convinced black servants would steal from them. It was in their nature, and thus blacks could not be held responsible. Since whites were the ones capable of such preventive actions as locking liquor cabinets or keeping a check on stockings, handkerchiefs, and food, they bore the responsibility for preventing such infractions (Davis, Gardner, and Gardner, 1941: 20).

Davis, Gardner, and Gardner indicated that certain social practices, which they called "rituals of subordination," maintained the caste system. These rituals included spatial separation, with southern blacks and whites always knowing that public facilities were segregated; and deferential behavior, which meant that blacks were always expected to respond respectfully to whites, using titles of respect and letting whites be served ahead of them in stores and offices.

Essential for maintaining the caste system was endogamy, the prohibition of interracial marriage. Had African Americans and whites been permitted to intermarry, it would have been much more likely that individuals could pass from the black to the white caste. Such a prospect represented a frontal assault on the caste system.

Blacks, the system dictated, needed to be kept in their place. When this occurred, whites received a variety of benefits. In a study conducted in another southern town during the 1930s, John Dollard (1937) suggested that local middle-class whites received three principal gains from their dominant position in the caste system. First, there was an economic benefit. Middle-class whites were able to avoid menial, often physically demanding jobs. Generally they did not mow their own lawns, cook their own food, or clean their own houses. In what was largely an agricultural area, most of the farming, including the backbreaking work of cotton picking, was blacks' responsibility. Furthermore, while blacks' work was more taxing physically taxing than whites', it also paid considerably less. Thus many whites could use advantages they obtained from blacks' low-paid employment to maintain a luxurious lifestyle.

Second, Dollard discussed whites' sexual gain, meaning that because of their superior position in the caste structure, white men had unchallenged sexual access to both African American and white women. Dollard suggested that southern white men's traditional outlook toward white women enhanced the significance of this issue. Southern white men were expected to idealize the white women, celebrating their beauty and chastity and restraining erotic feelings and behavior. While sexual activity with their wives was necessary to produce children, southern white men felt guilt ridden about it. For uninhibited, passionate sex, freed from "cares, threats, and duties" (Dollard, 1937: 144), they often turned to black women, many of them prostitutes.

Third, southern whites received a prestige gain. Simply because people were white, they were able to demand forms of deference from blacks that would enhance their self-esteem. For whites, Dollard suggested, the prestige gain created an illusion of greatness similar to alcohol's intoxicating effect. The difference was that this benefit was not an illusion but "a steadily repeated fact." Dollard wrote:

> From the standpoint of the white man the crucial thing may be that his aggressive demands are passively received; this gives the gratification of mastering the other person. Still more important perhaps is to receive the deference in advance of demanding it, a submissive affection which is freely and automatically yielded. (Dollard, 1937: 174)

The prestige gain, in short, provided whites gratification on the spot, and it also served to emphasize the legitimacy of the caste system, in which blacks were classified as distinctly inferior to whites and controlled by them.

During the same era, Oliver Cromwell Cox (1959), an African American, Marxist sociologist, analyzed the relations between African Americans and whites. As a supporter of Marxist thought, Cox accepted Marx's claim that under capitalism, modern societies would be divided into two basic classes—the ruling class, whose members owned the factories and farms that were sources of wealth, and the working class, whose members depended on wages. Capitalism, Marx emphasized, was exploitative, paying workers barely enough to survive and forcing most of them to do assembly-line work that was repetitive and boring. Eventually, Marx indicated, workers would recognize that as a class they shared common grievances against the ruling class and the capitalist economic system. Organizing themselves into an army, workers would overthrow the ruling class and establish a new economic system—socialism—in which all citizens would own the means of producing wealth (Marx and Engels, 1959).

Writing in the 1940s, Cox extended the Marxist analysis to include blacks' oppression. He suggested that as members of the working class, blacks in capitalist society faced all the limitations and problems imposed on white wage earners. In addition, they were racially exploited, designated inferior to whites, and denied many of the modest rights available to members of the white working class. In Richard H. Thompson's phrase, blacks faced "double exploitation" (Thompson, 1989: 151).

Cox concluded that the core of the American racial problem was that blacks wanted to assimilate, obtaining equitable opportunities in modern society and reducing greater exposure to disease, unemployment, poverty, and illiteracy. The white ruling class, however, opposed blacks' assimilation. Its members felt that it was to their advantage to keep blacks and other racial minorities economically, politically, and socially underprivileged.

While whites used various techniques to keep blacks in an oppressed state, Cox believed that lynching was the "fundamental reliance" of the white ruling class. Although the practice occurred more frequently in the South than in the North, Cox contended that support for the practice—what he called "the lynching attitude"—existed among whites throughout the country.

Cox defined **lynching** as one group's use of mob action to kill a member of an oppressed group, thereby warning members of that oppressed group either to accept an even more lowly status or to forsake any budding plans to rise above their subordinated position (Cox, 1959: 549).

Because of the purpose lynching served for whites, the actual victim was unimportant: What was necessary was that some black person's violent death conveyed a warning. Cox believed that sending a warning to local blacks was a central element in the cycle producing lynchings. The process involved the following steps.

First, a growing belief developed among local whites that in some respect, such as gaining wealth or acting self-assertively, local African Americans were getting out of hand.

Second, discussing the issue among themselves, whites reached the conclusion that blacks in the area represented a distinct, immediate threat.

Third, there was a rumored or actual occurrence of some outrage committed by a black person against a white individual. If tensions among whites were extreme, some of them simply created an incident. For instance, they falsely accused a black man of making sexual advances toward a white woman or of stealing from his employer.

Fourth, once the real or imagined incident took place, the white mob mobilized, and a black victim was burned, hanged, or shot publicly, preferably before the courthouse to emphasize the legitimacy of the savage act; then the victim's remains were dragged through the black section of town. In the fury of mob violence, other African Americans were often killed or beaten, and considerable property belonging to blacks was destroyed.

Fifth, within two or three days, the mob had achieved its emotional release, and a movement for judicial investigation occurred. Sometimes on the Sunday following the violence, courageous local ministers preached that lynching was barbarous and un-Christian. Eventually a grand jury returned the finding that the deceased individual met death by burning, hanging, or shooting at the hands of unknown parties.

Sixth, a new racial adjustment developed, with blacks becoming very cautious in dealing with whites and accepting even more oppressive conditions than previously. If, at this time, some black people dared to defend their rights against whites, most local blacks were much more likely to be critical than supportive. For most black citizens, the major task at hand was to get on with life and to convey to whites a sense of normalcy—that they, the blacks, bore whites no malice. Cox wrote, "The lynching had accomplished its purpose, . . . and the cycle . . . [was] again on its way" (Cox, 1959: 551).

Cox suggested that the extraordinary violence whites inflicted on blacks might have been necessary to overcome "possible inhibitions of conscience" occurring because of black and white workers' common plight as exploited wage earners within industrial capitalism. Cox asserted that one of the significant effects created by racism was that it prevented black and white workers from appreciating that, under capitalism, they shared common grievances that could have served as the basis for an organized interracial effort to overthrow the ruling class and the capitalist system. Were Cox alive today, he might conclude that modern outbreaks of violence against racial minorities have produced a similar divisive effect.

Cox believed that in order to encourage structural changes that would eliminate violence against them and permit them to seek a full share of the rights and privileges of modern society, African Americans needed effective leadership. Cox indicated that in spite of many blacks' lamenting the fact that no great leader had emerged among them, the absence of such leadership was inevitable. Why? The key, Cox claimed, was blacks' position in society: "The destiny of Negroes is cultural and biological integration and fusion with the larger American society" (Cox, 1959: 572). Like other Americans, blacks were pursuing their individual destinies, seeking assimilation into the economic, political, and social structures of modern American life. A leader who either promised to carry the entire race to glory or who negatively represented whites and white dominated society would work against individual blacks' efforts to obtain success and satisfaction.

According to Cox, Marxist analysts of race relations needed to appreciate that black workers were only a small part of the larger American workers' struggle for political and economic power. Cox believed that for blacks and whites alike, the most effective leadership would undoubtedly come from white leaders who sought to improve downtrodden poor people's lives, regardless of color. Cox contended that without any undue concern for "the Negro problem," President Franklin D. Roosevelt did more to elevate blacks' status than any other leader of the first half of the twentieth century (Cox, 1959: 582).

A study of Cox's writings concluded that in his later years, he became more willing to make concessions about American society, moderating his earlier position about the necessity to overthrow capitalism and declaring that racial equality would most readily be produced by reforming current political and economic systems (Snedeker, 1988).

Cox's ideas, however, had little impact at the time they were written. From the 1930s until the late 1960s, structural-functional theory remained dominant, with its emphasis on cohesion, conformity, and cooperation. As we have noted, its applications to race relations—the assimilation and pluralism theories—were widely accepted. Then, in the middle and late 1960s, widespread protests, which included a deep concern for racial and economic injustice, promoted a sharply increased interest in conflict theory in general and conflict theories of race and racism in particular (Monk, 1994: xvii–xviii).

Sidney Wilhelm (1983) is a modern proponent of a conflict theory of racism. He has developed an extension of an idea already mentioned twice in this book: Like Marx before them, modern Marxist thinkers have failed to recognize that racism exists independently of economic forces. Marx believed that as capitalism advanced, narrow allegiances that produced racism would disappear. Modern Marxist theorists have tended to conclude that socialism would provide that benefit. According to Wilhelm, these theorists indicated that "the destruction of capitalism will immediately eliminate any economic necessity for the continuation of racism" (Wilhelm, 1983: 129). But Wilhelm suggested that racism is also the product of noneconomic factors. Currently racism cuts across all social classes, with blacks and other racial minorities who are spared oppressive economic conditions nonetheless vulnerable to racism. Certainly ample evidence in this book supports that claim.

Wilhelm's second principal conclusion is that many African Americans represent a special category of disadvantaged people—those who are permanently unemployed. Historically blacks have had uniquely restricted educational and occupational opportunities, and as a result many of them have been much less prepared than other groups to prosper in the computerized, automated postindustrial world. Wilhelm indicated that African Americans "are not so much oppressed as unwanted; not so much unwanted as unnecessary; not so much abused as ignored" (Wilhelm, 1983: 233). Both past and present Marxist theory, Wilhelm claimed, have failed to appreciate how historical conditions have placed poor modern African Americans in a position of unique economic exploitation.

Modern Marxists have continued to explore the combined impacts of race and social class, sometimes corroborating Cox's conclusion that in the United States, race has served to inhibit working-class solidarity and the development of a racially unified protest movement. Another issue modern Marxists concerned with race have been exploring has been the interplay of politics and race—for instance, the precise role of government in structuring race relations and in implementing antiracist policies. A third area of current exploration revolves around the question of whether a Marxist approach is inevitably Eurocentric, that perhaps its link to western European philosophic traditions is so fundamental it cannot effectively analyze the experiences of groups not originating from that tradition (Solomos and Back, 1995).

Patricia Hill Collins, a black feminist sociologist, has addressed the applicability of Eurocentric theories to black women's lives. While Collins has borrowed extensively from Marxist theorists as well as other theoretical traditions, her fundamental claim is that black feminist thought must be grounded in the lives and experiences of black women. Much of her writing originates from personal experience.

Collins indicated that as a child, she was in a preschool pageant where, like her, the children came from black working-class families. She recalled that "[a]ll of the grown-ups told me how vital my part was and congratulated me on how well I had done. Their words and hugs made me feel that I was important and that what I thought, and felt, and accomplished mattered" (Collins, 1991: xi). Beginning in adolescence, however, Collins was in schools and work settings where she was largely isolated from other blacks. She drew into herself and became silent. Her book, *Black Feminist Thought: Knowledge, Consciousness, and the Politics of Empowerment*, represented the effort to become vocal once again, not just for herself but for black women generally.

Black women, Collins contended, have always been able to define themselves in ways that have opposed the definitions supplied by Eurocentric, male-controlled culture. To some extent the very tyrannies imposed on blacks—slavery and later their ghettoization—provided a separate space where an independent, Afrocentric worldview could develop. Living isolated from whites, black women have promoted a self-definition stressing self-reliance, self-esteem, and independence—traits diametrically opposed to the stereotypic images of African American women that originated under slavery and have been supported ever since (Collins, 1991: 11, 73–78).

Black women's lives and experiences have contributed to an Afrocentric feminist pursuit of truth and knowledge that emphasizes such qualities as the use of concrete experience and an ethic of personal accountability. On the last point, Collins indicated that in a class composed entirely of African American women, she asked the students to evaluate a prominent black male scholar's analysis of black feminism. Instead of employing a conventional approach that would focus on his work without linkage to his personal life, these students wanted biographical information. Collins wrote:

> They were especially interested in concrete details of his life, such as his relationships with Black women, his marital status, and his social class background. . . , [refusing] to evaluate the rationality of his ideas without some indication of his personal credibility as an ethical human being. (Collins, 1991: 218)

Collins developed an intimate, provocative approach to theory that can apply to women and men in all racial groups. The insights provided by her analysis can suggest means of both understanding racism more fully and subduing racist structures and patterns in our society (Collins, 1996).

Some commentary on conflict theories of race relations seems appropriate. To begin, it should be emphasized that some of the observations about racism offered here are dated; for instance, the southern caste system with its associated lynching and other horrors has been largely dismantled. Nonetheless, we might consider the possibility that some oppressive social patterns described in this section are still applicable; for instance, while lynching no longer occurs, a similar process of terror and intimidation occurs in modern situations in which whites initiate violence against African Americans and other racial minorities.

Many conflict-theoretical analyses of American racism, such as Oliver Cox's and Patricia Hill Collins's work, are compatible with internal colonialist theory, emphasizing that whites have systematically controlled and exploited racial minorities in the areas of governance, freedom of movement, work, and cultural evaluation. In this section devoted to conflict theory, it seems appropriate to evaluate internal colonialism, which was introduced in the previous chapter and is discussed throughout the book. If you wish to review the theory's content, turn to pp. 12–14.

It appears that three criticisms most frequently directed against internal colonialism are that (1) its analogy between colonialism and internal colonialism is inaccurate, (2) it fails to address class divisions among dominant whites (Feagin and Feagin, 1993: 39–40; Kitano, 1997: 62), and (3) it underestimates minorities' ability to determine their own destiny.

First, we consider the criticism that the analogy between colonialism and internal colonialism is faulty. Supporters of this point emphasize that, unlike colonial subjects, American minorities are not confined to a restricted territory nor subjected to control imposed by an intermediate elite similar to the indigenous leaders within a colony that help the colonial power exploit the local people. Minorities, in short, have more opportunities to free themselves from oppressive conditions than do colonial subjects.

Advocates of internal colonialism concede that the situation faced by American racial minorities is different from that confronted by the indigenous African, Asian, and American peoples subjected to colonial exploitation. However, they emphasize that the theory highlights modern inequities. For instance, while minorities are not confined to a specific territory, they are subjected to significant restrictions of movement; furthermore, although American minorities do not need to deal with an intermediate elite, they often face a highly controlled governance process.

Second, critics claim that internal colonialist theorists fail to address class differences among whites. After all, they contend, not all minority group members are subordinate to whites. American minority groups have sizable numbers of people whose educational, occupational, and income levels are above the white averages.

This conclusion is true. Like any social theory, internal colonialism does not address the totality of social reality. In fact, the theory's emphasis is not on class differences among whites but on the power that whites as a group can impose on a given minority group: that because of the greater political and economic resources whites possess, they can readily insult and harm many minority group members. Supporters of internal colonialism recognize that American minorities have improving opportunities and achievements. However, the proponents emphasize, these accomplishments often fail to protect them from racist oppression.

Third, critics of internal colonialism have indicated that the theory underestimates racial minorities' ability to control their own destiny. While analysts must consider harsh realities of racism, they should not overstate their case, failing to acknowledge minority individuals' capacity to confront or surmount those harsh realities and obtain various successes.

Some theorists have been wary of this point. For instance, one writer contended that any theory of race and racism produced within American society will fail to fully grasp the structural limitations historically imposed on minorities and is likely to describe ineffectual or illusory means to escape racial oppression. It is essential, she concluded, to evaluate racial issues from a perspective rooted outside of traditional American culture—in her case, from an Afrocentric perspective (Van Dyk, 1993).

It seems that the modern observer of racism must steer a narrow course: on the one hand, thoroughly examine the devastating impact of racism—and internal colonialism proves useful here—and, on the other hand, acknowledge minority group members' successful efforts to control their own lives, quite possibly with strategies developed from their group's unique cultural perspective.

Let me conclude the commentary on conflict theories of racism with a personal observation. Frequently sociologists find that both structural-functional and conflict theories offer useful analysis of major sociological topics. For instance, in my own introductory sociology text (Doob, 1997), the two theories have complemented each other effectively in examining the functions of religion, the impact of education in modern society, and the concentration of political authority. But while structural-functional theory's perspective emphasizing stability and harmony and downplaying conflict and wealth and power inequities can provide some insight, I find such emphases especially hard to accept when the cruel, crippling realities of modern racism are readily apparent. Or, to phrase it differently, the only way I could comfortably write this book was if a conflict perspective permeated it.

We now shift from the macro level to the micro level and examine social psychological theories of racism.

Micro-Level Theories of Racism

Theories in this section examine the small-group context encouraging prejudice and discrimination. In *The Nature of Prejudice,* Gordon Allport (1954: 307–310) suggested that prejudice is a three-stage learning process to which children in American culture are exposed. The following situation illustrates the first stage: Janet, a 6-year-old girl, comes running home and asks, "Mother, what is the name of the children I am supposed to hate?" In Allport's apt phrase, Janet "is stumbling at the threshold of some abstraction" (Allport, 1954: 307). She identifies with her mother, seeks her approval, and wishes to fuse her obedience to her mother with appropriate feelings toward her own social contacts. The child, Allport contended, engages in *pregeneralized* learning, having accepted the information that a certain African American boy is dirty or a particular Native American woman is not to be trusted, but is still unable to generalize her prejudice toward entire racial or ethnic groups. Language is the key to the development of racist thought. Listening to her mother, father, other adults, and older children express their prejudices toward different groups, Janet will gradually be able to grasp which racial and ethnic groups are the culturally approved objects of prejudice.

In Janet's case the second stage in learning prejudice begins with her mother's response to the question about the children Janet is expected to hate. The mother might reply, "I told you not to play with black children. They are dirty; they have diseases; and they will hurt you. Now don't let me catch you playing with them." Such a directive can initiate the period of *total rejection:* Prompted by parental order, the child vigorously rejects all members of a certain racial or ethnic group—in this case African Americans. For Janet and other 6-year-olds, total rejection of a particular group might prove unsystematic since, according to research, until children are 8, they do not have a clear, stable sense of people's race and ethnicity (Aboud, 1984). By 10 or 11, white children subjected to a prejudiced upbringing answered a series of questions comparing blacks' and whites' qualities by scoring the whites higher on every question. Allport concluded that these children "had learned to reject the Negro category *totally*" (Allport, 1954: 309).

The third stage involves *differentiation.* Now the child has become more sophisticated, learning to make gracious exceptions when it seems appropriate: "Some of my best friends are Puerto Rican." Or: "How could I be prejudiced against Asians? The woman who took care of me when I was a kid was Chinese, and I loved her dearly." By about age 15, young people have become sophisticated enough to turn the racism faucet on and off at will. As part of the package, they have learned what Allport called "the peculiar double-talk appropriate to prejudice in a democracy"—speak in favor of individual rights and equality and simultaneously support prejudice and discrimination (Allport, 1948: 310). It appears that the cultural camouflage for modern racism discussed in Chapter 1 is an outgrowth of this double-talk.

Studies have generally supported but refined Allport's theory. Surveys and observational research in natural settings have indicated that by the time children are 3, they have developed "constant, well-defined, and negative biases toward racial and ethnic others" (Van Ausdale and Feagin, 1996: 791). For adolescents, the pattern is not as distinct. More independent than young children, they appear much more capable of combatting the impact of racial stereotypes imposed on either their own racial group or other groups (Aboud, 1988; Spencer and Markstrom-Adams, 1990).

A provocative article has raised a critical point, questioning whether the process of prejudice Allport described is universal. Psychologists Stanley Gaines and Edward Reed (1995) suggested that Allport's analysis might simply describe the modern-day legacy of the specific historical situation where white Americans have exploited various minorities, particularly African Americans. In fact, limited available research has indicated that blacks' prejudice and discrimination toward whites tends to be less extensive than whites' toward blacks.

Another social-psychological perspective is the frustration-aggression theory. Consider the following situation. A 4-year-old is scolded by an angry father. The child, in turn, is angry and frustrated and glances up at dad, momentarily wondering whether she might risk kicking him in the shins. His towering height convinces her that dad is much too formidable, and so, taking a less but still somewhat satisfying action, she slugs her innocent 2-year-old brother. The **frustration-aggression theory** emphasizes that people blocked from achieving a goal are sometimes unable or unwilling to focus their frustration on the true source, and so they direct the aggression produced by frustration toward an accessible individual or group. The displacement of hostility from the true source of frustration to this substitute—a so-called "scapegoat"—permits a release of tension called "catharsis."

Three conditions make it likely that a racial or ethnic group will become a scapegoat. First, the group must be easy to identify, whether by skin color, a tattoo, or some insignia such as the Star of David Nazis forced Jews to wear. Second, the group selected must be weak enough so that it is unlikely to retaliate. Third, to qualify as a scapegoat, a group must be physically accessible (Simpson and Yinger, 1972: 66–69).

For racist individuals, scapegoating is often an emotionally charged process, quickly meeting their needs at a given time and place. In his study of poor southern whites in the 1930s, Leonard W. Doob indicated that at least a half-dozen white men informed him that when farmers for whom they were working forced them to leave the cabins in which they were living and replaced them with blacks, their immediate impulse was to kill the blacks. Before pursuing the impulse, however, each concluded that "killing the nigger wouldn't get me anywhere, since there are plenty of other nigger families for the place" (Doob, 1937: 471). The quotation is notable because it suggests that even though the frustrated poor whites eventually toned down their initial aggressive reaction toward blacks, they were still in the grips of the frustration-aggression perspective, which protected them from facing the painful truth that the real source of their frustration was the powerful, inaccessible farmers.

While the frustration-aggression theory is a useful analytic tool, it could be refined. Sometimes frustration does not produce aggression, and thus it would be useful to determine when a frustrating situation produces an aggressive act and when it does not. Furthermore, even when aggression is the outcome, it is not necessarily focused upon a scapegoat. For instance, the theory does not specify the conditions under which aggression is directed against a scapegoat or against the true object of frustration. In addition, the theory specifies little about the process of scapegoating—in situations where several potential scapegoats are available, it is not clear what social factors encourage oppressors to tyrannize one particular group and not another (Marger, 1997: 94; Schaefer, 1993: 44).

Our discussion now shifts from the analysis of theory to a case study. In the following section, we consider how internal colonialism, conflict theory, and frustration-aggression theory help to explain the real-life extermination of a racial minority.

Ishi, the Last Surviving Yahi

Early in the morning of August 29, 1911, in a small northern California town, the sharp barking of dogs made workers at a slaughterhouse aware of a man crouching against a nearby fence. He was emaciated, dying of starvation, and his hair was closely shaved—a sign that he was in mourning. In the months that followed, it became apparent why Ishi was in mourning. He was the last surviving member of the Yahi tribe, whose other members had been mercilessly hunted down. Ishi's story is a stark account of what can happen to a highly oppressed group whose members are brutalized victims of internal colonialism.

With the discovery of gold in northern California in 1848, whites began coming to the area by the thousands. Some were law-abiding citizens and others were not, but the new settlers shared a sense of racial and cultural superiority, believing Native

Americans were inferior beings who should be exploited as servants, slaves, or sex objects. Any white man who actually married a Native American was viewed with contempt. Thus early white settlers drew what conflict theorists would consider to be caste distinctions. Indians, even so-called "good" Indians who lived on or near white homesteads, were always classified as lower caste members.

Inevitably stereotypes accompanying this classification process proved deadly for northern California Indians. White immigrants had come across the plains where they had encountered Indians who were mounted on horses and often armed with rifles. These were formidable opponents, and the whites adopted the convenient rationalization that the Yahi and other northern California Indians would be equally dangerous. Significant differences—that these Indians were on foot and without guns—apparently escaped the new settlers. Many whites made little or no effort to distinguish different Native Americans' abilities and motivations, and some killed Indians with little or no discretion. No saying more clearly demonstrates Indians' stigmatized status than the well known, nineteenth century phrase, "The only good Indian is a dead Indian."

Given such an outlook, no Indians were safe. The Yahi and other northern California tribesmen sometimes responded to the frequent threat of being tracked and killed by turning against whites and robbing or killing them. Following such acts trigger-happy whites were likely to murder any Indians, including "good" Indians. Frustration-aggression theory would observe that because of their inability to fight back and their accessibility, these Indians served as scapegoats for the whites.

Until the 1880s, however, the Yahi had few encounters with whites. Certainly the members of this tribe were aware of the invaders and viewed them as an oppressive force. However, their nomadic life, which kept them gathering fruits, nuts, and berries and hunting game, confined them to hilly country, far from the new settlements. Eventually whites' livestock began roaming the hills, destroying many plants that were a major source of the Indians' food. At the same time, settlers began to pollute the streams, which provided salmon and other fish. For the Yahi survival had always been precarious, but now it became even more so. Using all the skills developed living close to nature, they fought back. They raided the whites' homesteads and stole livestock and other food. When whites began killing them, they too killed in return. Theodora Kroeber indicated that the Yahi image "of the white man became fixed during those days when it was a careless boast that 'You can't tell one Indian from another.'" The Yahi "found themselves, too, indifferent to making distinctions between one white person and another" (Kroeber, 1969: 49–50). This situation illustrates how stereotypes can create a self-fulfilling prophecy. When whites and Indians began to stereotype each other as indiscriminate murderers, they became convinced it was necessary to kill or be killed. As a result members of each group became even more committed to indiscriminate murder.

Ishi was probably born in 1862. By that time the surviving Yahi had grasped one of the central ideas of internal colonialism—that their freedom of movement was highly restricted and that they could only survive if they used all their skills to avoid whites. But avoidance was sometimes impossible. When Ishi was about 3, a raiding party attacked the Yahi camp. Most of the Yahi were killed, but he and his mother escaped. As Ishi grew up, he learned to hunt and fish and to live on the run, hiding from whites. Always threatened by starvation, the diminishing band sometimes raided white farms and stole food. Such a difficult life took its toll. By 1870 only about 16 Yahi tribespeople survived, and by 1906 just four remained. At that point a surveying party discovered the hidden Yahi camp close to a stream. Three members fled, and the fourth, Ishi's crippled mother, was discovered by the whites. They took the Indians' food and weapons but left the old woman unharmed. Shortly afterwards Ishi returned and carried his mother to a secluded spot, where she soon died. Ishi never again saw the other two tribal members. He was convinced that they must have died, or otherwise he would have encountered them. For the last three years in the wild, Ishi was entirely alone—the sole survivor of a tribe that had been systematically reduced to a single person by whites' genocidal efforts.

Certainly the plight of Ishi and the Yahi is more in tune with conflict theory than structural-functional theory. Unfortunately, as we examine the history of American racism in the next chapter and then move on to consider current racism in later chapters, we see considerably more evidence of racial oppression. The role of theory for analyzing racism will also remain apparent.

Discussion Questions

1. Indicate one positive and one negative quality of the assimilationist and pluralist theories. Do you prefer one theory? Why?

2. Discuss the meaning of Davis, Gardner, and Gardner's rituals of subordination. Do they occur in modern society?

3. Does Cox's analysis of lynching make sense? Are you aware of situations fitting his specific steps?

4. Can you describe a hypothetical or real interracial situation where both the structural-functional and conflict theories would apply?

5. Discuss whether Allport's second and third stages in learning prejudice occur in modern times.

Sources

Aboud, Frances E. 1984. "Social and Cognitive Bases of Ethnic Identity Constancy." *Journal of Genetic Psychology* 145 (December): 217–230.

Aboud, Frances E. 1988. *Children and Prejudice.* New York: Basil Blackwell.

Allport, Gordon W. 1954. *The Nature of Prejudice.* Cambridge, MA: Addison–Wesley.

Bulmer, Martin. 1993. "The Apotheosis of Liberalism? An *American Dilemma* after Fifty Years in the Context of the Lives of Gunnar and Alva Myrdal." *Ethnic and Racial Studies* 16 (April): 345–357.

Collins, Patricia Hill. 1991. *Black Feminist Thought: Knowledge, Consciousness, and the Politics of Empowerment.* New York: Routledge.

Collins, Patricia Hill. 1996. "Toward a New Vision: Race, Class and Gender as Categories of Analysis and Connection," pp. 213–223 in Karen E. Rosenblum and Toni–Michelle C. Travis (eds.), *The Meaning of Difference: American Constructions of Race, Sex and Gender, Social Class, and Sexual Orientation.* New York: McGraw–Hill.

Cox, Oliver Cromwell. 1959. *Caste, Class & Race: A Study in Social Dynamics.* New York: Monthly Review Press.

Davis, Allison, Burleigh B. Gardner, and Mary R. Gardner. 1941. *Deep South: A Social Anthropological Study of Caste and Class.* Chicago: University of Chicago Press.

Dollard, John. 1937. *Caste and Class in a Southern Town.* New Haven: Yale University Press.

Doob, Christopher Bates. 1997. *Sociology: An Introduction, 5th ed.* Fort Worth, TX: Harcourt Press.

Doob, Leonard W. 1937. "Poor Whites: A Frustrated Class," pp. 445–484 in John Dollard, *Caste and Class in a Southern Town.* New Haven: Yale University Press.

Feagin, Joe R., and Clairece Booher Feagin. 1993. *Racial & Ethnic Relations, 4th ed.* Englewood Cliffs, NJ: Prentice–Hall.

Forbes, J. D. 1990. "The Manipulation of Race, Caste, and Identity: Classify Afroamericans, Native Americans and Red–black People." *Journal of Ethnic Studies* 18 (Winter): 1–51.

Gaines, Stanley O., Jr., and Edward S. Reed. 1995. "Prejudice: From Allport to DuBois." *American Psychologist* 50 (February): 96–103.

Glazer, Nathan, and Daniel Patrick Moynihan. 1963. *Beyond the Melting Pot.* Cambridge, MA: M.I.T. Press and Harvard University Press.

Glazer, Nathan, and Daniel Patrick Moynihan. 1975. "Introduction," pp. 1–26 in Nathan Glazer and Daniel Patrick Moynihan (eds.), *Ethnicity: Theory and Experience.* Cambridge, MA: Harvard University Press.

Gordon, Milton M. 1964. *Assimilation in American Life: The Role of Race, Religion, and National Origins.* New York: Oxford University Press.

Gordon, Milton M. 1978. *Human Nature, Class, and Ethnicity.* New York: Oxford University Press.

Kitano, Harry H. L. 1997. *Race Relations, 5th ed.* Upper Saddle River, NJ: Prentice–Hall.

Kroeber, Theodora. 1969. *Ishi in Two Worlds: A Biography of the Last Wild Indian in North America.* Berkeley and Los Angeles: University of California Press.

Marger, Martin N. 1997. *Race and Ethnic Relations: American and Global Perspectives, 4th ed.* Belmont, CA: Wadsworth Publishing Company.

Marx, Karl, and Friedrich Engels. 1959. "Manifesto of the Communist Party," pp. 1–41 in Lewis S. Feuer (ed.), *Marx & Engels: Basic Writings on Politics & Philosophy.* Garden City, NY: Anchor Books. Originally published in 1848.

May, Ann Mari. 1992. "Caste, Class, and Social Change: An Institutionalist Perspective." *Journal of Economic Issues* 26 (June): 553–560.

Merton, Robert K. 1968. *Social Theory and Social Structure, 3rd ed.* New York: Free Press.

Monk, Richard C. 1994. "Introduction: Issues in Race and Ethnicity," pp. xiv–xxi in Richard C. Monk (ed.), *Taking Sides: Clashing Views on Controversial Issues in Race and Ethnicity.* Guilford, CT: Dushkin Publishing Group.

Oommen, T. K. 1994. "Race, Ethicity and Class." *International Social Science Journal* 46 (February): 83–93.

Park, Robert Ezra. 1950. *Race and Culture.* Glencoe, IL: Free Press.

Roberts, Sam. 1990. "Moving Beyond the Melting Pot 25 Years Later." *New York Times* (May 17): B1.

Schaefer, Richard T. 1993. *Racial & Ethnic Groups, 5th ed.* New York: HarperCollins.

Scott, George M., Jr. 1990. "A Resynthesis of the Primordial and Circumstantial Approaches to Ethnic Group Solidarity: Towards an Explanatory Model." *Ethnic and Racial Studies* 13 (April): 147–171.

Simpson, George Eaton, and J. Milton Yinger. 1972. *Racial and Cultural Minorities: An Analysis of Prejudice and Disrimination, 4th ed.* New York: Harper & Row.

Smith, M. G. 1965. *The Plural Society in the British West Indies.* Berkeley, CA: University of California Press.

Snedeker, George. 1988. "Capitalism, Racism, and the Struggle for Democracy: The Political Sociology of Oliver Cox." *Socialism and Democracy* 7 (Fall/Winter): 75–95.

Solomos, John, and Les Back. 1995. "Marxism, Racism, and Ethnicity." *American Behavioral Scientist* 38 (January): 407–420.

Spencer, Margaret Beale, and Carol Markstrom–Adams. 1990. "Identity Processes among Racial and Ethnic Minority Children in America." *Child Development* 61 (April): 290–310.

Thompson, Richard H. 1989. *Theories of Ethnicity: A Critical Appraisal.* Westport, CT: Greenwood Press.

Van Ausdale, Debra, and Joe R. Feagin. 1996. "Using Racial and Ethnic Concepts: The Critical Case of Very Young Children." *American Sociological Review* 61 (October): 779–793.

van den Berge, Pierre L. 1978. *Race and Racism: A Comparative Perspective, 2nd ed.* New York: Wiley.

Van Dyk, Sandra. 1993. "The Evaluation of Race Theory: a Perspective." *Journal of Black Studies* 24 (September): 77–87.

Wilhelm, Sidney M. 1983. *Black in a White Society.* Cambridge, MA: Schenkman.

CHAPTER 3

Passage to Racism

The best-known estimates of the number of slaves brought to the New World range between 9 and 15 million, with perhaps half dying during the infamous "middle passage" from Africa to the Americas. Is it surprising that so many died? Consider the prevailing conditions.

After being branded and chained, the captured Africans were rowed out to slave ships, where they were packed into areas sometimes no more than 18 inches high. One captain said, "They had not so much room as a man in his coffin, either in length or breadth." Here they lived from six to ten weeks, in conditions horrible enough to drive people mad and often worsened when epidemics of dysentery, smallpox, or the flux, an illness which spared whites, swept the ships.

Suffocation in the unbearably close quarters was frequent, and in the frenzy to obtain more air, some men strangled those next to them. So many dead slaves were thrown overboard that reports indicated sharks would pick up a ship off the coast of Africa and follow it for its entire journey (Bennett, 1982: 49).

How could one group of people treat another so savagely? To analyze the historical development of racism, we can use a final theoretical framework. It is Donald L. Noel's (1968) theory of ethnic stratification, which concerns how ethnicity and race become central factors for determining people's access to valued political, economic, and social rewards of their society. This represents an additional conflict theory perspective. While the theory can apply to diverse ethnicities, including different white ethnic groups, our focus is on race.

According to Noel, three conditions permit racial stratification to develop. First, there must be **ethnocentrism,** which is the automatic tendency to evaluate other cultures by outsiders' cultural standards. Ethnocentric individuals believe that their way is the correct or most appropriate way, and if other cultures have different standards or ways, they invariably are inferior. The more one culture differs from another, the more likely it is that people's ethnocentric tendencies will appear. Nineteenth century white Americans were ethnocentric toward African slaves because slaves differed from them in many ways—language, clothing and appearance, social norms, religion, and other cultural standards.

Second, competition for scarce resources is a necessary factor. Competition can be between or among different racial groups or simply within the dominant group. Two conditions affecting the extent to which competition produces racial exploitation are (a) whether or not custom or law puts limits on how much the minority can be oppressed and (b) whether the dominant group's opportunities are static or expanding. Both conditions favored extensive exploitation of slaves. Owners' treatment of slaves was almost completely unrestricted, and during the first half of the nineteenth century, use of slaves in the South greatly increased agricultural production and profit.

Third, as we have noted with internal colonialism, for racism to occur, one racial group must possess superior power. Without it there will be intergroup relations ranging from peaceful coexistence to conflict, but one group will not be able to consistently impose its will on the other. When one group possesses superior power, it is often likely to try to produce structures and practices that permit it to keep control indefinitely. When blacks were brought to America, they were at the mercy of their masters, who went to great lengths to create a slavery system that would last forever.

In analyzing the process by which whites subordinated racial minorities, Noel's scheme proves useful. Internal colonialism seems more appropriate for analyzing events after the minority group's subordinate status has been established. So we return to internal colonialism in discussing the late industrial stage.

Race Relations in the Preindustrial Era

Whether Dutch, English, Portuguese, or Spanish, Europeans who encountered racial minorities used their superior power to deprive them of two precious resources—their material wealth or their labor. Physical conditions determined the most efficient means of exploitation. When inhabitants were fairly sparsely settled, as in the Americas, they were either driven back—the North American technique—or exterminated—the approach in the West Indies and the South American lowlands. When the population was densely settled, a more practical or efficient policy was to enslave the local people—the approach used widely in Africa and in Indonesia (Cox, 1976: 9–10).

Given the opportunity to exploit the minority members of technologically simple cultures, Europeans used ethnocentric stereotypes as rationalizations. By the middle of the sixteenth century, the Spanish declared that they enslaved Indians to work in tropical mines "because, among other things, of their 'barbarous natures,' 'their sins,' their need of religious instruction, and because their labor was naturally due to a people of such 'elevated natures' as the Spaniards" (Cox, 1976: 26).

During the preindustrial era, European explorers and settlers of what is now the United States dealt primarily with two minority groups—Native Americans and African Americans, originally slaves from Africa.

The Art of Making Breakable Treaties

The Tainos Indians who received Columbus on the island of San Salvador made a very favorable impression on the explorer. Writing to the King and Queen of Spain, he enthusiastically noted how peaceful they appeared, observing, "They love their neighbors as themselves, and their discourse is ever sweet and gentle, and accompanied with a smile; and though it is true they are naked, yet their manners are decorous and praiseworthy" (Brown, 1972: 1).

To Columbus, like the European hoards that followed, these positive qualities were clear signs of weakness. The Indians were sweet, pliable, but definitely savage children, who, Columbus believed, should be "made to work, sow and do all that is necessary and to *adopt our ways*" (Brown, 1972: 2). Columbus initiated a policy where white explorers, colonists, and settlers pursued a system of racist exploitation that incorporated the three factors in Noel's scheme: They used their greater power to seize what they considered the Indians' most precious commodity—land. This land permitted whites to steadily expand their economic activity, and neither law nor custom imposed much regulation on land take over and other dealings with Indians. In addition, ethnocentrism helped rationalize the take over: The Indians benefited greatly, the ethnocentric argument went, because they were now recipients of whites' supposedly superior cultural offerings.

For the millions of European settlers arriving in what was to become the United States, land acquisition was the basic necessity. To facilitate this process, Europeans and later Americans began establishing treaties with Native Americans and then invariably breaking them. The first treaty between Indians and Europeans occurred in Massachusetts. When English settlers landed in Plymouth in 1620, they received aid from several Indians, who gave them corn and taught them where and how to fish. Without this help the Pilgrims undoubtedly would have perished. Five years later the colonists asked one of these Indians, a Pemaquid chief named Samoset, if they could have an additional 12,000 acres of Pemaquid land for accommodating the steady stream of English settlers. Like other Native Americans, Samoset believed that people could no more own land than they could the sky, but he was willing to humor the colonists, with whom relations had been good, by putting his mark on a piece of paper.

In the following half-century, most arriving colonists did not bother with treaties, simply appropriating land to meet their needs. Metacom, the chief of the Wampanoags and the son of one of the four men who aided the original Plymouth settlers, realized that Indians would be pushed relentlessly westward unless they resisted, and so even though the colonists flattered him by crowning him King Philip of Pokanoket, he dedicated himself to establishing military alliances with the Narragansetts and other local tribes. In 1675 under Metacom's leadership, the Indians attacked 52 English communities, completely destroying 12 of them and suffering substantial losses themselves. After being captured, Metacom was drawn and quartered, and as a warning against further rebellion, his skull was displayed on a pole in

Plymouth for the next quarter-century. Meanwhile European settlement expanded, and many tribes continued to resist (Brown, 1972: 3–4).

During the seventeenth century, some Indian tribes allied themselves with the French, who were more inclined to hunt and trap than settle the land. When the British defeated the French after a 10-year war, they had to confront an array of hostile tribes. In 1763 these uprisings encouraged a Royal Proclamation in which the King of England declared that exploration and settlement of all lands west of the western slope of the Appalachian Mountains would cease until completion of negotiations with all tribes involved. The settlers, however, kept appropriating land.

More than 20 years later, in 1787, the U.S. Congress was also conciliatory, offering the following solemn pledge:

> The utmost good faith shall always be observed toward the Indians; their land and property shall never be taken from them without their consent; and in their property, rights, and liberty, they shall never be invaded or disturbed, unless in justified and lawful wars authorized by Congress; but laws founded in justice and humanity shall from time to time be made, for preventing wrongs being done to them, and for preserving peace and friendship with them. (Deloria, 1972: title page)

In the early 1800s, Supreme Court decisions established the principle that Native American societies were self-governing nations with a right to their land and that the American government must abide by the treaties that it made with them. But the steady influx of settlers to the frontier undermined that position. Congress passed what became known as "Pre-emption Acts," which validated settlers' claim to lands that treaties had assigned to Indians. In 1824 the Bureau of Indian Affairs was established to coordinate relations between Indian tribes and the federal government. Its major task became Native Americans' relocation. The "utmost good faith" expressed in the lofty statement of 1787 was discarded under what Noel's theory would consider the pressures of an expanding, competitive society.

In 1829 Andrew Jackson became president. Known as "Old Hickory" by whites and "Sharp Knife" by Indians, Jackson exhibited a tough, adversarial approach to Indians, whom he had fought throughout the southern states and considered incapable of living peaceably with whites. Jackson claimed that the best solution for all concerned was to move all Indians west of the Mississippi, where, he promised them,

> your white brothers will not trouble you; they will have no claim to the land, and you can live upon it, you and all your children, as long as the grass grows or the water runs, in peace and plenty. It will be yours forever. (Bailyn et al., 1977: 441)

To any Native Americans who were students of diplomatic relations with whites, this message must have seemed ominously familiar and provided little sense of consolation or security. Though phrased in peaceful terms, its author was an enthusiastic advocate of imposing whites' superior military power on Indians. Certainly it was realistic to be pessimistic, because within a few years settlers were streaming into territories west of the Mississippi, and so what had once been considered "the permanent Indian frontier" was steadily shifted westward.

Reading this material, you might begin to wonder whether racism is the central issue. After all, you might say, the primary motive for removing the Indians was economic—the settlers' need for land. A critical point is that if settlers and officials had not classified Indians as inferior, they could not have so easily exploited them economically. Racist and ethnocentric assessments were apparent from colonial times. The first settlers' written records indicated that they considered Indians "depraved, savage brutes," "impious rascals who lived in filth and ate nasty food" (Jacobs, 1985: 110). A major element in the eighteenth and nineteenth century stereotype of Indians was that they were all nomadic hunting people wandering free as the wind over thousands of acres of virgin wilderness. While this image simply ignored the obvious fact that many of the eastern tribes lived in stable villages, such prominent individuals as President John Adams and General William T. Sherman found it a fine rationalization for depriving Indians of their land (Jacobs, 1985: 111).

The most famous racist rationalization was the concept of "manifest destiny," which described Indians' culture as inferior to whites' and then suggested that this supposed inferiority should serve as the basis for their exploitation. According to the concept of manifest destiny, God ordained that Americans should liberate the continental territory and direct native people's movement toward participation in modern political and technological life. The idea proved convenient when gold was discovered in California in 1848, and many thousands of fortune seekers once again violated treaties and annihilated the idea of "the permanent Indian frontier" as they pushed nearly to the Pacific.

So it was clear that no treaties would stop the whites' advance. During the second half of the nineteenth century, the Sioux, Cheyenne, Arapaho, Kiowa, and Apache under such leaders as Sitting Bull, Crazy Horse, Cochise, and Geronimo felt compelled to fight soldiers and settlers in a vain effort to retain their land and way of life. Eventually they were killed or pacified and placed on reservations. Ethnocentrism was apparent in systematic efforts to destroy Native American cultures. Officals compelled many Indian children to attend boarding schools, where they had to abandon their native languages and customs. In 1892 the Commissioner of Indian Affairs issued a directive requiring all male Indians to keep their hair short; he also banned wearing paint and holding tribal dances and feasts and discouraged wearing blankets (Lyon, 1996; Nichols, 1986: 133–134). Native American cultures were inferior, the whites argued, and so such measures were believed beneficial for everyone, including the Indians.

During preindustrial times whites were equally systematic in oppressing blacks.

Behind the Cotton Curtain

As we noted earlier in the chapter, the American slavery system is a stark illustration of Noel's theory of racial stratification. Whites used their power to establish a system of nearly complete control which thrived in an expanding economy and involved almost no controls on owners' conduct toward slaves. Whites' ethnocentric attitudes towards blacks also contributed.

For the first 40 years of American settlement, there was little slavery. Instead of slaves early colonists were more likely to have indentured servants, whose passage to the New World and room and board were financed in exchange for a specified number of years of unpaid employment.

But eventually settlers became convinced that for several reasons slavery was more efficient. First, since slaves were owned, they could be forced to accept whatever living conditions would be most advantageous to their owners. Second, even though settlers could recruit a fair supply of servants, there simply were not enough of them to work on the steadily growing number of tobacco, rice, and indigo plantations in the South. These first two points are consistent with the Noel theory's emphasis on the significance of competition: Lack of regulation and the need for a vast supply of laborers in an expanding economy encouraged the development of slavery. Third, indentured servants' contracts were often a source of dispute, with servants either suing their masters or simply running away. In contrast, slaves could be purchased outright and thus contracts with them were unnecessary. Finally, maintaining slaves was distinctly cheaper than hiring indentured servants (Franklin and Moss, 1988: 32).

Why were Africans chosen as slaves? First, ethnocentrism contributed. Considered "heathens" in an age when Christianity was the only acceptable religion and possessed of dark skin, Africans were readily identified and stereotyped as "people who were believed to be defective in religion, savage in their behavior, and sexually wanton" (Marger, 1997: 229). But wouldn't all these attributes have been considered to fit Native Americans? Yes, they would have. There is, however, a second factor peculiar to the African captives—the fact that these slaves had been uprooted physically and culturally, leaving them completely isolated from outside support. Indians, in contrast, would have been much more difficult to enslave. Efforts to do so undoubtedly would have produced retaliation from the Indian nations whose members were being taken, and furthermore, Indian slaves might have escaped quite easily into the familiar, friendly wilderness (Marger, 1997: 229–230).

Slavery existed through the seventeenth and eighteenth centuries and was always most widely practiced in the South, which, unlike the New England and Middle Atlantic states, had large plots of agricultural crops that could effectively use the labor of a large slave population; by the early nineteenth century, the northern states had outlawed slavery. Until the end of the War of 1812, in fact, the growth of slavery was relatively slow, even in the South. Then, with the virtual elimination of war in the Western world, trade with Europe flourished, and a great demand for cotton developed. Massive cotton production depended on large numbers of unskilled laborers, and with the growing demand, slavery expanded. In 1790 there were fewer than 700,000 slaves; by 1830 the number had reached 2 million; at the last census before the Civil War, the slave population had nearly doubled to 3,953,760 (Franklin and Moss, 1988: 112–113).

According to one historian, the American slavery system developed into "a social system as coercive as any yet known." Most slaves served on farms and plantations, and about two-thirds of them worked on cotton plantations. These plantations varied considerably in size. In 1860 about 88 percent of slaveowners possessed fewer than 20 slaves, and evidence suggests that the most profitable economic unit contained between 30 and 60 slaves. While not maximally efficient, large plantations were enormously productive, especially in the states where King Cotton prevailed—Mississippi, Alabama, Louisiana, and Georgia (Bennett, 1982: 86–87).

Slavery was an economic system that permitted owners to use fellow human beings brutally to maximize profits, and the cotton plantation, which was a totalitarian system established with this goal in mind, controlled slaves' lives from birth to death.

Generally there was a nursery where a slave often designated an "aunty" cared for young black children while their mothers worked in the fields. At about the age of 6 or 7, slave children started working, and when they reached 10 or 12, they received a full set of adult tasks. An ex-slave described her childhood work experiences:

> I was four years old when I was put on the block and sold; and I had to sit by the cradle and rock my old mistress' baby, and keep the flies off her before I was five years old. Then, of course, you know from time to time I had to learn how to cook and do most everything about a house. (Rawick, 1972: 60)

One ever-present danger slaves faced was the possibility that the owner would find it economically productive to sell or hire out a family member, and thus many children were torn from their parents and often never saw them again. Frederick Douglass, who later became a prominent opponent of slavery, recalled seeing his mother only four or five times. She lived 12 miles away and had to receive permission to walk the distance on foot after a full day's work in the fields; she faced a whipping if not back before sunrise. Douglass wrote:

> I do not recollect of ever seeing my mother by the light of day. She was with me in the night. She would lie down with me, and get me to sleep, but long before I waked she was gone. Very little communication ever took place between us. Death soon ended what little we could have while she lived, and with it her hardships and suffering. (Douglass, 1968:22)

Like Douglass's mother, most slaves on large plantations were field hands. The cultivation of crops was a demanding undertaking, and planters felt that the system proved most successful when slaves were scrupulously supervised by the owner or a hired overseer. Planting, cultivation, and harvesting of cotton, tobacco, rice, and sugar cane required minimal skill but considerable time and effort. For slaves the most demanding time of the year came during the harvest season. Worried about inclement weather destroying crops, planters sometimes forced slaves to work 18 to 20 hours a day (Franklin and Moss, 1988: 116–117).

Discipline was harsh. Slaves were often beaten when they broke the rules, or, in some situations, even if they had not. One slave described his plantation, where every Thursday all the slaves were whipped:

> Yes'm, every Thursday was when you got your beating. . . . They had men hired to do the whipping; everybody got one on Thursday whether you have been bad or not during the week. Well, they had a log and they would tie your hands together and tie you to the log, a hand and arm on each side of the log, and whip you. (Rawick, 1972: 220)

Slaves experienced different degrees of misery. It was generally preferable to be on a small plantation than a large one, because then one would work directly with the master, and they tended to be less ferocious than overseers. Masters also differed markedly, ranging from cruel and sadistic to, if one might use the words loosely, kindly and caring. Yet one should remember that simply by owning fellow human beings, even the most benevolent masters were committed to the slavery system, and when faced with a situation where they had to choose between their economic welfare and their slaves' well-being, they seldom opted for the latter (Bennett, 1982: 94).

Besides work, other daily issues in slaves' lives were food, clothes, and housing. Slaves' food was often a problem for planters, who were preoccupied with producing their staple crops and frequently had to purchase food both for themselves and their slaves. Food for slaves was carefully rationed—a week's supply was about a peck of corn meal, three to four pounds of bacon or salt pork, and sometimes supplements of sweet potatoes, peas, rice, syrup, and fruit. Some slaves maintained their own gardens but risked possible punishment if they spent too much time at this activity. On most plantations slaves were fed fairly well because owners recognized that decent food was necessary for efficient work. An ex-slave explained:

> Well, old marster was called one of the best marsters in the county. He had five hundred darkies. Everybody had enough to eat; there wasn't no other family of people what done work like we done, 'cause you see, we was well fed and clothed and everything. We did real farm work, good work, I mean. (Rawick, 1972: 221)

Generally slaveowners were much less concerned about slaves' clothes than about their food. Most slaves wore crude, homespun garments known as "Negro clothes" and poorly made, skimpy shoes called "Negro brogans." Housing too was poor, with slaves generally living in small, crudely made huts that had no windows, little furniture, and usually no beds. Worse than the absence of comforts, however, was the crowding (Bennett, 1982: 89–90; Franklin and Moss, 1988: 120–121). An ex-slave said, "We all lived in the same cabin; men and women all together. They didn't care how we was treated. Stock was treated a great deal better" (Rawick, 1972: 217).

Like whites dealing with Indians, slaveowners used racist rationalizations to justify the oppression in which they engaged. Slaveowners claimed that blacks were inferior and destined to occupy subordinate positions and that southern whites, far from being corrupted by the practice, had developed a uniquely refined culture that could not have evolved without slaves performing the menial tasks (Franklin and Moss, 1988: 174–175).

To legitimate slavery, southern whites cited the biblical accounts of Cain and Ham. These stories helped slaveowners rationalize that blacks were evil, cursed by God, and fully deserved to be condemned to slavery (Allahar, 1993: 46).

Southerners further legitimated slavery by enacting what became known as Slave Codes, a body of laws covering every aspect of slaves' lives. While the Slave Codes differed from state to state, the general point of view was that slaves were property, not people—that the laws were supposed to protect ownership of that property and to ensure that slaves were maintained under repressive conditions that would promote a maximum level of production. Thus most of the laws focused on exclusion, indicating activities slaves were not permitted to do—for instance, leave their plantations without authorization, possess firearms, hire themselves out without owners' permission, buy or sell goods, or visit the homes of whites or free blacks. Most of the petty offenses were punished with whippings while the more serious ones produced branding, imprisonment, or death. Arson and conspiracy to rebel were capital crimes in all slave-owning states (Franklin and Moss, 1988: 114–115). The Slave Codes made it clear that owners' rights were carefully protected while blacks' were scrupulously denied.

In spite of slaveowners' intimidating control, resistance occurred. Diaries, logs, and historical accounts indicate that some blacks opposed enslavement in a variety of ways, including armed insurrection, physical attacks on masters or overseers, escape, starvation, and suicide (Forbes, 1992). Furthermore, research has suggested that a larger group of whites opposed slavery than historians generally acknowledge.

According to Herbert Aptheker, these courageous people were more likely to be women than men and more frequently poor than affluent. In his book Aptheker provided evidence of persistent white opposition to slavery and racism in the writings of preachers, teachers, anti-slavery workers, and ordinary people as well as whites' support for slave flights from servitude and active involvement in slave uprisings (Aptheker, 1992; Solomon, 1993).

Controversy has surrounded the contemporary presence of symbols from the slavery era. For instance, should "Carry Me Back to Old Virginia," which refers to "darkies" and "old massa," remain the state's official song? Should the Georgia flag continue to incorporate the Confederate pattern? Should the Confederate battle flag still be raised over the capitol in Columbia, South Carolina? And should obelisks and statues to the Confederate dead be kept standing in almost every southern courthouse square? Christopher M. Sullivan, the executive director of the Southern Heritage Association, declared that racial matters are not the central issue. "It's about the courage and valor of Confederate soldiers on the battlefield," he said. The problem, many black and white critics point out, is that the Confederacy represented an era of white supremacy and that symbols alluding to that era glorify a time when African Americans were brutalized. Historian Dan T. Carter concluded that if ours is truly a caring society, "you have to look at symbols from the point of view of the people who are most hurt by them, and [in this case] that's African Americans" (Sack, 1997: 8).

Sometimes major historical figures become embroiled in the modern controversy about slavery. Consider, for instance, the now hotly debated subject of Thomas Jefferson's life. In 1997 legal researcher Annette Gordon-Reed published a book systematically presenting the factual evidence supporting the claim that Jefferson had a 38-year relationship with Sally Hemings, a black woman who was a slave on his plantation. While prominent white historians have claimed that it would have been inconsistent with Jefferson's character to have maintained such a liaison, Gordon-Reed reviewed the evidence and came up with an opposing conclusion. In an interview Gordon-Reed explained, "At so many levels, what historians have done—what they really want to do—is sort of have Jefferson in slavery but not really of it." She added:

> There's a whole range of sexuality, relations between men and women, fathers and children. The whole thing. It's the wickedness of the whole enterprise that puts you in these kinds of positions. And historians want to deny that, to say that somehow Jefferson was above all that. (Alexander, 1997: 7)

In the early industrial stage, new economic and political conditions produced some changes in racial minority group members' lives.

The Early Industrial Stage

According to Oliver Cox (1976: 14–15), industrial leaders have always been willing to accept racist outlooks and practices. Their dominant motivation has been to expand their economic enterprises, and racism has often assisted that expansion.

Soon after the Civil War, Herbert Spencer thrilled most prominent Americans with the doctrine of social Darwinism, which loosely built upon Charles Darwin's research done with plants and animals. Spencer declared that as a fundamental scientific principle, the most intelligent and capable people would invariably rise to dominant economic and political positions, and that society would evolve most rapidly and efficiently if citizens recognized that this "survival of the fittest" was the natural and proper order of things. Those who failed to rise to the top—some whites and all racial minority group members—were simply proving their inherent inferiority. The timing of social Darwinism was perfect for wealthy and powerful whites, appearing just when American industry was rapidly expanding and justifying its leaders' success and prominence. We wouldn't be at the top if we didn't deserve it, they triumphantly declared, and John D. Rockefeller enthusiastically lectured about social Darwinism to children in Sunday school while industrialist Andrew Carnegie felt privileged to consider Herbert Spencer a close friend (Hofstadter, 1955).

Spencer and the other social Darwinists, of course, had never heard of the self-fulfilling prophecy and, if they had, undoubtedly would have dismissed it as the muddled thinking of sentimental, unscientific minds. There is little doubt, however, that what social Darwinism did was to offer a giant boost to those already well placed and, conversely, a shove toward the bottom for those who were not.

It was not just the leaders who subscribed to this doctrine. Members of various social classes read and applauded Spencer's work (Hofstadter, 1955: 34), and it seems likely that the racist position inherent in social Darwinism must have readily blended with racist views already firmly fixed in American culture. Whether recently arrived or already settled, it was not a good time to belong to a racial minority in America.

We next consider experiences for Indians, African Americans, Chinese, Japanese, Mexican Americans, and Puerto Ricans during the early industrial era.

Native Americans' Reservation Life

Throughout this period Native Americans continued to experience the racist treatment inflicted on them since Columbus's time: In their passion for what they considered the Indians' one precious resource—land—white Americans used their superior power to subdue the native inhabitants and to relocate them to reservations, where they fell under the control of the Bureau of Indian Affairs. Meanwhile, whites' ethnocentric outlook drove them to provide their victims with a new and "better" culture and way of life.

Native Americans were hardly convinced. Always objects of exploitation, they were located on reservations with land that was often arid and infertile. When Indians were fairly successful agriculturally, they were vulnerable to white encroachment. For instance, Apaches on the San Carlos Reservation had their water supply diverted upstream by Mormon settlers, which destroyed their farms. If, against heavy odds, Indians developed products for sale, they found themselves isolated from white markets. Almost invariably the result was that Native Americans were forced to become wards of the state, subject to control imposed by the Bureau of Indian Affairs (Kivisto, 1995: 264–265).

In 1887 the passage of the Dawes Act mandated the end of common land holdings on reservations; instead, each single Indian adult or family was supposed to receive a 160-acre plot. One immediate effect of the Dawes Act was that millions of acres of so-called "surplus" reservation land not included in the allotments was taken from the Indians and sold to white farmers, miners, and corporations.

For many Indians the 160-acre allotment provided inferior land that was inadequate for crops or grazing animals. In other instances, however, land quality was good, and Native Americans were able to lease the land to farmers and ranchers for substantial income. While many Indians were pleased with this arrangement, white reformers obsessed with the work ethic were disturbed, feeling that such a system made Native Americans unproductive and lazy. These people reasoned that if the Indians could sell at least some of their land, then they could buy machinery and homes that would allow them to become effective, hard-working farmers in the best American tradition.

The reformers convinced congressional members of the righteousness of such an approach, and between 1902 and 1910, Congress passed legislation permitting the sale of all Indian-owned land. Within a decade over half the Indians who had received allotments under the Dawes Act had sold their land at far below market value and were both landless and penniless. Landless Indians were in a much more economically deprived state than landless whites, because they were unprepared educationally and culturally to face the white work world, whose members tended to respond violently to Native Americans venturing outside of reservations (Berthrong, 1986: 204–209).

During this era missionaries, officials of the Bureau of Indian Affairs, reservation teachers, and personnel at federally funded boarding schools tried to impress the importance of dropping traditional ways and learning white people's culture. Indian boys and young men were supposed to receive training as farmers or laborers while Indian girls and young women were prepared for housekeeping and domestic tasks.

In the late nineteenth century, boarding schools, which supposedly trained young Native Americans for jobs in the industrial world, reached their highest level of enrollment, with 25 schools enrolling over 6,000 students. The schools had major deficiencies, however. The young people were lonely living in a culturally alien atmosphere, and they were repelled by the inevitable emphasis on military organization: By the middle 1890s, both girls and boys were placed in drill companies on the first day of school, were required to wear uniforms, and were led by student officers following army drill regulations. Ethnocentric in outlook, most school officials praised the military structure, contending that it

> served to develop a work ethic; it broke the students' sense of "Indian time" and ordered their life. The merits of military organization, drill, and routine . . . were explained by one official who stated that "it teaches patriotism, obedience, courage, courtesy, promptness, and constancy." (Trennert, 1986: 225)

Imbued with a sense of cultural superiority, teachers often humiliated their students. In an autobiographical account, one Native American indicated that in class a teacher asked him to read a paragraph, and he did so without error. The teacher, however, criticized the performance and demanded that he read it again, and again, and again. After the eleventh reading, "everything before me went black and I sat down thoroughly cowed and humiliated for the first time in my life and in front of the whole class" (Luther Standing Bear, 1978: 146).

By the early 1920s, the Indian boarding schools ceased. Gradually educational officials recognized that while government officials might have established the schools with the intention of preparing Indians for work in the white world, actual training occurred in an atmosphere conveying a sense that they were racially and culturally inferior beings. Furthermore, jobs for which they were trained were rarely available, and Indians' condemnation of the boarding schools was growing (Trennert, 1986: 229–230).

Meanwhile, during the late nineteenth and early twentieth centuries, blacks faced new forms of oppression.

African Americans' Survival in the "Survival-of-the-Fittest" Era

While the end of slavery meant that blacks were technically free, an oppressive system of racial stratification continued. Whites were still much more powerful than blacks, using them to financial advantage in the expanding, early industrial economy.

After the Civil War, most ex-slaves found little reason to celebrate their recent freedom. The land had been devastated, with many blacks and some whites suffering from disease and starvation. Furthermore, southern whites, determined to retain as much power as possible over the newly freed blacks, passed the infamous Black Codes, which provided blacks scarcely more rights and opportunities than under slavery. In addition, President Andrew Johnson was sympathetic to white southerners, declaring that African Americans were not ready for the privileges of citizenship and vetoing legislation that would have benefited them. A fight between Congress and the president broke out, and in spite of Johnson's strenuous campaign for his program, the people sided with Congress, providing an overwhelming mandate to Thaddeus Stevens and other Republican congressmen supporting blacks' rights.

For blacks, it appeared to be a great moment. Historian Lerone Bennett, Jr., concluded, "Never before had the sun shone so bright" (Bennett, 1982: 214). The Reconstruction Act of 1867 passed, and all southern states had to convene racially mixed constitutional conventions, which outlawed slavery, eliminated race as a criterion for determining a person's right to possess and inherit property, permitted blacks to seek legal recourse for crimes against them or denial of rights, and extended the vote to all black males. Suddenly whites' overwhelming political power was threatened. In the next few years, blacks served as lieutenant governors in Mississippi, South Carolina, and Louisiana, as secretary of state in Florida, on the state supreme court in South Carolina, were a majority in the South Carolina House of Representatives, and held a host of less influential but important posts in southern state and municipal governments (Edwards, 1996; Franklin and Moss, 1988: 206–220).

Change was social as well as political. In South Carolina, probably the most racially liberal southern state, dramatic developments were occurring. One account noted:

> The social life was gay, glittering and interracial. A dashing militia captain gave a ball, and blacks and whites—some of them native South Carolinians—glided across the polished floor. At official balls, receptions and dinners, blacks and whites sat down together and got up in peace. (Bennett, 1982: 216)

But it was no more than a quick burst of sunshine. American public opinion was turning against people of non-Anglo-Saxon background in what soon became the heyday of social Darwinism. The Supreme Court adopted the tone of the times, emasculating the Fourteenth Amendment, which ensured that African Americans were citizens with full rights and privileges, by ruling that the amendment prohibited states but not individuals from discriminating. Many whites expressed their racism less elegantly. A group of South Carolina whites appeared before Congress in 1868, protesting African Americans' participation in politics and vowing to carry on the fight until blacks were once more subordinated. Expressing their racism proudly, they declared:

> That is a duty we owe to the land that is ours, to the graves that it contains, and to the race of which you and we alike are members—the proud Caucasian race, whose sovereignty on earth God has ordained. (Bailyn et al., 1977: 766)

Faced with white southerners' continuous resistance, northern congressmen gradually grew indifferent to the long struggle for blacks' rights, and in 1877 federal troops meant to ensure the implementation of Reconstruction-era laws were removed from the South (Smith, 1997). The message was clear. No lasting economic, political, or social reforms would emerge—no guaranteed 40 acres of land and a mule (as one congressional supporter had promised), no guaranteed citizens' rights, no guaranteed boost in social position, but only a full share of racism and terror.

The terror struck with full force at the turn of the century, primarily in the South. Two general factors seemed to lie behind the beatings, shootings, and lynchings—the desire to drive blacks out of political activity initiated during Reconstruction and into terrorized submission; and a general sense of social crisis generated by economic depression, with blacks serving as scapegoats for fearful, frustrated whites. A study of lynchings occurring in Georgia between 1890 and 1900 found that counties demonstrating intense economic competition between blacks and whites had a greater number of lynchings than counties where that competition was less intense. Between 1882 and 1901, 1,914 African Americans were lynched. While still alive, victims were sometimes roasted slowly over fires or had limbs or sexual organs amputated. Castration occurred in hundreds of lynchings, with the impulse to castrate black males popularized in white literature and folklore. After death, pieces of the victim routinely were distributed to onlookers who wanted souvenirs of the notable event (Marable, 1994: 71; Shapiro, 1988: 30–31; Soule, 1992).

During that era whites often believed that most lynching victims had raped white women. Records do not support this conclusion, however. In the first 14 years of the twentieth century, just 315 lynching victims were accused of rape or attempted rape while over 500 were accused of homicide and others of robbery, insulting whites, and a variety of nebulous "offenses" (Franklin and Moss, 1988: 282).

How did the people of that era feel about lynching? Unfortunately, systematic survey research did not start for several decades. In 1905 one writer, however, did have the initiative to record the following data: In the trial of white men accused of burning two black men to death, 76 of 110 prospective jurors (69 percent) indicated that even if evidence clearly demonstrated that the defendants had taken part in the murders, they would not have favored their conviction (Baker, 1973a). Such sentiment was consistent with the Slave Codes and other norms for whites' unregulated treatment of blacks established during slavery.

Even more threatening to blacks than lynchings were race riots, which were not directed at individuals but ranged across large areas and could involve any African Americans unlucky enough to be in the vicinity. In the early 1900s, while the number of lynchings slowly decreased, the frequency of riots rose in both southern and northern cities. As black immigration to the North increased, hostilities grew proportionately; the riot that occurred in 1908 in Springfield, Illinois, during which two black men were killed within a half-mile of the only home Abraham Lincoln ever owned, was as ferocious as any that occurred in the South (Franklin and Moss, 1988: 282–286).

Violence against African Americans was simply the most vicious example of the racism they encountered. In 1908 a writer asked blacks in both the North and South to summarize their chief complaints. In the South the first problem cited was almost always the separate and inferior railroad cars or facilities in railroad stations, followed by references to injustice in the courts, the low quality of schooling, and the prospect of physical violence. In contrast, in the North, overwhelmingly the most frequent complaint involved discrimination in the workplace, even though job opportunities were much more extensive than in the South. To the southern black man, the North proved to be a shock. He was seeking work where he would be "judged at his worth as a man, not as a Negro: this he came North to find, and he . . . [met] difficulties of which he had not dreamed in the South" (Baker, 1973b: 279).

Black leaders responded in different ways to the violence and discrimination their people suffered. On September 18, 1895, Booker T. Washington, a very moderate leader, made a famous speech that became known as the "Atlanta Compromise." Appearing before a segregated, all-white crowd, Washington drew loud applause when he described blacks as "the most patient, faithful, law-abiding people the world had seen" and promised the increasingly enthusiastic audience that in all social areas, blacks would accept racial separation. A decade later W. E. B. DuBois and a group of black militants repudiated this position, claiming for themselves "every single right that belongs to a freeborn American, political, civil, and social; and until we get these rights we will never cease to protest and assail the ears of America" (Bennett, 1996: 150). To help accomplish such goals, these black leaders founded the National Association for the Advancement of Colored People. It was the first major organization formed to promote blacks' interests—certainly a formidable task at a time when most African Americans were poor and powerless.

Until World War I, most blacks lived in the South, but then several conditions encouraged them to leave. Because of a series of disastrous floods, the devastating impact of the Mexican boll weevil, and low cotton prices, many southern planters shifted from cotton to food crops and livestock, which required fewer workers. With declining demand for workers, wages plummeted. A noneconomic factor—the threat of lynching—also spurred a number of southern blacks to head north. A study covering the years 1910–1930 found that African Americans' migration was heaviest in southern counties where more lynchings had occurred.

While some factors pushed blacks to leave the South, others pulled them to the North. The outbreak of World War I contributed to a northern labor shortage in two ways. A sharply increased demand for northern industrial production of war supplies coincided with a curtailment of European laborers. This combination of conditions encouraged black laborers to respond favorably to recruiters who came south seeking workers.

Southern whites were alarmed by African Americans' flight and took measures to limit it. In Jacksonville, Florida, a local ordinance declared that all labor recruiters needed to pay a license fee of $1,000. In many southern towns and cities, whites threatened departing blacks, and the local newspapers urged that they remain. But blacks recognized that this was their chance to participate, if modestly, in the bounty of the industrial age. Northern employers appreciated the influx of African Americans at a time when otherwise they would have remained understaffed. Furthermore, patriotic Americans realized that without blacks the labor shortage would have significantly hampered the country's war effort. In the decade 1910–1920, the black population in the northern and midwestern states increased by about 525,000 people; during the 1920s about 877,000 African Americans left the South (Franklin and Moss, 1988: 251–252, 305–306; Massey and Denton, 1993: 29; Tolnay and Beck, 1992).

In the 1890s the typical African American resident of a northern city lived in an area that was 90 percent white. When large numbers of southern black workers started to arrive, whites' views toward African Americans quickly hardened. Northern newspapers participated enthusiastically, using such racist terms as "nigger" and "darky." Between 1900 and 1920, race riots broke out in a number of northern and midwestern cities. The worst riots occurred during the so-called "red summer" of 1919; throughout the country 26 riots broke out as returning white soldiers feared competition for jobs from African Americans. Blacks living outside recognized "black" neighborhoods had their homes ransacked or burned. To survive, African Americans had to move to recognized black areas. By about 1940 the segregated urban pattern leading to modern black ghettoes had been established (Massey and Denton, 1993: 29–31; Schaefer, 1993: 196).

While the racist atrocities of the early 1900s seem remote, their legacy can stretch to the present as the following situation indicates. The Tuskegee study, which began in 1932, was a research project in which the Public Health Service (and later the Centers for Disease Control) decided to record the natural course of syphilis by observing 400 black men with the disease without treating them. Recruited from churches and clinics throughout the South, the men were simply told they had "bad blood" and were not provided the standard 1930s treatment involving mercury and arsenic compounds nor penicillin when in 1947 it was found effective for treating syphilis.

The Tuskegee study continued for 40 years, ending abruptly in 1972 when a lawyer informed about the research went public with his knowledge. That would appear to have been the end of the damage done, but not so. For many southern blacks, the Tuskegee experiment created a legacy of distrust. For instance, one woman being treated for AIDS told her doctor that as a child she was warned to get home before dark because otherwise the Tuskegee researchers "would snatch her off the street and experiment on her in the basement at night" (Stryker, 1997: 4). Such stories were common, symptomatic of a massive, persistent mistrust. Many blacks, particularly those living in the rural South, have believed that HIV, the virus causing AIDS, was produced in laboratories to kill African Americans; that AZT, a prominent drug for treating AIDS, was meant to poison blacks; and that both condom use and needle-exchange programs have been part of the conspiracy to wipe out African Americans. A 1990 poll conducted among 1,956 black churchgoers provided consistent information, indicating that 35 percent of the respondents believed that AIDS was meant to produce genocide for blacks (Stryker, 1997).

Now we move from the macro-level analysis to the micro-level, considering one young African American's struggle during the early twentieth century.

Perils of Being Black in the Early Twentieth Century South

When famed writer Richard Wright was growing up in the South, the Civil War had been over for about a half-century. For those 50 years, African Americans had been technically free, but, in the well-known phrase, they were expected "to know their place"—to accept that they would be deprived of full rights and privileges in society.

As the introduction to a book of short stories entitled *Uncle Tom's Children,* Wright wrote an autobiographical essay that showed how perilous the lives of young black people could be. One tenet of internal colonialism is the colonial labor principle, stressing that racial minorities are expected to perform tasks that primarily benefit majority group members. But what if a young black man ignored this principle and considered work a personal growth experience? Such an approach represents a direct challenge to the current racial order. It illustrates what Erving Goffman called **normification**—behavior that gives the impression that an individual widely considered inferior is trying to deny being different (Goffman, 1974: 115).

Wright applied for a job at an optical company in Jackson, Mississippi. The interview went well, with Wright careful to show the expected deference by pronouncing his "sirs" very distinctly. He was hired, and the new boss indicated that Wright would be able to learn about the business. As a result the new employee had visions of working his way up. The first month went well enough, but while cleaning the shop and polishing lenses, Wright gradually realized that he had no opportunity to learn anything, in spite of the boss's claim.

So one day Wright approached Morrie, a young white colleague about his own age, and asked about his work. Morrie grew red and asked, "Whut yuh tryin' t' do, nigger, git smart?" No, Wright replied, he wasn't trying to get smart. "Well, don't, if yuh know what's good for yuh!" Morrie replied.

Puzzled, Wright concluded that Morrie simply did not want to help him, and so he went to Pease, the other employee, and asked him about his work.

> "Say, are you crazy, you black bastard?" Pease asked me, his gray eyes growing hard.
>
> I spoke out, reminding him that the boss had said I was to be given a chance to learn something.
>
> "Nigger, you think you're white, don't you?"
>
> "Naw, sir!"
>
> "Well, you're acting mighty like it!" (Wright, 1938: xv)

Pease went on to warn Wright to stay away from "white man's work."

From then on both Pease and Morrie treated Wright differently. They ignored him unless he was a bit slow performing some task. Then they called him "a lazy black son-of-a-bitch" and told him to hurry up.

Wright faced other dangerous situations in which normification became an issue. One day, entering an elevator along with some white men, Wright had an armload of packages. Because of the packages, he could not remove his hat as whites always expected of African Americans in their presence. After staring at him coldly, one of the white men removed Wright's hat and stuck it under his arm.

Had Wright thanked the white man, he would have risked a punch in the mouth since such a response would have suggested normification—implying a situation of racial equality in which the white man had done him a favor. The safe course of action would have been to look at the white man out of the corner of his eye and grin. Wright refused to demean himself by taking the easy way out, but he also wanted to avoid the punch in the mouth. So as soon as the hat was placed under his arm, he used another strategy—acting as though the packages were slipping and seemingly making a highly concentrated effort to prevent it from happening (Wright, 1938: xxx).

In his youth Richard Wright had several painful experiences making it clear that when dealing with whites, black people put their physical safety on the line if they even hinted at normification. In the early twentieth century South, African Americans were safe only if their words and actions constantly reassured whites that they, the blacks, accepted the caste system and its rituals of subordination (discussed in Chapter 2).

During the preindustrial era, other racial minorities began arriving in the United States.

Chinese, Japanese, Mexican, and Puerto Rican Pioneers

In the late nineteenth and early twentieth centuries, the four groups examined in this section started arriving in the United States. The factor in Noel's scheme most saliently affecting their situation is the issue of competition. Workers from these countries were welcomed when it proved beneficial to businesses to obtain cheap labor. On the other hand, frequently white workers found themselves in competition with these immigrants for jobs, and as a result resentment and even violence against them developed, with the law providing minority groups little protection. Noel's two other factors also are relevant: At times whites' ethnocentrism helped make it acceptable to oppress a particular racial minority, and whites' superior power allowed them to establish policies and pass laws limiting newly arrived minorities' opportunities.

Chinese immigrants, who were escaping the ravages of the Taiping Rebellion in southern China, reached the West Coast when gold was discovered in California. At first relations between the races were amiable because the Chinese were willing to work the areas already abandoned by whites who had moved on to more profitable sites. Eventually, however, the Chinese workers' willingness to put in long, arduous, but productive days proved abrasive to whites; even though the recent arrivals were restricted from the richest areas, they simply were too successful. The remedy was to pass a special foreign mining-license tax imposed once a month almost exclusively on the Chinese. Still they kept coming to California and, by 1860, represented nearly 10 percent of its population.

By the early 1860s, the gold supply had started to dwindle, and most Chinese had little to do. White leaders wanted to exploit this eager, hard-working labor source. Would the seemingly puny Chinese be strong enough to lay track for the transcontinental railroad? Widespread debate developed, and eventually Charles Crocker, a contractor for the Central Pacific Railroad, decided to give them a trial. Although scornfully called "Crocker's pets," 1,200 Chinese were hired for construction and between 1864 and 1869 proved to be excellent workers. But then the job was done, and along with about an equal number of non-Chinese, they were out of work. Meanwhile about a million people had moved to California on the transcontinental railroad, and the result was a distinct labor surplus.

In the context of racist, late nineteenth century America, it was not surprising that the Chinese became scapegoats for white workers' economic plight. At a miners' meeting, the participants concluded that any means necessary should be used to stop the "Asiatic inundation" and that the ruling class and the Chinese shared responsibility for job scarcity. The miners produced a fierce, racist statement flatly declaring that

> the Capitalists, ship-owners and merchants and others who are encouraging or engaged in the importation of these burlesques on humanity would crowd their ships with the long-tailed, horned, and cloven-hoofed inhabitants of the infernal regions. (Daniels and Kitano, 1970: 36)

In the 1870s and 1880s, hostility toward the Chinese became more than verbal. Violence started in the mining districts and surged into the cities. Chinese were robbed, beaten, and sometimes killed, but because of the laxity of law enforcement and a statute prohibiting Chinese from testifying against whites, almost no criminal prosecution occurred. Mark Twain wrote,

> I have seen Chinamen abused and maltreated in all the mean, cowardly ways possible to the invention of a degraded nature, but I never saw a Chinaman righted in a court of justice for wrongs thus done him. (Twain, 1868)

One analyst suggested that supporters of the Chinese were "the rich, the good, and the wise"—merchants seeking trade with the Far East, ranchers and farmers looking for cheap laborers, most Protestant clergy, and individuals searching for low-paid, docile servants. The anti-Chinese forces were composed of white working-class people competing against Chinese immigrants for jobs and two groups who needed support from working-class whites to survive occupationally—politicians seeking their votes and journalists requiring their patronage (Daniels, 1988: 51–52). Thus the economic factor played a major role in whites' response to early Chinese immigration.

Eventually Congress decided to take a decisive step to quell the violence and to protect jobs for white workers. The Chinese Exclusion Act of 1882 halted the immigration of laborers and helped to alleviate if not eliminate anti-Chinese violence, which continued through the 1880s (Knoll, 1982: 24–27).

The Japanese arrived on the West Coast several decades after the Chinese, and they inherited much of the racist feeling. "Now the Jap is a wily an' a crafty individual—more so than the Chink," warned a writer in the *Sacramento Bee* (quoted in Okimoto, 1971: 15). To many white Americans, newly arrived Japanese workers willing to work at the most menial, lowest-paying jobs simply extended the "Yellow Peril," threatening employment, housing, and even American culture itself. As Japanese immigration reached a peak of about 50,000 in the first decade of the twentieth century, Congress passed the United States Immigration Act of 1907, which authorized the president to restrict entrance of foreign workers if he deemed that their arrival would jeopardize opportunities for American workers. The following year President Theodore Roosevelt negotiated a deal with the Japanese government, permitting only the families of Japanese men already owning land or families headed by professionals to immigrate. This arrangement precluded the embarrassment of legislation similar to the Chinese Exclusion Act of 1882 (Ima, 1982: 263–264; Knoll, 1982, 53–58).

Unlike Asian Americans, the earliest Mexican Americans (Chicanos) did not immigrate to the United States. They were living in Texas when, following the

Mexican War, the United States gained permanent possession of the land that currently constitutes the states of Texas, New Mexico, and Arizona. As late as 1910, however, only about 250,000 Mexican Americans, people of Spanish descent sometimes combined with Native American heritage, were residents of the United States.

At that time a pair of events in Mexico—the release of workers from forced labor on large haciendas (ranches) and the violence produced by revolution—encouraged many Mexicans to flee their homeland. Along the U.S. border, work was available because legislation had compelled many large cattle and sheep ranchers to give way to crop farmers who badly needed laborers. In the 1920s Mexicans also moved to such northern manufacturing cities as Chicago, Detroit, and Milwaukee, where they became factory employees. By the early 1930s, there were nearly 1.5 million Mexican Americans in the United States. During that decade, however, there was a great surplus of workers because of high unemployment accompanying the Great Depression. About 400,000 out-of-work Mexican Americans either returned to Mexico voluntarily or were forced to leave by government officials intent on reducing welfare roles.

With the outbreak of World War II, the employment picture once again changed dramatically. Mobilizing for war, the United States badly needed workers to fill farm-labor jobs left by departing soldiers. In 1942 the *bracero* program, which had existed briefly during World War I, was reestablished. It involved a bilateral agreement between Mexico and the United States about the supply of labor. The American government underwrote Mexicans' travel costs and promised both a minimum wage and just treatment for *braceros* (temporary laborers) working on privately owned farms in the United States. Essentially, the program provided a federal subsidy for agricultural interests, and while originally intended only to meet wartime labor shortages, it continued for a quarter-century after the war because it proved useful on both sides of the border. For Mexico the *bracero* program served as a partial solution for high unemployment, and for U.S. farmers it produced a steady supply of cheap labor.

Frequently employers violated the program's conditions, and although the Mexican government protested the violations, few official efforts sought to prevent them; the federal government, in fact, permitted agricultural interests almost complete control of wages, housing conditions, and other factors affecting workers' welfare. Although the *bracero* program was officially discontinued in 1964, many American farmers still maintain it informally, illegally hiring Mexican farmworkers.

At present about 90 percent of Chicano citizens live in urban areas, particularly in the Southwest. A substantial number, however, live elsewhere, especially in the Midwest (Feagin and Feagin, 1993: 262–264; Heyman, 1990; Keefe and Padilla, 1987; Maldonado, 1982; Stoddard, 1973: 2–30).

Puerto Ricans, another major Hispanic group, began reaching the United States in the nineteenth century, but their relations with whites began much earlier. On November 19, 1493, on his second voyage to the New World, Columbus arrived in Puerto Rico. At that time the island inhabitants were members of the Tainos tribe, and when the Spanish conquered the island, most of the Tainos died because of exposure to European diseases. As a result of this annihilation of indigenous people, the Spanish had no source of cheap labor. In 1511, to remedy the situation, they started bringing in African slaves, and the practice of slavery continued for over three and a half centuries until it was abolished in 1873.

In 1898, following Spain's defeat in the Spanish-American War, the island became a possession of the United States. American-owned sugar plantations dominated the economy until after World War II when the local government started a program of economic expansion that produced over 1,000 factories by 1970. For American businessmen, it has been very profitable to establish factories in Puerto Rico since local workers could be hired for considerably less than mainland laborers (Fitzpatrick, 1987: 28–29, 33–34). Commenting on 500 years of white exploitation, Jesus Colon wrote:

> The first thing we must realize is that . . . strangers have been knocking at the door of the Puerto Rican nation for centuries always in search of something, to get something or to take away something from Puerto Ricans. This has been done many times with the forceful and openly criminal way of the pirate. (Colon, 1961: 147)

Before the Spanish-American War, most of the Puerto Rican immigrants were political exiles who used New York as a base for seeking support for the island's independence. Obviously these people were disappointed when the United States took over the island instead of granting independent status.

The greatest influx of Puerto Ricans to the mainland occurred in the 1950s when the American economy was flourishing. For instance, in 1953, nearly 75,000 people left the island for the mainland, compared to only about 1,000 in 1940. By the 1970s, however, a stagnating economy meant the decline in low-skilled jobs, and migration to the mainland slowed but still occurs at present. Through the years a rapidly growing population in an undeveloped economy where unemployment has remained high has spurred the migratory flow. Furthermore, as American citizens, Puerto Ricans do not face legal restrictions on entering the country, and since the island is close to the mainland, flights from and to the island are fairly cheap.

Race and racism have been complicated issues for Puerto Ricans. While firmly established segregation patterns never existed on the island, Puerto Ricans have been aware of racial differences. Traditionally, upper-class individuals prided themselves on what they claimed to be their pure Spanish lineage, and among other social-class groups, there has been a similar preoccupation with color. But while a concern with people's skin color and other racial characteristics has existed, Puerto Ricans claim that social class, not race, determines how one person will treat another. In Puerto Rico, they say, an upper-class white Puerto Rican will treat lower-class Puerto Ricans the same way, regardless of whether they appear to be white or racially mixed. In the United States, in contrast, people's color often determines their treatment, regardless of their social class. For Puerto Ricans with an African and Indian heritage, such abruptly explicit racial discrimination can be painful to encounter (Fitzpatrick, 1987: 18-19, 105–106; Marger, 1997: 287–288).

Located at the nexus of two very different cultural traditions, modern Puerto Ricans often must face problems and challenges to which most Americans are oblivious. For Puerto Rican women, this situation is particularly difficult.

Stereotyped in Everyday Life

Riding an English bus one day, poet Judith Ortiz Cofer suddenly found herself facing a young man, clearly fresh from a pub, who kneeled in the aisle and with both hands over his heart broke into an Irish tenor's version of "Maria" from *West Side Story*. The amused passengers clapped politely and, though less amused, Cofer gave her version of a restrained English smile. She wrote:

> I was at this time of my life practicing reserve and cool. Oh, that British control, how I coveted it. But Maria had followed me to London, reminding me of a prime fact of my life: you can leave the Island, master the English language, and travel as far as you can, but if you are a Latina, especially one like me who so obviously belongs to Rita Moreno's gene pool, the Island travels with you. (Cofer, 1995: 203)

Throughout her life, Cofer indicated, she has been the brunt of stereotyping. Sometimes, as in the previous example, the stereotyping was fairly gentle; in other instances the representation was distinctly consistent with internal colonialism's emphasis on the inferiority of minority group culture and social organization.

Certainly Cofer's childhood took place outside the cultural mainstream. During the 1960s her family lived in urban New Jersey, speaking Spanish at home, eating Puerto Rican food, and practicing strict Catholicism.

Growing up in a Puerto Rican subculture, Cofer felt unprepared for many conventional American experiences. For Career Day at her high school, the teachers told the students to dress as if for a job interview. But except for television actresses, Cofer had no mainstream models. She was left to agonize over what to wear, and while she couldn't recall her actual outfit, it was clear that she and the other Puerto Rican girls received teachers' criticism for wearing too much jewelry and overly tight skirts.

In addition, Cofer pointed out, she and other Latinas have been the object of media-promoted stereotypes describing them as "sizzling" and "smoldering"—stereotypes that fail to recognize that Puerto Rican women have traditionally grown up in communities where the extended family and the church provided standards of purity as well as protection from men's sexual exploitation.

Going to school and working in mainstream society, Cofer was exposed to the stereotypes but was without the traditional protection of family and church. At her first formal dance, the Anglo boy who brought her leaned over to plant a kiss on her mouth and was disturbed when she showed insufficient passion. The boy, Cofer recalled, said resentfully, " 'I thought you Latin girls were supposed to mature early'— my first instance of being thought of as a fruit or vegetable—I was supposed to ripen, not just grow into womanhood like other girls" (Cofer, 1995: 205).

Cofer indicated that stereotyping incidents remain common in her life. Several years ago she was staying at a very classy metropolitan hotel patronized by young professional couples for their weddings. Walking through the lobby with a colleague, Cofer found a middle-aged man in a tuxedo accompanied by a young girl dressed in satin and lace blocking her path. Raising his champagne glass toward her, he shouted "Evita!" Then, still blocking the way, the man bellowed the song, "Don't Cry for Me, Argentina." Afterwards the young girl said, "How about a round of applause for my daddy?" At this moment the man, who seemed encouraged by the growing crowd, broke into a ditty sung to the tune of "La Bamba" with lyrics about the exploits of a girl named Maria and each line rhyming with her name or gonorrhea. As the man sang, his daughter kept saying, "Oh, daddy" while her pleading eyes implored Cofer to laugh along with the others. But Cofer just waited silently for him to finish. Then, without looking at the man, she turned to his daughter and calmly told her never to ask him what he had done in the army. As they left, Cofer's companion complimented her on how coolly she handled the situation. Cofer admitted that she would have preferred pushing him into the swimming pool—that had she been white he probably

> would have checked his impulse by assuming that she could be somebody's wife or mother, or at least *somebody* who might take offense. But to him, I was just an Evita or a Maria: merely a character in his cartoon-populated universe. (Cofer, 1995: 206)

Part of the stereotype imposed on Latina women, Cofer found, was the conviction that invariably they fill lowly roles—in the language of internal colonialism, they are the objects of the colonial labor principle. A friend working on her Ph.D. at a major university said her doctor shook his head in amazement at all the big words she used.

Cofer's most vivid memory of her first public poetry reading, which occurred at a boat-restaurant in Miami, involved an older white woman who motioned Cofer to her table. Mistakenly thinking that the woman wanted her to autograph her slim volume of poetry, she went. The woman ordered a cup of coffee, apparently assuming that any Puerto Rican woman in the restaurant must be a waitress. Cofer recalled:

> Easy enough to mistake my poems for menus, I suppose. I know that it wasn't an intentional act of cruelty, yet of all the good things that happened to me that day, I remember that scene most clearly, because it reminded me of what I had to overcome before anyone would take me seriously. (Cofer, 1995: 207)

Yet, Cofer conceded, she was one of the lucky ones—a woman whose parents had supported her pursuit of education, which had made possible a life much less exposed to the prejudice and hardship the majority of Latina women must face.

Majority group members, Cofer argued, perceive these women in a highly stereotyped way. She wrote:

> My personal goal in my public life is to try to replace the old pervasive stereotypes and myths about Latinas with a much more interesting set of realities. Every time I give a reading, I hope the stories I tell, the dreams and fear I examine in my work, can achieve some universal truth which will get my audience past the particulars of my skin color, my accent, or my clothes. (Cofer, 1995: 207)

Cofer's experiences bring us to modern times, where we consider the events and conditions that have set the stage for race relations in the late industrial era, which will be discussed in detail in other chapters.

The Late Industrial Period

By the middle of the current century, all racial groups examined in this book had substantial membership in the United States. While significant changes have continued to occur, it appears that the racial-stratification system was essentially in place. Thus, at this juncture, it seems reasonable to suspend the use of Noel's theory on the development of racial stratification and employ the internal colonialist theory. Table 3.1 summarizes the relationship of theory to events in the three historical sections examined in this chapter.

During World War II, an executive order banning discrimination in defense plants and government agencies, along with an acute labor shortage, permitted blacks and other racial minorities to move into semiskilled manufacturing jobs and some white-

Table 3.1 Historical Stages of American Racism

I. Preindustrial Stage (analyzed by Noel's theory of the origin of racial stratification)
   A. Ethnocentrism stressing Native Americans' and blacks' cultural inferiority
   B. Competition, with whites experiencing an expanding, unregulated economy: Indians' loss of land and traditional subsistence patterns; blacks' slavery
   C. Whites' superior power, permitting complete control of Native Americans and blacks

II. Early Industrial Stage (analyzed by Noel's theory)
   A. Social Darwinism, ethnocentrically declaring racial minorities "less fit" racially and culturally
   B. Competition pursued by whites in an expanding, largely unregulated economy
   C. Whites' greater power, allowing nearly complete control of policies and practices affecting racial minorities

III. Late Industrial Stage (analyzed by internal colonialism)
   A. Whites controlling the political structure and determining the policies dominating racial minorities' lives
   B. Ghettoes and segregation forcing racial minorities to live in certain areas and making them highly vulnerable to economic downturns; sporadic violence against minorities limiting freedom of movement
   C. Consistent with the colonial labor principle, racial minorities highly overrepresented in low-paid, menial jobs
   D. Blaming-the-victim ideology ignoring institutional racism and emphasizing that poor members of racial minorities possess cultural inferiority

collar positions. While some individuals belonging to racial minorities lost their positions to returning veterans after the war, the expanding economy provided improved opportunities for many of them.

At the time the economy was starting to shift from one focused on goods-producing industries (manufacturing, construction, mining, and agriculture) to one primarily concerned with services (government, transportation, public utilities, trade, and later, information transmission). In this new economy, members of racial minorities with appropriate educational and training credentials, sometimes assisted by affirmative action standards, could often locate well-paying jobs (Wilson, 1978: 88–93).

But in recent decades racial discrimination has continued to be widespread, and protest against it has been extensive.

Racial Minorities' Protest in Modern Times

On February 1, 1960, four black students from the Negro Agricultural College in Greensboro, North Carolina, entered a variety store, bought several items, and then sat down at a lunch counter and ordered coffee. At the time their action was remarkable, because the lunch counter, like other public facilities then in the South, was officially segregated. The students were refused service, but they continued to sit at the counter until the store closed. This was the opening attack of the sit-in movement, which was a peaceful effort to destroy segregation in stores, libraries, hotels, buses, and other southern public facilities.

During the early 1960s, peaceful protests demanding full civil rights for blacks spread throughout the South. In May 1961 the Congress of Racial Equality, a prominent civil rights organization, sent "freedom riders" into the South to challenge segregation laws in interstate transportation. In several Alabama cities, the interracial teams encountered violence when their buses were attacked. Eventually Attorney General Robert Kennedy sent 600 federal officers to the scene to restore order (Franklin and Moss, 1988: 439–444). While blacks' civil rights were not high on the agenda for either Robert Kennedy or his brother, the president, the Kennedys basically supported freedom riders' efforts. Martin Luther King, Jr., suggested that the attorney general seek a ruling from the Interstate Commerce Commission establishing the rights of all interstate travelers. At first Robert Kennedy branded the scheme naive, but then he changed his mind, ordering Justice Department lawyers to keep after ICC commissioners until they issued a ruling protecting the rights of interstate travelers. In September, Kennedy received the ICC statement. Taylor Branch indicated that Kennedy and his assistants had "telescoped a process that normally took years—even if the commissioners like the proposal, which in this case they did not—into less than four months. Experts considered the lobbying feat a bureaucratic miracle" (Branch, 1988: 478).

The unstable partnership between protesters in the South and the federal government also involved school integration and voting rights. Although black and white protesters were sometimes attacked, beaten, and even killed, government forces offered some protection and support. Advances occurred, most notably the Civil Rights Act of 1964 and the Voting Rights Act of 1965, which we discuss in the next chapter.

It took enormous conviction and courage to be a prominent participant in southern civil rights protests. In 1963 Medgar Evers was the best-known civil rights leader in Mississippi, initiating organized drives for integration in general and equitable employment in particular. More than 30 years later, his wife recalled:

> We both knew the end was near. You don't challenge a system like that without knowing the price to be paid. We lived with threats on a daily basis, and both of us knew in the last three weeks that it wasn't going to be long. (Applebome, 1994: 30)

On June 12, 1963, Medgar Evers was assassinated.

Outside of the South, intentionally segregated facilities was not the core problem. In those regions blacks and other racial minorities were victims of institutional racism in politics, work, education, and housing. In 1966 Stokely Carmichael, a prominent civil rights leader, started speaking about "black power"—that only if blacks provided strong, militant leadership for their own people would they obtain a fair share of the society's political, economic, and social rewards. Black leaders' style changed, and many began to predict that unless African Americans started receiving equal rights, massive violence would occur. Riots in Los Angeles, Detroit, Newark, Washington, DC, Cleveland, and a host of other cities indicated that the black-power leaders were not making idle statements.

Studies of American riots occurring between 1960 and 1993 indicated that they were more likely to occur at times of rapid social change: when black residents were more involved in competition for jobs and housing during years of rapid population growth (Olzak and Shanahan, 1996; Olzak, Shanahan, and McEneaney, 1996).

In the late 1960s, other racial groups besides African Americans became involved in protests. Among Native Americans the best-known protest group was the American Indian Movement (AIM). Founded in 1968 in Minneapolis, it had over 70 chapters four years later and played a major part in several large protests, including the 71-day, armed occupation of reservation land on the Pine Ridge reservation in Wounded Knee, South Dakota (Farley, 1988: 143; Nagel, 1993: 10). In the late 1960s and early 1970s, disgusted with the failure of established political organizations to oppose discriminatory policies against Mexican Americans, a group of radical Chicanos formed *La Raza Unida,* which ran candidates for statewide and local offices, winning a number of contests and initiating educational and social programs that helped their primarily low-income constituents. In the spring of 1969, some Puerto Rican men in Chicago started the Young Lords, a militant organization, which soon established chapters in other cities. The New York City branch, for instance, occupied the First Spanish Methodist Church for 11 days and started a day-care center, a breakfast program, and a clothing distribution program. In the 1960s an Asian American movement, led by Japanese American students, began to challenge older leaders and traditional ways. Programs in Asian American studies were established, and in their own journals, Asian Americans started to encourage their people to discover new ways of developing group pride and collective consciousness (Feagin and Feagin, 1993: 191–182, 276–277, 315–316, 351).

The accomplishments of minority group organizations, however, were offset by the dismemberment of various progressive social programs and policies during the Reagan/Bush presidential years. As a result many middle-class African Americans became deeply disillusioned about what they had started to believe might be an inevitable path toward racial integration and equality. Without faith in black nationalism and having lost faith in American democratic institutions, they found themselves, in the words of sociologist Robert Washington, "ideologically adrift, groping for a different, more practical conception of black America's place in American society" (Washington, 1993: 259). Unfortunately, during the past two decades, one prominent reality has encouraged such pessimism.

The Double Whammy: Racism and Poverty

Since the 1970s a new complex of destructive economic and social conditions has affected many minority group members, particularly poor African Americans and black Puerto Ricans. These groups, often labeled members of the so-called "underclass," now seem to have little opportunity to escape poverty. One contributing factor has been the loss of jobs for unskilled minorities produced by the decline of manufacturing and the suburbanization of blue-collar employment (Wilson, 1987). Douglas Massey and his associates (Massey, 1990; Massey and Denton, 1993; Massey and Hajnal, 1995) have argued that the most significant cause of blacks' poverty has been racial segregation in housing.

Focusing on African Americans, Massey analyzed the significance of racial segregation in housing. He indicated that in a largely integrated area, particularly if it has diverse income groups, an increase in poverty (such as the one occurring during the economic downturn of the early 1970s) will adversely affect the area but will not alter its basic functioning. The economic strengths of the district will offset increased poverty, which will be dispersed throughout it.

In contrast, if African Americans face segregated housing, they will be forced to live in a restricted number of locales, which, given blacks' history of job discrimination, are likely to be in no better than fair economic condition in the best of times. An economic downturn will not only affect black residents more readily than whites, since blacks' greater poverty makes them more vulnerable to the downturn, but given housing segregation, poor blacks from other locales may be forced by the downturn to move into the area, contributing significantly to its economic decline. As a result many businesses will fail or be forced to leave; local opportunities for work will decline or virtually disappear; with the loss of local income, clinics and hospitals will leave the area; schooling, which is highly dependent on district funding, will sharply decline in quality; local residents will be less able to maintain their homes, landlords will be less motivated to do so, and with deterioration of residential buildings, the number of deserted buildings will increase; and, because of the growth of poverty, crime and violence will accelerate. Over the past 30 years, this process has contributed substantially to the rapid increase in the number of poor African Americans.

But many people pay little attention to structural conditions producing poverty and racism. They focus on somebody's inability to be successful, to avoid poverty. Social Darwinist or hateful references no longer prevail. The common approach is what we noted in Chapter 1—"symbolic racism"—a combination of traditional American values and anti-minority feeling. Individuals engaging in symbolic racism are likely to indicate how African Americans or members of other minorities often lack the work ethic to succeed in conventional educational or occupational structures. Minorities, such people conclude, simply are not sufficiently motivated.

William Ryan (1976) has called this approach "blaming the victim." The failure to achieve success is described as an individual's personal deficiency, and the economic and political conditions severely limiting that person's full participation in society—in short, conditions promoting institutional racism—are downplayed or ignored. In modern times politicians, policy makers, and social scientists have often endorsed the blaming-the-victim approach, emphasizing racial minorities' cultural inferiority. Widespread support for such a perspective is hardly surprising in a culture that has placed a premium on the importance of individuals' strivings and success in competitive settings.

What is to be done? As I suggest throughout the book, the first step is to determine the sources of a race-related problem and then propose a solution.

Let's consider the situation for urban black males—statistically speaking, the most oppressed category of all American minorities. Sociologist Ronald L. Taylor noted that "because of a complex set of mutually reinforcing factors, black males start life with serious disadvantages" (Taylor, 1995: 327). The disadvantage begins at or before birth. Their mothers are disproportionately unwed teenagers, who are poorly educated and more likely than other categories of mothers to neglect or abuse their children. The disadvantage extends into such prominent areas as schooling, jobs, and involvement in crime and drug abuse.

In our society, where so much emphasis is placed on individual success, such people are devalued and invariably devalue themselves. Two lines of thought converge here: In a society which claims to embrace equal opportunity, those who are significantly disadvantaged *deserve* the chance to live well. Then there's the social good. If our society does not provide such opportunities, then a long host of social ills will persist and worsen: more children with serious problems, more delinquency, more crime, more drugs, more violence.

We can look to history for some guidance. In the 1960s and 1970s, job-training and employment programs for young African American men made it possible for thousands to earn their first steady income and become familiar with the world of work. Admittedly some programs were plagued with political and administrative problems, but the successful ones demonstrate how promising this direction can be. Taylor, who has studied these programs, wrote:

> As the employment crisis among inner-city black male youths deepens across the country, such programs may play a decidedly more important role in helping to reduce high levels of joblessness, crime, school truancy, and early parenthood among these men, provided such programs effectively address their personal and educational, as well as their employment needs. (Taylor, 1995: 333)

Unfortunately, it is highly questionable that the American public and the federal and state governments recognize that such programs represent both a humane and a practical, cost-effective investment in the nation's future.

Discussion Questions

1. Indicate how the art of making breakable treaties illustrates Noel's theory of ethnic stratification.

2. Some analyses of slaveowners distinguish between those who were harsh and those who were fairly humane. Discuss whether such a distinction is meaningful.

3. Define *normification* and indicate how it worked in Richard Wright's case. Describe any situation you know of in which it occurred.

4. Using the text and other sources, discuss major dangers and challenges faced by two of the pioneer groups described on pp. 61–66.

5. Explain why the combination of racism and poverty represent a "double whammy."

Sources

Alexander, Daryl Royster. 1997. "Looking beyond Jefferson the Icon to a Man and His Slave Mistress." *New York Times* (June 29): sec. 4, 7.

Allahar, Anton L. 1993. "When Black First Became Worth Less." *International Journal of Comparative Sociology* 34 (January–April): 39–55.

Applebome, Peter. 1994. "A Hot Summer of Bloodshed and Change." *New York Times* (February 6): 30.

Aptheker, Herbert. 1992. *Anti-Racism in U.S. History: The First Two Hundred Years.* Westport, CT: Greenwood Press.

Bailyn, Bernard, et al. 1977. *The Great Republic.* Lexington, MA: D.C. Heath.

Baker, Ray Stannard. 1973a. "What Is Lynching?" pp. 304–328 in Donald P. DeNevi and Doris A. Holmes (eds.), *Racism at the Turn of the Century: Documentary Perspectives 1870–1910.* San Rafael, CA: Leswing. Article originally published in 1905.

Baker, Ray Stannard. 1973b. "The Negro's Struggle for Survival in the North," pp. 278–289 in Donald P. DeNevi and Doris A. Holmes, (eds.), *Racism at the Turn of the Century: Documentary Perspectives 1870–1910.* San Rafael, CA: Leswing. Article originally published in 1908.

Bennett, Lerone, Jr. 19082. *Before the Mayflower: A History of Black America,* 5th ed.Chicago: Johnson Publishing Company.

Bennett, Lerone, Jr. 1996. "10 Most Dramatic Events in African-American History," pp. 148–151 in John A. Kromkowski (ed.), *Race and Ethnic Relations 93/94,* 6th ed. Guilford, CT: Dushkin Publishing Group.

Berthrong, Donald J. 1986. "Legacies of the Dawes Act: Bureaucrats and Land Thieves at the Cheyenne-Arapaho Agencies of Oklahoma," pp. 204–217 in Roger L. Nichols (ed.), *The American Indian: Past and Present,* 3rd ed. New York: Alfred A. Knopf.

Branch, Taylor. 1988. *Parting the Waters: America in the King Years 1954–63.* New York: Simon and Schuster.

Brown, Dee. 1972. *Bury My Heart at Wounded Knee.* New York: Bantam Books.

Cofer, Judith Ortiz. 1995. "The Myth of the Latin Woman: I Just Met a Girl Named Maria," pp. 203–207 in Paula S. Rothenberg (ed.), *Race, Class, and Gender in the United States: An Integrated Study,* 3rd ed. New York: St. Martin's Press.

Colon, Jesus. 1961. *A Puerto Rican in New York.* New York: Mainstream Publishers.

Cox, Oliver C. 1976. *Race Relations: Elements and Social Dynamics.* Detroit: Wayne State University Press.

Daniels, Edward, and Harry Kitano. 1970. *American Racism.* Englewood Cliffs, NJ: Prentice-Hall.

Daniels, Roger. 1988. *Asian Americans: Chinese and Japanese in the United States since 1850.* Seattle: University of Washington Press.

Deloria, Vine, Jr. 1972. *Of Utmost Good Faith.* New York: Bantam Books.

Douglass, Frederick. 1968. *Narrative of the Life of Frederick Douglass.* New York: Signet Books. Originally published in 1845.

Edwards, Laura F. 1996. "The Disappearance of Susan Daniel and Henderson Cooper: Gender and Narratives of Political Conflict in the Reconstruction-Era South." *Feminist Studies* 22 (Summer): 363–386.

Farley, John E. 1988. *Majority-Minority Relations,* 2nd ed. Englewood Cliffs, NJ: Prentice-Hall.

Feagin, Joe R., and Clairece Booher Feagin. 1993. *Racial and Ethnic Relations,* 4th ed. Englewood Cliffs, NJ: Prentice-Hall.

Fitzpatrick, Joseph P. 1987. *Puerto Rican Americans: The Meaning of Migration to the Mainland,* 2nd ed. Englewood Cliffs, NJ: Prentice-Hall.

Forbes, Ella. 1992. "African Resistance to Enslavement: The Nature and the Evidentiary Record." Journal of Black Studies 23 (September): 39–59.

Franklin, John Hope, and Alfred A. Moss, Jr. 1988. *From Slavery to Freedom: A History of Negro Americans,* 6th ed. New York: Alfred A. Knopf.

Goffman, Erving. 1974. *Stigma: Notes on the Management of Spoiled Identity.* New York: Jason Aronson.

Heyman, Josiah McC. 1990. "The Emergence of the Waged Life Course on the United States-Mexico Border." *American Ethnologist* 17 (May): 348–359.

Hofstadter, Richard. 1955. *Social Darwinism in American Thought,* rev. ed. Boston: Beacon Press.

Ima, Kenji. 1982. "Japanese Americans: The Making of 'Good' People," pp. 262–302 in Anthony Gary Dworkin and Rosalind J. Dworkin (eds.), *The Minority Report,* 2nd ed. New York: Holt, Rinehart and Winston.

Jacobs, Wilbur R. 1985. *Dispossessing the American Indian: Indians and Whites on the Colonial Frontier,* rev. ed. Norman: University of Oklahoma Press.

Keefe, Susan E., and Amado M. Padilla. 1987. *Chicano Ethnicity.* Albuquerque: University of New Mexico Press.

Kivisto, Peter. 1995. *Americans All: Race and Ethnic Relations in Historical, Structural, and Comparative Perspectives.* Belmont, CA: Wadsworth.

Knoll, Tricia. 1982. *Becoming Americans.* Portland, OR: Coast to Coast Books.

Luther Standing Bear. 1978. *Land of the Spotted Eagle.* Lincoln: University of Nebraska Press.

Lyon, William H. 1996. "The Navajos in the Anglo-American Historical Imagination, 1807–1870." *Ethnohistory* 43 (Summer): 483–509.

Maldonado, Lionel A. 1982. "Mexican-Americans: The Emergence of a Minority," pp. 168–195 in Anthony Gary Dworkin and Rosalind J. Dworkin (eds.), *The Minority Report,* 2nd ed. New York: Holt, Rinehart and Winston.

Marable, Manning. 1994. "The Black Male: Searching beyond Stereotypes," pp. 69-77 in Richard G. Majors and Jacob U. Gordon (eds.), *The American Black Male: His Present Status and His Future.* Chicago: Nelson-Hall Publishers.

Marger, Martin N. 1997. *Race and Ethnic Relations: American and Global Perspectives,* 4th ed. Belmont, CA: Wadsworth.

Massey, Douglas S. 1990. "American Apartheid: Segregation and the Making of the Underclass." *American Journal of Sociology* 96 (September): 329–357.

Massey, Douglas S., and Nancy A. Denton. 1993. *American Apartheid: Segregation and the Making of the Underclass.* Cambridge, MA: Harvard University Press.

Massey, Douglas S., and Zoltan L. Hajnal. 1995. "The Changing Geographic Structure of Black-White Segregation in the United States." *Social Science Quarterly* 76 (September): 527–542.

Nagel, Joane. 1993. "American Indian Mobilization: Tribal, Intertribal, and Supratribal Strategic Political Action," pp. 3–14 in Young I. Song and Eugene C. Kim (eds.), *American Mosaic: Selected Readings on America's Multicultural Heritage.* Englewood Cliffs, NJ: Prentice-Hall.

Nichols, Roger L. 1986. "The Indian in Nineteenth-Century America: A Unique Minority," pp. 127–136 in Roger L. Nichols (ed.), *The American Indian: Past and Present,* 3rd ed. New York: Alfred A. Knopf.

Noel, Donald L. 1968. "A Theory of the Origin of Ethnic Stratification." *Social Problems* 16 (Fall): 157–172.

Okimoto, Daniel I. 1971. *American in Disguise.* New York: John Weatherhill.

Olzak, Susan, and Suzanne Shanahan. 1996. "Deprivation and Race Riots: An Extension of Spilerman's Analysis." *Social Forces* 74 (March): 931–961.

Olzak, Susan, Suzanne Shanahan, and Elizabeth H. McEneaney. 1996. "Poverty, Segregation, and Race Riots: 1960 to 1993." *American Sociological Review* 61 (August): 590–613.

Rawick, George P. (ed.). 1972. *The American Slave: A Composite Autobiography.* Vol. 18. *Unwritten History of Slavery.* Westport, CT: Greenwood Publishing Company.

Ryan, William. 1976. *Blaming the Victim,* rev. ed. New York: Vintage Books.

Sack, Kevin. 1997. "Symbols of Old South Feed a New Bitterness." *New York Times* (February 8): 1+.

Schaefer, Richard T. 1993. *Racial & Ethnic Groups,* 5th ed. New York: HarperCollins.

Shapiro, Herbert. 1988. *White Violence and Black Response: From Reconstruction to Montgomery.* Amherst, MA: University of Massachusetts Press.

Smith, Dinitia. 1997. "Reconstruction's Deep Imprint." *New York Times* (June 18): C13.

Solomon, Mark. 1993. "Racism and Anti-Racism in U.S. History." *Science & Society* 57 (Spring): 74–78.

Soule, Sarah A. 1992. "Populism and Black Lynching in Georgia, 1890–1900." *Social Forces* 71 (December): 431–449.

Stoddard, Ellwyn R. 1973. *Mexican Americans.* New York: Random House.

Stryker, Jeff. 1997. "Tuskegee's Long Arm Still Touches a Nerve." *New York Times* (April 13): Sec. 4, 4.

Taylor, Ronald L. 1995. "Black Males and Social Policy: Breaking the Cycle of Disadvantage," pp. 325–335 in Margaret L. Andersen and Patricia Hill Collins (eds.), *Race, Class, and Gender: An Anthology,* 2nd ed. Belmont, CA: Wadsworth.

Tolnay, Stewart E., and E. M. Beck. 1992. "Racial Violence and Black Migration in the American South, 1910 to 1930." *American Sociological Review* 57 (February): 103–116.

Trennert, Robert A. 1986. "Educating Indian Girls at Nonreservation Boarding Schools, 1878–1920," pp. 218-231 in Roger L. Nichols (ed.), *The American Indian: Past and Present,* 3rd ed. New York: Alfred A. Knopf.

Twain, Mark. 1868. "Persecution of the Chinese in California and Passage of the Burlinggame Treaty to Protect Their Rights," pp. 98–99 in Maxwell Geismar (ed.), *Mark Twain and the Three R's.* Indianapolis: Bobbs-Merrill, 1973.

Washington, Robert. 1993. "The Civil Rights Movement after Three Decades." *Politics, Culture and Society* 7 (Winter): 259–285.

Wilson, William Julius. 1978. *The Declining Significance of Race: Blacks and Changing American Institutions.* Chicago: University of Chicago Press.

Wilson, William Julius, 1987. *The Truly Disadvantaged: The Inner City, the Underclass, and Public Policy.* Chicago: University of Chicago Press.

Wright, Richard. 1938. *Uncle Tom's Children.* New York: Harper & Brothers.

CHAPTER 4

Under the Thumb: Politics, the Criminal Justice System, and Violence

On October 12, 1996, tens of thousands of marchers gathered in Washington, D.C., for the first mass protest by Latino people in the nation's capital. The march started in a park about a mile from the White House and wove through the streets, often appearing more like a festival than a protest. Many in the crowd danced to salsa music from compact disc players, and Danza Azteca performers in traditional costumes and feathers danced to the accompaniment of drums.

But behind the colorful atmosphere, the march's organizers were protesting a set of new laws initiated during a politically conservative era, including those cutting off benefits to legal immigrants who are not citizens and those making political asylum more difficult to obtain.

"Newt Gingrich was the wake-up call," said Representative Nydia M. Velazquez, a New York Democrat. "If we can't get engaged politically, we will be subjected to the abuses of the Washington establishment."

Geraldo Rivera, the television host, agreed that political action was necessary. He stressed that the Latino people had to avoid being divided by different national origins and learn to work together. He explained:

> What you're seeing now is the beginning of the 21st century in terms of Latino-American political activism. I think from now on, Washington will be confronted with a group that puts aside the differences of whether or not they came from this or that island, or this or that state in Mexico. (Holmes, 1996: 26)

Like the Latino individuals testifying here, many members of various American racial minorities recognize that political involvement is essential—that without it the pervasive shadow of internal colonialism continues. While in the past couple of decades racial minorities have progressed in the political realm, they remain relatively powerless, with their governance primarily in whites' hands. Meanwhile, in the areas of criminal justice and violence, some whites' sense of perceived threat to their established control still encourages destructive, racist outcomes.

The common factor uniting political activity, the criminal justice system, and violence is power. **Power** is the ability of an individual or group to implement wishes or policies, with or without the cooperation of others. **Authority** is power that people generally recognize as rightfully maintained by those who use it. In race relations people's sense of which concept applies to a given situation varies with their outlook. In dealing with minorities, white politicians have generally felt they exercised authority. Minorities, in contrast, have stressed that whites maintained control by power, not authority: Whites simply had the personnel and weaponry to enforce their dominance. The first major section of this chapter discusses the **political institution,** which is the system of norms and roles that concerns the use and distribution of authority within a given society.

Racial Minorities in the Political Process

A study comparing blacks to three white ethnic groups—the Irish, Jews, and Italians—concluded that in the area of politics, blacks were distinctly disadvantaged. The researchers indicated that to a much greater extent than the white groups, the African Americans were forced to battle for basic citizens' rights, such as access to schooling, jobs, and political activity, including the right to vote. Furthermore, once blacks were able to enter politics, they faced much stronger resistance from the white political establishment than did the three white groups (Cornacchia and Nelson, 1992). Nonetheless, while blacks have been particularly disadvantaged politically, their opportunities in politics have gradually improved.

With the urbanization of the South after World War II, whites were increasingly exposed to higher education and the national mass media—both of which often opposed continuing segregation. Recognizing that political opportunities were starting to develop, African American organizations initiated sit-ins and boycotts to protest the continuation of segregation. Meanwhile, during the 1950s and 1960s, an expanded, active black electorate was beginning to make an impact in northern cities. The increased black-voter strength in the North combined with civil rights protest in the South to give the assertion of African American political rights much greater prominence.

In the late 1950s and early 1960s, black leaders hoped that the media coverage of white southerners' violent reactions to their anti-segregation protests would encourage the federal government to overcome its traditional reluctance to interfere with southern local and state governmental practice. This, in fact, did occur. After racial violence in Birmingham, Alabama, President John Kennedy proposed the Civil Rights Act, which was passed in 1964 soon after his death, and in 1965 renewed violence against African Americans in Selma, Alabama, and the international uproar it produced helped ensure passage of the 1965 Voting Rights Act.

The Civil Rights Act of 1964 has been the broadest American legislative effort to eliminate racial discrimination. The act covers employment practices of all businesses with more than 25 employees, access to all public accommodations such as hotels, motels, and restaurants, and use of such federally supported organizations as colleges and hospitals. The Voting Rights Act of 1965 has suspended various qualifying tests for voter registration that many southern states used selectively to discriminate against African Americans. This act also authorized federal examiners to enter these states and register black voters, greatly increasing their number.

Significantly, these two pieces of legislation developed when Americans' support for civil rights issues was very high. At the time Congress was faced with these two bills, adult Americans indicated that civil rights was the "most important problem facing the country." By 1966 civil rights had lost that priority position, and it has never regained it (Jaynes and Williams, 1989: 221–223).

The Voting Rights Act has helped advance political interests of African Americans and other racial minorities. Results have been most striking in the South. In 1952, before the passage of the Voting Rights Act, 13 percent of black adults voted; in 1984 the figure had risen to 65 percent (Jaynes and Williams, 1989: 234).

Since 1965 African Americans have been elected to every major political office except for the presidency and vice presidency; in November 1989 L. Douglas Wilder was the first African American elected to the other major executive position when he became governor of Virginia. The national total of black elected officials was 7,984 in 1993, 540 percent of the 1,479 elected black politicians in 1970 (U.S. Bureau of the Census, 1996, Table 452). Table 4.1 provides more detailed statistics on this topic.

These figures must be viewed in perspective. The percentage of black elected officials is very small. As of 1985, 1.2 percent of elected officials were African Americans, with the South's 4 percent the highest of all regions. In a country with about a 12 percent black population, there is a distinct underrepresentation of elected black officials (Jaynes and Williams, 1989: 238).

The figures, in fact, probably overstate blacks' political impact. In a well-known study of policy-making in Cook County, Illinois (which includes the city of Chicago), Harold Baron (1968) concluded that the actual power held by elected and appointed African American officials in government, business, labor, education, and other major policy-making bodies was probably about one-third as great as the percentage of posts they held. The difficulty was that these officials primarily worked in black areas or interacted only with blacks and had little or no opportunity to make policy decisions in such critical areas as housing, jobs, and education.

Other racial minorities are also underrepresented politically. Among Native Americans political activity primarily involves reservation elections. Not until 1924 did Indians have the right to vote in elections outside of reservations. By 1967 15 Native Americans had served in legislatures in six western states. In the 1990s participation increased; in 1992, 35 Indians were elected as representatives in 14 state legislatures, and Larry Echo Hawk won office as attorney general in Idaho. Very few Native Americans have been elected to Congress, with about a half dozen representatives and two senators having some Indian ancestry (Feagin and Feagin, 1993: 189).

While underrepresented politically, a few wealthy Indians have taken steps that could lead to significant influence in politics. In 1993 and 1994, the Mashantucket Pequots, whose Foxwoods Casino has made huge profits, contributed about $315,000

Table 4.1 Black Elected Officials by Office, 1970 to 1993

Year	Total	U.S. and State Legislatures[1]	City and County Offices[2]
1970	1,479	179	719
1975	3,522	299	1,885
1980	4,963	326	2,871
1985	6,312	407	3,689
1990	7,335	440	4,481
1993	7,984	561	4,819

Year	Law Enforcement[3]	Education[4]
1970	213	368
1975	387	951
1980	534	1,232
1985	685	1,531
1990	769	1,645
1993	922	1,682

[1] Includes elected state administrators.

[2] Composed of county commissioners and councilmen, mayors, vice mayors, aldermen, and regional officers.

[3] Involves judges, magistrates, constables, marshals, sheriffs, and justices of the peace.

[4] Includes members of state education agencies, college boards, and school boards.

Note: While blacks are underrepresented in elected offices, there has been a significant increase over time in the number of elected black officials.

Source: U.S. Bureau of the Census. Statistical Abstract of the United States: 1996, Table 452.

to the National Committee of the Democratic Party as well as about $500,000 to Democratic campaigns in at least four states. Initially it was not clear what the Pequots sought in return for their donations. Lobbyists for the tribe simply said that Democrats had been good to American Indians generally and the Pequots in particular and that on a variety of issues, including health care and education, the Clinton administration seemed to be on the right track. State Senator James T. Fleming, a Republican and an opponent of casino gambling, could not find fault with the donations. He said, "I would imagine that all they're trying to do is expand their influence. As long as it's legal, I don't see anything wrong with it" (Johnson, 1994: B2). While contributions to individual candidates are limited, the Pequots can give as much as they want to state and national parties, thereby gaining tremendous goodwill from politicians.

An entirely different strategy for promoting tribal objectives has developed among the Inuit of Nunavik in northern Quebec, Canada. Following a lands claim settlement in 1975, the Inuit received a large tract of territory along with control over local and regional government and education as well as participation in resource and land management. But very quickly the Inuit leaders discovered that they lacked the information to manage these activities effectively. So they created the Makivik Corporation, a research organization that would identify their research needs, develop a well-structured database for the entire region, encourage local Inuit participation through programs of training and education, and recognize the relevance of traditional Inuit knowledge for the success of the program. The four main topics on which the Makivik Corporation concentrated were land use and harvesting, traditional Inuit knowledge about the environment and local resources, studies of wildlife in the region, and the planning of environmental and social impacts in the first three areas. Such information can be invaluable for the future of Indian groups. A pair of researchers who worked for the Makivik Corporation indicated that:

> indigenous peoples must not just support "salvage" operations of what now is often referred to as "a rapidly disappearing knowledge base." It is not just a question of recovery and recording indigenous knowledge; it is one of respect and revitalization. (Kemp and Brooke, 1996: 99)

In short, this example illustrates the well-known claim that knowledge is power.

Less tyrannized than Native Americans, Asian Americans, especially Japanese Americans, have been more successful politically. In Hawaii they have dominated congressional positions, with both senators and both representatives usually Japanese Americans. In the middle 1970s, a Japanese American senator and representative were elected in California, but in 1990 Asian Americans, who were 10 percent of the state population, were vastly underrepresented. Only two members of the state's 47-member congressional delegation were Asian American, and only 1 percent of city council and school board seats were held by Asian Americans. In 1993 Tony Lam became the first Vietnamese American elected to a local government seat when primarily non-Vietnamese Republicans chose him for a seat on the city council in Westminster, California (Feagin and Feagin, 1993: 350; Mydans, 1994).

Asian Americans have encountered a pair of distinct disadvantages concerning participation in the political process. First, Asian Americans' membership in at least a half-dozen ethnic groups, that are further subdivided according to social origins, time of arrival, and religious affiliation, can make finding common political interests difficult. Second, many foreign-born Asian Americans grew up in cultural traditions in which taking public positions on political issues could endanger one's economic standing or physical safety. Changing countries does not necessarily eliminate those old fears, and in many cases American-born children are reared with the idea that politics is a dirty, dangerous business that should be scrupulously avoided (Awanohara, 1993: 112–113).

Mexican Americans have had a comparable level of political success. At any given moment, there are about 10 Mexican American members of the House of Representatives. In the 1992 California election, Mexican Americans won 10 seats in the state legislature. The growth of the Chicano population, along with the elimination of discriminatory statutes, such as a California law requiring English literacy for voters, have encouraged steady expansion of Mexican American voting turnout (Feagin and Feagin, 1993: 274–275; Maharidge, 1993). A study conducted in Texas provided two reasons why the Chicano population is increasingly likely to vote. First, Mexican Americans' level of education has been rising, and voting studies indicate that level of education is the factor best predicting people's inclination to vote. Second, both major parties have increased their effort to mobilize support from the growing Chicano population, in particular offering Chicano candidates on statewide ballots (Longoria, Wrinkle, and Polinard, 1990).

In some areas, notably urban sections of California, Mexican Americans face a complicated political future. Illegal Mexican migrants are restricted residentially, moving into low-rent districts that become filled with people who, because legal access to jobs is barred, have little chance to move into mainstream society. While elected officials in such districts are assuredly Mexican American, low voter turnout hardly establishes them as major vote getters in veteran politicians' eyes. Meanwhile the districts they serve usually become increasingly poor and in need of costly services. In the 1970s and 1980s, the prevailing idea was that the Voting Rights Act, which attacked discriminatory actions against racial minorities, would overcome their political disadvantage; for Mexican Americans, however, the reality of illegal immigration has produced significant new political problems (Skerry, 1994). As we noted at the end of Chapter 3, the combined impact of poverty and racism have led to negative conditions not previously anticipated.

Puerto Ricans have been fairly successful at winning state and local offices. In 1992 in New York state, two state senators, four members of the state assembly, and eight members of the New York City Council were Puerto Rican. In addition, there was one Puerto Rican in the lower houses of the state legislatures in New Jersey, Massachusetts, and Pennsylvania and three in Connecticut. In the early 1990s, lawsuits initiated by Puerto Rican activists led to two new congressional districts, one in Chicago and the other in New York City. At this time Puerto Ricans have three districts where their numerical domination makes the election of Puerto Rican candidates nearly inevitable (Feagin and Feagin, 1993: 313).

In modern times sociologists have recognized that within a given racial minority, variations in background as well as current experience promote different political stances. Among Asian American groups, for instance, Chinese Americans split roughly equally between Democratic and Republican affiliation, Indian Americans lean somewhat toward the Democrats, Japanese Americans and Filipino Americans have been largely Democratic, and Korean Americans and Vietnamese Americans have primarily gone Republican (Awanohara, 1993: 113).

Conditions Affecting Racial Minorities' Political Success

Minority politicians must be aware that they face limitations seldom imposed on whites. One of the two major political parties—the Republican Party—has remained committed to the governance principle contained in internal colonialism, regarding itself almost exclusively as a white party. While a few conservative or very moderate minority group individuals will receive political appointments or party backing in an election bid, African Americans and most other racial minorities realize that Republicans represent white Americans, defend their interests, and win most elections without minority—particularly black—support. Andrew Hacker suggested that by sending this message, the Republican Party "feels it can attract even more votes from a much larger pool of white Americans who want a party willing to represent their racial identity" (Hacker, 1992: 201).

Many whites simply refuse to support an African American candidate, and the darker the skin, the less likely the support. A random sample of white adult Americans participated in an experiment in which they were told they would assess policy issues in a gubernatorial race occurring in a neighboring state. Each subject received a two-page packet containing information about a candidate's political experience, personal characteristics, and positions on different political issues. These convincing but fabricated portraits presented either a moderate or liberal political position. In addition, the packet contained a portrait of the candidate—either a light-skinned black male, a dark-skinned black male, or a white male, with the photos carefully adjusted to be equal in physical attractiveness. The packets randomly distributed candidates' political positions and the three photos, thus permitting the experimenters to determine whether skin color and tone had an independent impact. They did. The findings showed that the three variations made significant differences: Both black candidates lost to the white one, but the dark-skinned black man finished a decisive third (Terkildsen, 1993).

Because of the disadvantages they encounter seeking political office, minority candidates are usually dependent on heavy voting support from their own racial group. A study of mayoral and city council elections between 1965 and 1986 in New Orleans indicated that in elections where less than 40 percent of registered voters were African American, most candidates were white and those elected overwhelmingly white, with few blacks supporting black candidates. When between 40 and 55 percent of registered voters were black, there were candidates of both races, and generally voting broke along racial lines. In elections with over 55 percent of registered voters African American, the majority of candidates were African American, and, in fact, in districts with over 60 percent black registered voters, both candidates were invariably black (Vanderleeuw, 1990).

Sometimes members of racial minorities can be elected even when their group is small. A study of the conditions permitting the election and reelection of Federico Peña, the Mexican American mayor of Denver, suggested two factors that can help accomplish this goal. First, the candidate must obtain almost complete support from his or her own racial group. Even though he did not present himself as a "minority" candidate, Pena was able to perform this task by stressing such issues as "neighborhoods" and "openness"—abstract concerns that had great meaning to Mexican Americans traditionally denied effective political participation but would not offend whites. Second, the minority candidate must make special efforts to appeal to nonminority voters or, at least, to lessen their opposition. One way Peña accomplished this goal was to emphasize prominent citywide concerns, such as more and better city planning and sounder government management (Hero and Beatty, 1989).

Current evidence suggests that black candidates elected to office in areas with many white voters tend to be mild-mannered people possessing a distinctly middle-class background and style who are perceived to be running more as individuals than as representatives of their racial group. Many, perhaps the majority, of whites are frightened when they hear or think they hear a black candidate referring to "our turn" in politics: To such individuals this candidate seems to be an insurrectional leader who will use an elected office to subject whites to the range of inequities African Americans suffered in the past (Hacker, 1992: 206–209). It is a situation where the cultural camouflage for modern racism can appear: Behind some whites' publicly stated claims of equal opportunity in politics lies a sense of racial threat—the fear that what black candidates really want is to take over and grind all whites into the dust.

Besides the difficulty of seeking political leadership positions, racial minorities face another important challenge in the political arena: Are they able to accomplish significant political goals? A study of black and Chicano urban leadership in 12 northern California cities produced a notable result: Researchers found that the extent of minority representation in city government was not a decisive indicator of whether local government was responsive to minority needs.

Much more significant was what researchers called **political incorporation**— inclusion of racial minority group members as significant players in political coalitions that contained some whites and successfully challenged established white conservative groups for control over a city's political activity. When African Americans and Mexican Americans achieved substantial political incorporation, significant improvements for their groups were likely to occur. These included:

1. A sharp increase in the city employment of minorities
2. The creation of police review boards, which investigated cases in which racial minority group members claimed police abuse
3. A significant rise in the numbers of minority representatives appointed to city boards and commissions
4. The establishment of many minority-oriented programs
5. City governments' greater responsiveness to minority interests in the delivery of services and the formation of city policies in such key areas as economic development and education (Browning, Marshall, and Tabb, 1986)

The link between political incorporation and internal colonialism seems clear. The colonial mentality persists among whites, notably the governance principle emphasizing whites' control of racial minorities in political situations. Thus, as political leaders, African Americans and other minority group members are only able to produce significant political change when allied with whites.

For African American mayors, economic impediments to political incorporation can be formidable. Blacks tend to be elected mayors in cities with large African American populations, and these cities tend to be poor. A recent study of seven cities with populations of more than 150,000 citizens indicated that all seven had suffered significant population loss and that unemployment, underemployment, and poverty were widespread problems. With declining economic resources, these mayors' ability to provide effective governance and service delivery or to attract business will suffer (Swain, 1993). Because of such limitations, the mayors' support from citizens is likely to dwindle. Once they lose influence with the voters, black mayors' capacity to generate political incorporation sharply declines.

An overview of political incorporation in American cities found just one economic or political benefit for blacks: in government employment. After African Americans were elected mayors in Atlanta, Chicago, Detroit, and New York City, there was a sharp rise in government employment even though those cities already had strong black representation in civil service jobs.

In general, however, political incorporation cannot compensate for distinct minority disadvantages. Whether cities are black- or white-controlled, low-income African Americans and other minorities benefit little from economic development. A central drawback has been that planners have generally believed that the most profitable enterprises involve the construction of downtown offices and the pursuit of retailing, business activities providing a modest number of jobs tailored for minorities, especially for black males (Fainstein and Fainstein, 1996).

The reality of urban politics can be very frustrating for African Americans. A study of the 26 states in which blacks comprise over 5 percent of the population found that the higher the proportion of black voting in state political races, the less policy outcomes favored blacks. The most plausible explanation is that as African American voter turnout increased, the white-controlled leadership at the state level mobilized against black interests, producing a backlash in such key areas as education, work, housing, and social services. For supporters of minority rights, this seems a discouraging outcome. However, this apparent pattern in state politics probably doesn't apply in cities, where elected black mayors seem able to gain greater control over political policy (Radcliff and Saiz, 1995).

Minority Politics outside of Government

One racial minority—Native Americans—has conducted much of its political activity outside of the established governmental structure. Forced to confine most of their political involvement to reservations and supported by governmental emphasis on the revival of tribalism, many modern Indians have started to mobilize politically around issues of tribal identity and reservation roots (Hagan, 1986).

The federal government recognizes the sovereignty of Indian nations, supporting their right to choose their political and judicial leaders and also maintain their own police forces, but are the tribes truly independent political entities when crises develop? Consider, for instance, the troubles encountered by the Cherokee Nation, which has 186,000 members, second only to the Navajo. When, following a dispute about the Nation's finances, the tribe's highest court issued an arrest warrant for Joe Byrd, the Principal Chief, Byrd sought help from the Federal Bureau of Investigation and the Federal Bureau of Indian Affairs to keep the situation from escalating. "It's humiliating, it's embarrassing," said Chad Smith, a leader of the opposition to Chief Byrd. "And it makes the Cherokee people sick to their souls" (Verhover, 1997: 10). Considering the tremendous military strength of the United States and its tradition of intervening in Indian affairs, however, such an action should hardly be a surprise.

A strategy of some Indian tribes has been the initiation of lawsuits to reclaim tribal lands that were illegally purchased from their ancestors. In 1972 two Indian tribes in Maine claimed thousands of acres of land, and state officials had a good laugh. By 1985, however, they were no longer laughing. In that year the U.S. Supreme Court ruled that a 1790 law stating that no Indian land could be bought or sold without federal approval needed to be honored in various cases where it had either been ignored or misunderstood.

The claims in question involve land purchases made in either the late eighteenth or early nineteenth centuries in eight eastern states. While in the past state negotiators tended to believe that Indians had little basis for their claims, they now realize that federal officials have frequently ruled in favor of Native Americans. Therefore, state representatives, such as those in the previously cited Maine case, are likely to display a spirit of compromise, settling out of court and bringing various bargaining chips to the table—for instance, offers to build school, roads, or bridges if Indians will relinquish certain land claims. In some states, however, the Interior Department has been unwilling to participate in such negotiations, and this creates a major difficulty. Without that department's support, Congress is not likely to provide its approval as the 1790 law requires (Wagar, 1993).

In other locales the treaties were negotiated legally, but the government has not enforced them. Thus members of the tribes that signed the treaties are in a strong legal position to demand that the government maintain these official agreements. In 1984 Ojibway men renewed the practice of spearfishing, which had been a tradition-al spring practice of the tribe. The fishing is done in the Upper Great Lakes area on land sold to the United States. Treaties signed in 1837 and 1842 permitted the Indians to fish the land, but for over a century, the state of Wisconsin refused to recognize those rights, imposing its fish and game laws and jailing Ojibway people who violated them. In recent years court orders have allowed the activity to continue while the issue is being litigated. Although the tribe's legal efforts have permitted the Ojibway to return to this traditional practice, at least temporarily, there has also been a negative development—extensive, sometimes violent non-Indian resistance to the Ojibway fishing practices (Harjo, 1989).

While pursuing political rights through the courts does not always produce desired results, other benefits can emerge. Since 1920 a string of court cases have been initiated by the tribes deprived of control of the Black Hills, a huge tract of west-ern land. Although this series of lawsuits has been unsuccessful, it has helped maintain a strong sense of unity among members of participating tribes and has won a number of admissions from the Supreme Court, such as its 1975 statement that Indians' treat-ment in this giant land deal represented "a national disgrace." Such admissions have produced much more national support for these tribes than they could have obtained if they had just made a one-sided presentation of their case (Churchill, 1990).

Like Native Americans, Chicanos have also pursued political goals by using orga-nizations outside of the established political process. In 1929 the League of United Latin American Citizens (LULAC) was founded in southern Texas to use moderate political means to oppose discrimination against Mexican Americans. Currently the organization has active councils in 28 states, a national headquarters in Washington, D.C., and a professional staff. White politicians have seldom criticized LULAC's efforts because its heavily middle-class membership has made strenuous efforts to strongly support most American political and economic practices and has never con-demned the society as discriminatory. LULAC has approached political activism cau-tiously, avoiding demonstrations or disruptive practices but using such widely supported techniques as voter registration drives, petitions, and legal pressure (Marquez, 1989).

In the middle and late 1960s, the Chicano movement developed, with its mem-bers viewing themselves as oppressed because of their race and social class. The idea of internal colonialism seems relevant. One writer noted that Chicanos have been "socially, culturally, and economically subordinated and territorially segregated by white America" (Gutierrez, 1993: 46). As part of the Chicano movement, Cesar Chavez used the union of the United Farm Workers of America to organize agricul-tural workers throughout the Southwest and fight for higher wages and better working conditions. In addition, in northern New Mexico and southern Colorado, Reies Lopez

Tijerina created the Alianza Federal de Mercedes, and this organization was able to win land settlements for some Mexican Americans making such claims. Men's concerns within the Chicano movement focused on such issues as the elimination of job discrimination, access to political power, entry into higher education, and community self-determination. While concerned about these issues, female members of the movement tended to emphasize demands for birth control, welfare rights, protection against male violence, and sexual pleasure (Guttierez, 1993).

For African Americans a major political event outside the established political arena has been the Million Man March, which occurred in Washington, D.C., in October 1995. The hundreds of thousands of marchers were primarily African American men who, according to a survey conducted at the scene, provided three principal reasons for participation: to indicate support for the black family; to encourage black men to take more responsibility for their families and communities; and to demonstrate black unity (Brossard and Morin, 1996). There is some indication that the Million Man March produced significant effects. Six months after the march, it was reported that 350 cities had Million Man March organizing committees, with many engaged in productive activities; for instance, Atlanta's committee registered 28,000 people to vote and increased deposits in black-owned banks by $2 million while in Chicago 100 black men joined a mentoring program (Brooke, 1996). A year after the march, Louis Farrakhan, the leader of the Nation of Islam and the march's chief organizer, spoke to a crowd of about 38,000 in New York City. In a three-hour speech, Farrakhan both praised the successes produced by the original rally and exhorted the continuing need for black men's renewed commitment to their families and communities (Jones, 1996).

Can racial groups from fundamentally different locations within the society work well together? Some evidence suggests that a useful, perhaps necessary step is for the participants to be fully honest with each other: that those advantaged be willing to examine their privilege while those disadvantaged have the chance to expose the anger, pain, and frustration of racial oppression (Cole and Stewart, 1996: Smith, 1995). Then, with some mutual understanding created, the groups might have the trust to work together.

As the following situation illustrates, minority group politicians often face special challenges.

PACs and African Americans in Congress

By the middle 1990s, political action committees (PACs) had a bad name among American voters, invoking images of wealthy businessmen giving huge sums of money to politicians who would then champion the donors' corrupt drive for even greater wealth. In the long run, the dominant wisdom ran, taxpayers must foot the increasingly burdensome bill. Leading politicians have been responsive to the public's discontent. In 1993 President Bill Clinton urged Congress to curb the power of PACs, and in June of that year, the Senate passed a bill that would get rid of them.

But the issue was not settled. In the House of Representatives, most Democrats vowed to fight to keep PACs, arguing that these organizations created for the express purpose of meeting campaign expenses were an essential source of funding.

Black members have been particularly committed. The black caucus, which in 1993 was comprised of 38 House members, indicated that it must defend PACs because minority candidates are particularly dependent on them. Disproportionately representing poor districts, minority politicians generally lack white candidates' frequent access to wealthy schools and corporations that can be major funding sources. As Representative Eva Clayton, a first-term Democrat representing the district with the lowest per capita income in North Carolina, said, "If your district is poor, you're not wealthy and you're excluded from affluent circles; it's hard to raise money" (Donovan, 1993: 2523).

Compared to whites, blacks are less inclined to oppose PACs, seeing these organizations not as potential sources of corruption but as useful means to counter wealthy interests. Reflecting the latter outlook, Representative Melvin Watt, another first-term member of the black caucus, noted, "The whole rationale for having PACs was to enable small contributors to have an influence. What is wrong with that?" (Donovan, 1993: 2524).

Commenting on African American House candidates, Ronald Walters, a political scientist at Howard University, said, "They're no different than anyone else. They're trying to protect their political base" (Donovan, 1993: 2524). The difference is that in the case of black candidates, PACs serve a more central funding role than they do for many of their white colleagues.

While PACs are important for members of the black caucus, they traditionally have received limited support from them. One reason for this disinterest has been that potential contributors have recognized that African American House members, who tend to have been recently elected to office, generally have lacked seniority on key committees. As a result they did not possess the ability to influence the outcome of significant legislation that could benefit PAC sponsors, and so potential sponsors stayed away. That situation is starting to change. Three blacks now chair full committees, and 10 head subcommittees. As major policy players, these senior black House members can steer PAC contributions not only toward themselves but toward junior members who might otherwise be overlooked. As a result, PACs have started to show a true interest in black caucus members.

For White House leaders, an alliance with the black caucus on the PAC issue permits them to sound like progressive legislators and not simply politicians concerned about the possible loss of a lucrative source of campaign funds. Thus, House Speaker Thomas Foley declared, "I don't think it's a . . . reform to cut off the opportunity of women and African Americans and Hispanics and other minorities to seek office and be elected" (Donovan, 1993: 2525). Certainly members of the black caucus will pursue this line of thought. Representative John Lewis noted that in spite of the corrupt uses of PACs that have occurred, people should remember that they were originally intended as part of a campaign reform package. Lewis said, "They allow working people to pool their dollars so the millionaires and the big-money interests won't be in the game alone" (Donovan, 1993: 2526).

The relationship between our current topic—political activity—and the next subject—the criminal justice system—is intimate if often unexamined. For instance, about 950,000 African Americans are ineligible to vote because they are in prison, on probation, or on parole while an additional 510,000 are permanently barred from voting because they live in states depriving convicted felons of the right to vote. Thus a total of 1.46 million, or about 14 percent, of black men are currently barred from voting because of convictions for crimes (Butterfield, 1997).

Racial Minorities and the Criminal Justice System

On December 31, 1994, American federal and state prisons contained 1,054,774 inmates. Of that total, 464,157 were white, 501,672 black, 158,908 Hispanic, 9,283 Indian or native Alaskan, and 6,005 Asian Americans (U.S. Department of Justice, 1996, Tables 6.26 and 6.27).

It is revealing to compare racial groups' representation in the prison population, adjusted for their numbers in the overall American population: African Americans stand out. Blacks are 25 times more highly represented at state and federal prisons than Asian Americans; 7.1 times more than whites; 2.6 times more than Hispanics; and 3.7 times more than Native Americans (U.S. Department of Justice, 1996, Table 6.26 and Table 6.27; U.S. Bureau of the Census, 1996, Table 21 and Table 23). With their members so heavily represented in the criminal justice system, many young black men are as inclined to consider prison an inevitable part of their life experience as many young white men do college (Mauer, 1994: 90). We need to consider why African Americans are disproportionately represented in the criminal justice system.

Alfred Blumstein (1982) and Patrick Langan (1985) sought to determine whether racial discrimination explains African American overrepresentation in prisons. Their studies of state prisons produced similar results, with both researchers concluding that the disproportionate number of blacks arrested, particularly for major crimes carrying severe penalties, largely explained their overrepresentation in the prison population. Thus Langan indicated that his study demonstrated that "even if racism exists, it might explain only a small part of the gap between the 11% [currently 12%] black representation in the United States adult population and the now nearly 50% black representation among persons entering state prison each year in the United States" (Langan, 1985: 682).

Two comments on these studies seem appropriate. First, since both compare the number of individuals arrested with those who eventually end up in prison, they are not examining the issue of whether racism enters the criminal justice process during the arrest phase. Studies indicate some tendency to arrest blacks more readily than whites, with the additional suggestion that the very presence of observers might restrict discriminatory treatment. One notable finding is that black and Latino arrestees are more likely to be released than whites for the less serious offenses of prostitution, gambling, vagrancy, and public drunkenness, most likely indicating that in many cases the grounds for arrest were weak and that police harassment was a distinct possibility (Weitzer, 1996: 310).

Second, these investigations might have underestimated the extent to which racism exists throughout the entire criminal justice system. Marjorie Zatz (1987) suggested that such investigations may concentrate on readily detectable measures of bias and overlook less obvious racist displays—for instance, a prosecutor's request for a long sentence for a black man officially sought not because of his race but because of his history of criminal activity. In addition, Zatz emphasized that participants in the criminal justice system inevitably try to hide racist policies since such activities would cast doubt on the legitimacy and rationality of the entire system. Other researchers have indicated that most studies of racial discrimination in the criminal justice system have focused on specific points—arrest, arraignment, sentencing, and so forth. Such studies tend to ignore or deemphasize that accused people's involvement in this system is a process. Thus seemingly trivial bits of information or commentaries that are racially discriminatory can remain in an individual's file or be transmitted verbally, appearing to have no impact in the early stages of the criminal justice process but then impacting sentencing or incarceration (Bridges and Crutchfield, 1988; Swigert and Farrell, 1977).

Some experts, in fact, have become convinced that quantitative data assessing racism at discrete points in the criminal justice process are invariably superficial, even misleading. Instead they are much more inclined to favor participants' detailed observations of the criminal justice process. This qualitative information, they contend, can supply a much fuller sense of the extent to which racism resides in a given criminal justice system (Mann, 1994).

In 1991 the 17-member New York State Judicial Commission on Minorities composed of judges, lawyers, law professors, and an official from the State Education Department concluded that the state court system is "infested with racism." The commission concluded that minority group members are less likely than whites to receive favorable actions from the courts; that judges and prosecuting attorneys are more hostile and racially biased toward minorities than are other court employees; and that minority lawyers are often subjected to opposing attorneys' racial stereotyping and racist jokes (Gray, 1991).

Not surprisingly, blacks and whites have significantly different perceptions of how the American criminal justice system relates to blacks. While 54 percent of African Americans felt that the system was biased against blacks and 35 percent denied discriminatory treatment, whites' responses were much less critical of the system—33 percent perceiving bias and 58 percent not (Moore and Saad, 1995).

In short, there is the distinct possibility that racism is more prevalent within the criminal justice system than the Blumstein and Langan investigations concluded. Blacks and Puerto Ricans, whose incarceration rate is closest to blacks, are the most likely victims. Let's consider why racism permeates this system.

Sense of Threat: Key to Racism in the Criminal Justice System

Sociologist Darnell F. Hawkins (1987) wrote about the relationship between race and the criminal justice system. Hawkins made a specific point reminiscent of a more general issue discussed within the first chapter's introduction of internal colonialism—that conflict theorists have tended either to ignore the role played by race in relation to criminal justice or to subordinate its significance to social class. The result, Hawkins indicated, is that conflict theorists have simply lumped all poor people together, whether members of racial minorities or white, assuming that people's socioeconomic class is the major factor determining their treatment in the criminal justice system. For this issue, however, race appears to play a critical role.

Hawkins concluded that a sense of threat is the key factor encouraging racial discrimination in the criminal justice process. When whites see blacks' criminal behavior as threatening, they are likely to deal with them harshly. On the other hand, when whites do not see blacks' crimes as threatening, they will not subject them to discriminatory treatment (Hawkins, 1987). Other research has produced similar evidence. Thus investigators calculated relative arrest rates for blacks and whites; the percentage of blacks arrested for a given crime out of the total number known to have committed that crime was compared to the same data for whites. One study found that for robbery, the arrest percentage for blacks and whites was nearly identical. However, in cases of assault and rape, the black arrest rate was distinctly higher than the white one (Yu and Liska, 1993).

This evidence seems consistent with the internal colonialist perspective, suggesting that whites fixate on controlling racial minorities' activities. A sense of threat emerges when whites believe that blacks' actions would loosen their controlling grip, and criminal behavior, particularly violent criminal behavior, can often produce that sense.

Hawkins's thesis also receives support from other studies examining arrest rates. An investigation of 77 American cities with populations of over 100,000 people found no relationship between the cities' proportion of poor and their arrest rates. On the other hand, the proportion of minority group members and the extent of racial segregation within cities correlated to minority individuals' arrest rates. Thus the higher the proportion of minority group members and the more extensive racial segregation, the higher the arrest rate, both for minority group members and for whites. Why did this result occur? The researchers reasoned that the combination of a high percentage of minority group members and a low level of racial integration caused whites' perceived threat of crime to grow. These perceptions increased pressure on police to control crime, and the result was an accelerated rate of arrests for both racial minorities and whites (Liska, Chamlin, and Reed, 1985).

A study drawing its data from a representative sample of American 11- to 17-year-olds concluded that for serious offenses (in particular, felony theft, felony assault, robbery, hard drug use, and fraud), African Americans were two to three times more likely to be arrested and charged than whites. But this finding does not mean that racial discrimination definitely occurred. Perhaps black and white youths differed in some other significant respect besides race. Investigators examined several of the most likely possibilities. Did the youthful blacks have a more extensive history of delinquencies? No! Perhaps the blacks were more likely to have committed crimes involving either greater physical injury or the use of guns? Once again, no! The researchers concluded that young African Americans "appear to be at greater risk for being charged with more serious offenses than whites involved in comparable levels of delinquent behavior, a factor that may eventually result in higher incarceration levels" (Huizinga and Elliott, 1987: 221).

Another study found that black youths were not only more likely to be arrested than whites but were also more frequently held, charged, sentenced, and incarcerated. The researchers suggested that when black youths "discern differential and more lenient treatment for their Anglo counterparts, a bitter and ironic form of accountability is taught" (Fagan, Slaughter, and Hartstone, 1987: 253). A self-fulfilling prophecy develops. Motivated by their perception that young African Americans represent a greater threat than white youth, police, judges, and other court officials treat them more harshly. The black youth perceive their biased treatment, and, indeed, are likely to become a more substantial threat than they would have been without exposure to racism in the criminal justice system.

A number of other studies demonstrate racial bias in sentencing, with the relationship between threat and race apparent once more. An investigation done in 39 states found that blacks typically served longer sentences than whites for robbery, rape, and murder (Hacker, 1988). A growing body of research indicates that in many cases the key factor is the race of the victim. Evidence suggests that when the victim of rape or robbery is white, the sentence is likely to be more severe (LaFree, 1980; Thomson and Zingraff, 1981).

A related conclusion appears in murder cases. Researchers have found that when the level of seriousness is controlled—that is, when four possible racial combinations of offender and victim are compared for similar degrees of severity, such as whether only one person was killed or whether multiple killings were involved—prosecutors and juries are more likely to demand the death penalty if the victim is white and the offender is black than in any of the other three possible racial combinations—white offender/black victim, black offender/black victim, or white offender/white victim (Ekland-Olson, 1988; Jaynes and Williams, 1989: 488–489; Keil and Vito, 1989; Weitzer, 1996). Furthermore, this same pattern occurs with executions. Although most killings are intraracial, over two-thirds of the African Americans executed between 1976 and 1996 killed whites. In contrast, only two whites have been executed for killing blacks (Weitzer, 1996: 315). Once again the concept of threat seems relevant. When a black person kills a white person, he or she violates not only the individual, whom the state has an obligation to protect, but also the state itself by challenging whites' control of the social order. African Americans killing whites present the spectre of insurrection. White murderers generally create a similar sense of threat only if they kill public officials or law enforcement personnel (Hawkins, 1987: 726).

In a study of state prisons in 48 states, George S. Bridges and Robert D. Crutchfield (1988) found that African Americans were disproportionately imprisoned in states where the black citizenry was relatively poor compared to whites, primarily urban, and a fairly small percentage of the overall population. North-central states had the disproportionately highest number of black prison inmates and southern states the lowest. The researchers decided that while racial differences in arrest rates was a factor in the disproportionate imprisonment of blacks, it was a much less significant factor than indicated in the Blumstein and Langan studies.

Bridges and Crutchfield hypothesized that one factor that might have contributed to the high proportion of African Americans in the prison population in states where blacks were poorer and concentrated in urban areas might have been longer criminal records among blacks. But blacks' records were not longer than whites'. Like Darnell Hawkins, these researchers eventually endorsed the idea of threat, suggesting that an effective analysis of their findings needed to consider that disproportionate punishment is the dominant white group's means of signaling its determination to maintain control over African Americans and other racial minorities in a situation where it considers the stable social order threatened (Bridges and Crutchfield, 1988: 719).

But why, one might ask, do people in the north-central states—in particular, Minnesota, Nebraska, Wisconsin, and Iowa, according to the Bridges and Crutchfield data—appear to feel the strongest sense of threat from blacks? One possibility is that in such states many whites find racial confrontation a horrifying abstraction. They have had little or no contact with blacks but are painfully aware that not far away—in Minneapolis, Omaha, Milwaukee, or Des Moines—there is a heavy concentration of poor blacks who, their television news programs and newspapers daily inform them in gruesome detail, are heavily engaged in crime, much of it violent. As a result these people are frightened, and they react by pressuring their politicians, police, sheriffs, prosecutors, and judges to crack down on African Americans and other minorities.

In the late 1960s, I recall watching a news program during which a reporter standing in a remote corn field in one of the north-central states reported that where he was, 100 miles from the nearest city, residents were far more terrified of being victims of rioting inner-city blacks than any urban people he had ever encountered. Perhaps today in the era of the cultural camouflage for modern racism, their contemporary counterparts would be less willing to speak frankly to reporters about racial fears, but Bridges and Crutchfield's study makes it clear that the underlying sense of racial threat persists.

African Americans are not the only group affected by the sense-of-threat reality in the criminal justice system. A recent study found that when compared to whites, Native Americans were punished more harshly than whites for crimes involving robbery and burglary but less severely for murder. The key component was the victim. For the first two crimes, whites were victimized, and thus a threat to the white-controlled system was involved. With murder, however, Indians were more likely to kill Indians, who because of their minority status were considered devalued victims within the criminal justice system. Thus the sentences were less severe than when whites killed (highly valued) whites (Alvarez and Bachman, 1996).

For individual minority group members, the patterns discussed here have often come home to roost. In some cases they see that compared to whites who have committed comparable crimes, they received stiffer sentences. Or, the relevance of threat against whites can become apparent when they assess the penalties imposed on them. As an adolescent, Nathan McCall faced charges for two felonies, with very different results. In *Makes Me Wanna Holler*, he explained:

> I shot and nearly killed Plaz, a black man, and got a thirty-day sentence; I robbed a white business and didn't lay a finger on anybody, and got twelve years. I got the message. I'd gotten it all my life: Don't fuck with white folks. (McCall, 1994: 144)

Some observers might conclude that whites' sense of threat is regrettable but that, after all, blacks and other minorities represent a significant threat to whites' sense of security. However, consider a sobering comparative reality: In the course of an average hour, two Americans will be murdered, but four U.S. citizens will die of unhealthy or unsafe conditions in the workplace—events that were also precipitated by major criminal violations (Reiman, 1994: 294). In the latter situation, people end up just as dead, and the misery and suffering are similar. Yet while often illegal, the conditions causing those deaths are often not perceived as crimes. Even when considered crimes, the sense of threat is much less compelling for the general public. Undoubtedly the combined race and class factors help produce the difference: It remains difficult for most white Americans to consider wealthy white executives as a threat while poor black individuals readily qualify.

Judges are well aware that prisons are disproportionately filled with minority group members, representing a special level of threat to the numerical minority—white inmates. For this reason they are often more inclined to give whites than blacks probation instead of incarceration. One judge explained:

> This [consideration] is becoming more important all the time—especially with the prisons so overcrowded—you are reluctant to send white offenders especially younger ones, to a prison that is largely black. It seems the prisons are becoming more and more black and Hispanic, so judges are leery because they have heard horror stories about what has happened. (Kramer and Steffensmeir, 1993: 371)

Research done in North Carolina and New York prisons has supported this conclusion, showing that in both general assaults and sexual assaults the aggressors are disproportionately black and the victims primarily white. While African Americans' opportunities to retaliate against whites for their treatment outside prison may be a contributing factor, imprisonment itself appears to magnify racial tensions by forcing blacks and whites into situations where overcrowding, boredom, and deprivation dominate (Weitzer, 1996: 319).

Yet not all whites in prison are terrorized. In fact, some, such as political prisoners Alan Berkman and Tim Blunk (1995), have concluded that prison "can be one of the few places where we [middle-class whites] look at America from the bottom up" (Berkman and Blunk, 1995: 336). What one sees, they say, is a world disproportionately inhabited by young African American men and women who are poor, badly educated, and profoundly alienated. In prison dehumanization and disrespect are the dominant signs of the prevailing oppression. Berkman and Blunk wrote:

> For instance, we've consistently experienced the fact that you can be getting along okay with the guards and prison officials when they suddenly do something which is not only totally outrageous, but often a complete violation of their own supposed rule structure. You call them on it, and their response is to look at you—*through* you would be more accurate—as if you just weren't there. It doesn't matter a bit whether you're right or wrong. It cuts at the very core of your sense of humanity and self-worth. It is infuriating and degrading. (Berkman and Blunk, 1995: 337)

Some black or primarily black juries have contended that because of the racist oppression of the criminal justice system and the destructiveness of prison itself, the most humane treatment for African American defendants is jury nullification—a verdict of "not guilty" even though a traditional sifting of the evidence suggests otherwise. This approach has been most evident in such urban environments as the New York City borough of the Bronx, where black and Latino juries have acquitted African American defendants in felony cases 48 percent of the time—nearly triple the 17 percent national acquittal rate for all defendants (Holden, Cohen, and Lisser, 1996).

Debatable questions arise concerning this controversial topic. To what felony cases should jury nullification apply? Paul Butler (1996), a former prosecutor, has supported the use of jury nullification only in cases where nonviolent crimes occurred. Are the reasons why jurists engage in nullification justifiable? Randall Kennedy (1996) has argued that in many nullification cases the jurists have an unreasonable suspicion of police oppression of minorities and are simply trying to send a message that they will do everything possible to counteract such racist behavior, even if it means countermanding court procedures. How do you feel about the use of jury nullification?

Another response to racism in the criminal justice system shifts the focus from the system to young people's activity. "Prevention is the key," said Robbie Smith, a member of a Sacramento group dedicated to the curtailment of crime. "We have got to find things for kids to do before they get in trouble. We've seen what happens when you cut back on all the programs. It's time to turn that around before it's too late and they arrest my kid—or yours" (Anner, 1996: 134).

Sense of threat, which seems to be an important influence in the criminal justice system, also appears to be a factor encouraging racial violence.

Violence against Racial Minorities and Conditions Encouraging It

In his well-known study of a southern town in the 1930s, John Dollard (1937) summed up his perception of whites' motivation for aggression against African Americans with the following statement. He wrote:

> In the end it seems . . . [most accurate] to say that white people fear Negroes. They fear them, of course, in a special context, that is, when the Negro attempts to claim any of the white prerogatives or gains. . . . By a series of hostile acts and social limitations the white caste maintains a continuous threatening atmosphere against the possibility of . . . demands by Negroes; when successful, . . . the effect is to keep the social order intact. (Dollard, 1937: 316–317)

Sometimes whites' violence against racial minorities has served to keep the social order intact, and sometimes it has been a means of winning control over minorities.

From the seventeenth through the nineteenth centuries, white invaders battled Native Americans in the continuous effort to take over their land and their lives. Broken treaties and the slaughter of defenseless Indian women, children, and elderly people were common practices. Richard Maxwell Brown indicated that the effect of whites' dealings with Indians "has not been a healthy one; it has done much to further our proclivity to violence" (Brown, 1979: 34).

Even today, however, the public presentation of those violent events honors whites and either ignores or vilifies the Indians. At the Little Bighorn Battlefield in Montana, for instance, an obelisk stands at the site praising Lieutenant Colonel George Armstrong Custer, his troops, and their Indian scouts and describing their Sioux and Cheyenne opponents only as "the enemy." Now, however, the National Park Service plans a $2 million monument honoring the Indians who died in the battle—a rare, perhaps unprecedented, move (Limerick, 1997).

Like Indians, blacks have often been victims of whites' violence. With the end of slavery, some southern whites developed a special organization for dealing with African Americans—the Ku Klux Klan, which was discussed in Chapter 1. Three phases have occurred. In the 1860s, under the direction of Nathan Bedford Forrest, a former slave trader and Confederate general, the Klan developed as a central organization in the effort to restore the Confederacy. During the 1920s the Klan appeared once more, largely outside the South, as a white-supremacist structure intent on assuming political control. In some political districts, its influence was strong because candidates for office needed either to be Klan members or to receive the organization's endorsement. Finally, since the 1960s, the Klan has been revived once again, using the Confederate battle flag as its symbol and emphasizing the grandeur of the institutions of the segregated white South. At times the modern Klan has united with the American Nazi Party and other fascist groups (Lawrence, 1994: 23–24).

Even before the development of the Klan, racial riots served to intimidate blacks. Anti-black riots, which occurred in the North in the 1820s and 1830s and continued in both the South and North for about four decades after the Civil War, were one-sided attacks on blacks by whites. From about 1915 through the 1940s, whites still initiated riots, but blacks began to develop their own counterrioting gangs. From 1964 through 1967, some inner-city residents initiated riots. Generally the rioters were infused with black pride, frustrated by limited economic opportunities available to them, and mobilized by local incidents, such as a white policeman's beating or killing of a black resident.

Other racial minorities have also encountered extensive violence. For instance, in the 1870s and 1880s, Chinese workers competing with whites for jobs were often run out of town, beaten, or even killed. In Los Angeles in 1871, between 18 and 21 Chinese men were hanged or burned to death, and in 1887 in desolate Hell's Canyon on the Idaho-Oregon border, 31 Chinese gold miners were robbed and murdered (Kitano and Daniels, 1988: 22).

In recent years, to be sure, those who want to control racial minorities' advancement are no longer "successful" in Dollard's 1930s sense. The relationship between threat and violence, however, is probably similar—with whites who want African Americans or other racial minorities "kept in their place" using violence as a means of intimidation.

One issue that has received considerable attention has been the number of blacks killed by the police. In any given year, a disproportionate number of blacks will be killed by police—about a fourfold greater number than one would expect given their overall proportion of the population. In particular, researchers suggested that violence is more likely to develop when police arrest or attempt to arrest individuals for serious offenses. They pointed out that when analysts consider not only offenders' race but the seriousness of the crimes with which they are charged, the number of African Americans killed is not disproportionate (Jaynes and Williams, 1989: 477–478).

The same statistical murkiness discussed in the previous section develops once more: Since researchers do not systematically observe law enforcement officials on the job, they cannot determine to what extent racial bias enters at the arrest stage—in the decision either to arrest or to use deadly force.

What is known is that in inner-city areas, typical white police officers are modestly educated individuals, most likely high-school graduates who had never previously set foot in the districts they now patrol. Frequently they appear to judge individuals first and foremost by their color, and because of the ongoing barrage of poverty and crime with which they have to deal, many have become so disillusioned that they view even law-abiding African Americans as belonging to "the other side" (Hacker, 1992: 190).

Sociologist William B. Waegel did a study that uncovered at least some relevant, behind-the-scenes information. Waegel spent about ten months as a participant-observer in a police department in a northeastern city. He concluded that politicians' calls for the harsh treatment of criminals along with victims', friends', or family members' demands for revenge create a moral climate encouraging violence against offenders. Widespread racism, Waegel believed, plays into the process. In urban areas, where minorities are overrepresented in serious crimes, police are likely to feel that race itself is a major cause of crime. Frequently Waegel heard comments supporting such a position. For instance, during the investigation of a homicide involving a member of a racial minority (Waegel did not specify which group), the researcher heard one detective tell another, "Maybe Hitler was right; he just had the wrong group." And during another investigation in which all the parties involved were black, a veteran officer told Waegel, "You've got to understand, these people are animals, and we're here to keep peace among animals." In the aftermath of a police shooting, a colleague approached the officer responsible and asked what happened. The officer described the circumstances, which included shooting the suspect while he was lying unarmed on the ground, and then concluded, "What was I supposed to do?" Without hesitation the other policeman replied, "What's another dead nigger anyway?" (Waegel, 1984: 148)

A former police officer provided this comment in a paper he wrote about the criminal justice system:

> Throughout my 20 years in law enforcement, I have witnessed and at times even participated in cruel, repressive treatment of the have-nots of our society. Every police officer has his own kind of evil twin that when confronted with danger or anger can turn a gentle family man into a savage. Unfortunately this savagery is most often meted out on the heads of blacks and other minorities, who in the eyes of the police are committing all the crimes. (Krill, 1997: 8)

In March 1991 in Los Angeles, the most celebrated recent incident of police violence against a minority group member occurred. Following a high-speed pursuit, two police officers kicked and beat Rodney G. King, a local African American, for two minutes while 13 other officers and 20 local residents watched. What was unique about the incident was that one of the local residents filmed the beating, and it was widely shown on national television. The large number of police present during the beating and transcripts of squad-car communications, which indicated that such incidents occurred frequently, supported the widespread belief in the Los Angeles area that police violence against black and Chicano citizens is commonplace. Jerome Skolnick, a sociologist specializing in police behavior, indicated, "This is going to be the defining incident in police brutality; it's going to be the historical event for police in our time" (Mydans, 1991: B7).

Another celebrated incident occurred in August 1997 in New York City following a tense scuffle between police officers and a crowd outside a nightclub. Abner Louima, who supposedly had been trying to break up a fight between two women but then became involved in an altercation with police, was arrested and brought to the police station, where he was tortured. Apparently one officer shoved a toilet plunger deeply into his rectum, perforating both his small intestine and bladder. Then the officer forced the plunger's filthy end down Louima's throat, breaking several teeth. Following the torture, Louima was in critical condition, though he eventually recovered (Barry, 1997).

The fact that this incident occurred after a tense confrontation between police and citizens can remind us of one idea cited by the cultural camouflage for modern racism: that the tensions of specific race-related circumstances can draw people, including public officials, into racist acts. That recognition certainly does not alleviate the officer's responsibility for his vile act, but it does serve as a warning regarding the dangerous conditions that predictably promote the most virulent racism.

So what measures should be taken to address police violence against African Americans and other minorities? To begin, it should be recognized that all Americans, and perhaps particularly African Americans, make a distinction between legal and illegal police use of violence. Survey data have indicated that because they often live in areas with extensive violent crime, blacks are sometimes more prone than whites to support legal police violence. On the other hand, probably because they are considerably more likely to be victimized, they are more inclined to oppose illegal police violence (Cullen et al., 1996).

The key challenge involves training and supporting police to stay within the bounds of the law. Some issues would be to educate police forces, particularly white suburban officers with little exposure to minorities, on how to relate to blacks and Latinos; to make officers aware of how to avoid or at least to relieve the pressure of deadly encounters; and to encourage departments to eliminate or curtail high-speed chases except in the case of violent felonies where the chances of safely catching the subject are substantial.

What should be the guidelines for evaluating police use of violence? One suggestion is that police officers should be treated much like private citizens—that indictments should be made if circumstances suggest the possibility that officers acted illegally and that they should be punished if, in fact, evidence demonstrates that they killed when not exposed to "imminent danger." Presently few police officers pay such a price, even in cases where the threat to the officer's life was minimal or nonexistent. Usually grand juries or prosecutors are unwilling to issue indictments, thereby giving police the message that violence, particularly against minorities, is acceptable.

The circumstances under which a death occurs are critical. What if the officer made a "bad shoot," misreading the situation but not intentionally engaging in an illegal act of killing? Then, some legal experts have argued, the best course of action would be to pursue a civil court not a criminal court solution, with the city forced to write the victim's family a very large check and the department required to examine its relationship with minorities, probably increasing their number in its force and training its cops more effectively (Bass, 1997; Cullen et al., 1996).

In addition to the police, ordinary citizens sometimes engage in racist violence. Janet Caldwell, a member of the Center for Democratic Renewal, an Atlanta-based research group that monitors the Ku Klux Klan and other white-supremacist groups, suggested that in the modern world, a white skin no longer translates to automatic privilege. Caldwell said, "Young whites are facing things they never had to face before" (Johnson, 1989: Sec. 1, 32). No longer do whites monopolize high-paying, prestigious jobs. Many resent the situation, and they can find support from various media sources, notably white-power rock and roll groups such as Guns N' Roses, whose debut album sold nine million copies and included vicious putdowns of African Americans and other racial minorities (Pareles, 1989).

Life is precarious for minorities when their very existence poses a sense of threat to whites. Over the years many blacks in Chicago have known that they were risking their lives if they strayed into Bridgeport, a largely white neighborhood almost devoid of blacks. Then, in March 1997, Lenard Clark, a 13-year-old African American, rode along the area's edge, where three white adolescents attacked him and beat him into a coma. Later the teenagers bragged that they had helped keep blacks out of the neighborhood. "Over the years I've heard that people of color should be careful going to Bridgeport," Clark's aunt Tallulah Black explained, "but I never realized it was this bad. I never realized that a little boy couldn't ride his bike on a beautiful spring day without fearing for his life" (Terry, 1997: A18).

In a study of the Ku Klux Klan, researchers found extensive evidence of youthful racism, learning to their surprise that even though Klan membership had been greater in the past, support was unrelated to age—that "favorable attitudes toward the Klan are not dying out in the younger generation" (Seltzer and Lopes, 1986: 96). The investigators discovered that the social variable that most predicted support for the Klan was education, or actually the lack of it: the less formal education, the greater the expressed support. The researchers did not know whether this relationship resulted because better educated people have learned to tone down their racist expression or are actually less inclined to be racist (Seltzer and Lopes, 1986: 98).

Another study, conducted in Wilkes-Barre, Pennsylvania, illustrated how Ku Klux Klan members have learned to exploit whites' fears. When new owners of the local newspaper anticipated a workers' strike, they hired a security company, which deployed guards throughout the building—in rest rooms, on the shop floor, in most work areas, and in the places where workers gathered to talk or eat lunch. The workers deeply resented the guards' presence, feeling that the company was trying to intimidate them into not striking. The fact that the guards were primarily black while the newspaper workers were mainly white compounded the tension, and in the weeks that preceded the strike, the workers' frustration centered on the guards, whom they constantly threatened and insulted with racial slurs.

Eventually the strike occurred, and workers began mass picketing in front of the newspaper headquarters. At this point built-up frustrations were released on the guards, with many spat upon, hit by objects, and punched.

After the outbreak of violence, Klan organizers approached the strikers, suggesting that their fury toward the black guards should extend to the entire black community of Wilkes-Barre. What was particularly disturbing to local African American leaders was that few whites expressed alarm or even concern about the Klan actions. Eventually the security company was replaced with one using exclusively white guards. Tensions lessened, and finally the strike was settled. It appeared, however, that the events described placed a long-term strain on race relations in Wilkes-Barre (Keil, 1985).

When jobs are on the line in interracial situations, there is likely to be racially targeted resentment, which can turn violent. Visitors to Detroit-area auto plants found racist anti-Japanese posters and graffiti very prevalent. Some United Auto Worker locals ordered and distributed bumper stickers reading "Toyota-Datsun-Honda = Pearl Harbor" and "Unemployment—Made in Japan." A number of auto executives were equally unrestrained. In particular, Bennett E. Bidwell, Chrysler's executive vice president for sales and marketing, suggested that the most effective means of limiting car imports would be to charter the *Enola Gay* (the airplane that dropped the first atomic bomb on Japan) (Daniels, 1988: 342–343).

The most notorious violent incident emerging from this situation occurred on June 19, 1982. Vincent Chin, a Chinese American, went with three friends to a topless bar, where a white automobile industry foreman mistook him for Japanese and started making racial slurs, suggesting that Chin was responsible for his unemployment. A scuffle developed, and all participants were thrown out of the bar. Later that evening the white foreman and his stepson saw Chin at a restaurant, waited for him to leave, and then, while the stepson held Chin, the older man beat him with a baseball bat. Chin died four days later. Originally charged with second-degree murder, the whites were allowed to plead guilty to manslaughter; they were fined $3,780 each and put on three years' probation. The local Asian American community was outraged, charging that a racist deevaluation of Asian Americans led to the light sentences. Eventually their protests produced a federal investigation and a federal indictment of the older man, who was found guilty of depriving Chin of his civil rights. In September 1984 he received 25 years in prison, but upon appeal, witnesses' conflicting and vague testimony produced an acquittal (Kitano and Daniels, 1988: 189).

The Chin murder was hardly an isolated incident. Asian Americans have increasingly become the target of hate groups, with Navroze Mody killed in 1987 by 11 youths belonging to a gang whose stated purpose was to rid Jersey City of Asian Americans and Sam Nang Nhem kicked and beaten to death in 1993 in Fall River, Massachusetts, simply because he had the ill-timed misfortune of walking by a group of brawling young white men who instantly decided "to knock that gook out." The perpetrators of anti-Asian bigotry and violence are usually members of the racial or ethnic group living in the area where a given Asian American group has settled and started establishing an economic foothold in a variety of businesses. Thus in Texas those responsible have been whites and Chicanos, in Seattle and Tacoma African Americans and Hispanic Americans, in Boston whites, and in Philadelphia whites and blacks (*New York Times,* 1994; Wong, 1994).

Modern Native Americans sometimes are victims of violence when they use the court system to obtain illegally removed tribal rights. After the Ojibway of northern Wisconsin sued for return of traditional fishing rights, hundreds of whites gathered on different occasions to protest. During the 1987 fishing season, 12 Ojibway spearers were trapped on a small point of land by about 500 whites, who hurled rocks and racial insults and blocked escape until a tactical squad arrived and dispersed the mob. In the spring of 1989, several anti-Indian organizations with such names as Protect Americans' Rights and Resources, and Stop Treaty Abuses organized against Ojibway fishermen, throwing rocks, shooting ball bearings from high-powered slingshots, shouting racist vulgarities, and taking to the water to swamp the Indians' boats. Over 200 of the members of these anti-Indian organizations were arrested during a 12-day span. It is not readily apparent why the return of Ojibway fishing rights so angered whites. Did they feel threatened? One Native American writer stated:

> It seems to enrage white people whenever Indians manage to hold onto any vestige of their land, their heritage, their rights. The racist resentment unleashed in northern Wisconsin is never far from the surface in areas with an Indian presence. The thin veneer of civilization is easily stripped away. (Harjo, 1989: 25)

For racial minorities, negative living conditions can encourage violence. In a study conducted in Baltimore, Taylor and Covington (1990) found that murder and assault rates rose rapidly in largely black neighborhoods in which rapid growth of poverty indicated that residents' quality of life was declining.

James W. Balkwell provided consistent findings. In research done in 150 urban areas each containing 50,000 or more inhabitants, Balkwell (1990) found that what he called "ethnic inequality" was the social factor best predicting the homicide rate. Balkwell obtained income data from five ethnic categories—non-Hispanic whites; African Americans; Native Americans, Eskimos, or Aleuts; Asian Americans; and Hispanic Americans. He found that the greater the proportion of poor racial minority group members, the higher the homicide rate. Balkwell suspected that a version of the frustration-aggression theory applied here: Frustrated and angered by restrictions on achieving economic success and unable to confront the true sources of their frustration, poor members of racial minorities sometimes lashed out at the people at hand, who served as scapegoats.

Native American women, in particular, have been victims of this pattern. Evidence from a regional psychiatric center for women serving a five-state area in the Southwest suggested that at least 80 percent of the female patients had been victims of sexual assault, with a substantial number having suffered gang rape. Deprived of respect and self-respect in a world where they were systematically stripped of their traditional culture, Indian men were taught that emulation of the white man was the route to follow. That emulation included the brutalization of women—an act conspicuously missing from their traditional cultures (Allen, 1995).

The most dominant factor linked to violence is economic condition, and that linkage also occurs with violent crime. Research based on arrest rates in New York City found that black males and females had higher arrest rates for homicide, robbery, assault, and burglary than both their white and Hispanic counterparts. The investigators concluded that backgrounds featuring poor schools, a lack of legitimate job opportunities, and weak community organizations pushed young black men and women away from the mainstream job world and pulled them toward the criminal underworld, where violence is widespread. While many studies have analyzed how black males' disadvantaged status has promoted their disproportionate involvement in violent crime, little attention has been paid to the fact that a comparable pattern has developed for young black females (Sommers and Baskin, 1992).

A black police officer working in inner-city Chicago commented on children's frequent exposure to violence and death in a world where drug dealers' fight for control of turf is the dominant cause of violent activity. He said:

The little children growing up in our inner city have experienced more violence than many of our veterans of wars. Working in the projects, I can recall the children as somebody was shot on a playing field. By the time the ambulance arrived, there are all these children looking at a dying person. It's a hot day, everybody out playing. You see these little kids just looking. Most Americans never experience this. I didn't until I was an adult. It's just so ordinary, so everyday with them, seeing death. (Terkel, 1992: 253)

The officer went on to explain that several years earlier in a nearby upper-middle-class suburb, a disturbed woman killed several schoolchildren. For the surviving children, the school provided extensive psychiatric counseling. For inner-city children, in contrast, no psychiatric care is available to respond to their frequent encounters with violence. They simply must deal with such harsh realities the best they can.

Furthermore, once violent crime increases within an area, its racial composition is likely to change, with white flight a distinct prospect (Liska and Bellair, 1995). Businesses often respond the same way. Five years after the Los Angeles riots, the inner city was still suffering from the fallout. "I don't want to sound pessimistic, but, yes, we're losing the battle to keep companies here," said Ahmed Enamy, executive director of the Southern California Biomedical Council, which has sought to bring investment to the inner city. "There's an issue of image in these neighborhoods," Enamy added. "People don't want to locate there. Everyone we speak to says so" (Sterngold, 1997: D11). As a result the unemployment rate for black youth was over 30 percent, and the chances of bringing in jobs paying over $8 an hour were fairly remote.

Probably when most people think about groups promoting racist violence, they feel that those responsible are men. In some such groups, however, women are well represented.

Women in Contemporary Ku Klux Klan and Neo-Nazi Groups

Both scholarly and popular representations of women in racist groups suggest that women are on the fringe—"directionless, manipulated, and victimized" (Blee, 1996: 680). Seldom if ever do accounts indicate that they took purposeful steps to enter these organizations.

After interviewing 34 women in such white-supremacist groups as the Ku Klux Klan and the neo-Nazi movement, sociologist Kathleen M. Blee found that the women had rational, well-planned motives for their participation. She detected three strategies—conversion, selective adoption, and resignation—that created a "fit" between their personal perspectives and the goals of the racist organizations to which they committed.

To begin, conversion entailed the respondent claiming that a single, dramatic incident or set of incidents led to a fusion between her personal goals and the group's. For instance, Alice, a 23-year-old racist skinhead, interviewed on death row following her conviction for a series of murders and robberies, indicated that a car accident had led to her conversion. Awaking in the hospital following the accident, Alice felt surrounded by African American nurses, probing and invading her. She had been taught racist attitudes by her parents, but like them she had never felt moved to act on those beliefs. Now the situation had suddenly changed. Blee indicated that:

> bodily invasion thus took on a racialized cast for which her earlier belief system served as an ideological template [mold]: "I said [to the African American nurses] 'don't touch me. Don't get near me . . . leave me alone.'" It was this incident, she concluded, that brought her into permanent "racial awareness" and that set the stage for her subsequent involvement in neo-Nazi gangs. (Blee, 1996: 690)

Some other women in white-supremacist groups had a similar experience, indicating that conversion occurred when in their perception a traumatic incident such as an accident was closely linked to minority group individuals. In some cases supportive evidence simply didn't exist. For instance, one woman who increasingly felt that the problems in her "bad" neighborhood were produced by blacks' laziness contended that the car accident in which she was seriously injured must have been a black person's responsibility. The reason, she explained, was that she had been ignoring the African Americans in her neighborhood, and forcing the accident was their way of getting revenge. When pressed, this woman admitted that she had not seen the driver. Nonetheless her conviction was strong enough that once recovered, she concluded that the reality of the ongoing race war between whites and blacks had been revealed to her, and so she became an active member of a neo-Nazi group.

Selective adaptation is the second strategy. Whereas conversion involves a sudden realization that one's personal goals and those of the organization are the same, selective adaptation is less complete, with the women pursuing this approach recognizing that only some of their activities and goals coincide with the group's and that the rest must be disregarded. Blee's study indicated a fairly lengthy list of issues where her respondents disagreed with their organizations, including some Klanswomen's support for homosexuality; a neo-Nazi leader's positive feelings about racial intermarriage and lesbianism; Klan members' criticisms of their chapters for being too male oriented and sexist. As in the case of conversion, odd perceptions were often involved. One woman explained that her best friend was an African American man but that he was "really white." Apparently this woman had quite an unusual criterion for assigning race—on the basis of friendship (Blee, 1996: 694).

Resignation is the third strategy, with women pursuing an approach normally not taken by men. Studies have shown that when men participate in racist groups, they often display enthusiasm, even a swagger, when discussing their mission. Blee's respondents, in contrast, were much more reluctant. For one thing they questioned whether knowledge about their respective groups was desirable. One Nazi member said, "It's painful, it hurts, it's all consuming when you have the knowledge." A member of an Aryan supremacist group explained, "It's hard feeling this duty to alert other people" (Blee, 1996: 695). Almost none of the women interviewed wanted to recruit family members into their organizations.

Unlike their male counterparts, they were neither empowered by their activity nor boastful of involvement in racial violence. Why, one might reasonably wonder, did they join? The reality was that they saw this activism as a recourse for protecting their families or themselves. As a white supremacist said, "I would like my future to be a little house on the prairie picture . . . but it will not be like that. I think we'll be struggling my whole life . . . surrounded by immorality and corruption" (Blee, 1996: 696). So for these women, racist activism is a defensive stance, offering little to them personally but fending off the racial forces they see as threatening to engulf them and their families.

Analysis of these three strategies indicates that Blee's research subjects made rational decisions to join their racist groups—that these women were not simply men's irrational, passive followers. For foes of racism, this conclusion is instructive, suggesting that many female members of such groups might forsake racist activity if they could learn to examine and understand the sense of threat driving them to embrace racism.

Discussion Questions

1. Discuss any illustrations of political incorporation that have occurred in your locale.
2. Consider the pros and cons of minority political candidates developing PACs.
3. Do you have specific knowledge about racism in the criminal justice system that you can share with the class?
4. Should juries practice nullification and, if so, in cases involving what alleged crimes?
5. Examine local instances of interracial violence, indicating why the violence developed and whether similar incidents are likely to reoccur.
6. If you were mayor of a city in your region, what step(s) would you take to reduce the likelihood of interracial violence?

Sources

Allen, Paula Gunn. 1995. "Angry Women Are Building: Issues and Struggles Facing American Indian Women Today," pp. 32–36 in Margaret L. Andersen and Patricia Hill Collins (eds.), *Race, Class, and Gender: An Anthology.* 2nd ed. Belmont, CA: Wadsworth Publishing Company.

Alvarez, Alexander, and Ronet D. Bachman. 1996. "American Indians and Sentencing Disparity: An Arizona Test." *Journal of Criminal Justice* 24: 549–561.

Anner, John. 1996. "Linking Community Safety with Police Accountability," pp. 119-134 in John Anner (ed.), *Beyond Identity Politics: Emerging Social Justice Movements in Communities of Color.* Boston: South End Press.

Awanohara, Susumu. 1993. "Spicier Melting Pot," pp. 112–117 in John A. Kromkowski (ed.), *Race and Ethnic Relations 93/94,* 3rd ed. Guilford, CT: Dushkin.

Balkwell, James W. 1990. "Ethnic Inequality and the Rate of Homicide." *Social Forces* 69 (September): 53–70.

Baron, Harold M. 1968. "Black Powerlessness in Chicago." *Trans-Action* 6 (November): 27–35.

Barry, Dan. 1997. "Officer Charged in Man's Torture at Station House." *New York Times* (August 14): A1+.

Bass, Paul. 1997. "Cops Who Kill." *New Haven Advocate* (May 15): 11+.

Berkman, Alan, and Tim Blunk. 1995. "Thoughts on Class, Race, and Prison," pp. 335–338 in Margaret L. Andersen and Patricia Hill Collins (eds.), *Race, Class, and Gender,* 2nd ed. Belmont, CA: Wadsworth.

Blee, Kathleen M. 1996. "Becoming a Racist: Women in Contemporary Ku Klux Klan and Neo-Nazi Groups." *Gender & Society* 10 (December): 680–702.

Blumstein, Alfred. 1982. "On the Racial Disproportionality of United States' Prison Populations." *Journal of Criminal Law and Criminology* 73 (Fall): 1259–1281.

Bridges, George S., and Robert D. Crutchfield. 1988. "Law, Social Standing and Racial Disparities in Imprisonment." *Social Forces* 66 (March): 699–724.

Brooke, James. 1996. "Denver Is Proving Fertile Ground for Theme of Million Man March." *New York Times* (March 25): A1+.

Brossard, Mario A., and Richard Morin. 1996. "Leader Popular among Marchers," pp. 152–154 in John A. Kromkowski (ed.), *Race and Ethnic Relations 96/97*, 6th ed. Guilford, CT: Dushkin.

Brown, Richard Maxwell. 1979. "Historical Patterns of American Violence," pp. 49–76 in Hugh Davis Graham and Ted Robert Gurr (eds.), *Violence in America: Historical & Comparative Perspectives*, rev. ed. Beverly Hills: Sage Publications.

Browning, Rufus P., Dale Rogers Marshall, and David H. Tabb. 1986. "Protest Is Not Enough: A Theory of Political Incorporation." *PS* 19 (Summer): 576–581.

Butler, Paul. 1996. "Racially Based Jury Nullification: Black Power in the Criminal Justice System," pp. 334–338 in Richard C. Monk (ed.), *Taking Sides: Clashing Views on Controversial Issues in Race and Ethnicity*, 2nd ed. Guilford, CT: Dushkin.

Butterfield, Fox. 1997. "Many Black Males Barred from Voting." *New York Times* (January 30): A12.

Churchill, Ward. 1990. "The Black Hills Are Not for Sale: A Summary of the Lakota Struggle for the 1868 Treaty Territory." *Journal of Ethnic Studies* (Spring): 127–142.

Cole, Elizabeth R., and Abigail J. Stewart. 1996. "Meanings of Political Participation among Black and White Women: Political Identity and Social Responsibility." *Journal of Personality and Social Psychology* 71 (July): 130–140.

Cornacchia, Eugene J., and Dale C. Nelson. 1992. "Historical Differences in the Political Experiences of American Blacks and White Ethnics." *Ethnic and Racial Studies* 15 (January): 102–124.

Cullen, Francis T., et al. 1996. " 'Stop or I'll Shoot': Racial Differences in Support for Police Use of Deadly Force." *American Behavioral Scientist* 39 (February): 449–460.

Daniels, Roger. 1988. *Asian Americans: Chinese and Japanese in the United States since 1850.* Seattle: University of Washington Press.

Dollard, John. 1937. *Caste & Class in a Southern Town.* New Haven, CT: Yale University Press.

Donovan, Beth. 1993. "Black Caucus: PAC Funds a Must for Minorities." *Congressional Quarterly Weekly Report* 51 (September 25): 2523–2526.

Ekland-Olson, Sheldon. 1988. "Structured Discretion, Racial Bias, and the Death Penalty: The First Decade after *Furman* in Texas." *Social Science Quarterly* 69 (December): 853–873.

Fagan, Jeffrey, Ellen Slaughter, and Eliot Hartstone. 1987. "Blind Justice? The Impact of Race on the Juvenile Process." *Crime & Delinquency* 33 (April): 224–258.

Fainstein, Norman, and Susan Fainstein. 1996. "Urban Regimes and Black Citizens: The Economic and Social Impacts of Black Political Incoporation in U.S. Cities." *International Journal of Urban and Regional Research* 20 (March): 22–37.

Feagin, Joe R., and Clairece Booher Feagin. 1993. *Racial and Ethnic Relations*, 4th ed. Englewood Cliffs, NJ: Prentice-Hall.

Gray, Jerry. 1991. "Panel Says Courts Are 'Infested with Racism.' " *New York Times* (June 5): B1+.

Gutierrez, Ramon A. 1993. "Community, Patriarchy, and Individualism: The Politics of Chicano History and the Dream of Equality." *American Quarterly* 45 (March): 44–72.

Hacker, Andrew. 1988. "Black Crime, White Racism." *New York Review of Books* 35 (March 3): 36–41.

Hacker, Andrew. 1992. *Two Nations: Black and White, Separate, Hostile, Unequal.* New York: Charles Scribner's Sons.

Hagan, William T. 1986. "Tribalism Rejuvenated: The Native American since the Era of Termination," pp. 295–304 in Roger L. Nichols (ed.), *The American Indian: Past and Present,* 3rd ed. New York: Alfred A. Knopf.

Harjo, Suzanne Shown. 1989. "Rights of Spring: Racism in Wisconsin." *Daybreak* 3 (Spring): 24–25.

Hawkins, Darnell F. 1987. "Beyond Anomalies: Rethinking the Conflict Perspective on Race and Criminal Punishment." *Social Forces* 65 (March): 719–45.

Hero, Rodney E., and Kathleen M. Beatty. 1989. "The Election of Federico Peña as Mayor of Denver: Analysis and Implications." *Social Science Quarterly* 70 (June): 300–310.

Holden, Benjamin A., Laurie P. Cohen, and Eleena de Lisser. 1996. "Color Blinded? Race Seems to Play an Increasing Role in Many Jury Verdicts," pp. 244–246 in John A. Kromkowski (ed.), *Race and Ethnic Relations 96/97,* 6th ed. Guilford, CT: Dushkin.

Holmes, Steven A. 1996. "Hispanic March Draws Crowd to Capital." *New York Times* (October 13): 26.

Huizinga, David, and Delbert S. Elliott. 1987. "Juvenile Offenders: Prevalence, Offender Incidence, and Arrest Rates by Race." *Crime & Delinquency* 33 (April): 206–223.

Jaynes, Gerald David, and Robin M. Williams, Jr. (eds.). 1989. *A Common Destiny: Blacks and American Society.* Washington, DC: National Academy Press.

Johnson, Kirk. 1989. "Racism and the Young: Some See a Rising Tide." *New York Times* (August 27): 32.

Johnson, Kirk. 1994. "Pequots Invest Casino Wealth in a New Game: Party Politics." *New York Times* (August 30): A1+.

Jones, Charisse. 1996. "Thousands Rally on Anniversary of the Million Man March." *New York Times* (October 17): B1+.

Keil, Thomas J. 1985. "Capital, Labor, and the Klan: A Case Study in the Deterioration of Local Racial Relationships." *Phylon* 46 (Winter): 341–352.

Keil, Thomas J., and Gennaro F. Vito. 1989. "Race, Homicide Severity, and Application of the Death Penalty: A Consideration of the Barnett Scale." *Criminology* 27 (August): 511–531.

Kemp, William B., and Lorraine F. Brooke. 1996. "Toward Information Self-Sufficiency: The Nunavik Inuit Gather Information on Ecology and Land Use," pp. 97–100 in John A. Kromkowski (ed.), *Race and Ethnic Relations 96/97,* 6th ed. Guilford, CT: Dushkin.

Kennedy, Randall. 1996. "After the Cheers," pp. 339–42 in Richard C. Monk (ed.), *Taking Sides: Clashing Views on Controversial Issues in Race and Ethnicity,* 2nd ed. Guilford, CT: Dushkin.

Kitano, Harry H. L., and Roger Daniels. 1988. *Asian Americans: Emerging Minorities.* Englewood-Cliffs, NJ: Prentice-Hall.

Kramer, John, and Darrell Steffensmeir. 1993. "Race and Imprisonment Decisions." *Sociological Quarterly* 34 (May): 357–376.

Krill, Vern. 1997. "The Injustices within the American Criminal-Justice System." Research Project for Sociology 510, Southern Connecticut State University.

LaFree, Gary. 1980. "The Effect of Sexual Stratification by Race on Official Reactions to Rape." *American Sociological Review* 45 (October): 842–854.

Langan, Patrick A. 1985. "Racism on Trial: New Evidence to Explain the Racial Composition of Prisons in the United States." *Criminology* 76 (Fall): 666–683.

Lawrence, Ken. 1994. "Klansmen, Nazis, and Skinheads: Vigilante Repression," pp. 21–37 in Richard G. Majors and Jacob U. Gordon (eds.), *The American Black Male: His Present Status and His Future.* Chicago: Nelson-Hall Publishers.

Limerick, Patricia Nelson. 1997. "The Battlefield of History." *New York Times* (August 28): A31.

Liska, Allen E., and Paul E. Bellair. 1995. "Violent-Crime Rates and Racial Composition: Convergence over Time." *American Journal of Sociology* 101 (November): 578–610.

Liska, Allen E., Mitchell B. Chamlin, and Mark D. Reed. 1985. "Testing the Economic Production and Conflict Models of Crime Control." *Social Forces* 64 (September): 119–138.

Longoria, Thomas, Jr., Robert D. Wrinkle, and J. L. Polinard. 1990. "Mexican American Voter Registration." *Social Science Quarterly* 71 (June): 356–361.

Maharidge, Dale. 1993. "Did 1992 Herald the Dawn of Latino Political Power?" *California Journal* 24 (January): 15–18.

Mann, Coramae Richey. 1994. "The Reality of a Racist Criminal Justice System," pp. 249–253 in Richard C. Monk (ed.), *Taking Sides: Clashing Views of Controversial Issues in Race and Ethnicity.* Guilford, CT: Dushkin.

Marquez, Benjamin. 1989. "The Politics of Race and Assimilation: The League of United Latin American Citizens, 1929–40." *Western Political Quarterly* 42 (June): 355–375.

Mauer, Marc. 1994. "A Generation behind Bars: Black Males and the Criminal Justice System," pp. 81–93 in Richard G. Majors and Jacob U. Gordon (eds.), *The American Black Male: His Present Status and His Future.* Chicago: Nelson-Hall Publishers.

McCall, Nathan. 1994. *Makes Me Wanna Holler: A Young Black Man in America.* New York: Random House.

Moore, David W., and Lydia Saad. 1995. "No Immediate Signs That Simpson Trial Intensified Racial Animosity." *Gallup Poll Monthly* (October): 2–7.

Mydans, Seth. 1991. "Videotape of Beating by Officers Puts Full Glare on Brutality Issue." *New York Times* (March 18): A1+.

Mydans, Seth. 1994. "A Vietnamese American Becomes a Political First." *Migration World Review* 21 (September/October): 44.

New York Times. 1994. "Guilty Verdict in Slaying Linked to Racial Hatred." (September 19): A12.

Pareles, Jon. 1989. "There's a New Sound in Pop Music: Bigotry." *New York Times* (September 10): Sec. 2, 1+.

Radcliff, Benjamin, and Martin Saiz. 1995. "Race, Turnout, and Public Policy in the American States." *Political Research Quarterly* 48 (December): 775–794.

Reiman, Jeffrey. 1994. "A Crime by Any Other Name," pp. 294–302 in Kurt Finsterbusch and George McKenna (eds.), *Taking Sides: Clashing Views on Controversial Social Issues,* 8th ed. Guilford, CT: Dushkin.

Seltzer, Rick, and Grace M. Lopes. 1986. "The Ku Klux Klan: Reasons for Support or Opposition among White Respondents." *Journal of Black Studies* 17 (September): 91–109.

Skerry, Peter. 1994. "Not Much Cooking: Why the Voting Rights Act is Not Empowering Mexican Americans," pp. 107–109 in John A. Kromkowski (ed.), *Race and Ethnic Relations 94/95,* 4th ed. Guilford, CT: Dushkin.

Smith, Barbara Ellen. 1995. "Crossing the Great Divides: Race, Class, and Gender in Southern Women's Organizing, 1979–1991." *Gender and Society* 9 (December); 680–696.

Sommers, Ira, and Deborah Baskin. 1992. "Sex, Race, Age, and Violent Offending." *Violence and Victims* 7 (Fall): 191–201.

Sterngold, James. 1997. "5 Years after Los Angeles Riots, Inner City Still Cries Out for Jobs." *New York Times* (April 28): A1+.

Swain, Johnnie Dee, Jr. 1993. "Black Mayors: Urban Decline and the Underclass." *Journal of Black Studies* 24 (September): 16–28.

Swigert, Victoria, and Ronald A. Farrell. 1977. "Normal Homicides and the Law." *American Sociological Review* 42 (February): 16–32.

Taylor, Ralph B., and Jeanette Covington. 1990. "Ecological Change, Changes in Violence, and Risk Prediction." *Journal of Interpersonal Violence* 5 (June): 16–175.

Terkel, Studs. 1992. *Race: How Blacks & Whites Feel about the American Obsession.* New York: New Press.

Terkildsen, Nayda. 1993. "When White Voters Evaluate Black Candidates: The Processing Implications of Candidate Skin Color, Prejudice, and Self-Monitoring." *American Journal of Political Science* 37 (November): 1032–1053.

Terry, Don. 1997. "Chicago's Neighborhood Reveals an Ugly Side." *New York Times* (March 27): A18.

Thomson, Randall J., and Matthew T. Zingraff. 1981. "Detecting Sentence Disparity: Some Problems and Evidence." *American Journal of Sociology* 86 (January): 869–880.

U.S. Bureau of the Census. 1996. *Statistical Abstract of the United States: 1996,* 116th ed. Washington, DC: U.S. Government Printing Office.

U.S. Department of Justice. 1996. *Sourcebook of Criminal Justice Statistics, 1995.* Washington, DC: U.S. Government Printing Office.

Vanderleeuw, James M. 1990. "A City in Transition: The Impact of Changing Racial Composition on Voting Behavior." *Social Science Quarterly* 71 (June): 326–338.

Verhover, Sam Howe. 1997. "Cherokee Nation Facing a Crisis Involving Its Tribal Constitution." *New York Times* (July 6): 1+.

Waegel, William B. 1984. "How the Police Justify the Use of Deadly Force." *Social Problems* 32 (December): 144–155.

Wagar, Linda. 1993. "Reclaiming Tribal Lands," pp. 74-75 in John A. Kromkowski (ed.), *Race and Ethnic Relations 93/94,* 3rd ed. Guilford, CT: Dushkin.

Weitzer, Ronald. 1996. "Racial Discrimination in the Criminal Justice System: Findings and Problems in the Literature." *Journal of Criminal Justice* 24: 309–322.

Wong, Morrison G. 1994. "Rise in Anti-Asian Activities in the United States," pp. 417-422 in *Sociological Footprints,* 6th ed. Belmont, CA: Wadsworth Publishing Company.

Yu, Jiang, and Allen E. Liska. 1993. "The Certainty of Punishment: A Reference Group Effect and Its Functional Form." *Criminology* 31 (August): 447–464.

Zatz, Marjorie S. 1987. "The Changing Forms of Racial/Ethnic Differences in Sentencing." *Journal of Research in Crime and Delinquency* 24: 69–72.

CHAPTER 5

Knowing Your Place: Work and Housing

"Let's see, Chris." He paused to think. "It must have been about 1935. I was 5 or 6, and every day my old man and I would drive downtown to make food deliveries to black restaurants.

"He'd go by a club where there was a bunch of white guys on the street." He laughed half-audibly. "Now you've got to realize my old man hardly drove over 5 miles an hour. And with that rickety truck they'd hear him a mile off. So by the time we reached the club they'd be loaded up with every foul expression their little minds could conceive. They'd start by yelling nigger and head downhill from there."

"How'd you react?"

"I'd hide under the seat, and then when we'd get back home to where there was just black folks, I'd feel a great relief. But I was building up a powerful hatred for those dudes. And I couldn't abide how my father accepted everything they threw at him.

"Then some 10 years later I was driving downtown. There's this large white guy in a garbage truck, and he's yelling at someone I can't see. When I get around the truck, I find it's my father, and I went nuts.

"I grabbed a bowling pin I kept on the seat next to me and ran to the truck, pulled the guy out, and prepared to beat the hell out of him. 'Don't hit me,' he moaned. 'I'll do anything you want.' He, this large white man, and me, this skinny black kid! 'Stop yelling at my father,' I said and walked away.

"Somehow that incident cooled me off so I started looking at things more calmly. I realized I was at least as mad at my old man as at the white guys. And now I started watching more closely what he did."

"What do you mean?"

"Well, for one thing I noticed he'd always drive by that club regardless of where he was going."

"He went out of his way?"

"He went *way* out of his way."

"Why?"

He laughed. "Now this wasn't exactly the nineties, you know. My dad was never into heart-to-heart conversation and so I'm guessing. I think he was testing himself. 'Take your best shot, and in the end I'll still be standing,' he seemed to be saying."

"How'd his face look when they were yelling?"

"Peaceful, man, just as peaceful as could be." He laughed gently. "A pipeline to his soul."

This is a kind of success story. Living in segregated areas and working in segregated jobs, blacks and other minorities often could not attain the composure this man achieved. Hardship and heartache have been the standard hallmarks of segregated housing and work.

Internal colonialism applies all too well to the topics of this chapter. One of the theory's basic ideas is the colonial labor principle, which indicates that racial minorities must serve white controllers' interests and needs and relates to the upcoming discussion of work. The idea of racial minorities' restricted freedom of movement relates to housing, the second issue.

Racial Minorities' Work World

At the end of the nineteenth century, Horatio Alger wrote a series of best-selling novels about hard-working, clean-living boys whose perseverance paid off. Their virtuous efforts produced a rise from poverty and obscurity to wealth and fame. Horatio Alger never bothered to emphasize that all his young heroes were white. For racial minorities of that era, the road to economic and social success was virtually nonexistent.

Before World War II, African Americans still largely lived in the rural South. With the outbreak of war, they started moving to both southern and northern cities, where wartime industrial jobs paid much higher wages than they had previously received. The labor force transformation continued after the war, as we see by examining job categories in which African American men and women made their statistically largest shifts.

In 1939, 41 percent of black men were farmers or farmworkers; by 1984, the figure had dropped sharply to 5 percent. Meanwhile, the proportion in clerical and sales, machine operation, and crafts jobs rose from 19 percent to nearly 52 percent. During that period the proportion of women providing domestic service shifted from

60 percent to 6 percent while clerical and sales, machine operation, and crafts jobs went from less than 8 percent to nearly 48 percent.

The transition from rural to urban living also gave African Americans increasing access to American consumer technology—inside plumbing, electricity, automobiles, refrigerators, telephones, radios, and eventually television. They also benefitted from improved medical care, especially in the late 1960s after the establishment of government-subsidized health care for the poor (Medicaid) and for the elderly (Medicare).

Overall, however, African Americans' economic advancement in the past half-century has been at best mixed. Through the 1970s and the 1980s, blacks' wages rose relative to whites', but African Americans experienced higher unemployment rates than whites, with the least educated workers most adversely affected. Poverty among African Americans has become increasingly evident. For instance, keeping the dollar's buying power at the 1984 level, one finds that in 1984 about 40 percent of black men earned less than $10,000, up from 25 percent in 1969. For white men the respective percentages were 20 percent and 10 percent (Jaynes and Williams, 1989: 272–275).

Why have African Americans historically had lower incomes than whites? Differences of opinion exist. Wacquant and Wilson concluded that the dominant factors are the flight of manufacturing jobs out of northern and midwestern cities and the general economic shift toward service industries and occupations. When these conditions occur, they suggested, "even mild forms of racial discrimination—mild by historical standards—have a bigger impact on those at the bottom of the American class order" (Wacquant and Wilson, 1989: 11). For these observers poor blacks' poverty is largely the result of impersonal, color-blind factors, primarily affecting low-income people.

Many scholars more strongly emphasize the impact of racism, offering recent evidence that racial discrimination has been a significant factor affecting African Americans' work at all income levels: limiting them in management (Collins, 1997; Morrison and Von Glinow, 1990; National Committee on Pay Equity, 1996) and male-dominated professions (Sokoloff, 1988); pushing them into low-skilled as opposed to high-skilled work (Kaufman, 1986); holding down salary levels (Geschwender and Carroll-Seguin, 1990; Killian, 1990; Thomas, 1993; Tomaskovic-Devey, 1993) and advancement from low-paying jobs (Beauregard, 1990; Pomer, 1986; Wilson, 1997); and increasing the likelihood of unemployment or underemployment (Burstein and Pitchford, 1990; Farley, 1987; Johnson, 1990; Killian, 1990; Lichter, 1988; National Committe on Pay Equity, 1996; Tigges and Tootle, 1993).

Furthermore, as we noted in Chapter 3, racial segregation has played a major role in the creation of a black underclass. Forced to live in restricted urban areas, poor African Americans find their residential districts particularly hard hit by such economic downturns as the one occurring in the early 1970s, especially when segregation policies make it likely or inevitable that large numbers of poor blacks from other districts are funnelled into them. Businesses leave; vital services including medical care and schooling deteriorate, and crime and violence sharply increase (Massey, 1990). These are prime conditions fostering the **vicious cycle of poverty**—a pattern in which parents' minimal income significantly limits children's educational and occupational pursuits, thereby keeping them locked into the same low economic status. It is being argued here that in modern times, a poor minority member's residential area contributes significantly to the perpetuation of poverty. In inner-city areas, main-

Table 5.1   Minority Groups' Poverty[1]

Percentage of Members of Different Racial Groups below the Poverty Level: 1991

Puerto Ricans	40.6%
African Americans	31.9
American Indians	30.9
Mexican Americans	28.1
Asian Americans	12.2
Whites	10.7

Percentage of Black and White Individuals Living in Poverty 1959 to 1994

	African Americans	Whites
1959	55.1%	18.1%
1966	41.8	12.2
1970	33.5	9.9
1975	31.3	9.7
1980	32.5	10.2
1985	31.3	11.4
1990	30.6	10.0
1994	30.6	11.7

[1] The poverty index, which is updated each year, is an estimate of the money necessary to purchase basic consumer products and services. Individuals falling below the poverty line simply possess insufficient funds to make these purchases.

Note: While poverty has been an unrelenting American problem, data in this table make it clear that it has been a consistently greater threat to most racial minorities than to whites.

Sources: U.S. Bureau of the Census. Current Population Reports, "Characteristics of the Population Below the Poverty Level: 1980." Table 38; U.S. Bureau of the Census. *Statistical Abstract of the United States: 1992,* Table 41; U.S. Bureau of the Census. *Statistical Abstract of the United States: 1996,* Table 733.

stream jobs for minimally educated African Americans have often virtually disappeared (Wilson, 1997). Given these conditions it is not surprising that in 1994 the proportion of African Americans living below the poverty level was nearly three times greater than the white proportion—30.6 percent compared to 11.7 percent (U.S. Bureau of the Census, 1996, Table 733). Table 5.1 provides more information on racial minorities' poverty.

Research has also indicated that housing segregation affects middle-class blacks' job prospects. Often prevented from living in primarily white suburbs, which have become prominent sites for retail and service trade industries in the last couple of decades (Darden, 1990) or restricted to living in racially segregated suburbs that provide few such job opportunities (Schneider and Phelan, 1990), middle-class African Americans often have much less immediate physical access to good-paying jobs than whites. However, a recent study done in Boston and Houston suggested that the part played by residential location for black versus white employment has been overstated: that employer discrimination in hiring is more significant, at least for entry-level blue-collar jobs (Cohn and Fossett, 1996).

Like African Americans, other racial minorities have historically suffered job discrimination. For instance, during the 1950s and 1960s, increasing numbers of Japanese Americans and Chinese Americans graduated from college and obtained jobs outside their ethnic locales, but they tended to be denied supervisory and higher administrative positions. The most formidable barrier to their advancement seemed to be white employers' reluctance to put Asian Americans into positions where they could hire and fire whites (Daniels, 1988: 315–316).

To many white Americans, Asian Americans' occupational success is impressive, and, in fact, the success image has often become the dominant element in modern whites' stereotype of Asian Americans. Like any stereotype, however, this one provides a disservice to the group in question. Asian Americans' success image often over-shadows significant amounts of unemployment and underemployment, poverty among the elderly, mental illness, divorce and family disorganization, and juvenile delin-quency even in the most accomplished Asian American groups. Some recently arrived Asian Americans, especially those from the Philippines, Vietnam, and Cambodia, tend to arrive poor, limited in English proficiency, and, in the case of the Vietnamese and Cambodians, carrying the traumatic psychological burdens produced by extensive exposure to warfare. Because of the simplistic success image, however, government agencies, educational institutions, and private corporations have been less likely to address the often pressing problems among Asian Americans than among other racial minorities (Chua-eoan, 1993; Crystal, 1989; Hurh and Kim, 1989; United States Commission on Civil Rights, 1996).

Like Asian Americans, Chicanos have also suffered job discrimination, with work-ers in farming, oil, mining, and manufacturing jobs often classified as "nonwhites" and systematically paid less than their white counterparts. Many current employers have selectively hired illegal Mexican American immigrants, who could be forced to accept subminimum wages and oppressive working conditions to avoid being turned over to government authorities. Studies conducted primarily on Mexican Americans living in the southwestern states indicated that they are more likely to be successful occupa-tionally if they speak English, live in areas where they represent a substantial propor-tion of the population, and have elected representatives in local government (Mladenka, 1989; Stolzenberg, 1990).

Those without these attributes often find themselves at the mercy of the internal colonialist system. In 1994 California passed Proposition 187, a referendum which denied education and health services to illegal migrants and their families. Still des-perately needing work, impoverished Mexicans continued to arrive in the state, pro-viding somewhere between one-third and two-fifths of workers tending and harvesting the fields of lettuce, broccoli, mustard greens, grapes, and other crops. For growers, who have always given their illegal workers subminimum wages, the steadily increasing pool of Mexican workers has made it possible to pay their employees about 15 percent less than a decade ago, thus fattening their profits (Chavez, 1994; de Uriarte, 1997).

Research has indicated that Puerto Ricans are the only major racial group besides blacks suffering racial segregation so severe that they are locked into residential areas that have steadily deteriorated since the advent of the 1970s economic downturn (Massey and Eggers, 1990). In other words, besides blacks, Puerto Ricans have been the only other major racial group in which an underclass has been rapidly expanding. About two-fifths of the Puerto Rican population in the United States—40.6 percent in 1991—falls below the poverty line (U.S. Bureau of the Census, 1990, Table 53).

For Puerto Ricans, institutional racism has also been a common barrier. In New York City, for example, applicants for many low-level service jobs such as trash collection have been required to take tests written in English that are not job related and that could easily have been translated into Spanish. Another illustration of institutional racism is that Puerto Ricans, who tend to be smaller than average American citizens, find that height and weight requirements for police and fire department jobs can rule them ineligible (Feagin and Feagin, 1993: 306).

Research on Puerto Rican women in the New York City area indicated that respondents with 11 or more years of formal education, good ability to speak English, no children under 5, and previous work experience were considerably more likely to be employed than women without all or most of these characteristics. A related pattern applied to higher-level positions. Puerto Rican women with advanced educational credentials (some college credits or college graduation), English-language proficiency, and delayed childbearing (until the middle or late twenties) were more likely to be in white-collar positions than those without these qualities. About 30 percent of the women studied lacked the traits making employment likely, and as education and English-language skills become increasingly required for employment, such women's chances of getting a job will grow even more remote (Falcon, Gurak, and Powers, 1990; Madamba and De Jong, 1994).

A number of state and national studies indicated that Native Americans frequently suffer discrimination in employment in towns located near reservations. Indians' work difficulties have been compounded by limited amounts of formal education and by the fact that a surplus of potential workers on reservations has tended to keep wages for such positions as laborer, truck driver, and typist scarcely half what they would be off the reservation (Olson and Wilson, 1984: 186–187).

Do most Americans appreciate the conditions just discussed? When asked in July 1989 which is more often to blame if a person is poor—lack of effort or circumstances—38 percent of a national sample indicated lack of effort, 42 percent opted for circumstances, 17 percent selected both, and 3 percent had no opinion. Thirty-nine percent of whites chose lack of effort, compared to 32 percent of members of racial minorities; among whites, 41 percent selected circumstances while among minority members, 48 percent chose that option (Gallup, 1989). Clearly whites were more inclined than minority members to focus on individuals' failure and hold them responsible—to "blame the victim," in the phrase introduced in Chapter 3—while members of racial minorities were more likely to take a sociological perspective, focusing on conditions promoting poverty in people's lives. Why the difference? While the survey did not examine this issue, it seems probable that racial minorities' more intimate contact with poverty and, perhaps in particular, their knowledge of the role racism plays, encourage them to be aware of social conditions producing poverty.

Abundant evidence suggests that racism affects racial minorities in the economy. One way to examine the situation systematically is to analyze employment as a process involving three phases.

Racial Minorities and the Employment Process

When a national survey team asked Americans whether blacks in their community have as good a chance as whites to receive any job for which they are qualified, seven out of ten (70 percent) agreed that they did. Respondents' race was a significant factor. Compared to 73 percent of whites, only 43 percent of blacks replied affirmatively (Gallup and Hugick, 1990).

At each stage of racial minorities' work experience, evidence of racism is prevalent. We examine the job candidate stage, the job screening stage, and the job promotion stage. Then we consider black managers' experience.

Job Candidate Stage

Research has indicated that African Americans are often excluded from entire job areas, especially well-paid positions requiring minimal education and experience. For instance, blacks who seek jobs in large restaurants are usually kept out of such positions as waiter and cook that lead to promotion and supervisory roles. Instead they are pushed into low-paying, dead-end jobs—dishwasher and busboy. A 1985 study done in New York City found blacks were virtually unrepresented in 130 of 193 private-sector industries, and the few working in these industries were primarily in clerical positions (Steinberg, 1989: 49). Individual racism helps produce this outcome, but social networks, or rather the lack of such networks, also contribute significantly.

In a society where racial segregation permeates all major structures, members of different races are primarily involved in social networks—composed of friends, neighbors, and colleagues—containing members of their own race. This situation has a significant impact on job applicants. At the job candidate stage, there are fertile possibilities for institutional racism: Members of racial minorities are indirectly discriminated against because frequently they lack access to whites' social networks, which generally provide better leads and informal recommendations for jobs than their own.

When social networks are a chief means of job recruitment, minority members are more likely than whites to be denied employment or to receive low-paying jobs. For poor, young members of racial minorities, who live in residentially segregated areas, have limited schooling, and modest or no work histories, social networks for obtaining employment are deficient (Jaynes and Williams, 1989: 320–321). For this reason alone, they are at a distinct disadvantage compared to other groups competing for jobs.

As the prestige and pay of jobs increase, use of social networks for locating candidates declines. For positions requiring college degrees, employers are much more likely to place advertisements in the local mass media than they do when hiring people for lower-level slots.

Nonetheless, social networks are also used for higher-level jobs. In a study of 4,078 employers, the openings of those who said they relied on social networks as a chief means of recruitment for college-degree jobs were more likely to be filled by whites than were those of employers who indicated limited reliance on these networks.

Besides determining whether individuals will be hired, access to social networks appears to affect job candidates' income. In the same investigation, black high-school graduates who used segregated networks averaged $5.69 per hour, those who did not use networks averaged $5.74 per hour, and, in contrast, those who had access to desegregated networks averaged $6.45 per hour (Braddock and McPartland, 1987).

Sometimes by choice and sometimes because of legal pressure, government agencies, most major companies, and many smaller businesses have initiated formal written policies to recruit minorities. These affirmative action standards have produced major gains for African American job seekers, with the percentage of blacks in the work force increasing by 50 percent between 1965 and 1990. However, in recent years politicians like California's governor Pete Wilson have challenged affirmative action standards, claiming that they are no longer necessary and productive. In 1996 in California, Proposition 209, a ballot initiative scrapping affirmative action guidelines for employment and education, won majority support. Even before its passage, the state government had rolled back race and gender considerations in hiring (Boxall, 1997).

Cuts in minority hiring most often occur in areas where minorities' job candidacy has been most prevalent. Since the late 1960s, thousands of African Americans have entered city jobs in New York City, especially in areas like social services and health care, which were rapidly expanding then and are now under pressure to downsize. H. Carl McCall, the New York State Comptroller and a 30-year observer of blacks in city government, concluded, "Public sector jobs helped establish a stable middle class for the minority community, but the next generation will not have that opportunity" (Johnson, 1997: 36).

Job Screening Stage

When employers confront a pool of job candidates, they usually have certain desirable traits in mind. To begin, they are likely to set a minimum educational standard; this practice represents institutional racism when it is irrelevant to on-the-job performance and yet disproportionately eliminates racial minorities, whose members are on the whole less educated than whites. A study of equal employment opportunity cases brought to federal appellate court showed that employers were usually unable to demonstrate that educational credentials and test scores related to productivity (Burstein and Pitchford, 1990).

Screening candidates also involves an evaluation of individuals, and individual racism can appear at this time. In some job categories, minorities still are largely screened out. Political scientist Andrew Hacker suggested that perhaps the reason why blacks have largely been excluded as dental hygienists is that whites are probably not willing to accept African Americans' fingers in their mouths (Hacker, 1992: 110).

One study found that many companies frequently eliminated 30 to 40 percent of applicants via a screening interview. In such situations employers did not need to make direct reference to race, even among themselves. They could discuss impressions of candidates' "intelligence," "appearance," "vigor," and "self-confidence," with such references intentionally or perhaps unintentionally playing into interviewers' racial stereotypes (Lopez, 1976).

In the previously cited study of 4,078 employers, investigators found that whites were more likely to be chosen for jobs when employers valued such traits as quick learning, advanced reading skill, math excellence, and good judgment. This trend was most apparent for jobs requiring high-school certificates and less (though still) evident for jobs needing some college or a college degree (Braddock and McPartland,

1987). With such stereotypes prevalent, blacks seeking jobs that possess a distinct intellectual component have little hope of getting them unless they are fully qualified or overqualified educationally while for whites, educational criteria might be applied less stringently.

It is sobering to learn that when researchers asked members of the college class of 1957 from three Ivy League colleges, which have traditionally supplied about two-fifths of America's business elite, whether they agreed with the conclusion that blacks are as intelligent as whites, just 36 percent of the Princeton class, 47 percent at Yale, and 55 percent at Harvard agreed (Jones, 1986: 88). If a similar mindset exists throughout the business world, it is hardly surprising that blacks face widespread job discrimination.

Asian Americans are underrepresented in such occupations as journalism, law, and social sciences as well as in administrative positions in management. When interviewed about this pattern, Asian American job candidates say that they tend to avoid applying for positions requiring language skills and extensive person-to-person contact because they believe white employers feel they will only succeed in positions requiring technical knowledge (Chun, 1993). Whether or not this self-screening process reflects prospective employers' perceptions, it is widespread.

At the screening stage, Asian American women are likely to encounter stereotypes that can block their access to job opportunities. The most prominent pair of stereotypes are that Asian American women have manual dexterity along with endurance for routines and thus are well suited for assembly-line work; and that they are diligent, loyal, and attentive to detail and thus make good subordinates in clerical and service work but are ill-suited to function as supervisors (Lai, 1995).

Even over the telephone, employers sometimes screen out minority candidates. In an experimental study in which white and Hispanic pairs of applications responded to randomly sampled job vacancies listed in the newspapers and at employment agencies in Washington, D.C., and its surrounding suburbs, discrimination occurred. Although the qualifications the white and Hispanic applicants provided were similar, the latter group—whose members displayed a slight Spanish accent and Spanish surnames—received a less favorable response in 22.4 percent of the calls; in particular, the Hispanic applicants were less likely to be asked to appear for a job interview (Bendick, Jackson, Reinoso, and Hodges, 1993).

Another study produced a consistent result, discovering that Mexican Americans with distinct accents consistently earned less money than Mexican Americans without foreign accents—that in fact the accent "penalty" was distinctly greater for Mexican Americans than for either German Americans or Italian Americans. The suspected reason was that employers might be particularly suspicious that heavily accented Mexican Americans were illegal aliens who could be forced to work for low wages (Davila, Bohara, and Saenz, 1993).

The cultural camouflage for modern racism can appear at the screening stage. When confronted with what they might perceive as the strain of hiring minority group members, some majority group employers are inclined to turn their backs on current, everyday standards of racial equity and react in a racist way. The fact that the job screening process is largely hidden from public view, permitting deception and even self-deception, increases the likelihood of such a prospect.

Job Promotion Stage

The national study of 4,078 employers indicated that African Americans' chances for promotion were closer to whites' if candidates came from within instead of outside an organization. Nonetheless, blacks were not as likely to be promoted as whites when only internal candidates were involved; the researchers learned that within organizations, when workers' qualifications were held constant, blacks' salaries tended to be distinctly lower than whites' (Braddock and McPartland, 1987: 23).

Some companies apparently maintain blatantly discriminatory promotion policies. In November 1996 Texaco Inc. agreed to pay more than $140 million to resolve a federal lawsuit brought by minority employees (Eichenwald, 1996a). While Texaco's public statements about minority hiring and promotion strongly emphasized equal opportunity, only six—or 0.7 percent—of the jobholders making over $106,000 were black. A Labor Department audit indicated that minority employees did indeed need to wait far longer for promotions. During court testimony employees indicated that they were subjected to racially hostile behavior but did not report the infractions for fear of losing their jobs. One black employee noted, "Throughout my employment, three supervisors in my department openly discussed their view that African Americans are ignorant and incompetent, and, specifically, that Thurgood Marshall was the most incompetent person they had ever seen" (Eichenwald, 1996b: 1).

On the job African Americans and members of other racial minorities tend to face a "triple jeopardy"—*racial stereotyping*, the *solo role* (being the only member of a racial minority at the work site), and the *token role* (being considered inferior by whites if they obtained their positions through affirmative action). The impact of these three factors is likely to affect blacks negatively when they apply for promotion (Pettigrew and Martin, 1987).

Individuals who are the only or nearly the only representatives of racial minorities in an organization frequently encounter stereotypes. If an African American employee does something that an observer can interpret negatively, such as speaking somewhat harshly to a colleague, then that behavior is more likely to be attributed to a basic deficiency in the person's character than if a white person acted similarly. In the latter instance, the white colleague would probably attribute the harsh statement to a situational factor, saying, "Oh, she's just having a bad day."

Following his retirement from a 21-year professional basketball career, Robert Parrish indicated how this process had been applied to him. Pressed during an interview to explain whether he had ever been subjected to racism, Parrish, who is black, smiled. In his deep, gentle voice, he indicated that he had joined the Boston Celtics at about the same time as two celebrated white players—Larry Bird and Kevin McHale. While they all sought to establish themselves in the National Basketball League, each would inevitably have an occasional inferior performance. With Bird and McHale, Parrish explained, reporters would say it was "a bad game," but in his case they invariably labelled it "a slump" (ESPN, 1997).

On the other hand, when minority workers perform effectively, stereotypes rationalize the situation. White colleagues might say of an employee belonging to a racial minority, "He works so hard because he has to compensate for his lack of intelligence." Or they might claim that this person's success was the result of favoritism from a boss sensitive to pressures to incorporate minority individuals in high positions.

The second element in the triple jeopardy is the solo role. As the only or almost only member of their own group, African Americans or members of other racial minorities are likely to experience unrealistic evaluation from whites who have had little or no previous contact with racial minorities. White workers often expect poor performances from African Americans. One solo black worker reported, "They were astonished to find that I could write a basic memo. Even the completion of an easy task brought surprised compliments" (Pettigrew and Martin, 1987: 55). Sometimes minority solo employees find the opposite—that expectations are unrealistically high. In either case they face problems. Considered different from whites, they are not evaluated realistically and thus do not receive substantive feedback that provides a helpful evaluation of their progress on the job.

The third factor is the token role. If fellow workers or supervisors feel that a member of a racial minority received a position because of affirmative action, they are likely to assume the individual is incompetent, able to obtain the job only when given unfair advantage because of race.

It appears likely that the triple jeopardy is a major reason why the greatest disparity in income between black and white males occurs between the ages of 30 to 50. A study using national samples of black and white men found that in the 1980s black men in their thirties and forties obtained 86.6 percent and 86.7 percent, respectively, of white men's earnings—a smaller percentage than did blacks in both younger and older age categories. A similar pattern was apparent for each decade back to the 1930s. The researchers concluded that their data suggested that discrimination against black men accumulated over their working lifetimes. By the way, for black and white men in their fifties and sixties, income differences started to decline because white men were more inclined to move toward partial or total retirement, depending to a greater extent than blacks on their relatively greater amount of accumulated wealth (Thomas, Herring, and Horton, 1994). A recent study comparing black and white women aged 34–44 with similar education and work-related characteristics found that the African American women had lost the earnings parity attained in 1980. The principal factor contributing to this loss of parity was differential access to occupations, with black women more likely to be pushed into low-paying positions (Anderson and Shapiro, 1996).

An expert on race and wealth indicated that it will take much of the next century to close the financial gap between the black and white middle class. The best thing African Americans can do, William D. Bradford suggested, is to provide effective education for their children so that by the second or third generation, parity will develop. He added, "I don't see anything in the next 20 years. We're looking at 40 to 60 years" (Wilkerson, 1995: 161).

It should not be surprising to learn that research has shown little movement of minorities into top executive positions. A national survey of senior executives found that during the 1980s African Americans increased their miniscule percentage of top corporate positions from 0.2 to 0.6 percent, and Hispanics (three-quarters of whom were either Mexican American or Puerto Rican) expanded theirs from 0.1 to 0.4 percent (Sklar, 1995). The barrier faced by minorities and women seeking to move into top management has sometimes been called a "glass ceiling"—a barrier so subtle that it is nearly invisible but yet strong enough to block candidates from moving to the top rungs of the corporate ladder (Morrison and Von Glinow, 1990).

Perhaps no situation portrays racial minorities' special job pressures better than black managers' experiences.

Black Managers: The Dream in Jeopardy

As black managers move into the white corporate world, they must make major adjustments. Often they have come from very different backgrounds than their white colleagues. To be able to survive, they must learn norms governing behavior in what often feels like an alien world and make the necessary adjustments. Whites' stereotypes or discriminatory practices can complicate such adjustments.

Few if any people find business management an easy, tension-free experience. All executives must work hard and produce tangible results that lead to increased company profits. If unsuccessful, they will not advance and might lose their jobs. This issue alone is a source of considerable stress to many executives, both black and white. We see, however, that blacks face additional stresses.

Because African Americans entering executive positions often have very different backgrounds from whites', they are frequently unsure about standards of conduct and feel nervous and confused about interracial relations. As the solo African American management trainee in a department with over 8,000 employees, Edward Jones faced such problems. In a detailed account of his opening months on the job, Jones indicated that he worked very hard and did everything he could imagine to receive good evaluations, and yet to his surprise he was nearly fired, told that he lacked tact and was constantly rocking the boat.

In his evaluation of this experience, Jones concluded that his style of relating to co-workers and bosses was sometimes inappropriate—that the world of white business required a low-key behavioral style with which he was unfamiliar.

But, according to Jones, there was another issue. He was convinced that his

> peers and supervisors were unable to perceive me as being able to perform the job that the company hired me for. Their reaction to me was disbelief. I was out of the "place" normally filled by black people in the company, and since no black person had preceded me successfully, it was easy for my antagonists to believe I was inadequate. (Jones, 1973: 114)

As the colonial labor principle emphasizes, blacks have traditionally been assigned menial jobs, and Jones's placement in a management position contradicted whites' expectations. White colleagues responded to the confusing situation by unleashing their racial stereotypes on their solo black manager.

Entering corporations, black managers often find that the unrelenting emphasis on making profits means that corporate leadership often fails to establish clear standards about racial issues. To survive and do well, African American executives usually try to conform, but to what standards, in fact, are they supposed to conform? Sometimes top leaders within a corporation try to pretend that race is not an issue, and so all employees, regardless of race, are expected to support such a position. Moreover, some white managers become defensive if racism is ever mentioned. Jones wrote, "After all, it's un-American to be prejudiced, and who wants to be un-American? So white and black managers, fearful of confronting the issue, take part in a charade" (Jones, 1986: 90). The result is that communications between African Americans and whites become highly strained.

The isolated, confusing circumstances in which black managers often find themselves are special problems when they seek promotion, which requires effective relations with co-workers and superiors. A black middle manager described a situation in which a black manager working for her demanded an overdue merit raise. Convinced that he deserved it, the middle manager gathered relevant documentation and went to the appraisal meeting. That meeting involved several white male colleagues who spoke without documentation of their respective candidates, voted down her nominee, and awarded merit raises to several of their own people. According to the black middle manager, a "buddy system" existed. She explained, "It turned out to be a matter of 'Joe, you did a favor for me last week, so I'll support you in getting your person in this week. You owe me one, old buddy'" (Jones, 1986: 89). Within this system African Americans, who are new arrivals and widely considered "different" or inferior, are often victims of severe discrimination.

In business, high-level executives often become sponsors of younger subbordinates, but a prominent white consultant told Edward Jones that white managers are usually uncomfortable sponsoring African Americans, fearing negative reactions from other whites (Jones, 1986: 89). As a result, black executives often find themselves shunted into slots out of the corporate mainstream—into community relations, personnel, or anything to do with minorities. Furthermore, many black executives claim that their superiors withhold more strategic information from them than from their white colleagues. As a result African Americans claim that they cannot be as effective as their white colleagues (Campbell, 1982).

Most black executives believe that to obtain promotion they must demonstrate competence and loyalty in ways not required of whites. What happens, a black executive might wonder, if he hires a black secretary? He is likely to decide against it, realizing, as one black manager noted, that peers and superiors might say, "That's a black operation over there, so it can't be too effective" (Jones, 1986: 90). Or consider the case of Charlie, a junior executive who was straightforward and honest if not militant about racial issues. One day several lower-level black managers approached him, expressing concern about what they saw as a pattern of discrimination limiting their careers. Charlie felt that the top officers ought to hear their account and arranged a meeting with them. Two days before that meeting, the president took Charlie aside and said, "Charlie, I'm disappointed that you met with those people. I thought we could trust you" (Jones 1986: 90). Certainly this statement made it clear that Charlie's superiors were giving him little maneuvering room: If he were going to keep rising in the company, he would need to reject racial loyalties, making loyalty to his white superiors and the company his only concern.

An additional challenge now seems to confront black managers. A study of 76 high-ranking African American executives working in Chicago-based Fortune 500 companies found that about two-thirds have been in racialized jobs, focusing on black consumers or personnel or on civil rights issues like affirmative action or the development of minority business. An executive specializing in affirmative action noted, "You deal with 6 or 7 basic laws, or regulations, and once you know those there's not an awful lot more to learn" (Collins, 1997: 62). This narrow experience is a disadvantage for these executives when they seek promotion. One African American manager commented:

> I talked to [people] in various divisions that I was interested in, and I got the lip service that they would keep [me] in mind if something opened up. As it happened, that just did not develop. I can never remember being approached by anyone. Nothing [happened] that I can hang [onto] as an offer. People would ask, "Have you ever run a profit and loss operation?" (Collins, 1993: 442)

Black managers face not only the possibility of dead-end jobs, but also the distinct danger of losing those they have. In an era of business retrenchment and deteriorating national concern about minorities' advancement, job slots dealing with African Americans' needs and interests are likely to be eliminated or reduced.

For African Americans the move into the alien corporate world offers the same rewards of wealth, power, and prestige whites receive. It is a journey, however, that promises special difficulties and tensions: Often they need to learn new rules and to adjust to special, race-related demands made on them. Even when they adjust successfully, their rewards are likely to be less extensive than whites'.

As an alternative to seeking work in the mainstream economy, members of racial minorities have pursued some unique approaches.

Minorities' Special Strategies

One special strategy is to establish businesses that offer select products or services not provided by the mainstream economy, as Japanese Americans have done in farming and Native Americans in casino gambling. The other is to seek employment in areas where minorities' participation has traditionally been encouraged, as when blacks pursue professional sports.

Japanese Americans in Farming

How can a racial minority survive in a repressive, racist society? While there is no foolproof answer to this question, many Asian immigrants developed a response: find a business that provides a potentially profitable product or service that is minimally competitive with those supplied by established whites. Chinese opened restaurants, laundries, and garment factories (Sanders and Nee, 1987; Wong, 1987). Japanese produced a variety of agricultural products. The Japanese experience in California serves to illustrate this strategy for seeking economic success (Jiobu, 1988a).

In the 1890s Japanese immigrants, many with a background in farming, began to work as farm laborers. In the next two decades, government officials became concerned that the hard-working Japanese would dominate agriculture, and so their immigration was restricted, their political rights were removed, and, if not citizens, they were prevented from owning land.

Still Japanese farmers prospered. Often the laws prohibiting land ownership were poorly enforced, and white land owners and bankers were generally eager to do business with the Japanese, selling them marginal land at high prices. The Japanese approach to farming was to concentrate on crops that required intensive labor and specialized care and that could be grown in profitable amounts on fairly small plots of marginal land. Besides their farming expertise, Japanese efforts benefitted from an ancient cultural tradition emphasizing hard work, sacrifice for the future, and patience in the face of adversity. Their efforts paid off. By the early 1920s, in the Sacramento area, for instance, Japanese farmers grew 80 percent of the tomatoes, 61 percent of the asparagus, and 78 percent of the spinach. By the outbreak of World War II, estimates indicated that throughout the state Japanese Americans (who were about 2 percent of the population) were producing over 90 percent of snap beans, strawberries, and celery and about 50 percent of artichokes, cauliflower, cucumbers, and tomatoes.

Forced relocation of all Japanese Americans living on the West Coast during World War II produced significant economic losses for farmers, but their overall capital investment was fairly modest, and thus the majority managed to reestablish themselves in the farming business after the war.

In the past 20 or 30 years, there has been a steady decline in the proportion of Japanese Americans entering agriculture. But early success in farming seems to have served several important purposes: It provided funding that subsidized the education and training of many members of the next generation of Japanese Americans; it also established Japanese Americans as a hard-working, reputable people in the eyes of the majority group, thus making it easier for youthful Japanese Americans to enter the mainstream economy.

Native Americans in Casino Gambling

Unlike Japanese in farming, Indians involved in casino gambling have enjoyed a favored status. Two specific legal conditions have promoted casino gambling. First, the U.S. Supreme Court has supported Indian tribes' right to negotiate business deals as sovereign nations. Then the Indian Gaming Regulatory Act of 1988 required that states negotiate agreements, known as compacts, with tribes living on reservations. Since that time Native Americans have opened about 170 casinos, and dozens more are planned. More than 150 tribes, about half of those in the continental United States, are either involved in this business or in the near future plan to enter it (Clines, 1993; Meier, 1994; Schaefer, 1993: 167).

The largest of all the Indian gambling establishments, the Foxwoods High Stakes Bingo & Casino, is on the reservation of the Mashantucket Pequots in Ledyard, Connecticut. By the end of 1993, Foxwoods, which opened in February 1992, had 9,200 workers, making it one of the largest employers in the state. In the summer of 1994, Foxwoods was bringing in estimated revenues of about $800 million a year and clearing over $400 million a year in profit. Because of its ready access to a large, fairly affluent clientele as well as the absence of nearby competition, Foxwoods appears to be the most profitable casino in the world. When Foxwoods opened a new building in September 1993, the size of the operation doubled, and it became the largest gambling operation in the Western Hemisphere, edging out the Taj Mahal in Atlantic City. Like all Indian gambling operations, Foxwoods is exempt from federal and state taxes. However, deals can be made. Thus, in May 1993, Governor Lowell Weicker agreed to give the Pequots monopoly control of slot machines in the state in exchange for $113 million a year of aid to the state's cities (*Economist,* 1993; Johnson, 1993; Passell, 1994).

A major issue tribes involved in casino gambling must face is the extent to which they operate on their own or, in various ways, seek outside help. Richard (Skip) Hayward, the Mashantucket Pequot chief now widely regarded as a genius at casino development, hired as his chief executive G. Michael Brown, the former director of New Jersey's Division of Gaming Enforcement. Brown, a former prosecutor who forced the Atlantic City casinos to cut their ties with the underworld, has eased back on the absolute sovereignty so cherished by other tribes and sought to cooperate with state and federal law enforcement experts to keep out organized crime and stop other outsiders' illegal efforts to make money at Foxwoods.

It is one thing to bring in a single expert like G. Michael Brown, but it is quite another thing to permit outside casino businesses to run tribal operations. Some tribes, such as the St. Regis Mohawks in upstate New York and the Ak-Chin of Arizona, have already signed agreements with such companies permitting them to build and run the tribes' casinos for a share of their revenues. While federal regulators must review all these agreements, there is no guarantee that they will be run honestly or effectively. The Wisconsin Winnebago tribe, for instance, nearly went bankrupt after a corrupt businessman ran its casino for 20 months.

Clearly Native Americans are finding that the casino business can be precarious. Some opponents like Donald Trump have lobbied Congress to curtail the Indians' billion-dollar tribal power. They argued that tribes' designation as sovereign states, which permits them to escape normal governmental regulation of business and be exempt from state and federal taxation, provides enormous competitive advantage. In addition, the Indians recognize that these are perilous times—that if any major casino scandals occur, their future in this business could be jeopardized (Clines, 1993; Meier, 1994).

Success also produces significant growing pains. In the area around the Foxwoods Casino in Connecticut, many local residents are disturbed by the noise, traffic congestion, crowds, and crime the large influx of outsiders has brought to the area. They are hardly comforted by the Mashantucket Pequots' plan to use some of their profits to buy 8,000 acres of adjoining land and annex it to the reservation, quintupling its size and encircling the towns of Ledyard and Preston. If this purchase occurs, officials in those two towns would lose political control over that land, and as soon as it became part of the reservation, it would be exempt from property tax. Thus many whites living near Foxwoods tend to strongly oppose the annexation (*Economist,* 1993; Johnson, 1993).

Other controversies are developing. In Idaho the Coeur d'Alenes, who have a successful casino business, have decided to offer gambling on the Internet. While safeguards involve limits of $500 a month per person and the requirement that participants verify that they are over 18, have a credit card, and live in a state with legal gambling, opposition is strong. A spokesman for the governor of Idaho said, "This would be worse than Las Vegas. Instead of having a casino on every corner, you potentially have a casino in every living room of the state" (*New York Times,* 1997: 8). While a court battle is likely to develop, an expert on casino gambling indicated that a tribe that follows the legal standards scrupulously will probably be able to accept wagers over the Internet from people in states where lotteries are legal.

In spite of the economic gains casino gambling can mean for Indians, financial problems can also occur. The pie appears to be shrinking. While casino gambling is a huge business, the number of tribes starting their own operations has sharply increased in recent years. In some places the intake of revenues has already been adversely affected. The larger operations are probably firmly established, but some of the newer ventures are likely to find that the pieces of pie left for them are simply too thin to sustain them (Meier, 1994). Furthermore, in some remote reservation areas, the primary customers are likely to be poor Indians. On the Pine Ridge Reservation in South Dakota, for instance, the Ogalalas run a casino which "consists of three double-wide trailers stuck together on cinder blocks in a rutted lot with two rusty oil drums outside for trash." This casino earns about $1 million a year, Foxwoods' take for half a day (Kilborn, 1997: A1). Duane Beyal, the assistant to the president of the Navajo Nation, asked a troubling question. "When you have such a large population with high unemployment, all kinds of poverty and related problems like alcoholism, and you put a casino in the middle of it, what kind of problems do you have?" (Judson, 1994: 5).

Blacks in Sport

For African Americans two avenues to possible financial success have traditionally been open: entertainment and sports. The openness of entertainment and sports suggests the internal colonialist issue mentioned in the chapter title—knowing one's place. In the realm of the physical, whites experienced little sense of threat from blacks as long as blacks were merely strong or physically capable. The key issue for whites was maintaining control. In the well-known book *Soul on Ice*, Eldridge Cleaver analyzed racism in American society, classifying white men as "Omnipotent Administrators"—all mind and no body—and labelling black men "Supermasculine Menials"—all body and no mind (Cleaver, 1970: 166). According to Cleaver, the reality of modern sport, in which large numbers of black professional athletes perform impressive physical feats for primarily white audiences, simply confirms in the racist's mind the natural order of things.

But while blacks have found the world of professional sport open to them, the question remains as to whether they have experienced racial discrimination within it. We examine research involving professional baseball, football, and basketball.

Writing about Major League baseball, Robert M. Jiobu (1988b) suggested that for a number of reasons related to the game itself, one would expect baseball to be relatively free of racial discrimination. First, Major League baseball, which has been voluntarily integrated since 1947, has a longer history of integration than most American activities. Second, with constant exposure to the mass media, baseball officials are fully aware that incidents of racism will be exposed. Third, widespread agreement exists about the basis for evaluating good performance, and major statistics on batting, pitching, and fielding are well publicized. Fourth, the goal of winning dominates professional baseball, and there is general acceptance that regardless of race, the best players are the ones that most effectively help a team to win. So these four reasons would discourage racial discrimination in baseball.

To find out whether racism occurred in the game, Jiobu looked at the records of Major League baseball players involved in at least 50 games between 1971 and 1985. He learned that African Americans' performance levels were higher than those for either Hispanics or whites. Blacks' lifetime slugging average (total bases per thousand times at bat) was .381 contrasted to .337 for Hispanics and .348 for whites, and blacks' lifetime batting average (hits per thousand times at bat) was .258 compared to .245 for Hispanics and .241 for whites.

Because of their superior performances, African Americans last longer in the Major Leagues than the other two groups. For blacks, the median survival time is 11.8 years while for whites and Hispanics it is 10.0 years.

So far there has been no evidence of racism. According to the data, African Americans perform better and as a result maintain longer careers in Major League baseball. But Jiobu realized that another issue required analysis. What happens if performance levels among the three groups are controlled (kept constant)? When this occurs, it turns out that African Americans' careers are shorter than either Hispanics' or whites'. Jiobu concluded that blacks are "simultaneously rewarded for their performance and penalized for their race" (Jiobu, 1988b: 532).

Why are African Americans penalized for their race? Jiobu speculated that a major factor might be owners' and management's concern that the predominantly white fans will not support a largely black team. To prevent such a result and yet to produce a winning team, owners and managers appear to place a distinct limit on the number of black players, cutting African Americans as soon as their skills start to decline while keeping a certain number of white players of comparably marginal ability. Many prominent writers and academics have suggested that there is no activity more typically American than baseball. Jiobu's findings suggest the ironic truth of the observation.

Research on football players in the National Football League has examined another racism issue—whether a player's race affects his position. Investigators' basic assumption is that more central positions in a football formation—on offense, centers, quarterbacks, and guards—are central not only physically but also socially and politically: These positions are central to communication and leadership, and players at the seven other positions simply must follow orders. If professional football reflects the racial stratification system prevailing in American society, then one would expect that whites would dominate the central positions and African Americans the less central ones. Let's consider whether this process, which is called stacking, has occurred.

Between 1975 and 1985, the percentage of black players in the National Football League increased from 41.6 to 51.3. Nonetheless, during that time period, stacking remained disproportionately high on both offense and defense, with some impressive statistical increases in the pattern. Most notably, among quarterbacks, whose position is the most cerebral and most involved in decision making, stacking increased from 95.5 to 97.1 percent. While the researchers unfortunately did not distinguish centers and guards—the most central of offensive linesmen—from the other offensive linesmen, they did indicate that during the same 10-year span, the percentage of white offensive linesmen increased from 76 to 89 percent. (Since on a given team, the guards and center represent about 43 percent of the offensive line—it varies with the formation—one can guess that between 1975 and 1985, the proportion of central linesmen who were white increased.) In contrast, African Americans' participation in noncentral positions rose. The proportion of black running backs increased dramatically, from 65 to 86 percent, and the proportion of black receivers went from 55 to 62 percent. The authors concluded, "The positions requiring leadership and thinking ability have become even more 'white' and the positions necessitating speed, quickness, and 'instinct' have become even more 'black'" (Schneider and Eitzen, 1986: 260).

Research conducted in Major League baseball reached a similar conclusion about stacking. Between 1960 and 1988, blacks were most highly represented in the outfield, the least central positions, and least represented at pitching and catching, the most central positions. It appears that the major factor contributing to stacking in professional baseball has been the influence of white coaches, who have often encouraged developing black ballplayers to move to the less central positions (Lavoie and Leonard, 1994). Current research has not addressed what motivates white coaches' actions. Do they believe that black players are less capable of communicating than white players, do they feel less comfortable communicating with black players and thus locate blacks far from themselves, or do both issues apply?

In basketball a study found that as a group African American players outperformed white players and as a result were better paid. Discrimination was apparent when performance statistics were held constant for the 1984–85 professional season: Researchers learned that blacks as a group averaged about $26,000 less per year than whites (Koch and Vander Hill, 1988). The authors suggested that while it "is difficult to avoid the conclusion that race discrimination . . . is the cause" (Koch and Vander Hill, 1988: 92), other factors might also be relevant, such as the possibility that upon entering professional basketball blacks are less knowledgable or aggressive bargainers than whites.

Besides athletes, management personnel are significant participants in the world of professional sport. Although the proportion of black management personnel in professional basketball, baseball, and football remains considerably below the proportion of black athletes, their numbers have been slowly increasing. Since the 1970s there have been a few black managers in Major League baseball and head coaches in the National Basketball Association. In 1989—finally—the Oakland Raiders became the first team in the National Football League to hire a black head coach.

Commenting on Major League baseball, Hank Aaron, a senior vice president for the Atlanta Braves and baseball's all-time home run champion, indicated that blacks' involvement in baseball management has been minimal. Aaron cited the impact of social networks discussed earlier. He concluded, "Baseball was and continues to be a good-old-boy network." Aaron added that the commissioner of baseball and the president of the United States should push for significant change (Araton, 1991).

Whether it is baseball or some other professional sport, minorities seeking to enter management often find themselves subjected to a distinct double standard. Analyzing the characteristics of black men who have been head coaches in the National Basketball Association, journalist Harvey Araton (1992) noted that while many white coaches have been outspoken and aggressive, their black counterparts have consistently been "low-key, unthreatening personalities." The colonial labor principle suggests that minority group members are supposed to "know their place," accepting a subordinate role in the world. An outspoken black coach defies the image racists find comfortable.

Drew Pearson, a former All-Pro wide receiver for the Dallas Cowboys and now the president of a successful sportswear manufacturing company, has raised another issue involving blacks' participation in professional sport. Black athletes, Pearson argued, have been restricted in their range of roles. For example, while top black athletes have made large sums of money endorsing athletic products, they could make more money and even provide jobs for poor, inner-city African Americans if they started their own companies. Black athletes have not pursued this course of action because since their first years in organized sports, they have been brought up to see themselves narrowly—as just athletes. Pearson said:

> You don't really see yourself as a coach or as someone running these concession stands that generate money. Power people see us as being participants, not the ones that set up these leagues, not the ones making any decision concerning the welfare of the league. (Rhoden, 1990: B7)

According to Pearson, both for their own good and for the benefit of young, struggling African Americans, black athletes should try to become major players in the commercial and administrative areas of professional sport.

In professional basketball, Isaiah Thomas had an opportunity to take a significant step in that direction, becoming part owner of the new Toronto team in the NBA. As a five-year president of the NBA Players Association, Thomas had extensive administrative experience that undoubtedly prepared him to function in his new capacity. Journalist Harvey Araton indicated that while Thomas is tough and controversial, his new position was one that "even those who don't like Thomas should applaud. Black leaders in sports have said that executive entrenchment and ownership are the only true means of obliterating quotas and old-boy networks" (Araton, 1994: 5). He added that basketball's black superstars have sufficient power to demand access to such top positions.

Power relates to other issues involving blacks in sport. At a seminar run by the National Association of Black Journalists, Nike sponsored a discussion entitled "Are Pro Sports Bad for Black America?" When the session was opened to questions, audience members were very critical of the company, pointing out that Nike and other sports merchandisers have played a major role in perpetuating the false impression that professional sport is the only avenue for young black men to succeed in the United States. Some participants at the conference called on African American sportswriters to start questioning such conclusions. It would be much easier to do so, one journalist indicated, if there were more than five black sports editors of daily newspapers. Since the sports editors assign stories, they are in a much more strategic position than reporters to counter newspapers' misinformation on this topic (Fitzgerald, 1997).

As we shift from jobs to housing, we once again find ample evidence of racism.

Racial Minorities and Housing

One of the basic points in the internal colonialist perspective involves freedom of movement. To what extent are members of racial minorities restricted in where they go and, in particular, where they live?

In restricting minorities' freedom of movement in the area of housing, racists have often resorted to violence. Recall the recent incident (described in Chapter 4) in which three white teenagers who badly beat a 13-year-old black boy bragged that their brutal act was meant to keep blacks out of their neighborhood (Terry, 1997).

Since the 1920s sociologists have been interested in residential segregation. As they watched various European groups settling in this country, they predicted that as groups' socioeconomic status rose, residential restrictions would disappear. For white groups this proved true, and it has been generally accurate for Native Americans, Asian Americans, and Mexican Americans (Darden, 1990; Massey and Eggers, 1990; White, Biddlecom, and Guo, 1993).

For African Americans, the pattern has been different. At the end of the nineteenth century, the perhaps 200,000 blacks living in northern and midwestern cities were well integrated, with the typical black resident living in an area that was 90 percent white. But then, starting in the 1890s and continuing through the 1920s, the migration of southern blacks to northern cities sharply increased. Many whites became hostile, and between 1900 and 1920, riots occurred in a number of northern and midwestern cities. African Americans who lived outside what were considered "black" areas often had their houses burned or ransacked. To blacks the message was clear: To stay healthy, one needed to live in what were called "black belts," "darkytowns," or "bronzevilles." In subsequent decades the progressive segregation of blacks continued, and by 1940 the boundaries of the modern black ghetto were established in nearly every northern city (Massey and Denton, 1993: 29–31).

Following World War II, a major movement to the suburbs occurred. It was, however, a "whites only" movement. Bowing to local pressure, the federal government permitted suburban towns and cities to zone their own land, and invariably, under the guise of promoting health and safety, these municipalities prevented the entrance of public housing, which might have brought poor people—particularly poor minorities—into their midst. Furthermore, authorities for the Federal Housing Authority believed that racial segregation would establish neighborhood stability and housing values, and so they prevented blacks from receiving mortgages insured by the Federal Housing Authority—a major source of low-interest loans in those years (Weir, 1994).

In the modern era, many whites have continued to support housing discrimination against blacks. Nancy Denton and Douglas Massey, a pair of sociologists specializing in housing discrimination, wrote, "Blacks represent a major exception to the pattern of declining segregation with rising socioeconomic status" (Denton and Massey, 1988: 798).

Denton and Massey found that this conclusion about residential segregation for blacks held across different socioeconomic levels. For metropolitan areas with the largest black populations, they calculated the **index of dissimilarity**, which indicates the proportion of a particular racial group that would need to change residential location in order to achieve racial evenness—a condition in which that racial group's representation throughout a city's census districts would be dispersed proportionate to its overall representation in the city. Thus, high indexes of dissimilarity demonstrate high levels of housing segregation: Large numbers of blacks would need to relocate to establish racial evenness.

In the metropolitan areas with the 60 largest black populations, the index of dissimilarity for African Americans with zero to four years of schooling completed was 83 percent; with 12 years of schooling, 71 percent; and with 17 or more years of schooling (schooling beyond college), 68 percent. There was, in short, only a slight decline in the index of dissimilarity as African Americans' education increased. When the researchers calculated the index of dissimilarity for income in those same 60 metropolitan areas, a similar pattern emerged. For blacks making under $2,500 per year, the dissimilarity index was 80 percent. It dropped to 73 percent for those with

Table 5.2 Blacks' Residential Segregation

	INDEX OF RACIAL DISSIMILARITY FOR YEARS OF SCHOOL COMPLETED				
	0–4	8	12	16	17+
Mean for metropolitan areas with 10 largest black populations	84%[1]	84%	78%	72%	73%
Mean for metropolitan areas with 20 largest black populations	80	80	75	70	70
Mean for metropolitan areas with 60 largest black populations	83	81	71	68	68

	INDEX OF RACIAL DISSIMILARITY FOR YEARLY INCOME				
	$2,500	$5,000	$10,000	$20,000	$50,000+
Mean for metropolitan areas with 10 largest black populations	84%	82%	79%	76%	79%
Mean for metropolitan areas with 20 largest black populations	81	79	76	74	77
Mean for metropolitan areas with 60 largest black populations	80	78	74	73	80

[1] Figures are rounded off to the nearest percentage.

Note: This table concerns two measures of blacks' indexes of dissimilarity—the percentage of blacks that would need to change residential areas to achieve a racially balanced outcome in a given city. Two distinct trends are apparent. First, as blacks' years of schooling and income increase, there is little change in the index of dissimilarity; in fact, in all three classifications of metropolitan areas, the highest income group scored a higher index of dissimilarity than the second-highest income group. Second, the larger the black populations of metropolitan areas, the higher the indexes of dissimilarity across educational and income levels.

Source: Adapted from Nancy A. Denton and Douglas S. Massey. "Residential Segregation of Blacks, Hispanics, and Asians by Socioeconomic Status and Generation." *Social Science Quarterly.* V. 69. December 1988, pp. 797–817.

income of $15,000 to $20,000 per year, but then rose to 80 percent for those with income of $50,000 per year or more (Denton and Massey, 1988: 803). Table 5.2 presents blacks' indexes of dissimilarity for education and income in three sets of metropolitan areas.*

Another factor affecting blacks' residential segregation is the population density of the area in which they live. African Americans living in the suburbs do experience more segregation than other groups but less than blacks in the largest cities (Massey and Denton, 1988). The most profound residential segregation experienced by African Americans occurs in the following large cities—Baltimore, Chicago, Cleveland,

---

* One should emphasize that indexes of dissimilarity do not reveal residents' feelings about segregated housing. While many African Americans want to escape segregated housing areas, some undoubtedly have various reasons for wanting to remain in them.

Detroit, Milwaukee, and Philadelphia. They are closely followed by Gary, Los Angeles, and New York. In these cities massive physical areas are exclusively black. As a result residents are likely to be largely or completely isolated from whites, most decisively affecting black citizens' opportunities for effective education.

Only one other major group that suffers a high level of residential segregation across all socioeconomic levels—black Puerto Ricans and other black Caribbean Hispanics who do not identify themselves as white. While white Puerto Ricans become increasingly integrated as their socioeconomic status rises, this is decisively not the case with black Puerto Ricans, whose most frequent non–Puerto Rican neighbors are African Americans. It seems clear that many white Americans have a powerful desire not to live near black people (Denton and Massey, 1988, 1989; Massey and Fong, 1990).

In the opening chapter, we encountered William J. Wilson's thesis about the declining significance of race. Lower-class status is the dominant source of oppression for blacks, Wilson argued. But the data on residential location question this conclusion: For African Americans a high educational or income level does little to overcome residential segregation.

For Asian Americans and Mexican Americans, the situation is sharply different. In metropolitan areas containing the heaviest concentrations of these two racial groups, their indexes of dissimilarity declined more sharply with rising socioeconomic status than did blacks'. Well-educated Asian Americans and Mexican Americans are accepted as neighbors by most whites, even in metropolitan areas where they live in large numbers (Denton and Massey, 1988: 810–812).

The least segregated Asian American group is the Japanese, with the Chinese, Filipino, Korean, Indian, and Vietnamese following in that order. It appears that the proportion of immigrants in an Asian American group affects its residential integration: the smaller the proportion of immigrants, the higher the group's residential integration (Langberg and Farley, 1985). One team of researchers concluded that Asian Americans are able to "translate their socioeconomic achievements into residential assimilation" (White, Biddlecom, and Guo, 1993: 93). As Asian Americans' income rises, they are more inclined to live in the suburbs. In fact, Asian American suburban households have income that is nearly a quarter greater than that of those living in central cities (O'Hare, Frey, and Fost, 1994).

Studies on Mexican Americans indicated that they are slightly less likely than Asian Americans but much more likely than blacks to share a neighborhood with whites (Darden, 1990; Massey and Fong, 1990).

An investigation of the suburbs surrounding New York City revealed a similar pattern. With rising income, Asian Americans and Hispanics, particularly white Hispanics, are increasingly likely to live near whites. For African Americans, regardless of income, their race is a barrier to proximity to whites. It appears that while suburban whites are unconcerned about how many Asian Americans and white Hispanics live close by, they want a modest black presence (Alba and Logan, 1993).

Thus the dominant research finding is that African Americans' index of dissimilarity is much higher than other racial groups'. In the 10, 20, and 60 cities with the largest black populations, blacks with postgraduate schooling lived in more highly segregated areas than Asians with between zero and four years of schooling. In addition, in those same three sets of cities, African Americans earning $50,000 or more per year resided in more highly segregated neighborhoods than Hispanic Americans earning between $2,500 and $5,000 a year (Denton and Massey, 1988).

Not surprisingly, a study found that once a certain minority dominates a given area, new inhabitants of that area are increasingly likely to be members of that group (Rosenbaum, 1994)—a particular problem for poor minorites. Forced to live in a deteriorating area, poor African Americans and Puerto Ricans suffer low-quality housing, dangers and tensions produced by high crime rates, substandard schooling for their children, and a physically unhealthy environment (DeFrances, 1996; Massey, 1990; Massey and Denton, 1993; Massey and Eggers, 1990). On the last point, residents affected have increasingly protested the occurrence of environmental racism—the distinct tendency to locate hazardous waste plants and other polluting industrial projects in poor, largely minority residential areas (Schneider, 1993).

A mildly optimistic point is that segregation rates have declined slightly over time. Examining the 232 metropolitan areas with substantial African American populations, a pair of researchers found a modest drop in the index of dissimilarity, thus indicating a slight decline in housing segregation. They concluded that areas with new housing construction, which tend to be less segregated than other locales, largely account for this development. In the Northeast and Midwest, where small suburbs have traditionally been hostile to blacks, the desegregation trend has been least apparent (Farley and Frey, 1994).

At this point we move from an analysis of housing discrimination patterns to an examination of a process helping to produce them. As the focus shifts to acts of individual racism, a cautionary note seems necessary. While realtors and other key players sometimes discriminate against minorities, particularly African Americans, such institutional factors as poverty, joblessness, and inadequate schooling play a major, perhaps dominant role in perpetuating housing segregation (Clark, 1993).

Racist Tactics in Housing

We are now examining racism delivered with a smile, often with a distinct show of courtesy and even deference. A report issued by the Department of Housing and Urban Development estimated that realtors, bank officials, and personnel at other lending agencies subject African Americans and other minorities to about two million instances of housing discrimination annually (Minerbrook, 1996). Investigations have shown that realtors selling homes to blacks have often invested less time and energy toward them or steered them to restricted locales. In fact, research suggested that as economic barriers to blacks' buying homes in white areas have declined, realtors' and lending organizations' discriminatory treatment has become a more significant factor in perpetuating housing segregation (Farley, 1995).

Research on this topic has used what are called "fair housing audits," in which a black couple and a white couple with comparable incomes and credit ratings and seeking similar residence requirements contact the same set of realtors and are shown houses or apartments. Using this technique, investigators are able to determine whether differences occur in white and black couples' treatment. Robert Weink and associates (1979) pioneered this use of testers, studying real estate activity in 40 large cities throughout the country and finding that discrimination against African Americans appeared in both rental housing and home sales. The investigation concluded that black clients had a 50 percent chance with home sales and a 70 percent likelihood with apartment rentals of encountering discrimination.

Realtors have discriminated against black clients in various ways. The body of research using testers seeking to rent has indicated that racial discrimination against African Americans occurred with respect to the number of available units, number of units offered for inspection, and length of waiting lists. For home buying, black testers received less time, more limited information about houses in higher price ranges or more select neighborhoods, less discussion about financing, fewer house showings, and more discourteous or rude treatment such as realtors' cancelling appointments or showing up late (Leigh, 1989: 74–75).

A major factor in housing discrimination has been the issue of steering clients toward particular residential areas (Galster, 1990a). Research in Boston indicated that the most significant consideration seemed to be the prospective residential section— in particular, whether it was currently an all-white area or undergoing racial transition. In the latter case, African Americans were much more likely to be shown housing. This research suggested that the primary cause of housing discrimination against blacks was agents' catering to their white clients' racism (Yinger, 1986).

Not surprisingly, blacks are more attuned than whites to racial discrimination in housing. When in 1990 a national survey team asked Americans whether blacks have as good a chance as whites in their community to get any housing they could afford, 75 percent of whites answered affirmatively. Among blacks the figure was a much lower 47 percent (Gallup and Hugick, 1990).

Besides steering, realtors sometimes use a less subtle technique—"block busting." Once a few black families have moved into a residential area, a realtor can exploit white home owners' racial and financial fears, suggesting by telephone, mail, or personal visits that the neighborhood is starting to deteriorate rapidly, becoming a distasteful and dangerous place to live, and that they had better get out before their property becomes nearly worthless. Successful block-busting campaigns can transform an all-white neighborhood into an all-black neighborhood in just a few years (Galster, 1990b).

The success of such tactics suggests that in order to avoid living near African Americans, many whites readily leave an area when blacks move into their neighborhood. One investigation concluded that two factors determined whites' departure— their desire to live in racial segregation and the percentage of African American residents in the district (Galster, 1990b). In a study conducted in Detroit, the most segregated U.S. city with a population of one million or more, evidence indicated a persistent if slowly declining white negative reaction to black neighbors. Thus, when white respondents were asked if they would try to leave a neighborhood when 5 of 14 houses had black residents, 41 percent replied affirmatively in 1976 and 29 percent in 1992 (Farley and Frey, 1994: 29).

A study in Los Angeles produced a comparable result, with a full 80 percent of respondents expressing feelings of comfort when the neighborhood was one-third black. However, that percentage dropped to 57 percent when the neighborhood became 53 percent black and 47 percent white. In contrast, three-quarters of whites were willing to live in a neighborhood where the majority of residents was either Latino or Asian (Zubrinsky and Bobo, 1996: 255). The cultural camouflage for modern racism seems applicable to the Detroit and Los Angeles findings. In the contemporary

climate of harmonious race relations, most white Americans support the idea of integrated housing with blacks as long as the numbers of black families are small.
However, whites' sense of threat and accompanying desire for racial exclusion become
manifest as the percentage of blacks increases.

Not surprisingly, the sense of threat and desire for exclusion are likely to diminish
or disappear when the proportion of black residents is fairly small and their lifestyles
are compatible with majority group members. Montclair, New Jersey, has become a
magnet for young professionals. Its population of about 38,000 is roughly two-thirds
white and one-third black, and most residents take pride in the way the races get
along. Robin Ross, a lawyer married to a neurosurgeon, explained, "We moved here
because we wanted our children to grow up in a diverse, integrated town with a fully
integrated school system" (Cheslow, 1997: 5). But while race relations generally go
well, various interracial disputes do occur, raising the question of what specific conditions, even in Montclair, are likely to arouse whites' sense of threat and desire for racial
exclusion.

Along with many citizens and realtors, bank officials often support racist housing
policies. A study by the Federal Reserve System indicated that banks and savings
institutions in the Boston area were discriminating racially in the awarding of mortgages. After income, property values, and other nonracial factors were taken into
account, a sharp difference remained between the percentage of mortgages granted in
white and in African American neighborhoods (Gold, 1989). A recent study indicated
that the major factor explaining whites' greater home equity (wealth built through
homeownership) was banks' and other mortgage lenders' discriminating on loans to
homeowners (Myers and Chung, 1996). Research concluded that the greater the percentage of African American employees lending organizations employ, the more likely
black applicants' loans will be approved (Squires and Kim, 1995).

Further in-roads on housing discrimination occur if banks change policies. In
such major cities as New York, St. Louis, and Philadelphia, some bankers are deciding
that providing mortgages for low-income, largely minority inner-city residents not
only helps eliminate their organization's discriminatory image but also provides the
bank new business opportunities. Some banks work with housing advocacy groups like
Acorn, which has 70,000 primarily African American members and two decades of
active service. In Acorn's North Philadelphia office, counselors explain the program to
people who call in or drop by, and applications are also filled out there. Applicants for
mortgages never need to go beyond the Acorn office. Commenting on the organization, a federal banking official said, "Acorn is street-tough rough and they bedevil the
bankers. But they've gotten banks to commit millions they otherwise would not have
lent" (Wayne, 1992: 50).

In the near future, banks might come under growing pressure to provide more
loans to low-income residents. While the Community Reinvestment Act of 1977
required increased lending to individuals in low- and moderate-income areas, mount-
ing evidence has suggested that most banks have avoided compliance. However, the
Clinton administration has developed a plan to tighten the law's standards, and some
banks are already starting to cooperate. For instance, in August 1993, CoreStates
New Jersey National Bank opened a branch in Camden, New Jersey—the first new
bank outlet in 22 years in that depressed city. Working with a credit union run by the

Latin American Economic Development Association, the bank makes home mortgage and home equity loans to low-income, primarily minority residents (Scherreik, 1994).

Another factor that probably discourages discrimination in housing has been the punitive damages some participants in the housing industry have been forced to pay. Thus, in New York City, over 2,000 African American and Hispanic individuals were awarded $20 million when a ruling found that they were the victims of discrimination in public housing assignments (Zimmerman, 1992). In Washington, D.C., 40 real estate and advertising firms faced a lawsuit for using advertisements that steered both black and white buyers to selected neighborhoods. Most of the companies reached a financial settlement and changed their ads, but while altering its ads, Colonial Village, a major realty company, did not settle and ended up paying $850,000 in punitive damages (*News Media & the Law*, 1992).

The federal government can take other measures to reduce housing discrimination under existing laws. First, Housing and Urban Development (HUD) personnel could provide financial assistance to local fair housing organizations to investigate and prosecute claims of discrimination. At present those organizations tend to be weak, and cases against violators of housing discrimination laws are unlikely to be forcefully prosecuted. Second, housing discrimination cases require evidence. HUD could establish a permanent testing program, identifying realtors engaging in housing discrimination and then turning over the evidence for prosecution (Massey and Denton, 1993: 229–230).

Until such measures are taken, it is likely that the kind of racist treatment described in the following section will keep occurring.

What Happened When a Puerto Rican Tried to Sell His House in an All-White Neighborhood

In *Stigma*, Erving Goffman suggested that oppressed individuals often experience a "phantom acceptance," which means that the nonoppressed members of the society treat them like everyone else during superficial contacts as long as the latter support the charade. In order to establish the fantasy, oppressed people generally must keep their distance (Goffman, 1974: 122) or, as the phrase goes in this chapter, know their place.

When African Americans or black Puerto Ricans, the two groups most likely to suffer housing discrimination, attempt to move into a white neighborhood, they are rejecting the phantom-acceptance game. If members of these minorities pursue this course of action, they are likely to encounter discriminatory tactics.

Piri Thomas, a black Puerto Rican, bought two houses on Long Island, New York, from Don Baldwin, his white brother-in-law, and moved into one of them. At first both he and his wife were very happy and proud to have moved from an inner-city neighborhood to the suburbs, and Thomas worked hard getting both houses into shape. Soon, however, he noticed that the neighbors would walk by and stare, often insolently, apparently suggesting that he shouldn't have dared to move into their neighborhood.

Once Thomas overheard a couple discussing the situation. The wife wondered "who could have sold that nigger a house in her community" (Thomas, 1973: 199). The husband replied that it had been Don Baldwin and that the family was Puerto Rican, not black. Thomas was infuriated, noting that in their bigoted minds being Puerto Rican was a notch above being black. Thomas wrote:

> Who makes the damned rules of who's better than who? I looked back at the two so-called Christians walking with their child and just to get their attention, I let out a mighty yell. They looked back and I made a most exaggerated bow and the gesture let them know I'd heard the bullshit that they, white Christian God-loving God-fearing [people], had put down. (Thomas, 1973: 199)

Eventually the Thomases decided to move back to New York City. While local racism played some role, the primary reason was that Thomas was working in the city, and the commute on top of a long day's work was backbreaking. So, deciding to sell the houses, Thomas went to see Paul Hendricks, a realtor.

As soon as Hendricks saw Thomas, he tried to steer him toward an area where he indicated some of the best African American families lived. No, Thomas indicated, he didn't want to buy a house, he wanted to sell two of them. Hendricks was puzzled, not recalling what he believed to be a black family living in that locale. When Thomas mentioned that he had bought the houses from Don Baldwin, Hendricks's face lit up with recognition. "Oh . . . ha ha, of course, you're the Spanish family I've heard about" (Thomas, 1973: 208). Puerto Rican, replied Thomas. They talked some more, and in spite of distinct reservations about Hendricks, Thomas decided to use him as a realtor.

Hendricks brought a few people to see the houses, but none of them were interested in buying. Eventually Thomas himself found a buyer. At first Hendricks was enthusiastic that a buyer had been found. But as soon as Thomas handed him a piece of paper on which the buyer's name and address were written, the enthusiasm faded. "What was the matter?" Thomas wanted to know. "Was the family black?" Mr. Hendricks asked.

> "That's right. Why?" I asked knowing the why all the way.
> "Really, Mr. Thomas, I don't know quite how to say this, but you certainly must know that Silver View is a, er . . . white community and they wouldn't be happy there . . . and you bought your house from Mr. Baldwin, who's lived here many years and his parents before him, and, well, you being, er . . . Spanish is not like. . . ."
> My blood was tearing itself up into my eyeball.
> "Why don't you just come out with it, fella?" My eyes just stared into his.
> "Well, it's not that I mind, but the people, I mean their homes, they've worked hard and they do mind, ah . . . mixing, and well, Dammit, I have lived here all my life.
> "Real estate is my livelihood and if I sold to a colored family property in Silver View, well. . . . Can you understand? I mean, put yourself in my place." (Thomas, 1973: 210)

No, he wouldn't do that, Thomas replied. He got rid of the agent and prepared to sell the house directly to the black family, but threatened by members of the all-white Better Civic Improvement Committee, the prospective purchaser withdrew.

The Thomases moved back to New York City, still hoping to sell to whomever they wished. Returning during the winter, they found that the house in which they had been living had been broken into, many windows were smashed, water had been turned on in the unheated house, thereby bursting the pipes, and dog dung had been smeared throughout the house.

Piri Thomas challenged the phantom-acceptance game by attempting to sell his house to a black couple. Eventually he was defeated by the racist system he attempted to overcome. The couple to whom he planned to sell his house was intimidated and decided not to buy it, and Thomas was punished when his house was broken into and damaged.

Discussion Questions

1. Analyze the three stages of job discrimination described in this chapter, tying in any personal experiences or experiences of individuals you know.

2. Evaluate whether casino gambling has been beneficial for Native Americans in your region.

3. Examine the relationship of the colonial labor principle to blacks in sport.

4. Evaluate the following statement: The evidence indicates that as minority group members' income and educational levels increase, they invariably move to more integrated neighborhoods. Tie into the discussion the internal colonialist principle of restriction of a racial minority's freedom of movement.

5. Are you personally aware of instances of racial segregation in housing? How does the concept of the cultural camouflage for modern racism relate to housing discrimination?

Sources

Alba, Richard D., and John R. Logan. 1993. "Minority Proximity to Whites in Suburbs: An Individual-Level Analysis of Segregation." *American Journal of Sociology* 98 (May): 1388–1427.

Anderson, Deborah, and David Shapiro. 1996. "Racial Differences in Access to High-paying Jobs and the Wage Gap between Black and White Women." *Industrial and Labor Relations Review* 49 (January): 273–286.

Araton, Harvey. 1991. "Aaron Speaks with Vincent on Remarks about Hiring." *New York Times* (May 15): B5+.

Araton, Harvey. 1992. "Beard Finally Showing His Stuff." *New York Times* (March 11): B13.

Araton, Harvey. 1994. "He Bargains as He Plays: Smartly." *New York Times* (January 9): 5.

Beauregard, Robert A. 1990. "Tenacious Inequalities: Politics and Race in Philadelphia." *Urban Affairs Quarterly* 25 (March): 420–434.

Bendick, Marc, Jr., Charles W. Jackson, Victor A. Reinoso, and Laura E. Hodges. 1993. "Discrimination against Latino Job Applicants: A Controlled Experiment," pp. 86–93 in John A. Kromkowski (ed.), *Race and Ethnic Relations 93/94*, 3rd ed. Guilford, CT: Dushkin Publishing Group.

Boxall, Bettina. 1997. "Proposition 209 Is a Blueprint for Court Fights, Scholars Say," pp. 31–34 in John A. Kromkowski (ed.), *Race and Ethnic Relations 97/98*, 7th ed. Guilford, CT: Duskin Publishing Group.

Braddock, Jomills Henry, II, and James N. McPartland. 1987. "How Minorities Continue to Be Excluded from Equal Employment Opportunities: Research on Labor Market and Institutional Barriers." *Journal of Social Issues* 43: 5–39.

Burstein, Paul, and Susan Pitchford. 1990. "Social-Scientific and Legal Challenges to Education and Test Requirements in Employment." *Social Problems* 37 (May): 243–257.

Campbell, Bebe Moore. 1982. "Black Executives and Corporate Stress." *New York Times Magazine* (December 12): 36–39+.

Chavez, Lydia. 1994. "More Mexicans, More Profit." *New York Times* (December 9): A33.

Cheslow, Jerry. 1997. "Culture, Parks, and Broad Diversity." *New York Times* (August 10): Sec. 9, 5.

Chua-eoan, Howard G. 1993. "Strangers in Paradise," pp. 118–121 in John A. Kromkowski (ed.), *Race and Ethnic Relations 93/94*, 3rd ed. Guilford, CT: Dushkin Publishing Group.

Chun, Ki-Taek. 1993. "The Myth of Asian American Success and Its Educational Ramifications," pp. 175–185 in Young I. Song and Eugene C. Kim (eds.), *American Mosaic*. Englewood Cliffs, NJ: Prentice-Hall.

Clark, William A. V. 1993. "Measuring Racial Discrimination in the Housing Market." *Urban Affairs Quarterly* 28 (June): 641–649.

Cleaver, Eldridge. 1970. *Soul on Ice*. New York: Dell Publishing.

Clines, Francis X. 1993. "Indian Tribes Close Ranks to Protect Casinos from Cheats and Competitors." *New York Times* (December 25): 6.

Cohn, Samuel, and Mark Fossett. 1996. "What Spatial Mismatch? The Proximity of Blacks to Employment in Boston and Houston." *Social Forces* 75 (December): 557–572.

Collins, Sharon M. 1993. "Blacks on the Bubble: The Vulnerability of Black Executives in White Corporations." *Sociological Quarterly* 34 (August): 429–447.

Collins, Sharon M. 1997. "Black Mobility in White Corporations: Up the Corporate Ladder But Out on a Limb." *Social Problems* 44 (February): 55–67.

Crystal, David. 1989. "Asian Americans and the Myth of the Model Minority." *Social Casework* 70 (September): 405–413.

Daniels, Roger. 1988. *Asian Americans: Chinese and Japanese in the United States since 1850*. Seattle: University of Washington Press.

Darden, Joe T. 1990. "Differential Access to Housing in the Suburbs." *Journal of Black Studies* 21 (September): 15–22.

Davila, Alberto, Alok K. Bohara, and Rogelio Saenz. 1993. "Accent Penalties and the Earnings of Mexican Americans." *Social Science Quarterly* 74 (December): 902–916.

DeFrances, Carol J. 1996. "The Effects of Racial Ecological Segregation on Quality of Life: A Comparison of Middle-Class Blacks and Middle-Class Whites." *Urban Affairs Review* 31 (July): 799–809.

Denton, Nancy A., and Douglas S. Massey. 1988. "Residential Segregation of Blacks, Hispanics, and Asians by Socioeconomic Status and Generation." *Social Science Quarterly* 69 (December): 797–817.

Denton, Nancy A., and Douglas S. Massey. 1989. "Racial Identity among Caribbean Hispanics." *American Sociological Review* 54 (October): 790–808.

de Uriarte, Mercedes Lynn. 1997. "Baiting Immigrants: Heartbreak for Latinos," pp. 119-121 in John A. Kromkowski (ed.), *Race and Ethnic Relations 97/98*, 7th ed. Guilford, CT: Dushkin Publishing Group.

Economist. 1993. "Connecticut: A Tribal Dance." (September 18): 31.

Eichenwald, Kurt. 1996a. "Texaco to Make Record Payout in Bias Lawsuit." *New York Times* (November 16): 1+.

Eichenwald, Kurt. 1996b. "The Two Faces of Texaco." New York Times (November 10): Sec. 3, 1+.

ESPN. 1997. "Up Close." Interview with Robert Parrish. (August 25).

Falcon, Luis M., Douglas T. Gurak, and Mary G. Powers. 1990. "Labor Force Participation of Puerto Rican Women in Greater New York City." *Sociology and Social Research* 74 (January): 110–114.

Farley, John E. 1987. "Disproportionate Black and Hispanic Unemployment in U.S. Metropolitan Areas: The Role of Racial Inequality, Segregation and Discrimination in Male Joblessness." *American Journal of Economics and Sociology* 46 (April): 129–150.

Farley, John E. 1995. "Race Still Matters: The Minimal Role of Income and Housing Cost as Causes of Housing Segregation in St. Louis, 1990." *Urban Affairs Review* 31 (November): 244–254.

Farley, Reynolds, and William H. Frey. 1994. "Changes in the Segregation of Whites from Blacks during the 1980s: Small Steps toward a More Integrated Society." *American Sociological Review* 59 (February): 23–45.

Feagin, Joe R., and Clairece Booher Feagin. 1993. *Racial and Ethnic Relations,* 4th ed. Englewood Cliffs, NJ: Prentice-Hall.

Fitzgerald, Mark. 1997. "Sportwriters Urged to Examine Nike." *Editor & Publisher* 130 (July 26): 8–9+.

Gallup, George, Jr. 1989. *Gallup Report* (August).

Gallup, George, Jr., and Larry Hugick. 1990. "Racial Tolerance Grows, Progress on Racial Equality Less Evident." *Gallup Poll Monthly* (June): 23–32.

Galster, George C. 1990a. "Racial Steering in Urban Housing Markets: A Review of the Audit Evidence." *Review of Black Political Economy* 18 (Winter): 105–129.

Galster, George C. 1990b. "White Flight from Racially Integrated Neighborhoods in the 1970s." *Urban Studies* 27 (June): 385–399.

Geschwender, James A., and Rita Carroll-Seguin. 1990. "Exploding the Myth of African-American Progress." *Signs* 15 (Winter): 285–299.

Goffman, Erving. 1974. *Stigma: Notes on the Management of Spoiled Identity.* New York: Jason Aronson.

Gold, Allan R. 1989. "Racial Pattern Is Found in Boston Mortgages." *New York Times* (September 1): A1+.

Hacker, Andrew. 1992. *Two Nations: Black and White, Separate, Hostile, Unequal.* New York: Charles Scribner's Sons.

Hurh, Won Moo, and Kwang Chung Kim. 1989. "The 'Success' Image of Asian Americans: Its Validity, and Its Practical and Theoretical Implications." *Ethnic and Racial Studies* 12 (October): 512–538.

Jaynes, Gerald David, and Robin M. Williams, Jr. (eds.). 1989. *A Common Destiny: Blacks and American Society.* Washington, DC: National Academy Press.

Jiobu, Robert M. 1988a. "Ethnic Hegemony and the Japanese of California." *American Sociological Review* 53 (June): 353–367.

Jiobu, Robert M. 1988b. "Racial Inequality in a Public Arena: The Case of Professional Baseball." *Social Forces* 67 (December): 524–533.

Johnson, Gloria Jones. 1990. "Underemployment, Underpayment, Attributions, and Self-Esteem among Working Black Men." *Journal of Black Psychology* 16 (Spring): 23–43.

Johnson, Kirk. 1993. "Indians' Casino Money Pumps Up the Volume." *New York Times* (September 1): B1+.

Johnson, Kirk. 1997. "Black Workers Bear Big Burden as Jobs in Government Dwindle." *New York Times* (February 2): 1+.

Jones, Edward W., Jr. 1973. "What It's like to Be a Black Manager." *Harvard Business Review* 51 (July/August): 108–116.

Jones, Edward W., Jr. 1986. "Black Managers: The Dream Deferred." *Harvard Business Review* 64 (May/June): 84–93.

Judson, George. 1994. "Some Indians See a Gamble with Future in Casinos." *New York Times* (May 15): Sec. 4, 5.

Kaufman, Robert L. 1986. "The Impact of Industrial and Occupational Structure on Black-White Employment Allocation." *American Sociological Review* 51 (June): 310–323.

Kilborn, Peter T. 1997. "For Poorest Indians, Casinos Aren't Enough." *New York Times* (June 11): A1+.

Killian, Lewis M. 1990. "Race Relations and the Nineties: Where Are the Dreams of the Sixties?" *Social Forces* 69 (September): 1–13.

Koch, James V., and C. Warren Vander Hill. 1988. "Is There Discrimination in the 'Black Man's Game'?" *Social Science Quarterly* 69 (March): 83–94.

Lai, Tracy. 1995. "Asian American Women: Not for Sale," pp. 181–190 in Margaret L. Andersen and Patricia Hill Collins (eds.), *Race, Class, and Gender: An Anthology,* 2nd ed. Belmont, CA: Wadsworth Publishing Company.

Langberg, Mark, and Reynolds Farley. 1985. "Residential Segregation of Asian Americans in 1980." *Sociology and Social Research* 70 (October): 71–75.

Lavoie, Marc, and Wilbert M. Leonard, III. 1994. "In Search of an Alternative Explanation of Stacking in Baseball: The Uncertainty Hypothesis." *Sociology of Sport Journal* 11 (June): 140–154.

Leigh, Wilhelmina A. 1989. "Barriers to Fair Housing for Black Women." *Sex Roles* 21 (July): 71–84.

Lichter, Daniel T. 1988. "Racial Differences in Underemployment in American Cities." *American Journal of Sociology* 93 (January): 771–792.

Lopez, Felix. 1976. "The Bell System's Non-Management Personnel Selection Strategy," pp. 226–227 in Phyllis A. Wallace (ed.), *Equal Opportunity and the AT&T Case.* Cambridge, MA: M.I.T. Press.

Madamba, Anna B., and Gordon F. De Jong. 1994. "Determinants of White-Collar Employment: Puerto Rican Women in Metropolitan New York." *Social Science Quarterly* 75 (March): 53–66.

Massey, Douglas S. 1990. "American Apartheid: Segregation and the Making of the Underclass." *American Journal of Sociology* 96 (September): 329–357.

Massey, Douglas S., and Nancy A. Denton. 1989. "Segregation along Five Dimensions." *Demography* 26 (August): 373–391.

Massey, Douglas S., and Nancy A. Denton. 1993. *American Apartheid: Segregation and the Making of the Underclass.* Cambridge, MA: Harvard University Press.

Massey, Douglas S., and Mitchell L. Eggers. 1990. "The Ecology of Inequality: Minorities and the Concentration of Poverty, 1970–1980." *American Journal of Sociology* 95 (March): 1153–1188.

Massey, Douglas S., and Eric Fong. 1990. "Segregation and Neighborhood Quality: Blacks, Hispanics, and Asians in the San Francisco Metropolitan Area." *Social Forces* 69 (September): 15–32.

Meier, Barry. 1994. "Casinos Putting Tribes at Odds." *New York Times* (January 13): D1+.

Minerbrook, Scott. 1996. "Home Ownership Anchors the Middle Class," pp. 171–175 in John A. Kromkowski (ed.), *Race and Ethnic Relations 96/97*, 6th ed. Guilford, CT: Dushkin Publishing Group.

Mladenka, Kenneth R. 1989. "Barriers to Hispanic Employment Success in 1,200 Cities." *Social Science Quarterly* 70 (June): 391–407.

Morrison, Ann M., and Mary Ann Von Glinow. 1990. "Women and Minorities in Management." *American Psychologist* 45 (February): 200–208.

Myers, Samuel L., and Chanjin Chung. 1996. "Racial Differences in Home Ownership and Home Equity among Preretirement-Aged Households." *Gerontologist* 36 (June): 350–360.

National Committee on Pay Equity. 1996. "The Wage Gap: Myths and Facts," pp. 304-308 in Karen E. Rosenblum and Toni-Michelle C. Travis, *The Meaning of Difference: American Constructions of Race, Sex and Gender, Social Class, and Sexual Orientation*. New York: McGraw-Hill Companies.

News Media & the Law. 1992. "Jury Awards $850,000 in Fair Housing Case." 16 (Summer): 6.

New York Times. 1997. "Tribe Starts New Business: Gambling Site on Internet." (July 5): 8.

New York Times/CBS NEWS Poll. 1997. "Many Americans Reject Diversity's Means, Not Its Ends." (December 14).

O'Hare, William P., William H. Frey, and Dan Fost. 1994. "Asians in the Suburbs." *American Demographics* 16 (May): 32–38.

Olson, James S., and Raymond Wilson. 1984. *Native Americans in the Twentieth Century*. Provo, UT: Brigham Young University Press.

Passell, Peter. 1994. "Foxwoods, a Casino Success Story." *New York Times* (August 8): D1+.

Pettigrew, Thomas F., and Joanne Martin. 1987. "Shaping the Organizational Context for Black American Inclusion." *Journal of Social Issues* 43: 41–78.

Pomer, Marshall I. 1986. "Labor Market Structure, Intragenerational Mobility, and Discrimination: Black Male Advancement Out of Low-Paying Occupations, 1962–1973." *American Sociological Review* 51 (October): 650–659.

Rhoden, William C. 1990. "The Man Who Has His Own." *New York Times* (May 25): B5.

Rosenbaum, Emily. 1994. "The Constraints on Minority Housing Choices, New York City, 1978–1987." *Social Forces* 72 (March): 725–747.

Sanders, Jimy M., and Victor Nee. 1987. "Limits of Ethnic Solidarity in the Enclave Economy." *American Sociological Review* 52 (December): 745–773.

Schaefer, Richard T. 1993. *Racial & Ethnic Groups*, 5th ed. New York: HarperCollins.

Scherreik, Susan. 1994. "More Banks Taking Space in Ethnic Neighborhoods." *New York Times* (February 20): Sec. 10, 7.

Schneider, John J., and D. Stanley Eitzen. 1986. "Racial Segregation by Professional Football Positions, 1960–1985." *Sociology and Social Research* 70 (July): 259–261.

Schneider, Keith. 1993. "The Regulatory Thickets of Environmental Racism." *New York Times* (December 19): Sec. 4, p. 5.

Schneider, Mark, and Thomas Phelan. 1990. "Blacks and Jobs: Never the Twain Shall Meet?" *Urban Affairs Quarterly* 26 (December): 299–312.

Sklar, Holly. 1995. "Imagine a Country," pp. 121–130 in Paula S. Rothenberg (ed.), *Race, Class, and Gender in the United States: An Integrated Study,* 3rd ed. New York: St. Martin's Press.

Sokoloff, Natalie J. 1988. "Evaluating Gains and Losses by Black and White Women and Men in the Professions, 1960-1980." *Social Problems* 35 (February): 36–53.

Squires, Gregory D., and Sunwoong Kim. 1995. "Does Anybody Who Works Here Look like Me: Mortage Lending, Race, and Lender Employment." *Social Science Quarterly* 76 (December): 823–838.

Steinberg, Stephen. 1989. "The Underclass: A Case of Color Blindness." *New Politics* 2 (Summer): 42–60.

Stolzenberg, Ross M. 1990. "Ethnicity, Geography, and Occupational Achievement in Hispanic Men in the United States." *American Sociological Review* 55 (February): 143–154.

Terry, Don. 1997. "Chicago Neighborhood Reveals an Ugly Side." *New York Times* (March 27): A18.

Thomas, Melvin E. 1993. "Race, Class, and Personal Income: An Empirical Test of the Declining Significance of Race Thesis, 1968-1988." *Social Problems* 40 (August): 328–342.

Thomas, Melvin E., Cedric Herring, and Hayward Derrick Horton. 1994. "Discrimination over the Life Course: A Synthetic Cohort Analysis of Earnings Differences between Black and White Males, 1940–1990." *Social Problems* 41 (November): 608–628.

Thomas, Piri. 1973. *Savior, Savior, Hold My Hand.* New York: Bantam Books.

Tigges, Leann M., and Deborah M. Tootle. 1993. "Underemployment and Racial Competition in Local Labor Markets." *Sociological Quarterly* 34 (May): 279–298.

Tomaskovic-Devey, Donald. 1993. "The Gender and Race Composition of Jobs and the Male/Female, White/Black Pay Gaps." *Social Forces* 72 (September): 45–76.

United States Commission on Civil Rights. 1996. "Civil Rights Issues Facing Asian Americans in the 1990s," pp. 315–330 in Karen E. Rosenblum and Toni-Michelle C. Travis. *The Meaning of Difference: American Constructions of Race, Sex and Gender, Social Class, and Sexual Orientation.* New York: McGraw-Hill Companies.

U.S. Bureau of the Census. 1990. *Statistical Abstract of the United States: 1990,* 110th ed. Washington, D.C. U.S. Government Printing Office. 415.

U.S. Bureau of the Census. 1996. *Statistical Abstract of the United States: 1996,* 116th ed. Washington, DC: U.S. Government Printing Office.

Wacquant, Loic J. D., and William Julius Wilson. 1989. "The Cost of Racial and Class Exclusion in the Inner City." *Annals of the American Academy of Political and Social Science* 501 (January): 8–25.

Wayne, Leslie. 1992. "New Hope in Inner Cities: Banks Offering Mortgages." *New York Times* (March 14): 1+.

Weink, Ronald E., et al. 1979. *Measuring Racial Discrimination in American Housing Markets.* Washington, DC: U.S. Government Printing Office.

Weir, Margaret. 1994. "Race and Urban Poverty: Comparing Europe and America," pp. 193–197 in John A. Kromkowski (ed.), *Race and Ethnic Relations 94/95,* 4th ed. Guilford, CT: Dushkin Publishing Group.

White, Michael J., Ann E. Biddlecom, and Shenyang Guo. 1993. "Immigration, Naturalization, and Residential Assimilation among Asian Americans in 1980." *Social Forces* 72 (September): 93–117.

Wilkerson, Isabel. 1995. "Middle Class Blacks Try to Grip a Ladder While Lending a Hand," pp. 155–162 in Paula S. Rothenberg (ed.), *Race, Class, and Gender,* 3rd ed. New York: St. Martin's Press.

Wilson, George. 1997. "Pathways to Power: Racial Differences in the Determinants of Job Authority." *Social Problems* 44 (February): 38–54.

Wilson, William Julius. *When Work Disappears: The World of the New Urban Poor.* New York: Vintage Books.

Wong, Bernard. 1987. "The Role of Ethnicity in Enclave Enterprises: A Study of the Chinese Garment Factories in New York City." *Human Organization* 46 (Summer): 120–130.

Yinger, John. 1986. "Measuring Racial Discrimination with Fair Housing Audits: Caught in the Act." *American Economic Review* 76 (December): 881–893.

Zimmerman, Joseph F. 1992. "Housing Authority in New York City to Compensate Victims of Steering and Discrimination." *National Civic Review* 81 (Fall/Winter): 515–516.

Zubrinsky, Camille L., and Lawrence Bobo. 1996. "Prismatic Metropolis: Race and Residential Segregation in the City of Angels." *Social Science Research* 25 (December): 335–374.

CHAPTER 6

Blocking the Gateway: Education

Fifteen-year-old Mark Jenkins lives with his mother and two of his three siblings in the all-black Cabrini Green housing project in Chicago, a building that many feel looks like a prison. In 1987 he was caught in a crossfire between two gangs fighting outside his apartment building, and a bullet lodged in his left arm just below the shoulder, shattering the bone. Mark explains, "They sniped me. I couldn't get out of the way in time." It was an automatic rifle, Mark explains. He hears them every day.

Like thousands of young African Americans enclosed in the inner city, Mark finds himself surrounded by poverty, violence, and frustration, and he is a member of a statistical category—poor black male teenagers—that is more likely to commit crimes and sell and use drugs than any other population group.

Mark, however, is determined to avoid such an outcome. He has not joined a gang; he goes to school regularly; he sells newspapers on weekends; and he often surprises his mother by cleaning the apartment and then complaining when his siblings mess it up. The violence around Mark, however, has affected him. In 1987 he spent two weeks in a juvenile detention center on assault charges. Later the charges were dropped, with the probation officer reporting that Mark was wrongly accused.

Here is a young person struggling to survive and do well in an environment that makes his efforts difficult or perhaps even futile. What role has schooling played? Early in elementary school, Mark earned good grades, but later he had to repeat grades twice when standardized tests revealed that he was reading at only a second-grade level. Two grades behind, he had to transfer to Lincoln Park High School in spite of poor grades, because he had become too old for elementary school.

Mark labors at school work but does not do well. It would be miraculous if he did. All his life he has attended poorly financed, overcrowded inner-city schools. Seldom have teachers paid much attention to him; never have they systematically tried to overcome his lifelong educational disadvantage. The high school is little help in this regard. While it brings together students from varied backgrounds, Mark and other poor African American students with weak academic backgrounds tend to be in separate classes from students with stronger academic preparation. In the hallways Mark passes middle-class white and black students wearing tee shirts and sweatshirts representing top universities; he imagines that they live in nice homes where they don't need to dodge bullets and explains that they deserve a better life than he because "they're smarter than me." This, according to experts, is not an unusual analysis; while poor delinquents tend to blame society for their plight, poor nondelinquents are likely to blame themselves. Having grown up in an all-black housing project, Mark has had almost no contact with whites and is wary of them. He says that he has no white friends and adds, "We don't have nothing in common."

Mark's goals in life are modest by many Americans' standards. He would like to graduate from high school and go on to either college or the Navy. He would also like to visit New York. But he is failing several of his courses; the circulation manager is cutting back the number of paperboys, and so Mark is probably going to lose his job; and several of the local gangs are trying to recruit him (Wilkerson, 1988).

This is not a pleasant, inspiring account, and yet while working on the third edition of this book, I decided to retain it because it sums up the situation many minority children face all too well. Mark's case doesn't coincide with the American dream that hard-working, ambitious young men, in the Horatio Alger mold, are sure bets for success and glory. What that dream fails to recognize is that for people who are poor and belong to racial minorities, circumstances often dictate that the dream either never exists or starts to fade rapidly at an early age. And schools, we find, play a significant role in the absence or death of that dream.

At this point let us consider the role of education in American society and then assess how racism links to educational policy. To begin, in preindustrial life, education had relatively little career significance for most individuals. They pursued a line of work, often that maintained by their parents—farming, a trade, some activity where expertise developed strictly out of experience and credentials were seldom an issue.

But as society industrialized, literacy and other educational skills became increasingly necessary, or—equally important—policy makers and employers perceived them as necessary. For a large proportion of modern jobs, American citizens must have formal educational credentials—high-school certificates, college degrees, and frequently graduate degrees.

Supposedly American society endorses equal opportunity for all citizens. However, given the link between education and job success, equal opportunity is nothing but an abstract principle unless all children, regardless of race and family income, have access to sufficiently high-quality schooling that they will be eligible for respectable, good-paying jobs. Absence of such schooling produces the opposite condition—a society in which the economic and social status quo is maintained.

In Chapter 5 we noted that housing segregation has contributed to the growth of an urban underclass by funnelling large numbers of black and Puerto Rican citizens into segregated, already poor inner-city areas, causing those districts to deteriorate much more rapidly. Education is one of the important areas seriously affected by this

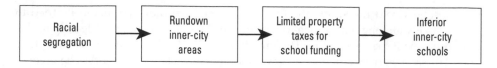

Figure 6.1   Factors Contributing to Inferior Inner-City Schools for Minority Children

deterioration. In the American public education system, the local property tax is a prominent contributor to public education, and in poverty-stricken areas, such funding will be minimal, perhaps nearly nonexistent. Thus local funding for education in such areas will be very low, and the quality will suffer seriously. One can readily argue that institutional racism is embedded in the public education system: The economic condition of a residential area affects the quality of education children receive, and racial minorities are disproportionately located in low-income districts, which receive inferior schooling. Figure 6.1 represents the relationship of factors described here.

A close relationship between racism and inferior schooling seems to exist. These are negative conditions that will be discussed frequently in this chapter. But as a foundation for this discussion, it seems necessary to convey some sense of the goals of effective schooling. Consider, for instance, the following statement issued by Cold Spring School, a widely acclaimed elementary school in New Haven, Connecticut.

> The cornerstone of Cold Spring School's program for elementary age child is active, personally fulfilling learning with an emphasis on inquiry and problem solving. The program encourages self-awareness and creativity. This approach to learning challenges children to think as well as act, finding alternative ways to reach solutions. At Cold Spring, children experience school as a stimulating, nurturing extension of family life. Children learn not only cognitive skills but also independence, responsibility, and sensitivity. . . . The sense of community enables them to take the intellectual risks necessary to stretch academically. (Fiss, 1989)

The statement suggests that an effective school establishes a nurturing environment that develops for children both a highly positive image and understanding of themselves, and also the intellectual and emotional tools to do well in the modern world.

Let's recall internal colonialist theory, with its emphasis on dominant whites continuing a colonial system of control. One tenet of the internal colonialist perspective is the colonial labor principle, which asserts that racial minorities' work is menial and low-status, simply serving the dominant group's interest. If members of racial minorities are deprived of effective education, their opportunity for achieving good-paying, satisfying work is minimal. Then there is the internal colonialist principle asserting that racial minorities' culture is invariably inferior. As we see at several places in this chapter, this tendency has appeared in the American education system as efforts to Americanize students, ignoring their cultural traditions.

In the next section, we survey the historical development of racial minorities' education in the United States. The second major part of the chapter assesses some of the complicated, contemporary issues involving the relationship between education and race—issues that demonstrate the relevance of internal colonialism to modern education.

A Brief History of Racial Minorities' Schooling

Most of the slave states passed laws prohibiting people from teaching slaves to read and write. Masters felt that if they became literate, slaves might read anti-slavery newspapers and become discontent or forge passes and escape (Rothenberg, 1988: 191). Still some, like Frederick Douglass, learned how to read. In his autobiography Douglass indicated that while working in Baltimore, he traded bread to poor white boys for "that more valuable bread of knowledge" (Douglass, 1968: 54).

In the mid-nineteenth century, northern public schools excluded African Americans. Many towns and cities made no provisions for blacks' education while others, including Boston and New York, supplied modest funding for segregated, highly inferior schools (Bailyn et al., 1977: 503).

Educational discrimination carried into the twentieth century, with inequality greater in the South than in the North. In 1940, for example, data compiled by the U.S. Department of Education from a dozen southern states indicated that per-pupil expenditures for whites averaged over three times those for blacks, with white students in Mississippi receiving seven times the amount provided blacks (Jaynes and Williams, 1989: 58). Clearly the southern states, operating under a legally mandated "separate but equal" doctrine, were supplying educational facilities for African Americans that were far short of equal.

Through the 1940s and early 1950s, an accumulation of legal precedents challenged the "separate but equal" doctrine, but the decisions used cautious, narrow wording. Then in 1954 in *Brown v. Board of Education,* the Supreme Court took a bolder step, declaring separate educational facilities for different racial groups unequal and inhumane. The following year the Supreme Court stated that school desegregation should proceed "with all deliberate speed" (Bailyn et al., 1977: 1219–1220).

But there was strong opposition from many southern whites. In 1957, in the first effort to desegregate southern public schools, Governor Orval Faubus of Arkansas ordered the National Guard to prevent nine African American students from enrolling in previously all-white Central High School. Each morning the students vainly tried to enter the school and were turned away by the Guard troops. An ever larger mob of angry whites gathered each day to make certain that the black students were stopped. Several times violence broke out, and one day two black reporters were beaten and school windows and doors were broken. President Eisenhower, a former general, saw the situation strictly in military terms—as an insurrection against the federal government. The solution, he decided, was to deploy a thousand riot-trained troops of the 101st Airborne Division. Through the school year, the troops occupied the school, and while violence declined, black students encountered countless incidents where they were mocked and ridiculed (Branch, 1988: 223–224).

School desegregation proceeded very slowly in the South. White groups like the White Citizens' Councils threatened and intimidated African American students integrating schools, and many administrators resisted the law or simply closed their schools. In 1954 in 11 southern states, the proportion of African Americans attending classes with whites was less than one-tenth of 1 percent. Ten years later the proportion had only risen to about 2 percent. The factor producing a major increase in desegregated schooling was the Civil Rights Act of 1964, which stated that until laws were obeyed, there would be no federal aid to local school districts. As a result the proportion of black students in formerly segregated southern schools rose to 18 percent in 1968 and then 46 percent in 1973. Since that time, however, there has been little or no increase in southern school desegregation (Jaynes and Williams, 1989: 75–76).

An explanation of this pattern seems instructive. Many southern school districts have been organized on a countywide basis, combining cities and suburbs, and thus a mandate to desegregate quickly produced a sharply increased racial mix of students. In some southern school districts, however, separation of cities and suburbs occurs, and as a result blacks, who are disproportionately located in cities, find themselves in largely segregated schools. In the North the latter pattern of school districting has dominated.

In the middle 1960s, the segregated nature of northern public schools became a publicized issue. As mandated by the Civil Rights Act of 1964, Congress ordered the federal Commissioner of Education to conduct a study of the availability of educational opportunities for Americans of different races, religions, and national origins, and sociologist James S. Coleman was put in charge. What became known as the Coleman Report was a massive study conducted throughout the country involving 600,000 children, 60,000 teachers, several thousand principals, and several hundred school superintendents. One major conclusion was that minority group students from poor areas could frequently improve their academic performance when they attended schools with students living in affluent districts (Coleman et al., 1966). This conclusion led directly to the practice of busing.

The plan was that busing minority students from inner-city to suburban schools and white students from suburban to inner-city facilities would produce an educational atmosphere that would prove beneficial for racial minorities. It has turned out that busing has provoked considerable controversy and even violence. Most white parents have not cited integrated classrooms as their reason for opposition. Instead they have claimed to be concerned about the inferiority of inner-city schools, their unfamiliarity with these facilities, lengthy school days that result from long-distance busing, the danger their children face by entering high-crime areas, and the destruction to community spirit produced by the loss of neighborhood schools (Armor, 1989: 26). One study concluded that nonracial factors like those just cited were at least as important as the racial composition of inner-city schools in predicting white students' refusal to be bused to inner-city schools (Rossell, 1988). Sixteen years after the Coleman Report appeared, James Coleman wrote about busing, acknowledging "the general unpopularity of this policy, greatest among whites, but also true for Hispanics and blacks" (Coleman et al., 1982: 197).

A study of pioneers of school integration also revealed negative reactions. Sociologist Leslie Inniss (1993) interviewed 20 individuals who along with her were in the first group of black students to integrate elementary and high schools in a southern city. Thirty years later the negative impact of the name-calling, vandalism, and general intimidation the students had experienced was still apparent. Two of them had suffered nervous breakdowns at the time and never effectively recovered. The others felt like "guinea pigs who were sacrificed with little or no regard for what might happen to them in the long term." Inniss continued:

> One desegregated school attender reported that she often wonders "what I would have thought like and been like before all those people impinged what they think and are on me." Another female lamented that "we gave up so much and got so little in return." Finally, an extremely angry and bitter male stated that "forced integration was the worst thing that happened to our race." He went on to explain that during school desegregation, "we were forced to play their game by their rules, but now my goal is to extract all their knowledge to use it to beat them at their own game." (Inniss, 1993: 9)

Given such sacrifices, one would hope that segregation no longer existed. However, because of segregated housing patterns and white resistance to school integration, nearly 70 percent of black students currently attend segregated schools. The principal change that has occurred in the past quarter-century is that school segregation is now more likely to occur in the Northeast and the Midwest than in the South; in the 1960s the South had this dubious leadership (Celis, 1996; Molnar, 1993). Consider a typical northeastern city. In Philadelphia, which has 19 new public schools that have been expressly established with the idea of promoting more racially balanced student bodies, the school system remains just about as segregated as it was a quarter-century ago (Hinds, 1994).

Still, some positive changes involving African Americans and the schools have occurred. Sociologist Peter I. Rose noted that in recent years

> those who were not African American were exposed to the fact that, besides being victims, those long called Negroes were, like all others, parts of complex, stratified, and far from monolithic systems in which people live and work and play and suffer. (Rose, 1997: 192)

In short, for the first time in mainstream society, blacks have been able to escape their stereotyped images as slaves, ex-slaves, and victims and have become more widely accepted as simply American citizens, with a wide range of outlooks, activities, and skills. Such recognition, Rose contended, has provided two functions both in the schools and in the general society: "strengthening communal ties among those celebrated and, simultaneously, teaching others that those whose stories are being recounted also had a noble past and are, like themselves, a proud people worthy of respect" (Rose, 1997: 192–193).

Like African Americans, early Asian American immigrants faced educational discrimination. In nineteenth-century California, the children of Chinese immigrants—the first Asians in the United States—were not permitted to enter public schools even though their parents, forced to pay extra taxes, contributed to them at a higher rate than most residents. To rectify the situation, Chinese immigrants sued to gain access to schools. In 1885 a judge in San Francisco ruled in favor of the Chinese, declaring that there was no legal basis for excluding Chinese children from the public school system and requiring the city to establish a special school for Chinese children.

Two decades later Japanese immigrants to the San Francisco area were more difficult to satisfy. Compelled to send their children to the Asian school originally established for Chinese children, Japanese parents rebelled, rallying support against school segregation from the Japanese government, which at the time had considerable influence with top American leaders. In 1907 President Theodore Roosevelt temporarily resolved the situation by negotiating with the Japanese government a "gentleman's agreement" whereby the segregation policy would be removed if the Japanese government agreed to block the flow of immigrants competing with Californians for jobs (Hsia, 1988: 11–12).

Since the second decade of the twentieth century, Asian Americans have been very successful educationally, surpassing whites in the number of years of schooling completed. Curiously, racism contributed to this success. Beginning with the Chinese Exclusion Act of 1882 and continuing with the Immigration Act of 1924, restrictive legislation relieved pressure on local Asian American communities previously forced to absorb new immigrants, permitting funds that would have been used to help new arrivals to be invested in children's education. In addition, those Asian immigrants allowed to come to the United States were highly selected, with educational qualifications well above the national average.

Prevented from entering most professions and excluded from the relatively well-paid craft industries, Asian immigrants devoted themselves to an ethnic economy centered in agriculture, trade, and services. They strongly encouraged their children to obtain a good education as a means of either entering a profession or preparing themselves to more effectively run the family business.

With declining discrimination, Asian Americans' level of educational attainment has increased markedly, with a college degree becoming the standard. Continuing emphasis on education, particularly higher education, seems to be the rational response of people who are less involved in ethnic industries than in the past, cherish professional careers, and recognize that in modern times these positions are unobtainable without appropriate degrees (Hirschman and Wong, 1986).

Mexican Americans have been more victimized educationally. Early in this century, education officials classified Mexican immigrants as farm laborers and decided that for them and their children schooling was a low priority. Language also played an important role in impeding their educational advancement. With Spanish as their first language, young Mexican American children often found themselves falling rapidly behind children whose native language was English. Evaluated by IQ tests given in English, Chicano children were often classified as EMR ("educable/mentally retarded") and placed in lower tracks that prepared them for low-level jobs requiring minimal formal education. Mexican American children whose parents had a fairly high level of education and used English in the home were more likely to do well in school. Until at least the early 1970s, school officials' principal response to this language problem was to blame victims, establishing a "no-Spanish" rule for Mexican American students. If caught speaking Spanish at school, they were punished. As internal colonialist theory indicates, such a move was a clear assertion of the inferiority of the Spanish language and created considerable resentment among Chicano students. Not surprisingly, in 1974, the U.S. Commission on Civil Rights concluded that the curriculum in southwestern schools did not meet Chicano students' needs; it effectively served just one group—white, middle-class, English-speaking children (Simpson and Yinger, 1985: 342–345).

For over three decades, Puerto Rican children have been having serious difficulties in the American public school system. A 1958 study indicated that two major sources of children's difficulties were language handicaps and ineffective relationships between teachers and parents. The report concluded with 23 recommendations, many stressing closer personal attention to the individual child and much greater contact with children's parents. A decade later a nationwide conference on Puerto Rican education indicated that instead of improving, problems were worsening (Fitzpatrick, 1987: 141–142). The trend has continued. More recent data have indicated that of all the groups discussed in this book, Puerto Ricans have the lowest Scholastic Aptitude Test (SAT) scores (*New York Times*, 1994) as well as the highest school-dropout rate (Fuentes, 1994).

From the early colonial era until well into the twentieth century, Native Americans have faced a relentless criticism backed by internal colonialism—that they suffer from an inferior cultural tradition. Early schools were run by the Bureau of Indian Affairs or religious groups that received government financing. As we noted in Chapter 3, many officials believed that the most efficient means of Americanizing Indian children was to send them to boarding schools where they could be systematically "civilized" as preparation for becoming submissive domestic workers or manual laborers. Between 1890 and 1930 in the Southwest, for instance, about one-quarter of Indian children attended such boarding schools. This sometimes brutal, often humiliating practice was never particularly successful, and it ended during the 1920s.

By the mid-1930s, the emphasis was on public schools for Native Americans. Nonetheless, after World War II, large proportions of Indian children were still not enrolled in school. Since the 1960s growing pressure from Native Americans has produced improved schooling and higher levels of attendance although widespread complaints persist about the quality of education and the emphasis on a curriculum that either ignores or denigrates traditional Indian cultures. A chilling reality is that after the tenth grade, about 36 percent of Native American pupils drop out of school—a figure twice that of whites.

Native American children generally fall below national averages on standardized tests. At the third-grade level, they are about one year below the national average, and that margin increases to two years for high-school students. What factors produce this result? Researchers have indicated that the environment in which Indian children develop plays a major role. Frequently their families offer limited effective preparation for school performance; many Native American parents are illiterate or minimally educated and speak little or no English. In addition, communities in which Indian children live provide mixed messages about doing well in school and seeking success in "the white world" (Feagin and Feagin, 1993: 200–201; Fuchs and Havighurst, 1972: 118–135; Lomawaima, 1993; Schaefer, 1993: 170–171; Simpson and Yinger, 1985: 348–351).

Recent figures show that among people over age 25, Asian Americans obtain more schooling than any other major ethnic or racial group, including whites. In 1991 39.9 percent of Asian Americans completed four years of college or more while for whites the figure was 22.2 percent (U.S. Bureau of the Census, 1993, Table 233). In the following section, we examine a number of topics involving race and education.

Table 6.1 provides information about different groups' number of years of schooling.

Table 6.1   Whites' and Racial Minorities' Amount of Schooling

	NUMBER OF YEARS IN SCHOOL FOR PEOPLE AGED 25 OR MORE [1]	
	Less than 4 Years of High School	College Degree or More
Group		
Asian Americans	18.2%	39.1%
Whites	17.0	24.0
African Americans	26.2	13.2
Puerto Ricans	40.6	9.7
Mexican Americans	53.3	6.3

[1] Figures in this table are the most recent available—1995 for whites, 1994 for Mexican Americans and Puerto Ricans, and 1991 for Asian Americans.

Note: The higher a group appears in this table, the greater the proportion of the group with a college degree or additional education. Thus it is apparent that Asian Americans have been more successful in obtaining higher education than whites, who, in turn, have graduated a higher proportion from college than African Americans, Puerto Ricans, and Mexican Americans.

Source: U.S. Bureau of the Census. *Statistical Abstract of the United States: 1993,* Table 233; U.S. Bureau of the Census. *Statistical Abstract of the United States: 1996,* Table 241.

Controversial Issues in Minorities' Education: Racism or What?

Recall the two points about the relationship between education and internal colonialism raised at the beginning of the chapter. Racial minorities have traditionally been forced to perform menial, low-status work and also been labelled culturally inferior. Both issues frequently arise as we examine in this section racial minorities' access to education and organizational policies affecting schooling.

Opening the Gate: Racial Minorities' Access to Education

We analyze two policy topics here—affirmative action and school desegregation. People feel strongly about both areas and raise arguments to support their respective positions.

Affirmative Action in Education   Affirmative action is a government-supported directive requiring employers and schools to develop timetables and goals for increasing employment and educational opportunities for women and minorities. The roots of affirmative action appear in the Civil Rights Act of 1964, an executive order issued by President Lyndon Johnson in 1965, and a Labor Department statement produced in 1970.

Supporters of affirmative action stress that this policy is traditionally American, representing our culture's emphasis on equal opportunity by helping to remedy historical disadvantages suffered by racial minorities concerning access to education. One team of writers noted that until the Civil Rights Act of 1964, there was "a legally sanctioned and pervasive system of discrimination" against blacks and other racial minorities (Wigdor and Hartigan, 1990: 12). African Americans and other racial minorities are especially disadvantaged because, unlike many of the white immigrant groups arriving in the nineteenth and early twentieth centuries, they seek educational advancement in a highly competitive time period against majority group members whose educational preparation has often been better than theirs.

Affirmative action can offset some subtle racist practices, advocates emphasize. For example, interviewers for college or graduate programs might claim that certain personality factors are the basis for dismissing some minority candidates, but in many cases such observations are nothing but coded references to candidates' race.

A final point stressed by advocates is that goals and timetables for affirmative action are not rigid. Goals need not become quotas specifying that an exact number of a certain minority must enter an upcoming college class; affirmative action procedures are flexible guidelines but nonetheless should be taken seriously (Bergmann, 1997; Chideya, 1996).

Like proponents of affirmative action, opponents might begin by stressing that theirs is the traditionally American position because it emphasizes that individuals must succeed in a competitive situation on their own, without governmental intervention.

One issue opponents raise is that goals might not start out as quotas but that over time they inevitably harden into them, and a quota system favoring minority educational candidates represents reverse discrimination. Reverse discrimination, in fact, is the central concern expressed by opponents of affirmative action. They feel that this policy establishes two classes—those who benefit from affirmative action and those who do not. According to opponents, this arrangement presents two major problems. First, its two-part division is impractical. Why, for instance, should Chinese Americans and Japanese Americans, who in spite of discrimination have done very well educationally, benefit from affirmative action programs? On the other hand, what about poor white males? They are judged solely on the basis of their ethnicity and sex, and no consideration exists for the fact that they are just as clearly victims of poverty as members of racial minorities. Second, the system undermines the time-honored American tradition of judging people as individuals. Affirmative action reestablishes the infamous "separate but equal" doctrine of the *Plessy v. Ferguson* case (Blits and Gottfredson, 1990: 9–10). When people are judged as members of separate categories, opponents argue, inequality—in this case reverse discrimination—is inevitable.

Finally, opponents of affirmative action indicate that not even the supposed beneficiaries gain from it. Since members of racial minorities receive an unfair advantage, their qualifications will always be suspect, and they might even have some doubts themselves (D'Souza, 1996; Kekes, 1997).

In recent years affirmative action programs have come under increasing attack, with California's Proposition 209 calling for an end to racial and gender preferences in education, state hiring, and contracts (*Economist*, 1996: 27; *Economist*, 1997a). The California board of regents approved a ban on affirmative action in admissions to state colleges and universities, and in Texas the state attorney general made a similar ruling against affirmative action.

The first evidence of this policy shift appeared in law school admissions. At the University of California at Berkeley, law school admissions dropped from 20 black and 28 Latino students in the Class of 1999 to 1 black and 18 Latino members in the Class of 2000. At the University of Texas, the respective numbers were 31 blacks and 42 Latinos in the Class of 1999 and 3 black and 20 Hispanic students in the following class. "It's so stunning it's almost unbelievable," Marjorie Shultz, a Berkeley law professor, said.

> What do we think? The leading public university in the most diverse educational system is going to just withdraw behind some siege wall and be a white institution? It's preposterous. (Applebome, 1997a: 22)

In Texas, Rodney Ellis, a black state senator who used affirmative action to attend the acclaimed University of Texas Law School, was as surprised as Marjorie Shultz. "Never in my wildest dreams," said Ellis, "would I have believed the clock could be rolled back that far that quick." He added:

> I clearly got in through an affirmative action program, and I don't apologize for it. I'm proud of it. It got me in, but it didn't get me out, didn't take the bar exam for me, didn't pass the 285 or so pieces of legislation I've authored. (Applebome, 1997a: A14)

A similar pattern has developed for college students in the California state system. At the University of California at Berkeley, the most selective public university in the country, the number of African Americans, Hispanic Americans, and American Indians admitted as members of the class of 2002 compromised 10.4 percent of the total pool—less than half the 23.1 percent of the previous year. The University of California at Los Angeles displayed similar figures, with the freshman class of 2002 containing 12.7 percent minority representation, much lower than the 19.8 percent a year earlier (Bronner, 1998).

Lani Guinier, a professor of law at the University of Pennsylvania, raised an important issue in her analysis of affirmative action for law students. Like other participants in this discussion, Guinier recognized the reality raised by conflict theory—that affirmative action has been one way of resolving the task of allotting positions when there are more candidates than available slots. While having been a long-term supporter of affirmative action, Guinier indicated that she would be willing to discard affirmative action in law school admittance but that the replacement system should be different from the one currently in use.

Presently, Guinier indicated, the emphasis is on test scores from the Law School Admissions Test. Two difficulties arise from this approach, with the first being that family income seems to be the best predictor of higher scores. Students with higher scores are disproportionately from white, affluent families; furthermore, for each racial and ethnic group, the higher the family income, the higher the test scores, perhaps because greater affluence promotes better test-taking preparation and more exposure to such score-enhancing experiences as books and travel. The second difficulty involves the significance of these test scores. At best they show a modest relationship to success in law school and beyond. So what factor(s) truly predict success, with success defined by income, community involvement, and professional satisfaction?

One three-decade study suggested that the key factor might be a student's drive to succeed. If indeed this factor is a better predictor of excellence than test scores, then an improved procedure for obtaining excellent students might involve placing more emphasis on a student's drive to succeed and other seldom-measured qualities considered valuable than on test scores (Guinier, 1997).

For high-school students applying to the University of Texas at Austin and Texas A&M University, standardized tests—in this case the SATs—are no longer required.

Now the top 10 percent of a high-school class are automatically admitted, raising in March 1998 the percentage of eligible African Americans by 7 percent and Mexican Americans by 21 percent. Rural whites, who tend to score low on SATs, have also gained (Guinier, 1998).

Desegregation and Racial Equality   "It's great to watch the kids interact with such freedom, such abandon and such joy," said actor Roy Scheider, who helped to found a school where the students are racially and economically diverse. "This is normal for them. I wish that we adults could have the same feeling" (Herbert, 1997: A15). But what, in fact, are the benefits, if any, that students receive from integrated schooling? A review of the hundreds of studies on school desegregation suggested that modest gains in African Americans' performance on standardized tests and in school grades result from one to two years in interracial schools (Jaynes and Williams, 1989: 373–374).

Braddock, Crain, and McPartland (1984) contended that the narrow relationship between school desegregation and blacks' academic performance has received too much attention. They examined 10 major studies on the connection between segregation in schooling and segregation in other basic activities and concluded that besides short-term academic performance, segregated schooling affected students' lives in other important ways. Black students who attended integrated elementary or secondary schools were more likely to enroll in integrated colleges, to complete those programs, to have white social contacts and friends, to work in desegregated businesses, and to live in integrated housing areas. The researchers indicated that "[d]esegregation puts majorities and minorities together so that they can learn to coexist with one another, not so that they can learn to read" (Braddock, Crain, and McPartland, 1984: 260).

But integration must be carefully planned so that individual students are not likely to be negatively affected. Attending Alford J. Mapp, a previously all-white junior high school, Nathan McCall was the only African American in most of his classes. When he sat down in class, whites would get up and move away. The looks they gave each other made it crystal clear that they deeply resented his presence. The teachers were hardly any better, avoiding eye contact and refusing to acknowledge student hecklers. McCall wrote:

> It was too much for an eleven-year-old to challenge, and I didn't try. Instead, I tried to become invisible. I kept to myself, remained quiet during class discussions, and never asked questions in or after class. I kept my eyes glued to my desk, or looked straight ahead to avoid drawing attention to myself. I staggered, numb and withdrawn, through each school day and hurried from my last class, gym, without showering so that I wouldn't miss the only bus headed home. (McCall, 1994: 18–19)

Such isolation does not generally occur on integrated campuses. In fact, there are now enough African Americans as well as members of other racial minorities to produce their own organizations and social centers. At the University of California at Berkeley, where minorities compose 55 percent of the enrollment, racial and ethnic organizations are highly specialized. For instance, if students have the appropriate combination of racial or ethnic status and career interest, they can join the Asian Business Association, the Black Sociology Student Association, or the Hispanic Engineering Society. Strong differences of opinion exist about whether separation is desirable (DePalma, 1991). On campuses people debate whether a largely separate existence strengthens minority students' self-image and performance or fosters suspicion and antagonism among different racial and ethnic groups. Can members of college and university communities establish a middle ground, nurturing both the solidarity of individual racial and ethnic groups and relations across racial and ethnic lines?

Counseling might contribute to minorities' effective adjustment. One researcher, whose analysis focused on black males, suggested that counseling centers should examine the informal networks available to black male students and, when they are weak, seek to strengthen them; furthermore, when possible, counselors should act as advocates for these students in their relations with various agencies and groups on campus (Bonner, 1997).

Sometimes whites are critical of blacks for sticking together, particularly at campus dining tables. Those who make such criticisms often fail to consider that whites also tend to prefer members of their own race. Furthermore, were these critics to examine the situation further, they would learn that like whites blacks do not habitually sit next to any members of their own race: Like whites they too have preferences based on shared outlooks and interests (Hacker, 1992: 151).

Research has indicated that for African Americans optimal achievement results when they comprise at least 20 percent of the student body. With such a proportion, blacks have a fair-sized pool of friends as well as recognition and support from both students and the school administration (Hacker, 1992: 166). It is very different for a small number of minority students forced to face a nearly all-white school.

About 20 percent of African American students attend all-black colleges. One advantage is that given the less effective educational preparation often available to blacks, they are likely to rank higher academically at all-black colleges than at integrated campuses (Hacker, 1992: 151, 158). Such advantages, in turn, mean that students at all-black colleges are more likely to graduate and will obtain higher incomes than African Americans at predominantly white schools (Constantine, 1994; Love, 1993). Finally, some African American students want to immerse themselves in black culture and study with black students and teachers. This outlook is particularly strong among some middle-class black students who attended largely white high schools. A senior at Howard University, an elite black school, stated, "My white friends from high school tried to talk me out of going to Howard. But I'd never had a black man teach me before, and when it happened, it made me feel kind of proud" (Alterman, 1989: 63).

All-black colleges do have disadvantages. They tend to obtain less funding, possess fewer academic programs, and rank lower in prestige than their integrated counterparts (Hacker, 1992: 158), with finances, according to one study, the most potent source of students' stress (Launier, 1997). An additional issue considered at the beginning of this section involves the basic nature of segregated education—that graduates of all-black colleges are less effectively prepared than African Americans from mainstream schools to function in the wider society.

Gary Orfield, director of the Harvard Project on School Desegregation, has been concerned about maximizing the quality of minorities' education when integration was difficult or impossible to achieve. Perhaps the best course of action, the researchers found, was to remove many established faculty members from segregated schools and replace them with teachers dedicated to effectively educating low-income students in a racially segregated setting. If integration cannot be achieved, the investigators declared, then high-quality instruction should (Berkman, 1994).

Mott Hall, a school for gifted children in grades four through eight, has produced very high standards without integration. Located in Harlem (New York City) and possessing a student body that is 99 percent black and Latino, Mott Hall has consistently ranked among the most distinguished public schools in the city. While the school is woefully underprovided with books, computers, and space, it has a highly committed faculty, whose interviews play a significant role in evaluating students' likelihood of being successful at Mott Hall and beyond. Seventy percent of Mott Hall's graduates go to exclusive public schools in New York City, and many of the rest end up in the most elite boarding schools (Staples, 1997a).

Successful though Mott Hall's graduates are, one wonders whether their eventual transition to integrated schools is a comfortable one. For them, like minority students generally, the emphasis is on adjustment to the new school. Integration has traditionally been a one-way process, with minority students adjusting to the integrated settings into which they move. But would it not make sense, one educational researcher suggested, to use a different approach where "the views and experiences of both the dominant group and minority groups . . . meet, informing and transforming each other"? (Powell, 1997: 21). The contention is that our contemporary integrated schools need to do more than just absorb minority students. In addition, those students' ideas, perspectives, and goals should play a prominent role.

In such mainstream schools, to be sure, racism frequently thrives.

The Terrible Twins: Racism and Alienation in School Policy

Florence Grier, a Sacramento community organizer, expressed frustration about school desegregation, noting that her all-black neighborhood had lost its junior high school. She observed, "I'm so frustrated and disillusioned with the whole integration bit. A lot of mothers are beginning to complain. Because what are the kids getting? They can't read. I have people coming to me saying, 'Let's organize and bring our kids back here and demand quality education. Quality teachers' " (Blauner, 1989: 192).

As we have already noted, different opinions exist about the desirability of school desegregation, but everyone concerned about education recognizes the importance of high-quality schooling. Conditions that systematically prevent high-quality education for minority children are racist, or at least institutionally racist.

We examine two topics that involve race and racism and that significantly affect educational policy.

Minority Subcultures and Education The internal colonialist perspective emphasizes that dominant whites declare racial minorities' cultures inferior. As a specialist in curriculum and instruction and a frequent observer of urban teachers, Carl A. Grant became convinced that white, middle-class students entering the teaching profession often have an unconscious belief in the superiority of white, middle-class cultural standards. For example, Grant observed a sixth-grade teacher, who was providing a lesson on topic sentences, telling his class of primarily African American students that having heard rap music, he was convinced that it wouldn't help them learn the English needed to get and keep good jobs. Grant wrote:

> The students silently tuned out this teacher and whatever instruction he might have offered on topic sentences. Had he introduced the lesson by using the words from rap songs to write a paragraph, the students would have remained interested. (Grant, 1989: 766)

Language issues, of course, are central concerns for bilingual schools, some of which have been very successful. For instance, in New York City, Public School 84 has provided alternate-day immersion in Spanish and English for both Hispanic and non-Hispanic children. Language itself is not taught but learned through informal classroom activities encouraging social interaction (Morison, 1990). In the Rock Point school, located on a Navajo reservation, students encounter both languages in all grades, with children gradually exposed to increasing amounts of English to help prepare them for participation in the outside world. The amount of class time conducted in Navajo declines from about two-thirds in kindergarten to 10–15 percent in junior high and high school (Holm and Holm, 1990). Computer technology can aid such bilingual efforts. In one New Mexico school which the Zuni tribe controls, such computer innovations as interactive videodisc and hypertext technology have been successfully used to help children learn the Zuni language and obtain knowledge about the Zuni culture (*Futurist,* 1994).

Whether educators or not, Americans sharply disagree about racial minorities' right to seek cultural diversity in schools. Proponents suggest that keeping African American music or the Spanish language out of the curriculum represents a racist display—the assertion that these cultural traits are inferior. Opponents of cultural diversity disagree, saying that they are not being racist but simply focusing on elements of the mainstream culture.

Asian Americans' educational progress has hardly helped those arguing for cultural diversity. People of Asian Indian, Chinese, and Japanese heritage currently obtain higher percentages of high-school and college graduation, higher test scores, and more prestigious prizes (such as in the Westinghouse Science Talent Search to identify the top 40 science students in American high schools) than whites. These accomplishments have occurred with Asian American students "playing by the rules"—not insisting that educators consider their linguistic or cultural background. People who compare Asian Americans' and African Americans' academic accomplishments often conveniently overlook the fact that Asian Americans have distinct background advantages over African Americans, other racial minorities, and even many whites. Asian American students are more likely than whites to have had fathers that graduated from college, attained postgraduate degrees, and were employed in professional or managerial positions. Compared to whites, Asian American students have had higher educational expectations and aspirations and have been more likely to aspire to professional careers (Divoky, 1988; Wong, 1990).

Some researchers have argued that there are serious problems with an educational approach that makes no allowance for participants' varied cultural backgrounds. Janice Hale-Benson (1986) surveyed research on child development in Africa and black America and concluded that behavioral similarities suggest that African American children grow up in a culture rooted in African tradition and that when attending school, they must adjust to a very different, often contradictory set of demands.

Like Africans, Hale-Benson suggested, African Americans are born into an expressive cultural setting which emphasizes close, emotional contact. Use of language seems different in black culture. At home and in their communities, black children encounter a strong emphasis on black slang and on extensive nonverbal communication, and their entire language experience is built around the idea of relationship—children interacting with adults and other children in a vibrant, emotionally and physically active environment. They master this body of skills and then, suddenly, they enter schools that primarily require analytic more than relational skills, written more than verbal expression, and much more constricted physical movement. What's the result? They are likely to receive such labels as "learning disadvantaged" or "hyperactive" and are destined to fail in the school system.

Black students, in essence, often face an educational process that stresses culturally "foreign" methods of teaching. Consider how this can hamper learning. William F. Tate (1994), a college mathematics teacher, entered a classroom where a student teacher was working with five second-grade students—four white and one black. To illustrate the workings of addition, the teacher provided the following example: Joe has five pumpkin pies. Karen has six pumpkin pies. How many pumpkin pies do Joe and Karen have together? While the white children seemed excited about solving the problem, the black child sat quietly and seemed uninterested. Tate asked the teacher about the African American student's behavior. He's a good kid, the teacher replied. He just doesn't like math. Asked about using pumpkin pies in her example, the teacher replied that Thanksgiving was arriving in two weeks, and she wanted a problem related to their holiday experience. Let's find out, Tate suggested, whether pumpkin pie is, in fact, a part of all the children's Thanksgiving experience. They asked the children, and it turned out that the four white children were expecting to have pumpkin pie, but that for the black child, sweet-potato pie would be the dessert of the day. Thus he approached this math problem at a distinct cultural disadvantage. While at Thanksgiving dinner not all white children have pumpkin pie nor all black children sweet-potato pie, the operative point raised here should be clear.

Native American children's subcultural experiences might also affect their adjustment to mainstream schools. Some Indian students, for instance, have grown up with an emphasis on visual learning, and so they will find the inclusion of drawings, building models, and other "hands-on" activities helpful in the classroom. Native American children who go to school from reservations often have had limited contact with a western time system, and thus they find timed tests confusing and difficult. As with exposure to other culturally strange experiences, the best approach is to permit a gradual adjustment (Soldier, 1997).

The above illustrations are distinctly consistent with the principle of cultural inferiority contained in internal colonialism. Educators battle over this issue. Some focus on the supposedly oppressive Eurocentric nature of American schools while others feel that to succeed in mainstream society, a child must obtain both an appreciation and a knowledge of the dominant culture (Macedo, 1994; Ravitch, 1994).

In 1997 a controversy involving black subculture and education developed when the school board in Oakland, California, declared that the schools in its district should be able to use the so-called "black English" spoken in the segregated, inner-city areas of American cities. Advocates of using black English, which has become known as "Ebonics," argued that African American students would start their educational experience feeling more comfortable and more readily make the switch to standard English (Golden, 1997; Williams, 1997). A particularly disturbing element in the school board's statement was the claim that black English is "genetically based."

Nearly all prominent individuals and groups concerned with race and education disagreed with the Oakland school board's decision. Jesse Jackson condemned the proposal as "an unacceptable surrender bordering on disgrace" (*Economist*, 1997b: 27). A spokesperson for the Clinton administration indicated that the Oakland school board should have no expectation of using Ebonics as a means for obtaining funding for bilingual education. Psychologist Brent Staples described the school board's plan as "idiotic and racist" (Staples, 1997b: A30).

Staples added that any effort to use black English in the Oakland schools would propel middle-class families to leave the district. He wrote, "Imagine yourself a parent with the Oakland resolution in one hand, an application to private school in the other—and a streetwise teen-ager to educate. What would you do?" (Staples, 1997b: A30). Internal colonialism warns about the disparagement of minorities' subcultures, but, at the same time, policy makers must remain clear-minded about the workings of their society—in this case the role of standard English in obtaining success in the mainstream culture.

Leaks in the Pipeline At critical points in the educational pipeline, African American, Mexican American, Puerto Rican, and Native American students drop out. Smaller proportions of these groups than either whites or Asian Americans complete high school, enter college, complete college, enter graduate school, attain graduate degrees, and enter the teaching profession at all levels (Blackwell, 1989; Haberman, 1989; Lang, 1988). Marvel Lang, a specialist on minority participation in higher education, pointed out that while equal educational opportunity has been a national policy since the late 1960s, most primarily white colleges and universities did little until the 1980s to ensure equitable access and retention of black students. Lang noted:

> Thus, the burden of historic exclusory and discriminatory racial practices is still being felt by black students attending predominantly white institutions. In practice, too few black students are being enrolled and too few graduating from these institutions. (Lang, 1988: 8)

This position asserts that the failure of administrators at white-dominated colleges and universities to take necessary steps to recruit and graduate a substantial number of African American students represents a clear illustration of institutional racism.

Institutional racism in higher education is a major issue. In the past two decades, changing governmental policies toward educational aid have disproportionately affected racial minorities, notably African Americans. Between 1975 and 1986, outright grants as a percentage of total financial aid declined from 80 percent to 46 percent while loans increased from 17 percent to 50 percent of the financial aid package. For two reasons, the change has probably reduced African Americans' college-going chances more than whites'. First, the reduction in outright grants seems to have had a greater impact on African Americans, because at equal levels of family income, black families are more vulnerable to unemployment and have fewer sources of wealth (economic assets such as stocks, bonds, and real estate) than white families. Second, African Americans are less likely than whites of comparable family income to seek government loans for education. It is probable that a major factor contributing to this greater reticence is that African Americans perceive more economic vulnerability than whites. Because of the history of discrimination against them, their more limited chances of obtaining good jobs, and their smaller probability for promotion, they are less inclined than whites to take a chance and seek a government loan (Jaynes and Williams, 1989: 343). On the surface, federal government cuts in grants and increased emphasis on loans to college students would appear to be color-blind developments, but with a little investigation it becomes apparent that these funding cuts disproportionately discriminate against blacks and are thus another case of institutional racism.

A recent study involving Mexican Americans found that their college completion rate peaked with the second generation and then declined with the third generation. The researchers discovering this troubling pattern were not certain why it occurred, but they felt that a particularly significant contributor for second-generation college graduates might have been their parents' educational level—that the first generation's limited schooling influenced the second generation's willingness to intervene and oversee their children's education (Zsembik and Llanes, 1996).

Consider an additional condition encouraging leaks in the pipeline. When colleges and universities have a small proportion of minority faculty, an arid climate for minority attendance results for two reasons. First, since minority faculty members are among the major recruiters of minority students, their absence deprives a school of this important recruiting resource. In addition, minority students are less inclined to apply to a college with few minority faculty, because students recognize that such a school is no more than modestly committed to equal opportunity for minority groups (Epps, 1989: 24). Thus the following statistics are instructive. In American higher education, whites represent about 90 percent of the teaching force. Asian Americans comprise about 3.9 percent, African Americans about 1.7 percent, Hispanic Americans 1.7 percent, and Native Americans about 0.3 percent (Blackwell, 1989: 8).

To obtain college and university faculty positions, candidates often need doctorates. Recent figures about minorities' achievement in this area are also instructive and do not bode well for blacks. Between 1982 and 1992, the number of African Americans earning doctorates declined by 9 percent. In contrast, for Native Americans, Asian Americans, and Hispanic Americans, increases occurred—of 92 percent, 83 percent, and 41 percent, respectively. While it is difficult to know exactly why black achievement of doctorates has been declining, sociologist Elijah Anderson suggested that

> [t]here is a subtle backlash against affirmative action and special treatment. The result is a whole complicated series of things. But the fact is that there are very few mentors. And the fact is that young blacks have no real role models. (Manegold 1994: A14)

Without question, mentoring is a significant issue. James Blackwell (1989), a leading authority on the subject, indicated that mentoring is a process by which people of higher rank and achievement instruct and guide the intellectual or career development of less experienced individuals outside of classrooms. Through mentoring, students obtain extensive knowledge of the mentor's field and also receive emotional support and stimulation to consider entering the field. Mentoring—actually the lack of it—is relevant to black students from the moment they become involved in the educational process. A government official who regularly visited inner-city schools indicated that he rarely met a black male teacher, especially in elementary schools, and that teachers and administrators regularly reported to him that the absence of black male role models is a major contributor to young black males' educational failure (Brooks, 1994: 268).

Blackwell's impression is that faculty members seeking to become mentors often want to reproduce themselves, thus subconsciously or even consciously choosing individuals whose social characteristics, including race, ethnicity, and sex, are similar to their own (Blackwell, 1989: 11). With small or even tiny percentages of minority faculty at most colleges, minority students have little or no opportunity to benefit from the unique opportunity provided by mentoring.

Does the absence of mentoring represent racism? The answer, it seems, depends on one's perspective. Certainly it would be difficult to accuse a white person of racism because he or she chooses to serve as mentor to an individual who happens to be white. On the other hand, one can argue that the entire higher education structure is institutionally racist, continuously failing in various ways to offer equal opportunity (including mentoring) to racial minorities.

The good news about mentoring is that opportunities to promote it with children do exist. For example, Fitchburg State College in Massachusetts established a course in which students receive college credit for spending 60 hours working to improve a single individual's literacy skills. Like the college students, the tutees were ethnically and racially diverse, and they included elementary, middle-school, and high-school students. Results showed younger tutees developing more positive attitudes toward reading and writing, and high-school participants usually raising their grades and improving the quality of their homework. Tutees of all ages developed increased confidence in attempting literacy-related tasks. The strength of the relationships between tutor and tutee, which were key to the program's success, were apparent in the graduation ceremony. The program initiators wrote:

> The powerful bond that develops is evident in the words spoken and tears shed as tutors and tutees tell about their learning relationships and their mutual accomplishments. An atmosphere of shared pride in the attainments of all participants prevails. (Flippo et al., 1997: 646)

From discussing upper levels of education, we shift to the opposite end of the age continuum and finish the chapter with a crucial issue—alienation and race in minority children's education.

Ghosts in the Classroom

In this section we take a detailed look at how minority children suffer institutional racism in the schools and often become victims of a self-fulfilling prophecy designating them inferior. We also examine some more optimistic material concerning successful schools or programs educators, parents, and children have produced.

For minority children going to schools where the learning process is ineffective, the self-fulfilling prophecy is particularly relevant: It is hammered home to the majority of them that they are "disadvantaged"—that it is unlikely that they will do well in school and that, even if they do graduate from high school, there is little likelihood that they will be able to obtain good jobs. So, many of them begin to withdraw emotionally from life at school. They participate minimally in classroom activity, are barely known by their teachers, start skipping school, and eventually drop out entirely—in Nat Hentoff's haunting term, they become "ghosts" (Hentoff, 1989: 138).

Ineffective public education is a problem throughout the country, in the primarily white suburbs as well as the heavily minority inner-city areas, and inner cities contain white as well as minority students. However, the most overcrowded, poorly funded schools tend to have a high proportion of minority students. The least effective schooling is in the inner-city areas of the nation's 100 largest cities, where 24 percent of all students attend 1 percent of the schools and up to half of the teachers are unqualified to do their jobs (Goldberg, 1997). For these children the process of stereotyping most readily comes into play. Cultural inferiority and perhaps even limited intellectual capacity are reasons given for early failures in school. These children often become trapped in a self-fulfilling prophecy.

We consider some of the major components affecting the production of ghosts— physical structure of the school, parents' role, teaching policy, and, finally, the children themselves. Throughout the discussion we should realize that the possibility of reforming urban schools always exists. The first step toward changing schools, one educator noted, is that teachers and administrators must initiate conversation about what they want the school to become and what steps must be taken to attain that goal (Rallis and Zajano, 1997).

The Physical Structure of Schools It might be possible to produce effective schooling in almost any environment, but pleasant, spacious surroundings certainly help. Inner-city schools are often old, deteriorating buildings that look like fortresses, with chunks of missing ceiling; broken windows; nonfunctioning toilets; collapsing desks; outdated texts; chronic shortages of pencils, chalk, and erasers; and, inevitably, serious overcrowding (Hentoff, 1989: 141; Lukas, 1985: 100–102). One writer observed, "Students in those schools hardly get the sense that education is valued or that *they* are valued. And the same message, of course, is delivered to the parents" (Hentoff, 1989: 141). The physical structure, in short, can help convey a negative sense of self to students.

While destroying many current buildings and replacing them with smaller, brighter, less intimidating structures might be ideal, sometimes carefully planned, program-oriented changes can compensate for physical disadvantages. If school administrators in old buildings can put the structures in running order and provide teachers up-to-date books and other basic supplies, schools can be effective environments for learning. Rafael Hernandez School uses an early twentieth-century building in an inner-city neighborhood. It is a so-called "school of choice," to which parents from different parts of the greater Boston community can send their children. Given the age of the building and the neighborhood, one might suspect that it would be unpopular. Quite the opposite. Its highly successful program, where African American, Puerto Rican, and white children are thoroughly integrated in all programs and expected to learn both Spanish and English, has produced a waiting list of children from all three groups (Glenn, 1989).

Parents When minority parents examine their children's schools, they are likely to be deeply concerned but feel powerless to do anything to improve the situation. For instance, a black man who had been a school dropout in the South had come to New York City, where he had worked various menial jobs and was earning $90 a week. He had a daughter, and he was disturbed to see that each year her test scores were falling farther and farther behind the average for her age. He could visualize his daughter's future being as bleak as his own, and so in frustration he stood up at a Board of Education meeting to speak.

> The father stared at the variously attentive members of the school board. "You people," he said, "operate a goddamn monopoly, like the telephone company. I got no choice where I send my child to school. I can only send her where it's free. And she's not learning. Damn it, that's *your* responsibility, it's the principal's responsibility, it's the teacher's responsiblity, that she's not learning."
> There was no answer from the board.
> "When you fail, when everybody fails my child," the father's voice had become hoarse with grief and frustration, "what happens? Nothing. Nobody gets fired. Nothing happens to nobody except my child." (Hentoff, 1989: 142)

Since parents are not the ones most responsible for education, they seldom are the prime movers. However, they can make a positive contribution when a school is effective. One elementary school in Brooklyn now stays open into the early evenings. As a result, working parents who normally are unable to pick up their children come into the school and chat with the teachers. Because of the extra effort produced by school administrators and teachers, parents are also willing to make a greater commitment. Visiting the Brooklyn school, the state commissioner of education was very impressed. Partly as a result of this experience, he decided to launch a pilot project in which 10 elementary schools in poor areas would become year-round centers of education open from early in the morning into the evening seven days a week (Hentoff, 1989: 145).

Psychiatrist James P. Comer's program provides a similar approach. After 22 years of research with black and Puerto Rican children in inner-city New Haven schools, Comer became convinced that such children "are in foreign territory" and that teachers and administrators are seldom aware precisely how students' cultural backgrounds make their adjustment to school life difficult. In New Haven, Comer established an inner-city educational program in which parents can provide significant assistance to their children, becoming classroom aides or tutors or joining school governance committees. With parental participation, students' needs can be more effectively identified and addressed, and as a result children are more likely to feel a welcome part of the school and confident about their activities in school. In recent years Comer's program has become nationally recognized and has been adopted by over 100 schools in eight states (Marriott, 1990).

The key to Comer's program has been effective parental involvement. Sometimes the means of eliciting it is quite simple. At Rock Point, the Navajo school mentioned earlier, the fact that the Navajo language played a prominent part in the school demystified the education process for parents who could speak little or no English and made them much more likely to participate in school board activities or join parents' committees (Holm and Holm, 1990: 183).

Parents' attitudes toward schooling can promote their children's educational success. A study of intergenerational relations revealed that when Mexican American mothers had high aspirations for their daughters, their daughters had a positive sense of maternal support, and this sense of support encouraged both an optimistic outlook about the personal benefit of education and effective performance in school (Hernandez, Vargas-Lew, and Martinez, 1994).

For many minority parents, however, efforts to influence their children's approach to schooling fail to yield positive results. According to John O. Ogbu (1990), poor black parents stressing the importance of education to their children often find themselves confronted by the harsh realities of an oppressive world, making it difficult to convey this message. These parents emphasize that success in school is a prerequisite to success in modern society, but children often see little evidence of such success. They observe parents struggling with low-level jobs, underemployment, and unemployment, and in their children's presence, parents are likely to complain to friends and relatives about "the system" they are encouraging their children to enter. Meanwhile, in their neighborhoods, these young people learn about such survival strategies as stealing, drug dealing, and pimping: Norms supporting these strategies emphasize that success is possible without schooling, which is considered part of "the white man's thing" (Ogbu, 1990: 158–159).

Teaching Policy A key—one might argue *the* key—to effective education is teaching policy. A positive, student-supporting policy makes a good teacher more effective. For both the policy and the individual teacher, the goal is to provide children an opportunity to develop a positive self-image and the emotional and intellectual tools that permit them to be successful in the modern world. Educational policies frequently discriminate against minority children's pursuit of these goals.

In American public education, the "graded school" remains prominent. Students are expected to master a certain amount of material in a given year. Those who succeed are passed on to the next grade; those who don't will be held back. Since the widespread use of standardized tests began in the 1920s, the system of classification has become more precise: Testers can obtain numerical scores representing intelligence and achievement levels, and as a result students can be classified gifted, superior, average, below-average, defective, or dull. Because of general cultural or language backgrounds that have left them relatively unprepared to do well in the American education system, many minority group members tend to score lower on these tests than whites and thus receive the less exalted, more stigmatized labels. As one educator wrote, "Their labels . . . [become] badges—filed away in cumulative folders to follow them every step of the way through public school" (Cuban, 1989: 783). A self-fulfilling prophecy has been set in motion, and the impact for many minority students is negative.

But as Robert Rosenthal and Lenore Jacobson (1968) demonstrated, self-fulfilling prophecies can also produce positive results. The researchers conducted an experiment at Oak School, a public elementary school in a low-income section of a medium-sized city. The first step was to give all of the 650 children a standard nonverbal test of intelligence. Rosenthal and Jacobson told the teachers that the test would predict intellectual "blooming" or "spurting"—students' rapid intellectual growth. Then, at the beginning of the following year, each of the 18 teachers of grades one through six received names of students who would supposedly be bloomers in the year ahead. While the researchers claimed that the list of names reflected test results, names actually had been chosen at random. Thus, at first, differences between designated bloomers and the remaining children existed only in teachers' minds.

Eventually, however, teachers produced a self-fulfilling prophecy: They believed the bloomers were superior, treated them as such, and thereby encouraged superior performances from them. After a year these children scored higher on an IQ test than the other children. The difference was especially pronounced among first and second graders. While 19 percent of the regular children gained 20 or more IQ points, 47 percent of the "special" children produced such a gain. For the follow-up year, during which the supposed bloomers no longer had teachers who believed that they were superior, "special" first and second graders lost any advantage shown over their peers. The expected bloomers in grades three through six, however, showed higher scores compared to other children. Thus the impact of the self-fulfilling prophecy took effect more slowly on the older children but lasted longer.

A type of blooming unfolds in effective schools. Nat Hentoff, a well-known writer, visited Clara Barton High School in Brooklyn, where the school body is predominantly African American, Puerto Rican, and Asian American. He was immediately struck with the way the students carried themselves and spoke, especially to their teachers. Hentoff indicated that at Clara Barton

> students looked directly at the teachers when they talked, and whether they were joking or in serious negotiation about an assignment, they were fully involved in the conversation. Their bearing showed considerable self-respect, not arrogance. They were comfortable with themselves, and so they were with others, including adults. (Hentoff, 1989: 137)

A consistent educational policy occurs in the Rafael Hernandez School, which was mentioned earlier. Throughout this school, children of diverse racial, ethnic, and linguistic backgrounds are expected to develop verbal and written proficiency in both Spanish and English. By state law the school can exempt from state testing those students who require bilingual education or special education services, but because of its policy emphasizing students sharing all activities, school officials have not done it. As a result the average test scores are fairly low, but the children are thriving emotionally and intellectually, building an understanding of each others' cultural backgrounds and all three major groups—African Americans, Puerto Ricans, and whites—finding their own cultural experiences objects of positive, thorough inquiry, with no students feeling stigmatized or isolated (Glenn, 1989).

Effective teaching requires commitment. A veteran of 29 years instructing inner-city children explained that "a teacher needs to remember only one thing: when the classroom door is closed and it's just you and them, give your students who you are and what you know. All of it. Not half. Not some. Everything" (Glasser, 1997: 505).

Students: Ghostlike or Alive? In sociology, a prominent concept related to socialization is Charles Horton Cooley's **looking-glass self**—the idea that individuals' understanding of what sort of person they are is based on how they think they appear to others. Members of racial minorities in inner-city schools have often received limited positive response from teachers, and thus their sense of self as students is diminished.

In ineffective schools most class time involves teachers' telling students what to do. For many inner-city students, like Alicia in an all-black Harlem school, classroom knowledge becomes something to which they do not relate. Alicia said, "I'm wise, not smart. I knows what people are thinkin' and what's goin' down, but not what he be talkin' about in history" (Fine, 1985: 47).

Once Hentoff read and discussed poetry with the primarily minority group children in an inner-city high school, acting against the advice of the regular teacher, who had explained that the children weren't interested in reading. At the end he was approached by an extremely shy young woman who asked if he could tell her something more about this Emily Dickinson. Later she told Hentoff that while it was weird, she felt some of the same things that Emily Dickinson had felt so long ago. Then, very hesitantly, she handed Hentoff some of her poems, indicating that she had never shown them to anyone because she had suspected that nobody would believe she could write poetry. It was the first time that anyone in the classroom had communicated with this young woman in a way that suggested the possibility of interest in her work and, as a result, drew her out of the ghost world.

John Simon is a teacher who regularly accomplishes such tasks. He has taken tough, often delinquent, inner-city, primarily minority group children and turned them into effective readers, writers, and even college students. Simon indicated that there is nothing special about his approach. It is neither revolutionary, nor does it require a charismatic personality, but it does take time. Simon told Hentoff:

> First of all, . . . you have to listen. When I start working with a child I don't know too well, I spend a lot of time listening to him before I try to suggest a course of study. I have never fallen in with that dumb notion that you have to start "teaching" from the very first day of class—as if teaching is something that happens in a vacuum without having to take account of where each student is, in his head, on that first day. (Hentoff, 1989: 145)

Such an approach not only provides useful practical information to teachers about their students, but it has the added value of reflecting back to the child an enhanced sense of personal worth as the teacher acknowledges the worthiness of what the child says.

The Georgia Institute of Technology (Georgia Tech), in essence, has grappled with the looking-glass-self issue. In the 1970s this engineering school developed several programs to assist minority students' development of math and science skills as well as their social adjustment. While these efforts helped produce less isolated and better adjusted black and Hispanic students, they did little to improve their academic performance or to keep them in school. The problem, according to President John Patrick Crecine, was that "[i]n the past we told them they were dumb, that they needed fixing, and we had them in remedial programs" (Smothers, 1994: A21). As the looking-glass-self concept suggests, the students were affected by the negative image imposed on them; often their behavior supported that image.

In 1989 the program was changed, making it a five-week mandatory introduction for all minority students. Now they take five demanding weeks of freshman math and chemistry with the same professors they will have in the fall, along with the option of a freshman psychology course to lighten the fall load. Perhaps most notable is the spirit of the program. Desi Bellamy, a senior from Athens, Georgia, said that its main strength "made it cool to be smart." He added, "You don't get the sense that they believe you need remediation coming in. And they tell you that you are the best of the best" (Smothers, 1994: A21).

With the looking-glass-self process altered, the results have been indisputable. Minority students' grade-point average has risen from 2.5 to 3.0, and retention has risen to nearly 100 percent. The results have been so dramatic that two other engineering colleges in the area have developed their own two-week program, and Georgia Tech will soon require a similar course of study for all entering freshmen.

Another prominent issue in modern urban education is children's home language. About one in seven of the nation's 5- to 17-year-olds speaks a home language other than English, and these students, who often enter school with limited English proficiency, are concentrated in cities in California, New York, Texas, Florida, Illinois, New Jersey, and the rural Southwest. Research done at eight successful schools for minority-language students in grades four through eight indicated that the best way to eliminate these students' linguistic disadvantage is to instruct them in science, social science, math, and language arts in their native languages and then provide language and academic support when they are later mainstreamed into all-English classes. This approach opposes the traditional stance that children's first task is to learn English and that all other subjects should remain on hold until they do so. That approach is dangerous, putting these students at an academic disadvantage that they might never overcome (Minicucci et al., 1995).

Some teachers effectively fight the stigma of racism. Now how does one bottle the prescription for eliminating ghosts in the modern classroom?

Conclusion

Martin Haberman (1997), a specialist on urban schools, has concluded that before teachers can begin transmitting positive values to their students, they must stop supporting negative, anti-work values that currently pervade the schools. Prevailing standards include handing out passing grades for simply showing up; an authoritarian style convincing students that teachers and administrators are in complete control; a setting where absence, nonperformance, or slovenly performance is tolerated as long as students provide doctors' or other "good" excuses; and the influence of peers who are often violent and opposed to constructive participation in school activities. The central reality of inner-city schools, Haberman argued, is a clash of socialization techniques. Will the values that lead to success in the mainstream dominate, or will the harsh, authoritarian values of modern inner-city schools prevail? At present, unfortunately, there is no contest.

But teachers, administrators, and students can turn the situation around. What's necessary is a full-fledged attack on the negative values and other debilitating characteristics. Officials at Boston's Lewenberg Middle School made such an attack. During the 1960s and 1970s, white flight occurred in the school's district, and minority families moved in. With a declining economic base in the locale, funding fell sharply. The school grounds deteriorated, with overgrown bushes giving cover to muggers, and the school property became a dumping place for old car batteries, appliances, and assorted junk. Inside the building, teachers struggled with discipline problems and parental nonsupport. Each year standardized test scores dropped. By 1983 Boston education officials considered closing down Lewenberg and sending children to schools in safer neighborhoods.

Then in 1984 Thomas O'Neill, a 14-year veteran of the Boston public schools, became Lewenberg's new principal. O'Neill's first act was to mobilize staff and parents to clean up the school yard, cut down the overgrown bushes, and plant flowers and trees. When the central office would not pay for the purchase of trees, O'Neill and his parent/teacher organization held fund drives to raise money. Because of the use of free labor, the custodians' union objected to the beautification program, sometimes threatening O'Neill and his family with bodily harm. O'Neill and his associates persisted, however, and the grounds are now very attractive. Furthermore, using materials donated by local merchants, O'Neill and a team of parent and staff volunteers have transformed much of the building, providing a reading and study area in the main foyer, an attractive kitchen, a small cafeteria, and a renovated gym.

The school's transformation, however, has been much more than physical. Members of the Lewenberg school community would appreciate Haberman's criticism of most inner-city schools' dominant standards. Instead of focusing on negative values, teachers in each classroom display a list of agreements. All members of the classroom will seek together; agree to work together to achieve individual and group goals; agree to give and receive honest feedback and to listen and learn; and agree not to devalue others or themselves and to keep all activities physically and emotionally safe.

The list of agreements resonates throughout the school. Instead of ordinary physical education, all children are expected to develop mountain-climbing skills. Not only do they learn the basics of rock climbing, but they overcome fear and self-doubt and acquire abilities that promote confidence and self-worth. As they assist each other, they develop trust, particularly trust in their teachers—a condition often missing with the adults in their personal lives.

In many classroom activities, where the emphasis is on pooling skills and talents, Lewenberg students learn to work well together, "discover[ing] that they can accomplish more than they ever dreamed possible" (O'Donnell, 1997: 512). What in the middle 1980s was a failing school has been turned around, with many graduates accepted in Boston's most prestigious high schools or provided scholarships to area private schools.

Discussion Questions

1. Consider the impact of institutional racism on American public education.
2. Comment on the direction in which affirmative action in education is currently headed.
3. If you were on a committee involved with school desegregation in a nearby city, what steps would you advocate?
4. What is your dominant personal position about minority subcultures and education?

5. Discuss leaks in the pipeline, providing any specific information you have obtained from people you know or from reading material.

6. If you were the local superintendent of schools, what specific policies would you establish to combat ghosts in the classroom?

Sources

Alterman, Eric. 1989. "Black Universities in Demand and in Trouble." *New York Times Magazine* (November 5): 60–63+.

Applebome, Peter. 1997a. "Affirmative Action Bar Transforms Law School." *New York Times* (July 2): A14.

Applebome, Peter. 1997b. "Minority Law School Enrollment Plunges in California and Texas." *New York Times* (June 28): 1+.

Armor, David J. 1989. "After Busing: Education and Choice." *Public Interest* (Spring): 24–37.

Bailyn, Bernard, et al. 1977. *The Great Republic.* Lexington, MA: D.C. Heath.

Bergmann, Barbara R. 1997. "Selections from *In Defense of Affirmative Action.*" *Academe* 83 (January-February): 29–34.

Berkman, Harvey. 1994. "Professor Studies, Acts on Equality/Reality Gap." *National Law Journal* (May 23): A12.

Blackwell, James E. 1989. "Mentoring: An Action Strategy for Increasing Minority Faculty." *Academe* 75 (September-October): 8–14.

Blauner, Bob. 1989. *Black Lives, White Lives.* Berkeley: University of California Press.

Blits, Jan H., and Linda S. Gottfredson. 1990. "Equality or Lasting Inequality?" *Society* 27 (March/April): 4–11.

Bonner, Wendell W. 1997. "Black Male Perspectives of Counseling on a Predominantly White University Campus." *Journal of Black Studies* 27 (January): 395–408.

Braddock, Jomills Henry, II, Robert L. Crain, and James S. McPartland. 1984. "A Long-Term View of School Desegregation: Some Recent Studies of Graduates as Adults." *Phi Delta Kappan* 66 (December): 259–264.

Branch, Taylor. 1988. *Parting the Water: America in the King Years 1954-63.* New York: Simon and Schuster.

Bronner, Ethan. 1998. "Black and Hispanic Admissions Off Sharply at U of California." *New York Times* (April 1): A1+.

Brooks, William C. 1994. "Black Males in the Work Force in the Twenty-First Century," pp. 263–270 in Richard G. Majors and Jacob U. Gordon (eds.), *The American Black Male: His Present Status and His Future.* Chicago: Nelson-Hall Publishers.

Celis, William, III. 1996. "40 Years after Brown, Segregation Persists," pp. 164–167 in John A. Kromkowski (ed.), *Race and Ethnic Relations 96/97,* 6th ed. Guilford, CT: Dushkin Publishing Group.

Chideya, Farai. 1996. "Ivory Towers: The African-American College and University Experience," pp. 304–315 in Richard C. Monk (ed.), *Taking Sides: Clashing Views on Controversial Issues in Race and Ethnicity,* 2nd ed. Guilford, CT: Dushkin Publishing Group.

Coleman, James S., et al. 1966. *Equality of Educational Opportunity.* Washington, DC: U.S. Government Printing Office.

Coleman, James S., et al. 1982. *High School Achievement.* New York: Basic Books.

Constantine, Jill M. 1994. "The 'Added Value' of Historically Black Colleges." *Academe* 80 (May/June): 12–17.

Cuban, Larry. 1989. "The 'At-Risk' Label and the Problem of Urban School Reform." *Phi Delta Kappan* 70 (June): 780–784+.

DePalma, Anthony. 1991. "Separate Ethnic Worlds Grow on Campus." *New York Times* (May 18): 1+.

Divoky, Diane. 1988. "The Model Minority Goes to School." *Phi Delta Kappan* 70 (November): 219–222.

Douglass, Frederick. 1968. *Narrative of the Life of Frederick Douglass.* New York: Signet Books. Originally published in 1845.

D'Souza, Dinesh. 1996. "The Failure of 'Cruel Compassion,' " pp. 316–320 in Richard C. Monk (ed.), *Taking Sides: Clashing Views on Controversial Issues in Race and Ethnicity,* 2nd ed. Guilford, CT: Dushkin Publishing Group.

Economist. 1996. "Not Over till It's Over." 341 (November 16): 27.

Economist. 1997a. "Ward Connerly's Trumpet Blast." 342 (March 29): 34.

Economist. 1997b. "The Ebonics Virus." 342 (January 4): 26–27.

Epps, Edgar R. 1989. "Academic Culture and the Minority Professor." *Academe* 75 (September-October): 23–26.

Feagin, Joe R., and Clairece Booher Feagin. 1993. *Racial and Ethnic Relations,* 4th ed. Englewood Cliffs, NJ: Prentice-Hall.

Fine, Michelle. 1985. "Dropping Out of High School: An Inside Look." *Social Policy* 16 (Fall): 43–50.

Fiss, Irene. 1989. "Why Cold Spring School?"

Fitzpatrick, Joseph P. 1987. *Puerto Rican Americans: The Meaning of Migration to the Mainland,* 2nd ed. Englewood Cliffs, NJ: Prentice-Hall.

Flippo, Rona F., et al. 1997. "Creating a Student Literacy Corps in a Diverse Community." *Phi Delta Kappan* 78 (April): 644–646.

Fuchs, Estelle, and Robert J. Havighurst. 1972. *To Live on This Earth: American Indian Education.* Garden City, NY: Doubleday & Company.

Fuentes, Luis. 1994. "Educating Puerto Ricans in the U.S.: The Struggle for Equity." *Equity and Excellence in Education* 27 (April): 16–19.

Futurist. 1994. "Tribes Go High Tech." 28 (January/February): 48–49.

Glasser, Perry. 1997. "Not Half, Not Some." *Phi Delta Kappan* 78 (March): 504–505.

Glenn, Charles L. 1989. "Just Schools for Minority Children." *Phi Delta Kappan* 70 (September): 777–779.

Goldberg, Mark F. 1997. "Maintaining a Focus on Child Development." *Phi Delta Kappan* 78 (March): 557–559.

Golden, Tim. 1997. "Oakland Scratches Plan to Teach Black English." *New York Times* (January 14): A10.

Grant, Carl A. 1989. "Urban Teachers: Their New Colleagues and Curriculum." *Phi Delta Kappan* 70 (June): 764–770.

Guinier, Lani. 1998. "An Equal Chance." *New York Times* (April 23): A25.

Guinier, Lani. 1997. "The Real Bias in Higher Education." *New York Times* (June 24): A19.

Haberman, Martin. 1989. "More Minority Teachers." *Phi Delta Kappan* 70 (June): 771–776.

Haberman, Martin. 1997. "Unemployment Training: The Ideology of Nonwork Learned in Urban Schools." *Phi Delta Kappan* 78 (March): 499–503.

Hacker, Andrew. 1992. *Two Nations: Black and White, Separate, Hostile, Unequal.* New York: Charles Scribner's Sons.

Hale-Benson, Janice E. 1986. *Black Children: Their Roots, Culture, and Learning Styles,* Rev. ed. Baltimore: Johns Hopkins University Press.

Hentoff, Nat. 1989. "Anonymous Children/Diminished Adults." *Proceedings of the Academy of Political Science* 37: 137–148.

Herbert, Bob. 1997. "Let Down the Barriers." *New York Times* (May 19): A15.

Hernandez, Arthur, Linda Vargas-Lew, and Cynthia L. Martinez. 1994. "Intergenerational Academic Aspirations of Mexican-American Females: An Examination of Mother, Daughter, and Grandmother Triads." *Hispanic Journal of Behavioral Sciences* 16 (May): 195–204.

Hinds, Michael deCourcy. 1994. "Judge Orders Desegregation of Schools in Philadelphia." *New York Times* (February 5): 6.

Hirschman, Charles, and Morrison G. Wong. 1986. "The Extraordinary Educational Attainment of Asian-Americans: A Search for Historical Evidence and Explanations." *Social Forces* 65 (September): 1–27.

Holm, Agnes, and Wayne Holm. 1990. "Rock Point: A Navajo Way to Go to School: A Valediction." *Annals of the American Academy of Political and Social Science* 508 (March): 170–184.

Hsia, Jayjia. 1988. *Asian Americans in Higher Education and at Work.* Hillsdale, NJ: Lawrence Erlbaum Associates.

Inniss, Leslie. 1993. "School Desegregation: Too High a Price?" *Social Policy* 24 (Winter): 6–16.

Jaynes, Gerald David, and Robin M. Williams, Jr. 1989. *A Common Destiny: Blacks and American Society.* Washington, DC: National Academy Press.

Kekes, John. 1997. "Against Preferential Treatment." *Academe* 83 (January-February): 35–37.

Lang, Marvel. 1988. "The Black Student Retention Problem in Higher Education: Some Introductory Perspectives," pp. 3–11 in Marvel Lang and Clinita A. Ford (eds.), *Black Student Retention in Higher Education.* Springfield, IL: Charles C. Thomas.

Launier, Raymond A. 1997. "Stress Balance and Emotional Life Complexes in Students in a Historically African American College." *Journal of Psychology* 131 (March): 175–186.

Lomawaima, K. Tsianina. 1993. "Domesticity in the Federal Indian Schools: The Power of Authority over Mind and Body." *American Ethnologist* 20 (May): 227–240.

Love, Barbara J. 1993. "Issues and Problems in the Retention of Black Students in Predominantly White Institutions of Higher Education." *Equity & Excellence in Education* 26 (April): 27–36.

Lukas, J. Anthony. 1985. *Common Ground.* New York: Alfred A. Knopf.

Macedo, Donaldo. 1994. "English Only: The Tongue-Tying of America," pp. 135–144 in Richard C. Monk (ed.), *Taking Sides: Clashing Views on Controversial Issues in Race and Ethnicity.* Guilford, CT: Dushkin Publishing Group.

Manegold, Catherine S. 1994. "Fewer Men Earn Doctorates, Particularly among Blacks." *New York Times* (January 18): A14.

Marriott, Michel. 1990. "A New Road to Learning: Teaching the Whole Child." *New York Times* (June 13): A1+.

McCall, Nathan. 1994. *Makes Me Wanna Holler: A Young Black Man in America.* New York: Random House.

Minicucci, Catherine, et al. 1995. "School Reform and Student Diversity." *Phi Delta Kappan* 77 (September): 77–80.

Molnar, Alex. 1993. "Facing the Racial Divide." *Educational Leadership* 50 (May): 58–59.

Morison, Sidney H. 1990. "A Spanish-English Dual-Language Program in New York City." *Annals of the American Academy of Political and Social Science* 508 (March): 160–169.

New York Times. 1994. "Gender Gap Continues to Close on S.A.T.'s." (August 25): A12.

O'Donnell, Mark D. 1997. "Boston's Lewenberg Middle School Delivers Success." *Phi Delta Kappan* 78 (March): 508–512.

Ogbu, John U. 1990. "Minority and Literacy in Comparative Perspective." *Daedalus* 119 (Spring): 141–168.

Powell, John A. 1997. "Is Racial Integration Essential to Achieving Quality Education for Low-Income Minority Students, In the Short Term? In the Long Term?," pp. 19–22 in John A. Kromkowski (ed.), *Race and Ethnic Relations 97/98,* 7th ed. Guilford, CT: Dushkin Publishing Group.

Rallis, Sharon F., and Nancy C. Zajano. 1997. "Keeping the Faith until the Outcomes Are Obvious." *Phi Delta Kappan* 78 (May): 706–709.

Rose, Peter I. 1997. *They and We: Racial and Ethnic Relations in the United States,* 5th ed. New York: McGraw-Hill Companies.

Rosenthal, Robert, and Lenore Jacobson. 1968. *Pygmalion in the Classroom.* New York: Holt, Rinehart and Winston.

Ravitch, Diane. 1994. "Politicization and the Schools: The Case of Bilingual Education," pp. 126–134 in Richard C. Monk (ed.), *Taking Sides: Clashing Views on Controversial Issues in Race and Ethnicity.* Guilford, CT: Dushkin Publishing Group.

Rossell, Christine H. 1988. "Is It Busing or the Blacks?" *Urban Affairs Quarterly* 24 (September): 138–148.

Rothenberg, Paula S. (ed.). 1988. *Racism and Sexism: An Integrated Study.* New York: St. Martin's Press.

Schaefer, Richard. 1993. *Racial and Ethnic Groups,* 5th ed. New York: HarperCollins.

Simpson, George Eaton, and J. Milton Yinger. 1985. *Racial and Cultural Minorities.* 5th ed. New York: Plenum Press.

Smothers, Ronald. 1994. "To Raise the Performance of Minorities, a College Increased Its Standards." *New York Times* (June 29): A21.

Soldier, Lee Little. 1997. "Is There an Indian in Your Classroom? Working Successfully with Urban Native American Students." *Phi Delta Kappan* 78 (April): 650–653.

Staples, Brent. 1997a. "The Battle for 'Gifted' Education." *New York Times* (May 3): 22.

Staples, Brent. 1997b. "The Last Train from Oakland." *New York Times* (January 24): A30.

Tate, William F. 1994. "Race, Retrenchment, and the Reform of School Mathematics." *Phi Delta Kappan* 75 (February): 477–480+.

U.S. Bureau of the Census. *Statistical Abstract of the United States: 1993*, 113th ed. Washington, DC: U.S. Government Printing Office.

Wigdor, Alexandra K., and John A. Hartigan. 1990. "The Case for Fairness." *Society* 27 (March/April): 12–16.

Wilkerson, Isabel. 1988. " 'Separate and Unequal': A View from the Bottom." *New York Times* (March 1): A12.

Williams, Robert L. 1997. "The Ebonics Controversy." *Journal of Black Psychology* 23 (August): 208–214.

Wong, Morrison G. 1990. "The Education of White, Chinese, Filipino, and Japanese Students: A Look at 'High School and Beyond.' " *Sociological Perspectives* 33 (Fall): 355–374.

Zsembik, Barbara A., and Daniel Llanes. 1996. "Generational Differences in Educational Attainment among Mexican Americans." *Social Science Quarterly* 77 (June): 363–374.

CHAPTER 7

All God's Children?
Minority Families

On January 25, 1986, Bill Moyers, a well-known newsman, hosted a prime-time, two-hour CBS Special Report titled *The Vanishing Black Family—Crisis in Black America*. Viewers were taken into a Newark, New Jersey, housing project for an intimate look at the supposed crisis in the modern African American family. They saw black teenage welfare mothers with their babies and children, with young fathers sometimes located on the fringe. When asked about their lives, some conceded that if it weren't for welfare, they wouldn't keep having children. One young man who had fathered six children by four women and supported none of them said, "So what I'm not doing the government does." While interviewing, Moyers generally appeared reasoned and nonjudgmental, but several times statements seemed to bring him close to losing his temper (Corry, 1986).

Jewell Handy Gresham suggested that beyond the already well-established conclusion that poor African American families have significant problems, two themes emerged. First, "a picture of 'jungle' immorality and degeneracy" was reinforced. Middle-class white viewers could look with horrified fascination at these young blacks and conclude that they were alien and inferior. Second, there seemed to be such "pervasive pathology" that it appeared no intervention could realistically alter the situation. Contributing to this conclusion was a significant omission—the failure to consider the economic and political sources of family crisis among poor blacks. The difficulty, Moyers and others on the program suggested, lay within the African American family itself. At the end of the program, an older African American woman delivered the clincher when she said, "If Martin Luther King were alive, he would not be talking about the things I think he was talking about—labor and all that. He would be talking about the black family" (Gresham, 1989: 119).

For many observers of race and poverty in the United States, this CBS program produced a powerful sense of *dèjá vu*. In this chapter we see that a celebrated 1965 government-sponsored report offered similar conclusions. Neither then nor now have the facts cited about the black family been incorrect. To be sure, statistics and studies indicate that serious problems of poverty and fragmentation exist. An effective sociological approach, however, needs to provide a thorough analysis of the sources of these problems.

Treatises that focus on the degenerate quality of black or other minority group families are racist in the tradition described by internal colonialism since they emphasize the cultural inferiority of blacks' family structure and fail to propose practical economic programs that would alleviate the problems. Recall a point raised in the discussion of institutional racism in Chapter 1: that the primary source of challenge for poor black families has been members' increasing difficulty since the early 1960s to obtain jobs that could maintain a family. The second major part of this chapter indicates that racism lies in both the dominant culture's outlook on racial minorities' families and in the steps taken to overcome crises associated with them.

But before confronting these issues, we briefly examine the history of minority group families, which begins to reveal why current problems exist.

History of Racial Minorities' Families in the United States

Slaves could not enter into binding contractual relationships, and since marriage is a contract, so-called "slave marriages" were not marriages in a legal sense. These arrangements required masters' approval, and masters could also dissolve them. Masters preferred marriages between their own slaves. The primary reason masters encouraged these unions was to perpetuate the slave population, and an owner considered it a waste if his male slave impregnated a woman on another plantation. In addition, if slave marriages involved workers on different plantations, then valuable working time was lost as slaves spent time away from their home plantations. Thus slaves were encouraged to marry individuals on their own plantations, and when this was not possible, masters often sought to purchase the spouse or sell their slave to the spouse's owner.

Frequently slaveholders' economic situation, such as bankruptcy or the need for funds, promoted the sale of a slave spouse or child. However, even some owners who were indifferent to slaves' interest felt that if the family stayed intact, the male slave would remain concerned about his family's welfare and be less inclined to rebel or attempt to escape.

The bearing of children was particularly difficult for slave women, who had little or no medical care during pregnancy, childbirth, and afterwards. Furthermore, they were required to work up to the moment they gave birth. During the week before childbirth, pregnant women picked three-quarters as much cotton as slave women of the same age who were neither pregnant nor nursing. Not suprisingly, over half of slave infants died during the first year—about twice the mortality rate for southern white infants. Survivors received little care from mothers, who were kept busy in the fields or household. Until the age of 14, the death rate for slave children remained twice that of white children. In spite of brutal conditions, slave mothers did what they could to stabilize the family, and its division was fiercely resisted. J. W. Loguen's mother, for instance, had to be tied to a loom when her children were taken from her to be sold.

Men also encountered many restrictions in slave families. Unlike free men, they could not economically support or protect their families. Frequently masters physically or sexually abused their slave wives, and a husband's effort to intervene invariably produced dire consequences, perhaps even death. In spite of the danger, slave narratives indicate that husbands intervened on behalf of their wives many times.

During the slave era, there were about half a million free blacks. Because they could own property and enter a variety of jobs, including skilled positions, their economic prospects were fairly good and their families tended to be stable. While some of them owned slaves, most of the men were former slaves who had purchased their wives and children. From this group the African American middle class began to develop.

In the late nineteenth century, racial discrimination made it difficult for most black men to find jobs. For black women, however, fewer restrictions existed, and so even though it was considered a mark of slavery for them to work, many did. In 1900 about 41 percent of African American women were in the labor force, compared to 16 percent of white women. Recent research indicates that the discriminatory pressures applied to southern black families did contribute to higher levels of nonmarital childbearing, less tendency to marry, and greater marital instability and disruption for black than for white families (Franklin and Moss, 1988: 127–128; Genovese, 1994; Johnson, 1989: 53–54; Pagnini and Morgan, 1997; Staples, 1984: 218–221). At all income levels, African Americans have endorsed stable, self-sufficient families (Furstenberg, Morgan, Moore, and Peterson, 1987; Parker and Kleiner, 1977).

For African American families, the impact of racism has extended beyond the economic dimension into the psychological arena. Writing about the middle-class black family in the post–World War II era, E. Franklin Frazier indicated that sometimes these parents tried to shield their young children from awareness of segregation in various public facilities, including schools. Frazier concluded that because of the persistence of racism, "the children of the black bourgeoisie can not escape the mark of oppression" (Frazier, 1957: 214).

Frazier's study of the black bourgeoisie is a prominent example of African Americans' long tradition of research on their own racial group—research that has often featured the black family. From W. E. B. DuBois's (1967) *The Philadelphia Negro*, which was originally published in 1899, this tradition extends to Andrew Billingsley's (1968) work and the current writings of Robert Staples (1994) and Charles V. Willie (1991, 1993).

Like blacks, Native Americans were the victims of whites' racism, which also drastically altered their family life. The Native Americans early settlers encountered often had considerable tolerance for diverse forms of marriage. Monogamy, polygyny (one man with two or more wives), and polyandry (one woman with two or more husbands) were all acceptable forms of marriage in many societies. Generally polyandry occurred because of unusual circumstances, such as the crippling of an older brother, encouraging that man's wife to form an additional marriage with her husband's younger brother, who then served as her chief means of economic support. Polygyny, on the other hand, was fairly common, with more than 20 percent of the Indians of the Great Plains and the Pacific coast engaging in the practice.

Another significant difference between Native Americans and whites was their relationship to the kinship structure, with this factor playing a much larger part in Indians' lives. When Native Americans married, the union was more a contract between two kinship groups (clans) than between two people. In addition, the type of kinship system determined significant relatives in an individual's life. The Crow, Hopi, and Choctaw Indians had a matrilineal system, in which people traced descent through the mother's kinship structure and the mother's relatives were recipients of prominent obligations and rights. Thus, within this system, a boy's father was not considered a significant relative. His mother's brother was his source of discipline and instruction, and this man provided food, clothes, shelter, and eventually an inheritance.

When European settlers encountered Indians, they readily adopted an internal colonialist standard, designating their customs barbaric and inferior, seldom taking them seriously, and thus not understanding why Native Americans continued to follow cultural patterns that were distinctly non-European. For instance, nineteenth-century missionaries, teachers, and government agents were disturbed that among the Choctaw tribe, fathers seemed unconcerned about providing materially for their own children. When the whites learned that the source of fathers' outlook was the matrilineal system, in which fathers were economically responsible not for their own children but for their sisters', they simply abolished that system. Clans were broken down or eliminated, and the nuclear family became the dominant kinship unit. In addition, a patrilineal system of obligation and inheritance replaced its matrilineal predecessor.

A law that helped impose these changes on Native Americans was the Indian Allotment Act, commonly known as the Dawes Act. Passed in 1887, it provided 160 acres of land to nuclear families and smaller amounts to individuals. Now the American government had made the nuclear family, not the extended family or the tribe, the dominant unit in Indians' lives. Alien standards abruptly replaced kinship patterns that had existed for hundreds, even thousands of years. Christian morality became the norm for assessment: Government officials did not consider whether a custom had historically contributed to individuals' welfare and a tribe's stability. Thus all forms of plural marriage were eliminated even though polyandry often provided economic provision for a woman or family that otherwise would have had no economic support. On the Pacific coast, the potlatch ceremonies, in which a lavish exchange of gifts occurred, were considered wasteful, heathen activities and were abolished even though these practices validated kinship titles and produced order among these groups (Kivisto, 1995: 265–266; Price, 1984: 246–252).

Unlike blacks and Indians, Asian Americans did not suffer forced change in family practices. They were neither slaves nor invaded people. Yet their situation, to be sure, was often not easy.

The Chinese Exclusion Act of 1882, which restricted Chinese laborers who were competing against whites for jobs, also prevented Chinese men from bringing their wives and children to the United States. The Immigration Act of 1924 further contributed to the problem, making it impossible for Chinese American men to have their spouses naturalized. Consequently Chinese men in the United States remained separated from their wives and children for many years (Daniels, 1988: 95–97; Li, 1982: 306).

In the early years of prejudice and isolation, the limited number of Chinese women meant that American Chinatowns largely contained single males. This situation existed until the 1940s when officials permitted Chinese to enter the country in larger numbers than during the previous 60 years.

In Chinese communities, individuals or families did not have isolated lives. Most immigrant Chinese belonged to a family association (clan), which had been village-centered in China and originally involved real blood relationships. When Chinese moved overseas, however, clans tended to broaden their membership. In the Chinese communities of many American cities, a single clan tended to dominate, with most residents obtaining membership in that clan and maintaining loyalty to it in exchange for protection and assistance at difficult or dangerous times. While other ethnic groups had organizations for their members, Chinese clans were more intense: Even though members were usually unrelated to each other, they considered these groups to be extended families, and all who belonged to an individual's association were designated "clan cousins" (Kitano and Daniels, 1988: 25–26). In an often violent new land, Chinese immigrants found their clans a major source of both psychological and practical support.

Modern immigrants continue to rely heavily on their families. A recent study indicated that foreign-born Chinese American women are considerably more inclined than their American-born counterparts to maintain extensive contact with their parents. The latter group is more likely to move out of the parental home before marriage, depart more sharply from the traditional close-knit parent-child relationships, and form significant relationships with non-family members (Ying, 1994).

Like the Chinese, early Japanese immigrants suffered discrimination, with a number of California newspapers agitating in 1905 for laws against their settlement in the United States. Three years later President Theodore Roosevelt negotiated the so-called "gentlemen's agreement" whereby the Japanese government would not issue any more passports to laborers if Japanese American children in San Francisco could enter local public schools. In public statements Roosevelt claimed that the result would be almost complete blockage of further Japanese immigration. Actually, for the next 16 years, female Japanese continued to enter the United States, and by 1930 the Japanese population, which in 1900 had been 3.9 percent female had become 41.1 percent female (Kitano and Daniels, 1988: 55–57). As a result,

compared to early Chinese communities, Japanese settlements had a smaller percentage of bachelors.

Still, the Japanese suffered intense hardships. In the past half-century, no other
American ethnic or racial group experienced forcible relocation as did Japanese
Americans when they were removed from the West Coast in 1942 and placed in 10 so-
called "relocation centers" (concentration camps) for the remainder of World War II.
While research did not systematically document the impact of living in the camps on
family life, it must have been considerable. Quarters were cramped, and centers were
surrounded by barbed wire and patrolled by armed soldiers who in several cases shot
and killed individuals they were guarding (Kitano and Daniels, 1988: 61–62).

One eloquent indication of the impact of camp life on individuals occurs when
elderly Japanese Americans living on the West Coast meet each other for the first
time. Conversation often begins with the question, "What camp were you in?" and
proceeds with exchanges of personal camp experiences that are so intimate and
detailed that listeners who were not in the camps feel excluded (Ima, 1982: 266).

Asian families that have recently arrived in the United States, particularly those
entering the country with few economic resources and contacts and little education,
find themselves mired in poverty. Refugee families from Cambodia, Laos, and
Vietnam tend to be poor, with about a third of the approximately one million
Southeast Asians on welfare. The stereotype of Asians as a model minority has excluded them from consideration in national policy debates on issues like poverty, economic
development, and health care. Paul M. Ong, a professor of urban planning at UCLA,
contended that this exclusion has been part of a larger pattern of failure. He noted,
"The country has not dealt very well with those on the margins. It's a tragedy and it
affects us all" (Dunn, 1994: A23).

Another stereotypic assumption is that Asian Americans' traditional respect for
their elders means that adult children inevitably address their elderly parents' various
needs. However, a study of Chinese Americans, Japanese Americans, and Korean
Americans found that the amount and quality of care children provided varied considerably depending on such factors as the physical distance between the two generations' residential locations and the adult children's level of affluence (Ishii-Kuntz,
1997).

Like Asian Americans, the majority of Mexican American families entered this
country under harsh conditions. Spurred by poverty and political instability, about a
half-million Mexicans immigrated to the United States between 1900 and 1930.
Working as farm or factory laborers, their jobs were usually unstable and low-paying;
frequently they found themselves objects of racial hatred or exploitation; and their
inability to speak English helped to isolate them (Maldonado, 1982: 172–173).

In this difficult situation, Chicanos tended to find the family a source of strength.
One prominent factor encouraging this trend was Spanish culture, which has taught
that close personal relationships are at the core of people's existence and that relationships establishing individuals' confidence, sense of security, and identity are those
formed within the family. From Spanish tradition Chicanos also adopted the use of
compadres—individuals who, whether related by blood or not, become ritualized kinship members after serving in ceremonies as godparents at a child's baptism or witnesses at a couple's wedding.

In modern times families play an important role in another way, with Mexican Americans tending to migrate to areas where relatives live. As young adults, Chicanos tend to have a wide range of kin in the vicinity—grandparents, parents, aunts, uncles, and cousins. Research has suggested that the higher their socioeconomic status, the more likely Mexican Americans will retain close relations with kinship members. In general, however, Chicanos tend to remain in the same area for many years, thus keeping open the distinct possibility of maintaining close contact with relatives (Keefe and Padilla, 1987: 142–143).

Some Mexican immigrants face a new problem. In November 1994, in response to the large number of illegal, primarily Mexican immigrants coming into the state, 59 percent of California voters supported Proposition 187, which denied social services, noncmergency health care, and education to illegal immigrants (Tolbert and Hero, 1996). One of the most publicized and criticized results of the referendum was the decision to force hundreds of college students, who had lived in the United States since arriving as infants, to leave state colleges and universities. Christina Bodinger–de Uriarte, a sociologist at California State University, Los Angeles, commented:

> Suddenly, within weeks of graduation, students were notified that unless they paid out-of-state tuition, they must leave school. Students who had worked full-time jobs for four or five years in order to finance their education and escape poverty were penalized. Some of my best students were in tears for days—then they simply disappeared from the student body. (de Uriarte, 1997: 119)

Like Mexican Americans, Puerto Ricans use *compadres.* Among Puerto Ricans *compadres* have a deep obligation to provide economic assistance, emotional support and encouragement, and even criticism and suggestions for personal improvement. While the Spanish provided a tradition that helped solidify family life, they also produced a distinctly negative influence on it. Between 1511 and 1873, Spanish rulers practiced slavery in Puerto Rico. Even though treatment of slaves was less brutal than in the United States, owners responded to the same economic pressures as their U.S. counterparts and thus bought and sold slaves with little or no regard for the impact on slave families (Fitzpatrick, 1987: 69–73). In spite of this ever-present threat, recent research has concluded that Puerto Rican slaves lived in stable relationships and, though not permitted to marry, spaced their children at intervals comparable to those of married women (Stark, 1996).

Like African Americans, Puerto Ricans have suffered the economic legacy of slavery. Often caught in the vicious cycle of poverty, they have experienced substandard education, high unemployment, poverty, and family fragmentation. In 1995, 33.2 percent of Puerto Rican families were living below the poverty level compared to 27.3 percent for African Americans, and the proportion of single-parent families with children under 18 was high for both groups—47.1 percent for Puerto Ricans and 58.9 percent for African Americans. Puerto Rican families have tended to concentrate in poor urban neighborhoods in northeastern and midwestern industrial centers that have suffered declining employment opportunities, especially for people with limited education and job training (Moore and Pinderhughes, 1995, U.S. Bureau of the Census, 1996, Tables 49 and 53).

Other factors can affect families. A significant negative reality is that across the nation, community life has declined, forcing families within all racial groups to fend for themselves to a greater extent. In the following excerpt, a group of elderly African American men suggest that in the 1920s and 1930s when they grew up in Chicago's black ghetto, adult neighbors took a much greater responsibility for other people's children than they do now.

> Ted began: "On our block you would get chastised by an old lady. 'Boy, what are you doing over here? Does your mother know you are over here?' She'd get you on your toes by the ear and she'd drag you home. 'I found him over on Lafayette.' You could get chastised by anyone in the neighborhood."
>
> "That's true," Slim said. "Oh, yeah. You had about twelve mothers, seventeen fathers. Everybody knew what you did."
>
> Ted continued. "We would be out on the corner. All the police would say is, 'I want this corner. I'll be back in five minutes.' If you weren't off the corner, they'd throw you up against the wall and go through this ritual. And your neighbor would come by and see this and say, 'Ted, what did you do?' 'Nothing, ma'am.' That would not be believed."
>
> "Yeah," Slim said, "you got looked out for in that old neighborhood." (Duneier, 1994: 61)

We now move into the present, assessing major problems in minority families and the impact of racism on their development and perpetuation.

Minority Families and Racism

In this section we examine two issues that relate to racism: The first concerns a celebrated racist analysis of the black family, and the second examines current racist outlooks on and programs for minority families.

The Moynihan Report

In 1965 a report titled *The Negro Family: The Case for National Action* appeared. While no individual was listed as author—the Office of Policy Planning and Research, United States Department of Labor received the designation—the public learned that the chief writer was Harvard professor, later New York senator, Daniel Patrick Moynihan.

The so-called Moynihan Report created a furor, because many readers considered it a simplistic indictment of the African American family and thus African Americans. William Ryan, whose concept of blaming the victim was introduced in Chapter 3, felt that the document served as a notable illustration of that process. Ryan wrote:

> Moynihan was able to take a subject that had previously been confined to the Sociology Department seminar room . . . and bring it into a central position in popular American thought, creating a whole new set of group stereotypes which support the notion that Negro culture produces a weak and disorganized form of family life, which in turn is a major factor in maintaining Negro inequality. (Ryan, 1976: 64)

Thus, the report emphasized, when African American families were not economically or educationally successful, the major problem was deficiencies within the African

American culture. The victims—African Americans—were designated the source of their own failure. Once again we see the internal colonialist perspective's emphasis on both a racial minority's supposed cultural inferiority and the necessity for its members to adopt standards of the dominant culture.

Since the Moynihan Report serves as the foundation for this section of the chapter, it seems reasonable to discuss the document in greater detail. The report contained five major conclusions.

First, it emphasized that while the white family had achieved a high degree of stability and was managing to maintain it, the black family—especially the lower-class black family—was highly unstable, with an increasing percentage of female-headed families and a sharp rise in welfare dependency.

Second, the report indicated that slavery had been a major influence on the development of the black family. Along with their cultural heritage and personal rights, slaves were deprived of the opportunity to produce and maintain a stable family. When slavery ended, blacks received liberty but not equality. In particular, the black man, widely seen as a threat by whites, was systematically deprived of rights, including the right to work. Thus black women became the breadwinners and also assumed the dominant role in family life.

Third, the Moynihan Report claimed that high levels of black unemployment, which have existed since the collection of unemployment data started in 1930, have contributed to the increasing fragmentation of African American families—a growing proportion of illegitimacy and female-headed families.

Fourth, Moynihan indicated that "the tangle of pathology"—the combined impact of poverty, the absence of fathers, and exposure to delinquency and crime—makes it impossible for poor black children, especially poor black males, to perform effectively in schools and in the workplace.

Fifth, the report concluded that "the case for national action" was clear. The United States needed an effective strategy, and because of the extent of current pathology in the black family, it could focus on only one place. Moynihan wrote:

> In a word, a national effort toward the problems of Negro Americans must be directed towards the question of family structure. The object should be to strengthen the Negro family so as to enable it to raise and support its members as do other families. (Office of Policy Planning and Research, United States Department of Labor, 1965: 47)

At this point perhaps you are wondering why the Moynihan Report deserves so much attention. After all, you might be thinking, the document is now over three decades old and probably forgotten by everyone except the fellow whose book I am presently reading.

Actually, the last conclusion is wrong. Detailed analysis of the Moynihan Report continues to appear in a variety of sources (see Besharov, Quin, and Zinsmeister, 1987; Blauner, 1989: 41; Brewer, 1988; Darity and Myers, 1984; Demos, 1990; Pagnini and Morgan, 1996; Stewart, 1994; Taylor, 1994).

But more significant than these references is the reason why writers on racism and the African American family continue to provide such analyses. As the opening of this chapter suggests, the plight of poor black families has not improved in the past quarter-century. In fact, as Table 7.1 indicates, over the past three decades, there has been an increase in the proportion of female-headed poor black families. For instance, in 1994, 70.4 percent of newborn African American children had unmarried mothers. All other major racial minorities had lower proportions of children born out of wedlock. For Chinese Americans, the figure was 7.2 percent; for Japanese Americans, 11.2 percent; for whites, 25.4 percent; for Mexican Americans, 40.8 percent; for Native Americans, 57 percent; and for Puerto Ricans, 60.2 percent (U.S. Bureau of the Census, 1997, Table 89).

Nobody disputes the statistics. At the national level, the practical necessity is to determine why minority family fragmentation has been so extensive and then to figure out what measures can alleviate destructive conditions imposed on black and other poor minority families.

But our agenda is more modest—simply to learn about the relationship between racism and minority families. One way to analyze this topic is to consider four major criticisms of the Moynihan Report. This approach not only provides information about current minority families but also points out the racism frequently found in official, government-sponsored investigations of racial issues.

Table 7.1 African Americans versus Whites: Family Fragmentation and Poverty

	PERCENTAGE OF CHILDREN UNDER 18 IN FEMALE-HEADED FAMILIES	
	African American	**White**
1960	22.4%	8.7%
1970	29.5	7.8
1980	46.9	13.4
1985	51.0	15.6
1995	58.3	18.0

	FAMILIES BELOW THE POVERTY LEVEL	
	African American	**White**
1959	48.1%	15.2%
1966	35.5	9.3
1970	29.5	8.0
1975	27.1	7.7
1980	28.9	8.0
1985	28.7	9.1
1991	30.4	8.8
1995	27.3	9.1

Note: In 1960 there were 14 percent more female-headed African American families than female-headed white families. By 1995 the difference had increased to 40 percent. While from 1959 to 1995, the proportion of both African American and white families below the poverty line declined, the ratio between the two sets of families has remained almost identical.

Sources: U.S. Bureau of the Census. *Statistical Abstract of the United States: 1961,* Table 34; U.S. Bureau of the Census. *Statistical Abstract of the United States: 1989,* Tables 71 and 739; *Statistical Abstract of the United States: 1990,* Tables 43 and 748; *Statistical Abstract of the United States: 1993,* Tables 73 and 743; *Statistical Abstract of the United States: 1996,* Tables 49 and 82.

Four Criticisms of the Moynihan Report and Their Application to Modern Minority Families

The four issues to be discussed are (1) the report's analysis of fragmentation in black families; (2) the role of welfare in the poor minority family; (3) stereotypes of minority, especially black families; and (4) deemphasis or omission of minority families' strengths.

Fragmentation of Poor Minority Families The Moynihan Report concluded that poverty produced "a tangle of pathology" that made it impossible for poor African American children, especially males to function effectively in schools and in the work world. This image—a tangle of pathology—creates the same sense of jungle immorality and dire hopelessness that Jewell Handy Gresham associated with the 1986 CBS Special Report on the supposedly vanishing black family.

Besides its negative imagery, the phrase is vague. To understand fragmentation within the poor black family, the analyst needs to move beyond slogans and examine concretely how economic conditions adversely affect poor African Americans. Hopefully, in the following pages, we can begin to untangle ideas related to this "tangle of pathology."

A useful place to start is Elijah Anderson's study entitled "Sex Codes and Family Life among Poor Inner-City Youths." In a poor inner-city black area, Anderson interviewed prospective and present teenage parents as well as their family members in an effort to understand the process producing an increasing number of out-of-wedlock children.

Anderson suggested that members of his peer group tend to be the most important people in the life of a young, inner-city black man. As in most young men's peer groups, there is a strong emphasis on obtaining high status. For these young men, good job prospects are remote or nonexistent, and so economic achievement and the status that goes with it are unrealistic. The most available means for achieving high status is sexual—the conquest of teenage girls.

So the teenage boy develops his sexual "game," focusing on his clothes, dancing ability, and, above all, his style of conversation, or "rap." Whether the young man is a winner or loser in his peers' eyes depends on the number of sexual conquests he obtains.

If a teenage girl is inexperienced, the boy's game might fool her. But even if she is not fooled, she is vulnerable to his advances. She has her own agenda—the American dream of living with a loving husband and children in a nice house in a pleasant neighborhood. This dream has been nurtured by the love songs she has heard since early childhood and by soap operas, which show affluent, comfortable middle-class housewives.

The dream is sufficiently powerful that, when approached by the boy, the girl simply tends to fit him into the dream. If successful at playing the romantic game, the boy knows what is on the girl's mind and exploits the knowledge. He might take her for walks, visit her family, even go to church with her family to show that he is an upstanding young man.

At times even the boy might get caught up in the dream, but then he recalls job prospects for young African American men in the inner city, and he rejects the idea of becoming the young woman's provider in the middle-class tradition. So he returns to the game, focusing on sexual conquest by playing the role of the "dream man," who appears to plan to marry the girl and live with her happily ever after. A 23-year-old respondent, who had become a single mother at 17, explained:

> Yeah, they'll [boys will] take you out. Walk you down to Center City, movies, window shop (laughs). They point in the window, "Yeah, I'm gonna get this. Wouldn't you like this? Look at that nice livin' room set." Then they want to take you to his house, watch some TV. Next thing you know your clothes is off and you in bed havin' sex, you know. (Anderson, 1989: 63)

Peers tend to accord high status to boys who can demonstrate extensive control or exploitation of their girlfriends. To achieve this, the boy is likely to try "to break the girl down" in front of his friends. The girl often accepts this treatment if she feels that it will help promote her dream of marriage and domestic happiness. On the other hand, if she believes that aggression or manipulation better serve her interests, then she follows an appropriate course of action. Each of them has a definite goal in mind and will do what's necessary to achieve it. As one respondent said:

> They trickin' them good. Either the woman is trickin' the man, or the man is trickin' the woman. Good! They got a trick. She's thinkin' it's [the relationship is] one thing, he playing another game, you know. He thinkin' she all right, and she doing something else. (Anderson, 1989: 64)

Ultimately the boy wants to demonstrate that he "has the girl's nose open"—that she is so sick in love with him that he has complete control.

Interestingly, at the time when the boy believes that he is achieving this objective, the girl is likely to give up birth control. She accepts what he told her about taking care of her and believes that if she becomes pregnant he will marry her or at least take care of her. She thinks little about the job market or the boy's job prospects; she also underestimates the impact of his peer group. She is in love, and the relentless dream of marriage and domestic happiness seems within reach.

When the girl becomes pregnant, the boy faces a decision. Should he accept the peer group ethic of "hit and run," or should he risk the loss of his friends' support by opposing the ethic? Actually, he can usually maintain prestige in peers' eyes if he acknowledges the paternity but provides the amount of financial support that he, not the girl, considers appropriate. With pregnancy the boy's economic situation becomes an even more critical reality. He recognizes that it is difficult simply to support himself. The prospect of maintaining at least two others seems difficult or impossible, especially in light of the peer group's contempt for settling down.

The young man's economic situation also creates ambivalence for the young woman. Upon giving birth she must decide whether or not to depend wholly upon the father. She might decide that she would be better off financially receiving regular checks from the welfare office instead of occasional support from a young man who is irregularly employed.

Frequently the expectant father decides that his best interest involves leaving the pregnant girl even if he knows that the baby is his own. His desire for freedom is very strong and receives peer group support. In addition, in a modern economy offering few job prospects, the young inner-city black man is unlikely to have sufficient funds to give him leverage to control the domestic situation, permitting him to "play house" in what he considers an enjoyable way.

Mercer L. Sullivan's (1989) research provides consistent evidence. Sullivan studied young men living in three low-income neighborhoods in Brooklyn, New York. One area contained primarily white, Catholic, third- or fourth-generation descendants of immigrants from Italy and Poland; the people in this district were among the poorest non-Hispanic whites in New York City, but their average income was considerably higher than that of the other two groups. The second neighborhood had predominantly black residents who were first- or second-generation immigrants from the southern United States. The final district was largely Puerto Rican, with a population whose members were first- or second-generation immigrants from Puerto Rico. In the latter two groups, about half the families were living below the poverty level and obtained Aid to Families with Dependent Children (AFDC), the largest government-subsidized welfare program. For the white group, about 12 percent of families were living below the poverty level, and less than 10 percent received AFDC.

Sullivan found that among young men in the three neighborhoods, economic prospects and culture combined to affect their responses to getting a young woman pregnant. Compared to young black men in the study, young white men who got young women pregnant were more likely to marry them. Better job possibilities seemed to be the major factor that produced the stronger inclination to accept marriage. Through family and neighborhood contacts—the informal networks influencing hiring discussed in Chapter 5—young white men tended to have fairly stable, decent-paying blue-collar jobs that permitted them to set up independent households. In contrast, young black men lacked such contacts and job opportunities, and so they were much less inclined than whites to marry young women they made pregnant. In many cases, however, black fathers did provide some support for their children.

In addition, culture played a role. Puerto Rican men in the study were as poor as blacks and had equally dismal job prospects, but coming from a cultural tradition that strongly emphasizes marriage, most of them married the young women they made pregnant. Because the majority were unlikely to find steady jobs that paid sufficiently well to maintain their families, it seemed likely that many of these marriages would soon end. Most Puerto Rican men, in fact, had fathers whose employment difficulties had caused them to leave home when the research subjects were still young children. Earlier in this chapter, we saw data on illegitimacy that showed Puerto Ricans' rate running a close second to blacks'. Those data suggest that in opposition to the results of this three-culture study, Puerto Ricans' illegitimacy rate is close to blacks'. Probably over time the economic factor plays a larger role than the cultural one, causing Puerto Ricans' family fragmentation to be statistically similar to blacks'.

In a third investigation, Mark Testa et al. (1989) also learned that the dominant issue affecting family fragmentation was the family's economic condition. Examining data from a survey of 2,490 inner-city residents in Chicago, this team of researchers found that black, white, Puerto Rican, and Mexican American unmarried male respondents were almost twice as likely to eventually marry the mother of their first child if they were employed than if he were unemployed. In addition, while researchers did not have income data, they learned that the higher the joint educational attainment of unmarried parents—and thus most likely their combined income—the stronger the likelihood that they would marry. Testa and his colleagues concluded their article by observing that "improvements in the economic status of both low-income men and women promise to enable most parents to marry and thus provide a financially and, it is hoped, socially better environment for themselves and their children" (Testa et al., 1989: 91).

A study of rates of murder and robbery in 150 American cities took the above conclusion a step further. Robert J. Sampson (1987) learned that as a result of a three-step process, African American men had greater involvement in these two violent crimes than white men. Because their fathers were more likely than whites' fathers to have been unemployed, there was a higher likelihood that they came from single-parent families. As a result African American males received less support, control, and supervision at home. Therefore they were more likely than white males to be vulnerable to involvement in delinquency and crime. Sampson concluded that to alleviate these problems, social policies need to address structural conditions that have maintained a high rate of joblessness among black men, encouraged the fragmentation of poor black families, and helped contribute to the high rate of violent crime among black men.

A recent study focusing on school attitudes and performance, did find that black high-school students coming from mother-only families had less discipline than their peers who had both parents at home. However, on other important issues, such as educational aspirations, grades, and the likelihood of staying in school, the differences between the two sets of students were very slight (Heiss, 1996).

Clearly not all single-parent families are the same. The greater parental ineffectiveness tends to occur when the mother is very young, inexperienced, and immature. An analyst noted that in poor areas with high illegitimacy rates, such as those described in the preceding studies, the pattern is likely to repeat in the next generation. He added, "High rates of illegitimacy also mean that there is not so much a breakdown in the black family as much as the black family not forming in the first place" (Williams, 1996: 97).

While no single, simple solution lies ahead, several of the studies already cited indicate that the development and promotion of effective education and employment prospects would certainly be productive steps.

The following research information relates to the previous discussion about family fragmentation.

Black and White Differences in Childbearing and Marriage

In the second edition of this text, I wrote:

> In spite of their poverty, black families in the late nineteenth and early twentieth centuries tended to be stable, with men, especially unemployed men, taking a significant role in domestic tasks. (Doob, 1996: 162)

Now new evidence suggests a different conclusion. Let's consider what has developed.

In the wake of the Moynihan attack on the black family, researchers mobilized, looking for evidence to dispute its conclusions. They found data seeming to indicate that black and white families were equally stable. However, a return to the actual studies from which those conclusions were drawn—studies involving census reports for the years 1880 to 1910—found substantial differences between blacks and whites in the areas of nonmarital childbearing, tendency to marry and to stay married, and the likelihood of children living separated from their parents.

It appears that in their concerted effort to invalidate the Moynihan Report's criticism of the black family the critics, in turn, distorted available data. Researchers Deanna L. Pagnini and S. Philip Morgan observed that while it was true that early researchers had found that black families were "strong and resilient," that did not mean they were necessarily structured like or behaved like white families (Pagnini and Morgan, 1997: 1697–1700).

Seeking new information on this topic, Pagnini and Morgan used data from the Federal Writers' Project Life History Program. While not a formal survey, this set of almost 1,200 interviews conducted by unemployed writers in the 1930s provided extensive information about the interviewees and a broad view of life in the South from the Civil War through the Great Depression. The interviews were fairly informal, not involving a standard set of questions or a rigorous sampling of respondents, thereby preventing the investigators from claiming that their findings were applicable to the entire southern region. But in spite of these difficulties, the data obtained was very informative, strongly suggesting greater differences between southern black and white families than generally believed a few years ago.

One area where these life histories provided useful findings involved nonmarital childbearing. Examining the incidence of nonmarital births for "nonwhite" and white American children in 1919, 1927, and 1936*, Pagnini and Morgan found the nonwhite percentage was about ten times as high as the white one. Excerpts from the Federal Writers' Project suggested that norms about nonmarital childbearing differed significantly for blacks and whites. While for unmarried white women who became pregnant, pressures to get married or to have an abortion were severe, black women encountered much less pressure. A black man named Mabry Shaw was critical of his parents, who, he claimed, had adopted whites' standards, urging him not to marry a woman with an out-of-wedlock child. Shaw said:

> I left and married her, in spite of all they could say about it. I loved her and I reckon I did a good day's work the day I married her. Her folks was tickled, and I don't see why mine won't because having the baby won't [be held] against her so far as the other Negroes was concerned. My folks had to try to be like white folks, though. (Pagnini and Morgan, 1997: 1707)

Different white and black norms toward nonmarital childbearing were apparent in the very terms used to discuss the issue. Tom Pugh, a black tenant farmer, explained, "I was what they called a off-child—my mother wasn't married to my father" (Pagnini and Morgan, 1997: 1708). While recognizing the difference between children born inside and outside marriage, the term "off-child" is softer, less condemning than the label "illegitimate" or "bastard."

Consider this contrasting statement from Carrie Black, a 42-year-old white woman whose childhood peers often ridiculed her because her mother wasn't married. Black said:

---

*In 1919, 19 states provided this information; by 1927 the total had risen to 36; and in 1936 all of the existing 48 states were included.

I started to school when I was six . . . but them wasn't no bright and happy school days. Not by no means! The other children picked on me all the time. They'd heard their folks talk, of course. One hateful boy used to set behind me and punch me and say I was a snotty little bastard. (Pagnini and Morgan, 1997: 1709)

In the survey, black women expressed a less positive feeling toward marriage and a greater willingness to divorce than their white counterparts. For instance, Ruby Childs, a 35-year-old black woman who had married at 14 and been deserted by her husband, was vehement when asked about marriage plans. She replied, "No God! I ain't got no husband. And what's more, I don't want one. I had one o' them once. But I sho' ain't lookin' for no more" (Pagnini and Morgan, 1997: 1710).

It seems probable that a major contributor to blacks' and whites' different standards toward marriage and childbearing was rampant job discrimination against black men, making work opportunities very scarce except for low-paying maintenance jobs. Just as we saw in such contemporary research as Anderson's and Sullivan's studies, the lack of work opportunities greatly discouraged a strong male presence in the family. Under the difficult economic circumstances black women faced, it is entirely reasonable that they were often committed to going it alone—as single people and single parents. While white women often found their marriages difficult, the fact that their husbands had considerably more extensive job opportunities than did black men provided an economic incentive to stay married that was often lacking in black families.

Welfare's Effect on Poor Minority Families   Besides focusing on the supposed fragmentation of African American families, the Moynihan Report suggested that welfare plays a destructive impact on poor minority families. One can examine three possible ways welfare might negatively affect minority families.

First, there is the claim that AFDC and other welfare programs promote fragmentation. A review of research on the topic indicated that there is a statistically detectable but modest relationship between levels of welfare benefits that different U.S. states provide and their proportion of female-headed families (Jaynes and Williams, 1989: 531).

Second, the possibility exists that women on welfare are likely to have an increased number of illegitimate children. A review of studies on the subject concluded that there is no evidence to support such a claim (Hayes, 1987).

Third, perhaps AFDC lowers or even kills poor parents' work incentive. In research on black, female-headed poor families throughout the United States, Jones (1987) found that higher proportions of these women were on welfare when the states in which they lived provided primarily low-paying clerical, service, and operative jobs to modestly educated black women. On the other hand, in states where jobs available to African American female heads of poor families offered higher wages, the proportion of these women supported by welfare dropped.

Reading the preceding paragraph, you might feel that even if wages are low, people should have the pride to work instead of seeking welfare support. The problem is that welfare recipients lose nearly a dollar in benefits for each dollar earned, and in some states they also lose health coverage. In addition, while working, they often need to pay for a babysitter or a child-care program. These economic realities help to explain why among the poorest female-headed families, AFDC and other welfare subsidies tend to encourage women to stay out of the work force (McLanahan and Garfinkel, 1989).

Policy makers often ignore or gloss over such economic realities, focusing instead on what the Moynihan Report considered the tangle of pathology dominating the poor black family. In 1988 Moynihan and senate colleague William Armstrong sponsored a "welfare reform" bill that was passed by the Senate. This legislation required all AFDC mothers with children over 3 to enter the labor force as cheaply paid workers. The bill simply failed to assess such practical problems as obtaining jobs in largely jobless areas, locating effective child care, and getting children to and from their caretakers.

Examining this legislation, a pair of writers wondered "how many of the men who sit in the halls of Congress have ever played a parenting role in which they had the opportunity to engage in such tasks for even, let us say, one week" (Wilkerson and Gresham, 1989: 128).

In July 1997 the 62-year-old federal welfare system ended, and states assumed the responsibility for dispersing subsidies to the poor. The program's name changed from Aid to Families with Dependent Children to Temporary Assistance for Needy Families. While the state programs differ, they "share a unifying theme [that] can be summarized in a word: work. States are demanding that recipients find it faster, keep it longer, and perform it as a condition of aid" (DeParle, 1997: A1). Generally state officials claim that even a low-paying, dead-end job is preferable to the traditional education and training programs.

Are there enough jobs for all former recipients? While it is highly doubtful that there are, particularly in areas where the economy is stagnant, few cities or states are willing to create large numbers of community-service jobs to make work universally available.

In the opening months of the state programs, recipients soon discovered that if they violated the new requirements for obtaining jobs, they could readily lose their current welfare support. Early evidence from Milwaukee, Wisconsin, and the state of Iowa indicated two broad developments for those losing benefits: While one group has used such sources as a secret job, a boyfriend, or a child's disability payment to equal or surpass previous levels of financial support, the other group—obviously already poor—suffered a sharp drop in income. In such areas, shelters have received a large influx of homeless families.

Wisconsin established one of the early, celebrated state programs shifting people from welfare to work. The core of its successful graduates were young, white women who generally had one child out of wedlock, were quite well educated, and had only brief exposure to welfare. Most of these women were fairly well prepared for the work world. However, they are hardly a cross section of women on welfare. About 39 percent of welfare mothers are black and an additional 17 percent are Hispanic; generally they have not finished high school and have at least two children; furthermore, many are as accustomed to receiving welfare as most citizens are to paying taxes. In the short term, such women simply are not ready to function effectively in the modern work world (Gage, 1997; Verhovek, 1995; Wilkerson, 1995). It is almost certain that many of these women and their families will suffer greatly within the new state programs and that the long-run expense will be greater than if the nation had established more humane, carefully planned welfare reform.

Stereotypes of Minority Families   Consider two titles— *The Negro Family: The Case for National Action* and "Vanishing Family: Crisis in Black America." These are the precise titles of the Moynihan Report and the CBS Special Report on black family problems. Both works, which appeared 21 years apart, refer to *a family*—singular. The analysts suggest that blacks have a single family structure. A stereotype emerges—in particular, Moynihan's idea of "a tangle of pathology." This stereotype has continued to thrive.

A study of 25 textbooks in the sociology of the family indicated that nine of the books analyzed black families under headings suggesting deviance or inadequate functioning. They stated that black families are more likely to be female-headed and to experience unemployment, illegitimacy, and break-up than white families. Such statements are factually correct, but without further explanation, they are misleading. Useful discussion would indicate how factors besides race, such as poverty and unemployment, have come into play. (Our earlier discussion of fragmentation in the poor minority family used such an approach.) Otherwise readers are likely to receive the impression "that black families are innately problem-ridden or dysfunctional" (Bryant and Coleman, 1988).

A review of the 283 data-based articles about black Americans published in the *Journal of Marriage and the Family* between 1939 and 1987 revealed a declining tendency over time to present a distinctly problematic, pathological image of the black family. However, research-related factors have contributed to a somewhat negative image of black families in this journal's articles. Since the early 1960s, the analysis indicated, articles about black families published in the *Journal of Marriage and the Family* were more likely than in earlier years to have been quantitative studies conducted by researchers at large, primarily white universities, and subsidized by government grants. These studies tended to present an abstract sense of black family issues, failing to represent respondents' point of view and often, with little or no explanatory analysis provided, highlighting statistical information indicating blacks to be more deviant or less successful than whites. Tendencies for this research to have been conducted at white universities and to have received government support have been consistent with this quantitative trend. White universities can best afford the mainframe computers necessary for this type of investigation, and government sponsors have been more inclined to fund large quantitative projects than qualitative studies. In short, all three trends have dovetailed in support of published studies that present an abstract, somewhat negative view of the black family (Demos, 1990). It would be instructive to know whether other prominent social-scientific journals with articles on minority families have produced similar results.

Some researchers have directly confronted stereotypes of the African American family. In *A New Look at Black Families,* Charles Willie (1991) suggested that his study of black families indicated that they can be roughly divided into three categories—affluent or middle-class blacks, working-class blacks, and poor blacks.

Affluent black family members tend to be well educated, with one or both spouses college graduates. Both adults generally work hard, obtaining positions in the public sector, industry, education, and in private business. Work is often a consuming experience; little time remains for recreation and other activities, with the possible exception of regular church attendance. Because of the income limitations of jobs available to blacks, wife and husband usually both work and as a result produce a total income at or above the national median. A study of 41 black professional couples concluded that while the respondents considered work a significant part of their lives, they heavily depended upon their marriages for happiness and psychological well-being (Thomas, 1990).

Middle-class African American families want the home to be a pleasant, often elegant place to live—"their home is their castle," Willie indicated—and so they emphasize modern furnishings and appliances.

Affluent African Americans tend to have two or fewer children and to encourage them to go to college directly after high school. The parents hope that their children will have more opportunities than they did, and they consider a college degree important for success in the work world. Middle-class African Americans try to develop in their children the same positive emphases on work and thrift that dominate their own lives.

Among working-class black families, life is a struggle requiring cooperative activity among all family members. Both spouses tend to be employed, with husbands sometimes maintaining two jobs. The sense of unity in this type of family is often less the result of understanding and tenderness than of the joint effort to avoid major economic hardship. Because their salaries tend to be low, working-class black families find that any reduction in their overall income is likely to push them below the poverty level.

Working-class African Americans consider children their special contribution to society, and they tend to have more of them than do affluent African Americans—sometimes five or even more. While these parents value education, they generally draw the limit at high-school graduation. Job expectations for their children are those requiring no more than a high-school or junior college education—for instance, employment as a secretary, nurse, or skilled manual worker.

The third category—poor black families—has already been discussed. As we have noted, these families have various problems rooted in poverty. Willie indicated that sometimes poor African American families are rebellious, rejecting the society that has rejected them, trusting few if any outsiders, and appearing uncommitted to anyone or anything. However, mothers remain loyal to their children, and brothers and sisters generally accept the obligation to help each other (Willie, 1991).

To break down stereotypes, analysts should keep in mind that minority group members' experiences can be diverse, producing a variety of outlooks and behaviors, not a single approach. For instance, a recent study of Mexican Americans' childrearing found not one but *two* distinct patterns produced by different sets of influences. Parents, especially mothers of first- and second-generation adolescents, tended to emphasize early autonomy, productive use of time, and strict adherence to rules while third-generation adolescents were reared with greater emotional support. These variations in outlook emerged because of diverse influences on the two sets of parents. The first- and second-generation parents were immigrants from a highly traditional culture and thus had grown up believing that their children's success in an alien world required a disciplined, dedicated approach. On the other hand, third-generation parents, who had all been born in the United States, had two experiences making them more inclined than earlier generations of parents to tune in to their children's emotional needs: First, better educated than their own parents, they had been more extensively exposed in school to the importance of providing emotional support during

Table 7.2   Black, Hispanic, Asian American, and White Family Income Levels: 1995

	PERCENTAGE IN EACH INCOME CATEGORY	
	Black Families	**Hispanic Families**
Under $9,999	24.7%	16.6%
$10,000–$24,999	29.7	34.3
$25,000–$49,999	27.4	31.6
$50,000 or more	18.1	17.4
Median income	$22,221	$24,530
	Asian American Families	**White Families**
Under $9,999	9.9%	6.8%
$10,000–$24,999	18.7	21.4
$25,000–$49,999	25.5	34.2
$50,000 or more	45.8	37.6
Median income	$45,251	$39,481

Note: While black and Hispanic families are less affluent than Asian American and white families, a fairly broad distribution of income exists within all four types.

Source: U.S. Bureau of the Census. *Statistical Abstract of the United States: 1996,* Table 715.

childrearing; second, unlike their own parents, they had been lifelong victims of discriminatory treatment and wanted to compensate their children for a similar exposure by providing extensive emotional support (Buriel, 1993).

Table 7.2 provides economic data on black, Hispanic, Asian American, and white families. Like the previous discussion, it suggests that all four sets of families are too diversified in income to fit an economic stereotype.

Deemphasis or Omission of Minority Families' Strengths   Stereotypes are negative, failing to consider possible positive qualities in a group. For the black family, Moynihan's "tangle-of-pathology" perspective is invariably negative. In contrast, research has suggested positive qualities about minority families.

A study of 41 black families that were poor, urban, and intact found that the husband played a prominent role. In at least seven out of ten cases, the husband was the main provider and was an active decision maker in such issues as choosing household appliances and selecting the residence (Robinson, Bailey, and Smith, 1985).

Since the days of slavery, African American families sometimes have informally adopted the children of fellow family members or friends when medical, financial, housing, emotional, or other emergencies have arisen (Littlejohn-Blake and Darling, 1993; McDaniel and Morgan, 1996). A large investigation revealed that when African Americans faced a serious emergency, eight out of ten had either a relative or friend available to help. Among respondents, 24 percent turned to parents or siblings, 21 percent to friends, 12 percent to their children, and 10 percent to in-laws (Taylor, Chatters, and Mays, 1988). A study of poor African American families indicated that resident grandmothers' parenting activity was substantial, second only to mothers in areas of control, punishment, support, and presence at bedtime (Pearson et al., 1990). Even when propelled into grandmotherhood at a relatively early age, 42 black mothers of teenagers indicated that while the grandchild's birth may have increased their responsibilities, it did not negatively affect their family relations, including their relationships with their daughters (Owens and Brome, 1997).

In reality, white, middle-class practitioners often lack the knowledge and experience to function effectively in this intergenerational context. Generalizing from their own social world, these individuals often believe that grandparents must be in their fifties or older. Thus, when a mother was held by the police and the 34-year-old grandmother showed up to take temporary possession of her grandchildren, the social worker in charge refused to release them, believing that the woman must be an imposter since she appeared too young to be a grandmother. Eventually the issue was resolved, but the incident "did irreparable damage to the relationship between the family and the agency" (Taylor, Chatters, and Jackson, 1993: 338).

Furthermore, city planner Walter Stafford (1996: 14–15) pointed out, when government decision makers develop policies and programs regarding poor families, including black and Puerto Rican families, they tend to ignore the values and functions provided by extended families. Certainly this represents a clear illustration of internal colonialism's claimed inferiority of a minority group's culture and social organization. While the lack of attention is demeaning, it is also impractical and disturbing: Extended family arrangements have often promoted effective survival and adjustment under demanding life conditions, and they could provide potentially valuable insights to political decision makers.

Native Americans also can often rely on support from a variety of relatives. In spite of government officials' historical efforts to undermine traditional extended family structures, many modern Indians continue to emphasize these family ties. Sometimes young people leave their parents' home and move in with other relatives. They do not need to pay rent, nor must they suffer inquiries about when they plan to leave. One Native American analyst noted that relatives accept that "the child will decide when it is right for him or her to go home" (Edmo, 1990: 3).

Findings on the Puerto Rican family suggest that when influenced by the desire for economic advancement on the mainland, second-generation adults are less familistic than parents who were born on the island and migrated to the United States. Such a comparison can be misleading, however, because even adult children who deemphasize family ties tend to turn to their parents for assistance when emergencies strike (Zayas and Palleja, 1988).

A recent analysis concluded that for most of the minority families examined in this chapter—African American, Native American, Chinese American, Japanese American, Mexican American, and Puerto Rican—the extended family has been both a problem-solving and stress-relieving system (Harrison et al., 1990).

Nonetheless, it is evident that oppressive conditions encourage victims to become oppressors themselves. Thus for minority-group members to interact effectively in families, they are well advised to understand the destructive factors impacting on their lives and to work together to overcome those influences. Consider the following statement from an analyst of the African American family:

Box 7.1   Major Conclusions about the Analysis of Minority Families

1. Family fragmentation: that limited educational and occupational opportunities have made a major contribution to this problem

2. Welfare impact: that analysts and policy makers often fail to assess effectively the complex relationship between welfare and poor minority families

3. Stereotypes of minority families: that many investigations, particularly large studies, tend to present a negative or abstract image of minority families; that analyzed by income level, black families divide into three broad types

4. Deemphasis or omission of minority families' strengths: that racial minorities' relatives provide considerable extended family support

---

The stereotypes imposed by white history and by the lack of knowledge of our own past often convince many younger Black males that their struggle is too overwhelming. Black women have a responsibility to comprehend the forces that destroy the lives of thousands of their brothers, sons, and husbands. But Black men must understand that they, too, must overcome their own deeply ingrained sexism, recognizing that Black women must be equal partners in the battle to uproot injustice at every level. (Marable, 1994: 77)

In this section we have examined the complex, primarily economic factors affecting minority families. We have also considered the role of racist, victim-blaming official outlooks on and policies toward minority families. Box 7.1 summarizes significant points about minority families raised in this section.

Minority Children at Risk

Recent statistics are impressive. Compared to white children, African American children are twice as likely to have been born prematurely, to have had a substandard birth weight, to live in inferior housing, and to die in their first year. Compared to white children, black children are three times as inclined to be poor, to live in a female-headed household, to have no employed parent, and to be murdered between the ages of 5 and 9. In addition, African American children are five times more likely to be dependent on welfare and nine times more inclined to live with a parent who has never been married. Not surprisingly, the highest rates of children's poor or fair health occur in black, low-income, single-mother families (Edelman, 1989: 22; Montgomery and Pappas, 1996; Taylor, 1990: 5–6). Thus it is no exaggeration to conclude that in various life-threatening or life-diminishing ways, black children are at greater risk than their white counterparts. Poor Puerto Rican and Native American children also experience a highly disproportionate exposure to life-threatening or life-diminishing circumstances.

Besides South Africa, the United States is the only modern industrialized nation that does not provide financial or medical aid when the birth or major illness of a child occurs (Rosewater, 1989: 11). Since African Americans, Puerto Ricans, and Native Americans are disproportionately poor, this omission clearly suggests institutional racism in government practice: This policy, or absence of a policy, systematically discriminates against a greater proportion of minority than white children.

The relationship between family income and race also affects child-care programs. Because of poverty, low-income parents, who are disproportionately members of racial minorities, must send their children to governmentally subsidized child-care programs. Middle- and upper-income parents enroll their children in fee-based services. The result is that in many residential areas, child-care programs are racially segregated. Because of the Supreme Court decision in *Brown v. Board of Education,* racial segregation of schools has been under attack since 1954. However, a similar concern has not developed for preschool child-care programs (Kagan, 1989: 77).

A situation that produces major difficulties for some children is homelessness. Among the hundreds of thousands of homeless American children, there are both whites and members of racial minorities. Because of more widespread poverty, minority youth—African American, Puerto Rican, and Native American children—are disproportionately represented.

In 1980 homeless children were rare, but several factors have altered that situation. During the 1980s chronic unemployment rose, especially for young black men. While explicit employment discrimination certainly played a role, the major cause was the restructuring of the American economy, with a shift toward a postindustrial work force most adversely affecting individuals with limited education and job training. (During the 1980s, minority group individuals were highly represented here.) In addition, the death and incarceration rates for African American males rose. All of these trends accelerated the growth of female-headed, single-parent families, which are the most common type of homeless families. Another factor contributing to increases in homeless families during the 1980s was a decline in inexpensive rental housing, with rent increases outpacing the growth of personal income. The disparity was particularly acute for welfare recipients, for whom the purchasing power of their grants was in 1990 only 64 percent of what it had been two decades earlier (Rossi, 1994). Policy makers and politicians often fail to assess the impact of these conditions on homelessness. As the following account suggests, they are more inclined to take a victim-blaming approach.

On March 6, 1986, David Bright, a 10-year-old, homeless black boy from New York City, testified before the House Select Committee on Hunger in Washington, D.C. When he grows up, David explained, he wants to become president so that he can make certain that "no little boy like me will have to put his head down on his desk at school because it hurts to be hungry" (Hayes, 1987: 58).

David's statement left few dry eyes in the hearing room. From Mayor Edward Koch, however, it aroused an angry reply. Koch indicated that David's testimony "simply doesn't reflect reality. New York does more for the homeless than any other city in America" (Rimer, 1986: 42). Koch took further action. Trying to prove that David's mother was directly responsible for her son's hunger, Koch had a spokesperson (whom he later appointed a judge of the New York Family Court) leak to the press confidential information from the Bright family's records about the mother's suspected drug abuse.

David Bright took the developing feud in stride, saying that the root of the problem might be jealousy produced by the fact that "I've got hair, and he doesn't." David's school principal declared that while Koch had an effective public presence, "he's no match for this kid" (Rimer, 1986: 42).

Although David Bright had his moment in the sun, much of his life has been dreary and painful. At the time of the hearing, he was living with his mother and three siblings in two small rooms in New York City's crowded Hotel Martinique, along with 1,500 homeless children and their families. Sometimes his mother would become so depressed that she would tell the children to leave her alone in one room so that she could cry.

But while adults suffer because of homelessness, children suffer perhaps more. There is no place—even though it might fall short of ideal—that provides a basic sense of stability, a home, during their early years. As one writer indicated, homelessness destroys "the inner beauty of a child" (Hayes, 1987: 66).

Racism and poverty are formidable realities that descend on many minority families. Another factor affecting family dynamics is women's perception of their roles. The final section of this chapter addresses that issue.

Women of Color : Through the Cultural Maze

During the late 1970s, Barbara Omolade became a part-time instructor at an evening college in New York City. The course she taught was on the topic of black women, for black women. Since Omolade was completing a master's degree on black motherhood, she was hired immediately in spite of minimum college teaching experience. She accepted the job reluctantly because she already had a full-time job and was a single mother of three school-aged children.

The course Omolade developed was entitled "The Histories and Experiences of Black Women," and it gave a historical over-view of African American women's lives and discussed contemporary challenges they faced. Soon she decided that since the students were about her age and came from working-class backgrounds similar to her own, it was most appropriate to act more like a sister than an instructor. As a sister it seemed inappropriate, arrogant in fact, to teach them. The best strategy, Omolade decided, was to present herself as one sister among many railing in a general way against the inadequacies of the current society. Much of the time, Omolade conceded, she simply lacked the background for such critical analysis, but she persevered.

Then one day she stopped in the midst of a lecture and stared at the students. Omolade wrote:

> There was silence. Every eye was on me. I was terrified. The students wanted—hungered, really—to know more. They wanted me to teach them, not just to be sisterly and befriend them or rant politics at them. (Omolade, 1993: 32)

Responding to the challenge, Omolade worked hard to improve the course. At that time, however, she found it difficult to obtain effective information because there were few available written works about black women.

Less than two decades later, the situation has changed impressively. Ann duCille, the chair of African American studies at Wesleyan University, indicated that she is "alternately pleased, puzzled, and perturbed—bewitched, bothered, and bewildered" by the extensive written analysis currently devoted to black women (duCille, 1994: 591). It is difficult, duCille suggested, to know just why this new interest has developed. Perhaps it is because white mainstream culture needs some spicing up.

For not only the topic of black women but also the larger subject of women of color, there is a growing body of literature providing a variety of information. Still, the challenges minority women face have not changed greatly in 20 years. In this section I focus on those special challenges, including the feminist option.

The Search for the Right Fit

How should a modern minority woman live? Certainly there is no simple, all-encompassing answer to that question. Comfortably or well, one might suggest. But what this outcome will entail might differ not only from one racial minority to another but for women with varying experiences and preferences within a given ethnic group. Let us consider some of the general social issues coming into play.

Many women of color come from cultures where they are expected to make the family their priority. First and foremost, traditional Mexican culture has emphasized, women are supposed to be mothers, centering their activities in the home. Not only women's own mothers but the entire kinship network along with the greater ethnic community support this orientation. When Mexican American women oppose this emphasis, they are seeking personal empowerment at the expense of a strongly supported traditional family pattern (Champion, 1996; Segura and Pierce, 1993). Such women can be considered deviants, even designated outcasts.

In cultures where women's lives are supposed to be centered in family activities, they are highly dependent on their families and thus vulnerable to familial changes, particularly divorce. A study of 50 divorced immigrant Asian American women found that since they had been socialized to believe that marriage is their highest goal and wife and mother their most important roles, they were often psychologically devastated by divorce, with 60 percent of the sample feeling that life was hardly worthwhile without a partner (Song, 1993: 188–189).

While women of color can be victimized by traditional conditions, they frequently find that the modern social world opens up new possibilities and options. Lynda Wright, a single black mother of four, was forced to go on welfare when she was divorced after 17 years of marriage and could not find a job. It was a long haul. Wright found welfare demeaning, with caseworkers telling her that she had been stupid and failed to plan her life well. She had to struggle to keep her children out of trouble and to find ways to get them the things they needed for a productive life. She had many fights with welfare personnel—over taking college courses, over preparing to be a teacher instead of settling for being a jackhammer operator. It was a difficult life, but through it all Wright extended herself. She explained:

> I have a rainbow coalition of friends. It took a lot of growth on my part, because in the sixties I became hostile to whites. I saw hate on people I didn't even know. They didn't try to know me; they just hated me instantly. I had a lot of anger. I did many sit-ins. As I've grown older, I've mellowed. It's all right if somebody else hates. I don't really have the time. I don't try to avoid hate; I just understand it better. (Terkel, 1992: 67)

Research indicates that among college-educated black women, an optimistic outlook toward work is common. When college-educated black and white women are compared, the former predict that their employment will produce fewer costs and more personal benefit for their children (Bridges and Etaugh, 1996) and that their professional success and income will be higher (Ganong et al., 1996).

Other minority women have found different kinds of opportunities opening up. In the Coast Salish communities of western Washington and British Columbia, Indian women have become increasingly active politically, now winning about a third of the seats in tribal councils. Several factors seem to have contributed. As some women have obtained more schooling and more jobs outside the home, they feel prepared to engage in political activity. A major contributor is that they often receive encouragement and child-care assistance from family members, allowing them to enter politics at an earlier age than can most women with families (Miller, 1992, 1994). Other considerations come into play. Before supporting a woman for council membership, tribal members analyze her social skills with her own children and with other people. One council member observed that the voters "have seen me work with kids the better half of my life, so I guess they trust in me, and elected me in" (Miller, 1992: 376). In many Coast Salish communities, the belief is strong that women become more emotionally involved than men and more readily will defend the tribe's interest to the outside world. As one female council member indicated, women are more inclined than men to "really go in and fight" (Miller, 1992: 377).

In the course of seeking their identity, some women of color are attracted to feminism.

The Feminist Option

Feminists' struggle is against **sexism**—the belief that actual or alleged differences between women and men establish the superiority of men. Sometimes minority women face barriers to engaging in feminist activity. One reason is that in many instances they find no feminist role models to observe.

Kesaya E. Noda, a Japanese American woman, has indicated that it has been much easier to establish her sense of self as a person of Japanese ancestry and as a Japanese American than to know herself as a Japanese American woman. The central problem, she explained, is that when she was growing up, her mother did not provide the kind of model that would have promoted a sense of herself as a competent, modern woman. Noda wrote:

> She was my dark self, a figure in whom I thought I saw all that I feared most in myself. Growing into womanhood and looking for some model of strength, I turned away from her. Of course, I could not find what I sought. I was looking for a black feminist or a white feminist. My mother is neither white nor black. (Noda, 1993: 48)

As an adult, Noda has come to value what she learned from her mother and to appreciate the ways that they are similar. Growing up, however, she felt confused without a more distinct feminist model.

Sometimes women of color deny the need for feminism, declaring that sexism does not exist in their group. Consider the relevance of a traditional African American stance about racism. Since the days of slavery, some African Americans have argued that while racist oppression has been relentlessly imposed on them, they have been able to battle it effectively: The proof has been the continued presence of many strong black families and communities. The basic defect of this analysis, feminist bell hooks suggested, is that it fails to consider that if black women battle only for racial liberation, then they face the distinct possibility that they help establish a society where they are subjected to a black patriarchal order (hooks, 1994).

Minority women considering the feminist option often face significant challenges. Sometimes they find that the white feminist world is hardly a hospitable place, with historical relationships between minorities and whites playing a role. For several centuries the chief relationship between black and white women was a hierarchical one, with the former in the role of slave or servant and the latter in the position of mistress. Such cultural patterns are not readily forsaken, and thus in spite of claims of equality, it appears that some white feminists still want to dominate black women, who readily conclude that a true sisterhood is impossible (hooks, 1994: 150). Another reason some black women reject feminism is that they feel that the white women's movement has promoted an image of a universal woman, "ignoring the ways that race, social class, age, and social ideologies produce differences among women" (Jackson, 1998: 46).

Nonetheless, many black and other minority women are interested in feminism and so must figure out how to pursue it. One place to start can be a discussion with a few immediate associates, perhaps friends or colleagues at work. In small-group settings, women can talk about their perceptions and experiences, learning that the "personal is political"—that only a critical self-evaluation can provide a starting point for a clear understanding of the nature of one's current existence. As women of different economic and racial backgrounds get together and discuss their experiences, they can begin to appreciate both their differences and their commonalities. Feedback from other group members is critical for the development of that understanding. This process is often difficult, requiring participants to evaluate and perhaps reject set ways of thinking, but it is essential for personal growth. Unless individuals' consciousness alters, they will be incapable of changing their actions or demanding change from others.

The key, bell hooks suggested, is that women belonging to different racial groups understand the "realities of sex, race, and class, the ways they divide us, make us different, stand us in opposition, and work to reconcile and resolve these issues" (hooks, 1992: 447). Throughout the 1980s an organization called the Southeast Women's Employment Coalition sought to unify black and white working-class women across the South. Researcher Barbara Ellen Smith indicated that "white women were willing to examine their racial privilege and black women were willing to share the anger and pain of racial oppression" (Smith, 1995: 694). Such experiences illustrate feminists' potential for overcoming differences and cooperating in mutually beneficial ways.

Conclusion

Throughout this chapter we have repeatedly encountered two points. First, minority families are often the victims of institutional racism, disproportionately suffering more limited educational and occupational opportunities and thus encountering greater risk of poverty and its associated problems than white families. Second, in the tradition of the Moynihan Report, a victim-blaming strategy has prevailed. For African

American and other minority families, this approach emphasizes, the source of serious problems resides in the family itself. If one focuses on the tangle of pathology or other supposed indicators of what internal colonialism labels racial minorities' cultural inferiority, then one can overlook economic and political roots of minority families' problems. To date this racist strategy has remained alive and well.

Discussion Questions

1. Did any historical material in this chapter surprise you? If yes, explain.
2. Evaluate the contribution of Anderson's study of inner-city teenage parents, mentioning the relationship of the research to the Moynihan Report.
3. From what you have read, heard, and seen, what has been the impact of welfare reform on poor minority families?
4. Are you aware of situations where minority families are represented in a stereotyped way?
5. Discuss whether women belonging to different racial groups can effectively work together on feminist issues. In your opinion, what are the greatest obstacles to overcome?

Sources

Anderson, Elijah. 1989. "Sex Codes and Family Life among Poor Inner-City Youths." *Annals of the American Academy of Political and Social Science* 501 (January): 59–78.

Besharov, Douglas J., Alison Quin, and Karl Zinsmeister. 1987. "A Portrait in Black and White: Out-of-Wedlock Births." *Public Opinion* 10 (May/June): 43–45.

Billingsley, Andrew. 1968. *Black Families in White America.* Englewood Cliffs, NJ: Prentice-Hall.

Blauner, Bob. 1989. *Black Lives, White Lives.* Berkeley: University of California Press.

Brewer, Rose M. 1988. "Black Women in Poverty: Some Comments on Female-Headed Families." *Signs* 13 (Winter): 331–339.

Bridges, Judith S., and Claire Etaugh. 1996. "Black and White College Women's Maternal Employment Outcome Expectations and Their Desired Timing in Maternal Employment." *Sex Roles* 35 (November): 543–562.

Bryant, Z. Lois, and Marilyn Coleman. 1988. "The Black Family as Portrayed in Introductory Marriage and Family Textbooks." *Family Relations* 37 (July): 255–259.

Buriel, Raymond. 1993. "Childrearing Orientation in Mexican-American Families: The Influence of Generation and Sociocultural Factors." *Journal of Marriage and the Family* 55 (November): 987–1000.

Champion, Jane Dimmitt. 1996. "Woman Abuse, Assimilation, and Self-Concept in a Rural Mexican American Community." *Hispanic Journal of Behavioral Sciences* 18 (November): 508–521.

Corry, John. 1986. "TV: 'CBS Reports' Examines Black Families." *New York Times* (January 25): 49.

Daniels, Roger. 1988. *Asian America: Chinese and Japanese in the United States since 1850.* Seattle: University of Washington Press.

Darity, William A., Jr., and Samuel L. Myers, Jr. 1984. "Does Welfare Dependency Cause Female Headship? The Case of the Black Family." *Journal of Marriage and the Family 46* (November): 765–779.

Demos, Vasilikie. 1990. "Black Family Studies in the *Journal of Marriage and the Family* and the Issue of Distortion: A Trend Analysis." *Journal of Marriage and the Family* 52 (August): 603–612.

DeParle, Jason. 1997. "U.S. Welfare System Dies as State Programs Emerge." *New York Times* (June 30): A1+.

de Uriarte, Mercedes Lynn. 1997. "Baiting Immigrants: Heartbreak for Latinos," pp. 119–121 in John A. Kromkowski (ed.), *Race and Ethnic Relations 97/98*, 7th ed. Guilford, CT: Dushkin Publishing Group.

Doob, Christopher Bates. 1996. *Racism: An American Cauldron*, 2nd ed. New York: HarperCollins College Publishers.

DuBois, W. E. B. 1967. *The Philadelphia Negro*. New York: Benjamin Blom. Originally published in 1899.

duCille, Ann. 1994. "The Occult of True Black Womanhood: Critical Demeanor and Black Feminist Studies." *Signs* 19 (Spring): 591–629.

Duneier, Mitchell. 1994. *Slim's Table: Race, Respectability, and Masculinity*. Chicago: University of Chicago Press.

Dunn, Ashley. 1994. "Southeast Asians Highly Dependent on Welfare in U.S." *New York Times* (May 19): A1+.

Edelman, Marian Wright. 1989. "Children at Risk." *Proceedings of the Academy of Political Science* 37: 20–30.

Edmo, Ed. 1990. "Cradleboards and Development." *American Indians for Development Newsletter* 5 (May/June): 2–3.

Fitzpatrick, Joseph P. 1987. *Puerto Rican Americans: The Meaning of Migration to the Mainland*, 2nd ed. Englewood Cliffs, NJ: Prentice-Hall.

Franklin, John Hope, and Alfred A. Moss, Jr. 1988. *From Slavery to Freedom: A History of Negro Americans, 6th ed.* New York: Alfred A. Knopf.

Frazier, E. Franklin. 1957. *Black Bourgeoisie*. Glencoe, IL: Free Press.

Furstenberg, Frank F., S. Philip Morgan, Kristin A. Moore, and James L. Peterson. 1987. "Race Differences in the Timing of Adolescent Intercourse." *American Sociological Review* 52 (October): 511–518.

Gage, Beverly. 1997. "Survival Tactics." *New Haven Advocate* (May 8): 14+.

Ganong, Lawrence H., et al. 1996. "African American and European American College Students' Expectations for Self and for Future Partners." *Journal of Family Issues* 17 (November): 758–775.

Genovese, Eugene D. 1994. "The Myth of the Absent Family," pp. 20–25 in Robert Staples (ed.), *The Black Family: Essays and Studies*, 5th ed. Belmont, CA: Wadsworth Publishing Company.

Gresham, Jewell Handy. 1989. "White Patriarchal Supremacy: The Politics of Family in America." *Nation* 249 (July 24/31): 116–122.

Harrison, Algea O., et al. 1990. "Family Ecologies of Ethnic Minority Children." *Child Development* 61 (April): 347–362.

Hayes, Cheryl D. 1987. *Risking the Future: Adolescent Sexuality, Pregnancy, and Childbearing.* Washington, DC: National Academy Press.

Heiss, Jerold. 1996. "Effects of African American Family Structure on School Attitudes and Performance." *Social Problems* 43 (August): 246–267.

hooks, bell. 1992. "Feminism: a Transformational Politic," pp. 441–448 in Paula S. Rothenberg (ed.), *Race, Class, & Gender in the United States: An Integrated Study,* 2nd ed. New York: St. Martin's Press.

hooks, bell. 1994. "Black Women and Feminism," pp. 148–153 in Richard C. Monk (ed.), *Taking Sides: Clashing Views on Controversial Issues in Race and Ethnicity.* Guilford, CT: Dushkin Publishing Group.

Ima, Kenji. 1982. "Japanese Americans: The Making of 'Good' People," pp. 262–302 in Anthony Gary Dworkin and Rosalind J. Dworkin (eds.), *The Minority Report,* 2nd ed. New York: Holt, Rinehart and Winston.

Ishii-Kuntz, Masako. 1997. "Intergenerational Relationships among Chinese, Japanese, and Korean Americans." *Family Relations* 46 (January): 23–32.

Jackson, Shirley A. 1998. "Something About the Word: African American Women and Feminism," pp. 38–50 in Kathleen M. Blee (ed.), *No Middle Ground: Women and Radical Protest.* New York: New York University Press.

Jaynes, Gerald David, and Robin M. Williams, Jr. (eds.). 1989. *A Common Destiny: Blacks and American Society.* Washington, DC.: National Academy Press.

Johnson, Michael P. 1989. "Upward in Slavery." *New York Review of Books* 36 (December 21): 51–55.

Jones, John Paul, III. 1987. "Work, Welfare, and Poverty among Black Female-Headed Families." *Economic Geography* 63 (January): 20–34.

Kagan, Sharon L. 1989. "The Care and Education of America's Young Children: At the Brink of a Paradigm Shift?" *Proceedings of the Academy of Political Science* 37: 70–83.

Keefe, Susan E., and Amado M. Padilla. 1987. *Chicano Ethnicity.* Albuquerque: University of New Mexico Press.

Kitano, Harry H. L., and Roger Daniels. 1988. *Asian Americans: Emerging Americans.* Englewood Cliffs, NJ: Prentice-Hall.

Kivisto, Peter. 1995. *Americans All: Race and Ethnic Relations in Historical, Structural, and Comparative Perspectives.* Belmont, CA: Wadsworth Publishing Company.

Li, Wen Lang. 1982. "Chinese Americans: Exclusion from the Melting Pot," pp. 303–328 in Anthony Gary Dworkin and Rosalind J. Dworkin (eds.), *The Minority Report,* 2nd ed. New York: Holt, Rinehart and Winston.

Littlejohn-Blake, Sheila M., and Carol Anderson Darling. 1993. "Understanding the Strengths of African American Families." *Journal of Black Studies* 23 (June): 460–471.

Maldonado, Lionel A. 1982. "Mexican-Americans: The Emergence of a Minority," pp. 168–195 in Anthony Gary Dworkin and Rosalind J. Dworkin (eds.), *The Minority Report,* 2nd ed. New York: Holt, Rinehart and Winston.

Marable, Manning. 1994. "The Black Male: Searching beyond Stereotypes," pp. 69–77 in Richard G. Majors and Jacob U. Gordon (eds.), *The American Black Male: His Present Status and His Future.* Chicago: Nelson-Hall Publishers.

McDaniel, Antonio, and S. Philip Morgan. 1996. "Racial Differences in Mother-Child Coresidence in the Past." *Journal of Marriage and the Family* 58 (November): 1011–1017.

McLanahan, Sara, and Irwin Garfinkel. 1989. "Single Mothers, the Underclass, and Social Policy." *American Academy of Political and Social Science* 501 (January): 92–104.

Miller, Bruce C. 1992. "Women and Politics: Comparative Evidence from the Northwest Coast." *Ethnology* 31 (October): 367–383.

Miller, Bruce C. 1994. "Women and Tribal Politics: Is There a Gender Gap in Indian Elections?" *American Indian Quarterly* 18 (Winter): 25–41.

Montgomery, Laura E., and Gregory Pappas. 1996. "The Effects of Poverty, Race, and Family Structure on US Children's Health: Data from the NHIS, 1978 through 1980 and 1989 through 1991." *American Journal of Public Health* 86 (October): 1401–1405.

Moore, Joan, and Raquel Pinderhughes. 1995. "The Latino Population: The Importance of Restructuring," pp. 227–236 in Margaret L. Andersen and Patricia Hill Collins (eds.), *Race, Class, and Gender*, 2nd ed. Belmont, CA: Wadsworth Publishing Company.

Noda, Kesaya E. 1993. "Growing Up Asian in America," pp. 45–50 in Anne Minas (ed.), *Gender Basics: Feminist Perspectives on Women and Men*. Belmont, CA: Wadsworth Publishing Company.

Office of Policy Planning and Research, United States Department of Labor. 1965. *The Negro Family: The Case for National Action*. Washington, DC: United States Department of Labor.

Omolade, Barbara. 1993. "A Black Feminist Pedagogy." *Women's Studies Quarterly* 21 (Fall/Winter): 31–38.

Owens, Michelle Deaneen, and Deborah Ridley Brome. 1997. "A Preliminary Examination of Family Environment and Social Support among African American Nongrandmothers, Grandmothers, and Grandmothers-to-Be." *Journal of Black Psychology* 23 (February): 74–89.

Pagnini, Deanna L., and S. Philip Morgan. 1997. "Racial Differences in Marriage and Childbearing: Oral History Evidence from the South in the Early Twentieth Century." *American Journal of Sociology* 101 (May): 1694–1718.

Parker, Seymour, and Robert J. Kleiner. 1977. "Social and Psychological Dimensions of the Family Role Performance of the Negro Male," in Doris Y. Wilkinson and Ronald L. Taylor (eds.), *The Black Male in America: Perspectives on His Status in Contemporary Society*. Chicago: Nelson-Hall.

Pearson, Jane L., et al. 1990. "Black Grandmothers in Multigenerational Households: Diversity in Family Structure and Parenting Involvement in the Woodlawn Community." *Child Development* 61 (April): 434–442.

Price, John A. 1984. "North American Indian Families," pp. 245–268 in Charles H. Mindel and Robert W. Habenstein (eds.), *Ethnic Families in America: Patterns and Variations*, 2nd ed. New York: Elsevier.

Rimer, Sara. 1986. " 'Hotel Kid' Becomes Symbol for the Homeless." *New York Times* (March 6): 42.

Robinson, Ira E., Wilfrid C. Bailey, and John M. Smith, Jr. 1985. "Self-Perception of the Husband/Father in the Intact Lower Class Black Family." *Phylon* 46 (June): 136–147.

Rosewater, Ann. 1989. "Child and Family Trends: Beyond the Numbers." *Proceedings of the Academy of Political Science* 37: 4–19.

Rossi, Peter H. 1994. "Troubling Families: Family Homelessness in America." *American Behavioral Scientist* 37 (January): 342–395.

Ryan, William. 1976. *Blaming the Victim*, rev. ed. New York: Vintage Books.

Sampson, Robert J. 1987. "Urban Black Violence: The Effect of Male Joblessness and Family Disruption." *American Journal of Sociology* 93 (September): 348–382.

Segura, Denise A., and Jennifer L. Pierce. 1993. "Chicana/o Family Structure and Gender Personality: Chodorow, Familism, and Psychoanalytic Sociology Revisited." *Signs* 19 (Autumn): 62–91.

Smith, Barbara Ellen. 1995. "Crossing the Great Divides: Race, Class, and Gender in Southern Women's Organizing, 1979–1991." *Gender & Society* 9 (December): 680–696.

Song, Young I. 1993. "Asian American Women's Experience in the Crossfire of Cultural Conflict," pp. 186–203 in Young I. Song and Eugene C. Kim (eds.), *American Mosaic: Selected Readings on America's Multicultural Heritage*. Englewood Cliffs, NJ: Prentice-Hall.

Stafford, Walter. 1996. "Black Civil Society: Fighting for a Seat at the Table." *Social Policy* 27 (Winter): 11–16.

Staples, Robert. 1984. "The Black Amerian Family," pp. 217–244 in Charles H. Mindel and Robert W. Habenstein (eds.), *Ethnic Families in America: Patterns and Variations*, 2nd ed. New York: Elsevier.

Staples, Robert. 1994. *The Black Family: Essays and Studies*, 5th ed. Belmont, CA: Wadsworth Publishing Company.

Stark, David M. 1996. "Discovering the Invisible Puerto Rican Slave Family: Demographic Evidence from the Eighteenth Century." *Journal of Family History* 21 (October): 395–418.

Stewart, James B. 1994. "Neoconservative Attacks on Black Families and the Black Male: An Analysis and Critique," pp. 39–58 in Richard G. Majors and Jacob U. Gordon (eds.), *The American Black Male: His Present Status and His Future*. Chicago: Nelson-Hall Publishers.

Sullivan, Mercer L. 1989. "Absent Fathers in the Inner City." *Annals of the American Academy of Political and Social Science* 501 (January): 48–58.

Taylor, Ronald L. 1990. "Black Youth: The Endangered Generation." *Youth and Society* 22 (September): 4–11.

Taylor, Ronald L. 1994. "Black Males and Social Policy: Breaking the Cycle of Disadvantage," pp. 147–166 in Richard G. Majors and Jacob U. Gordon (eds.), *The American Black Male: His Present Status and His Future*. Chicago: Nelson-Hall Publishers.

Taylor, Robert Joseph, Linda M. Chatters, and James S. Jackson. 1993. "A Profile of Familial Relations among Three-Generation Black Families." *Family Relations* 42 (July): 332–341.

Taylor, Robert Joseph, Linda M. Chatters, and Vickie M. Mays. 1988. "Parents, Children, Siblings, In-Laws, and Non-kin as Sources of Emergency Assistance to Black Americans." *Family Relations* 37 (July): 298–304.

Terkel, Studs. 1992. *Race: How Blacks & Whites Think & Feel about the American Obsession*. New York: New Press.

Testa, Mark, et al. 1989. "Employment and Marriage among Inner-City Youths." *Annals of the American Academy of Political and Social Science* 501 (January): 79–91.

Thomas, Veronica G. 1990. "Determinants of Global Life Happiness and Marital Happiness in Dual-Career Black Couples." *Family Relations* 39 (April): 174–178.

Tolbert, Caroline J., and Rodney E. Hero. 1996. "Race/Ethnicity and Direct Democracy: An Analysis of California's Illegal Immigration Initiative." *Journal of Politics* 58 (August): 806–818.

U.S. Bureau of the Census. 1990. *Statistical Abstract of the United States: 1990*, 110th edition. Washington, DC: U.S. Government Printing Office.

U.S. Bureau of the Census. 1996. *Statistical Abstract of the United States: 1996*, 116th edition. Washington, DC: U.S. Government Printing Office.

U.S. Bureau of the Census. 1997. *Statistical Abstract of the United States: 1997*, 117th edition. Washington, DC: U.S. Government Printing Office.

Verhovek, Sam Howe. 1995. "States Are Already Providing Glimpse of Welfare's Future." *New York Times* (September 21): A1+.

Wilkerson, Isabel. 1995. "An Intimate Look at Welfare: Women Who've Been There." *New York Times* (February 17): A1+.

Wilkerson, Margaret, and Jewell Handy Gresham. 1989. "Sexual Politics of Welfare: The Racialization of Poverty." *Nation* 249 (July 24/31): 126–130+.

Williams, Walter E. 1996. "Myth Making and Reality Testing," pp. 93-98 in Richard C. Monk (ed.), *Taking Sides: Clashing Views on Controversial Issues in Race and Ethnicity*, 2nd ed. Guilford, CT: Dushkin Publishing Group.

Willie, Charles V. 1991. *A New Look at Black Families*, 4th ed. Dix Hills, NY: General Hall.

Willie, Charles V. 1993. "Social Theory and Social Policy Derived from the Black Family Experience." *Journal of Black Studies* 23 (June): 451–459.

Ying, Yu-Wen. 1994. "Chinese American Adults' Relationship with Their Parents." *International Journal of Social Psychiatry* 40 (Spring): 35–45.

Zayas, Luis H., and Josephine Palleja. 1988. "Puerto Rican Familism: Considerations for Family Therapy." *Family Relations* 37 (July): 260–264.

CHAPTER 8

Distorted Image: Racial Minorities in the Mass Media

Convicted of armed robbery, Nathan McCall was sent to the Norfolk jail to await transmission to a prison. Time hung heavily on his hands, and he decided to relieve the boredom by volunteering for one of the jail jobs. Eventually he became the inmate librarian.

Besides reading a few short stories in high school, McCall had done very little recreational reading. Now, however, with books all around him, he started leafing through a number of them. One day he picked up a book with a black man's picture on the cover. It was Richard Wright's *Native Son,* and once he started reading it, McCall couldn't put it down.

The story was about a confused, angry young black man named Bigger Thomas, whose racial fears led him to accidentally suffocate a white woman. Knowing that nobody would believe that her death was accidental, he dismembered the body and tried to incinerate it in the furnace. Soon, though, he was apprehended, tried, and sentenced to die.

McCall identified with Bigger. They were both 20 years old and had ended up in prison. They shared the same conflicting feelings: "restless anger, hopelessness, a tough façade among blacks and deep-seated fear of whites—that I'd sensed in myself but was unable to express." Like Bigger, McCall had felt himself "headed down a road toward a destruction that I couldn't ward off, beaten by forces so large and amorphous that I had no idea how to fight back" (McCall, 1994: 157). He was surprised to find that someone had written a book that so clearly represented his experiences and feelings.

Not accustomed to books, McCall read slowly—through the days and during the nights by the dim light of the hall lamps. Toward the end of the book, there is a passage in which a lawyer talks to Bigger shortly before his execution. The man explains that while Bigger was trying to find a way to feel good about himself, his mind kept getting in the way. All through his life people had told him he was bad. Invariably, when a person receives that message over and over, he will have doubts about himself. The challenge, the lawyer continues, is to help people to understand and accept their feelings and to appreciate that they are just as significant and worthy as anybody else's.

After reading that passage, McCall sat up in his bunk, buried his face in his hands, and wept. The tears, however, brought relief. Finally he was releasing feelings that he had held in for years—feelings that he was unaccustomed to dealing with and that he didn't understand. McCall wrote, *"Native Son* confirmed for me that my fears *weren't* imagined and that there were rational reasons why I'd been hurting inside" (McCall, 1994: 158).

In school nearly all of the books were about whites' feelings and experiences. The only time African Americans' lives received any attention was during Black History Week, and then time was spent only on "Booker T. Washington and a few other noteworthy, dead black folks I couldn't relate to" (McCall, 1994: 158). Reading *Native Son* was a very different experience, however, and McCall was now stimulated to look for more books that could help him learn more about himself and about a society where so many young black men ended up in prison.

While Nathan McCall's encounter with *Native Son* was dramatic, we see that it was hardly unique. In various ways books and other forms of mass media can affect people's perceptions of race and racism and also how they feel about themselves.

The central subject in this chapter is the **mass media,** which are the instruments of communication that reach a large audience without any personal contact between senders and receivers. Books, records, newspapers, radio, television, videos, and movies are the most significant mass media.

Prominent in these discussions is a concept we have already used extensively. A **stereotype** is a highly exaggerated, greatly oversimplified image, maintained by prejudiced people, of the characteristics of the group members against whom they are prejudiced.

In this chapter we discuss mass media from the internal colonialist perspective. Then we consider the impact of mass media on racial minorities.

Mass Media and Internal Colonialism

Three tenets of internal colonialism apply to racial minorities' relationship to the mass media. The colonial labor principle is relevant: Members of racial minorities tend to be kept out of powerful, desirable jobs, with few minority group members in leadership positions in the popular mass media. The second principle of internal colonialism is restriction of racial minorities' freedom of movement. In this chapter we see how minorities' stereotyped portrayal in the mass media has helped impose restrictions on them. Finally, stereotyped representations of racial minorities in the media have served to represent them as culturally and even genetically inferior.

Racial Minorities' Participation in Mass Media

Starting on an optimistic note, some newspapers have implemented a high level of racial diversity in employment. Beginning in 1986, the *Washington Post* decided that 25 percent of new journalists hired would be minorities. In the first nine years, the paper brought in 98 minority group members and 232 whites, thus attaining a 30 percent overall level of minorities among new hires (Downie and Graham, 1996: 132).

Moving on to the larger picture, one finds that compared to their white colleagues, minority print journalists are less optimistic about their prospects. According to a survey conducted by the Minnesota Opinion Research Institute, 63 percent of whites believed that minorities spent the same or less time at entry-level positions as did whites while 66 percent of the minorities surveyed felt they spent more time at the bottom. Forty percent of whites believed that standards for promotion were lower for minorities, but 75 percent of minority staff felt they faced higher standards. Whites were more likely than minority groups to expect to be in their same position at the same newspaper in five years and also to desire that outcome (Cohen, 1996).

In 1997 a survey by the American Society of Newspaper Editors indicated that for the first time in 19 years the number of minority group members working in newspaper newsrooms had levelled off. In a nation where minorities comprise 24 percent of the population, the survey indicated they comprised 11.35 percent of newsroom employees, with 5.4 percent African Americans, 3.4 percent Hispanic Americans, 2.1 percent Asian Americans, and less than half a percent Native Americans. While various factors come into play, two of particular significance seem to be that recruitment is difficult because people of color often distrust the media, and minority journalists often become frustrated by the sense that their work is undervalued (Fitzgerald, 1997a, 1997b).

In spite of the growing market of Spanish-speaking readers, the American Society of Newspaper Editors indicated that only 3 percent of reporters on U.S. newspapers are Hispanic and that 44 percent of these papers have no Hispanics in the newsroom. The Hispanic journalists working in the mainstream press are primarily in the lower and middle ranks, with very few holding top executive jobs. Observers cite various reasons for the low numbers, including racism in hiring practices and Hispanic Americans' distrust of mainstream newspapers. Regardless of the reasons for the low representation, it increases the possibility that Hispanic-related issues will be covered sparsely or simply ignored (Stein, 1997a, 1997b).

Statistically, African Americans have done well as characters in network television programs. In the late 1960s, they represented 6 percent of the characters, with their share rising to 8 percent in the 1970s, 12 percent in the 1980s, and then 14 percent in the early 1990s. The latter figure actually meant that black characters were represented in a greater proportion than within the population at large—perhaps because Nielsen ratings have indicated that African Americans average more TV-watching time than most other groups. In contrast, there were several Asian characters in the 1980s but none in the 1990s, and Hispanic numbers went from 1 percent of characters in the 1970s to less than half a percentage in the 1990s (Greenberg and Collette, 1997).

Throughout all mass media, African Americans and other minority group members have had low representation in leadership positions such as editors, managers, and, in particular, owners. At present about 2.7 percent of the nation's television and radio stations are minority owned, and frequently these are among the weakest in their markets. One distinctive impact of minority ownership is that a greater number of minorities is likely to be hired. Research, however, has not established to what extent minorities' presence on the job affects programming. While some observers believe that an increase of minorities in radio and TV invariably influences news coverage and entertainment choices, others argue that career pressures on the decision makers have the dominant impact (Fabrikant, 1994). Most likely both factors come into play.

People belonging to different minority groups tend to support their own members' involvement in the mass media. When representative samples of African Americans, Hispanic Americans, and Asian Americans across the country were asked whether a news story primarily involving their respective group should receive coverage by a reporter belonging to their ethnic group, 58 percent of African Americans, 54 percent of Hispanic Americans, and 61 percent of Asian Americans indicated that it was very important or somewhat important to provide that same-group coverage (McAneny, 1994: 35).

Since the 1940s a number of black novelists, playwrights, poets, and other writers have had their work published or produced widely. One specialist in African American literature suggested that white Americans have met more black men through their portraits in novels and autobiographies than they have encountered in person (Andrews, 1994: 60). Following World War II, talented and versatile black actors performed on the stage and on the screen, and since the 1940s black actors have appeared on television, starting to play major characters in situation comedies during the early 1950s. By the late 1980s, Bill Cosby and Oprah Winfrey were the highest paid entertainers on television.

Perhaps African American artists have been best known in popular music. During the 1950s a number of African American singers and singing groups were commercially successful. In the past three decades, such performers as Ray Charles, Stevie Wonder, Diana Ross, and Michael Jackson have achieved the "crossover" effect, becoming as popular with white as with African American audiences (Abarry, 1990; Franklin and Moss, 1988: 374–375; 431–432; Jaynes and Williams, 1989: 101–102). But the number of successful African American singers and entertainers is relatively small.

Other racial minorities, for instance Asian Americans, have also had limited prominence in the major mass media. In such low-budget movies as *Dim Sum, Chan Is Missing, and Hito Hata,* Asian American filmmakers have had some popular and commercial success portraying the Asian American experience. It appears, however, that most white Americans do not want Asian Americans represented in dominant roles in the popular media (Kitano and Daniels, 1988: 176).

Even when they are successful, some minority artists face an indifferent, even hostile commercial world. Rudolfo Anaya's novel *Bless Me, Ultima* was first published in 1972, selling over 250,000 copies and still producing 13,000 sales annually. While the book remains popular among Mexican Americans, no major publisher has issued a mass-market edition. John Randall, who runs a bookstore featuring Chicano and Native American material, feels that censorship is common with writers like Anaya, whose writings help members of their racial group understand and rebel against political and economic oppression. Referring to Chicano writers breaking into mainstream publishing, Anaya said, "It's just that we see how important it is for the culture that our voices be heard and known to a wider readership. So while we're struggling to maintain our culture, lack of attention to it helps ensure that cultural genocide goes on" (M. Jones, 1990: 30).

Sometimes modern minority group members can identify an area where they have been excluded from media participation and then take decisive actions to alter the situation. For example, in 1992, three African American women formed a company called Black Books Galore!, which conducts book fairs and festivals providing hundreds of children's books about blacks, Native Americans, and other racial minorities. Such books do exist, but they are not well publicized or distributed. Christine Dina, a black woman who had grown up without such books and was experiencing the same deficiency with her 15-year-old daughter, explained:

> I never imagined there were so many books about different ethnic groups. Before we had the book fairs, which have been tremendously successful, I just thought there was not that much good literature about blacks and other minorities. I was wrong. (*New York Times*, 1994b: 42)

In November 1996 Dina and the rest of the staff at Black Books Galore! planned the Multi-Cultural Children's Book Festival at the John F. Kennedy Center for the Performing Arts. The result was 5,000 books for sale, 20 authors and illustrators reading, performing, and autographing, and 3,500 attendees (Wexler, 1997). With mainstream bookstores often failing to meet the needs of African Americans and other minorities, a company like Black Books Galore! has a continuing opportunity to resolve a glaring need.

While Black Books Galore! addresses a failure to present African Americans' contribution, sometimes minorities' welfare would be better served if they were not represented. For instance, Steven C. Dubin (1987) studied African Americans' representation on objects like salt and pepper shakers, cookie jars, lawn statues, and ashtrays. These media often portray African Americans with grossly distorted features and dressed like slaves ready to perform menial domestic tasks. Dubin described the representations as "symbolic slavery." Such a designation conveys a sense of the colonial labor principle: that the purchasers would be comfortable with a world where blacks and members of other racial minorities were restricted to menial, slavelike jobs. Such stereotyped images on objects were most popular from the 1890s to the 1950s and have become much less prevalent in the past four decades as whites have realized that they are insulting to blacks.

In contrast, a fairly recent event—the overthrow of South Africa's oppressive *apartheid* system—has produced minority group members' triumphal representation on objects. In the spring of 1994, South Africans could buy a four-foot-high wall clock picturing Nelson Mandela, the most prominent black hero. Mandela's likeness was also featured on a sun visor produced by his political party. In addition, *Oppression,* a Monopoly-style game, replicated the segregationist rules of *apartheid:* Draw a card and pay a $10 fine for letting your children play at an all-white playground; or roll doubles and reclassify a rival as a minority group member—black, Indian, or Colored (Keller, 1994).

Back in the United States, many of us have observed that over the past several decades suburbanites with lawn statues of black lackeys have either removed them or painted the face white, thereby preserving the statue and a sense of the elitist lifestyle it implies. The latter action seems to represent such people's sensibility about racism—that all that's needed to remove racism is a symbolic coat of paint, representing both a physical and cultural camouflage for modern racism.

From the material in this section, what expectations should one have about the career of an independent-minded black woman writer whose first literary works appeared in the 1920s?

Zora Neale Hurston: Against the Colonial Labor Principle

Zora Hurston was born in 1891 in a small Alabama town where her parents were sharecroppers. While she was still a young child, the family moved to Eatonville, Florida, the first incorporated black town, where her father both became a preacher and served three terms as mayor. Later, in writing novels, she used this experience, like so many in her life, as a source of information.

After her mother died in 1904, Hurston had little opportunity for education. Instead she had to clean house and mind children, and yet she persevered, eventually finishing high school in 1918 and then going on to Howard University. In 1925 she arrived in New York City with no job, no friends, and a dollar and fifty cents to her name. She managed to get a job working for Fannie Hurst, a best-selling novelist, and also studied under anthropologist Franz Boas, whose emphasis on the importance of southern black culture inspired her. Boas sent Hurston back to the South to study her people's language and culture—things she had previously taken for granted and now was encouraged to value strongly. The results of her fieldwork were apparent in the stories, plays, musical reviews, and academic articles she wrote throughout the early 1930s.

While many of Hurston's novels were published in her lifetime, she was hardly a major hit. In the 1930s and 1940s, few whites were interested in black people, and so blacks' novels, no matter how well written, received little attention. The distinct exception was Richard Wright. Hurston strongly disagreed with his emphasis on racial violence, suggesting that it would appeal to black male readers but that it obscured many of the complex realities in southern African Americans' daily lives. Wright, in turn, sharply criticized Hurston's work, saying that her description of blacks' lives in southern small towns, including her dialogue in black dialect, served simply to support the status quo. At the time his approach was much more popular with both blacks and whites.

The colonial labor principle suggests that a black writer's work would sell only if it appealed to majority group audiences. In her lifetime Hurston's didn't, and she was never a financial success, dying in 1960 in a welfare home in Fort Pierce, Florida. Hurston's success has come only since the 1970s, when black writers, particularly

Alice Walker, began to write and speak about her contributions. By the middle 1990s, all her major works had been republished, most recently by the Library of America, and her novel *Their Eyes Were Watching God* has sold more than a million copies since 1990, with the movie rights bought by Oprah Winfrey and Quincy Jones.

Reading Hurston's work, one is struck by its complexity and individuality. Those expecting to find evidence that she was an unrelenting champion of black people's strengths will discover mixed results. While many of her African American characters show generosity, nobility, intelligence, and other desirable traits, others are stupid, brutal, and racially rivalrous, believing that lighter-skinned blacks were superior to their darker companions. Furthermore, Hurston showed whites as diverse, presenting some as humane and insightful about blacks' actions and goals.

Feminists often have a mixed reaction to Hurston's work. During the 1970s, when *Their Eyes Were Watching God* was rediscovered, some literary critics considered Janie Crawford, the book's heroine, a candidate for the first heroic black woman in African American literature. But later on, other observers wondered why she couldn't go it alone and was always waiting for a man to provide the lead. The reality is that Janie was not meant to be a feminist model but simply a woman whose only ambition was to live as well as possible.

One of Hurston's most enduring contributions has been her characters' use of language. In an article about the author and her work, Claudia Roth Pierpont wrote:

> "It's sort of duskin' down dark" observes the otherwise unexceptional Mrs. Sumpkins, checking the sky and issuing the local evening variant of rosy-fingered dawn. "He's uh whirlwind among breezes," one front-porch sage notes of the town's mayor; another adds, "He's got uh throne in de seat of his pants." The simplest men and women of all-black Eatonville have this wealth of images easy at their lips. This . . . is a record of the unique explosion that occurred when African people with an intensely musical and oral culture came up hard against the King James Bible and the sweet-talking American South, under conditions that denied them all outlet for their visions and gifts except the transformation of the English language into song. (Pierpont, 1997: 80)

In 1995 when the Library of America published two large volumes containing all Hurston's major work, I read both. At first I found it difficult to understand some of the dialogue. Soon, when stumped, I began to read aloud, and usually the meaning became clear. Like Claudia Pierpont I soon was immersed in the material, captivated by its poetic, musical sound.

Media Stereotypes and Restriction of Minorities' Activity

Why have stereotypes been used in the mass media? One answer is that through the centuries their use has proved profitable (Clifton, 1990: 19-20). By the middle of the nineteenth century, writers learned that they could become wealthy writing Indian captivity narratives that barraged readers with sensationalized accounts of tortures and sexual abuse inflicted on captives, especially female captives (VanDerBeets, 1984).

Early films about Indians grew out of this tradition, recognizing that lurid, bloodthirsty sensationalism would bring patrons streaming into the theatres just as it had sent them running to the bookstores. Once filmmakers obtained proof that flaming arrows, burning forts and wagons, and screaming, soon-to-be-raped white women would effectively sell tickets, they gave up efforts to produce historically accurate portraits of Native Americans. Sensationalism in Indian films caught on so quickly, in fact, that in 1911 members of four western tribes travelled to Washington, D.C., to protest their treatment in films to Congress and to President William Howard Taft (Stedman, 1982: 157–158). Whether whites' opponents in film were Indians or some other minority group, Hollywood traditionally stereotyped them as the bad guys, giving them no chance to tell their own story and thus making it impossible to appreciate their resistance to whites' invasion, exploitation, and slaughter (Kitano, 1997: 70–71).

Filmmakers would not have produced such stereotyped representations of minorities if they were not popular. So it seems useful to speculate about what conditions in American society have encouraged support for stereotypes. Once more the internal colonialist perspective seems relevant: Stereotypes prove useful in controlling racial minorities' activities.

The mass media, especially written accounts, played a role in this endeavor. Mary Rowlandson, a seventeenth-century homemaker, authored the earliest effort. Captured during an Indian raid in 1675, Rowlandson was held by her captives for 12 weeks, then released after a ransom payment. Rowlandson's book described the atrocities she supposedly observed—the torture and killing of numerous white women and children. For decades the book was reprinted, and it became the prototype for later Indian captivity novels. Unlike later, fictionalized victims, Mary Rowlandson apparently was not sexually violated by her captors. Nonetheless, Raymond William Stedman indicated, even modern readers have found her account gruesome and terrifying.

> How much more unsettling it must have been when the depicted menaces were still only a night's march away from frontier cabins. It is well to remember that for two centuries and more the Rowlandson capture reflected elements of actual threat to many Americans—and a convenient excuse for land grabbing and Indian damning to others. (Stedman, 1982: 75)

Indian attacks ceased about a century ago. Undoubtedly African Americans have been the source of contemporary white Americans' greatest racial fears. Sometimes those fears have been so great that they have even affected whites trained to provide calm, objective analysis. During the 1960s urban riots, many journalists claimed that strategically placed snipers launched carefully planned and coordinated attacks on whites. Professional investigators looked into 25 such reports and found little or no supportive evidence. This research, however, received almost no publicity. The press's accounts of systematic insurrection carried the day and contributed substantially to a stereotype of brutal blacks dedicated to the systematic murder of whites (Hartmann and Husband, 1974: 156). Obviously the idea that such people had to be controlled by any means necessary was readily forthcoming. The same implication applies to the following situation.

In late 1989 in Boston, a highly publicized murder occurred. Carol Stuart, a pregnant white woman, was shot and Charles Stuart, her white husband, was wounded. Stuart claimed that the assailant had been black. The police systematically searched an African American neighborhood where Stuart claimed the assailant had forced him to drive before shooting Stuart and his wife. Even though Stuart's story had suspicious overtones, journalists accepted his account, not following the standard procedure of seeking verifying sources. One reporter indicated that press coverage was "voluminous and dramatic" (A. Jones, 1990: A21). On its front page, the *Boston Globe* published a picture of Mrs. Stuart's shattered head, and local radio and television kept replaying Mr. Stuart's desperate conversation with the police dispatcher, in which he referred to an unknown black assailant. Eventually evidence made it clear that Stuart should be the chief suspect, and at this point he committed suicide. African American leaders were enraged that the police and press so readily mobilized to seek a black suspect when from the beginning there was ample reason to regard Stuart suspiciously (Butterfield, 1990). The cultural camouflage for modern racism was apparent here: Apparently Stuart's account of a brutal murder produced by an unknown black killer resonated for many journalists, encouraging them to succumb to a racist interpretation.

As Table 8.1 indicates, many members of three minority groups believe that when covering crime stories, the local daily newspapers as well as local and national television news treat their group unfairly.

Other evidence has addressed the issue of controlling racial minorities, albeit in a more subtle manner. A study of African Americans' portrayal in popular magazines' advertisements produced between 1950 and 1982 found that whites and African Americans were much more likely to appear together on equal social terms in later ads. However, even recently the chances were substantially greater that the people in the pictures would be interacting with each other if all were white than if they were both black and white (Humphrey and Schuman, 1984). Thus, in the course of three decades, advertising specialists have concluded that popular magazines' primarily white audiences have been increasingly willing to support African Americans' entrance into their social world but have continued to want limited interaction with them.

Table 8.1   Response to Media Coverage of Crime Stories Involving One's Own Group: 1994

	African Americans	Hispanic Americans	Asian Americans	Whites
Local newspapers				
Fair	38%	61%	69%	85%
Unfair	47	30	10	10
No opinion	15	9	21	5
Local TV news				
Fair	35%	64%	73%	83%
Unfair	53	31	15	10
No opinion	12	5	12	7
National TV news				
Fairly	34%	60%	75%	77%
Unfair	55	34	14	17
No opinion	11	6	11	6

Note: Among the four groups represented here, distinct differences exist in the extent to which members feel that media coverage of crime stories involving their group is unfair. African Americans are the most inclined to perceive unfair coverage, followed by Hispanic Americans, Asian Americans, and whites.

Source: Leslie McAneny. "Ethnic Minorities View the Media's View of Them." *Gallup Poll Monthly.* August 1994, pp. 31–41.

Media Stereotypes of Racial Minorities' Cultural Inferiority

In a history of the relationship between American blacks and television, J. Fred MacDonald wrote, "In terms of utilization of black professional talent, and in the portrayal of Afro-American characters, TV as a new medium had the capability of ensuring a fair and equitable future" (MacDonald, 1983: 21).

So far it has not succeeded in this regard. In the late 1940s, as TV became popular, African Americans appeared in very selected roles as singers, dancers, and clowns. One of the most popular programs was *Amos 'n' Andy*, a televised recreation of a radio show that had been very popular in the 1920s and 1930s with both black and white audiences. In spite of NAACP protests, the program premiered on CBS television in June 1951, bringing "the old minstrel stereotype of blacks as slow, footshuffling, fun-loving, slightly dishonest people from the radio to television for all the world to see" (Staples and Jones, 1985: 12). While such individuals as Kweisi Mfume, the president of the NAACP, have continued to criticize the show, Video Bargains did sell over 40,000 tapes of 10 episodes until in June 1997 the company ran into a dispute with CBS over ownership of the episodes (Elliott, 1997).

As a child I sometimes watched the show, and the character who most vividly comes to mind is George "Kingfish" Stevens, a clumsily deceitful man who inevitably managed to trick Andy and all the other dumb nice guys portrayed on the program. I can remember thinking that if this slow-talking lightweight could outwit the others, then they must be dense indeed. It didn't consciously come to mind that these characters might be considered representative of all blacks, but psychically speaking, that idea couldn't have been very far away.

During the 1950s African Americans were generally limited to small roles on television. In one exception, Ethel Waters and later Louise Beavers starred in *Beulah*, which started in 1950 and was the first television program with a black actor in the lead. The show contained many stereotypes. Beulah was a maid for a prosperous white family and in that role she served as an update of the southern domestic slave—the "mammy" who was warm, loving, dedicated, and so accepted in her role that she could scold and lecture the children. In 1956 the *Nat King Cole Show* premiered on NBC. It was the first time that an African American appeared on TV in a dignified, unstereotyped way, and the program never did well, expiring in 1957 when it could no longer obtain sponsors. Apparently the American public simply was not ready to accept an African American entertainer in anything but stereotyped roles.

Bill Cosby was the first person to break that particular barrier on television. In 1965 he starred with Robert Culp in *I Spy*, playing a basically nonstereotyped role in a successful, three-year program where race was not the central issue. Racist overtones to the role did exist, however. As a spy Cosby's cover was trainer for a tennis player, casting him in a subordinate role within one of blacks' traditional realms—sport. Furthermore, the show's producers permitted Cosby no explicit romantic involvement, thereby reducing whites' possible anxieties about displaying a black man's sexual activities.

Perhaps the late 1960s was the heyday of African Americans' prominence on television. Diahann Carroll, Teresa Graves, Leslie Uggams, and Flip Wilson obtained their own shows, and a host of other programs had African Americans in supporting roles. While the percentage of black actors did not approach their proportion of the population, they had an unprecedented chance to display their abilities relatively unhampered by stereotyped roles.

By the early 1970s, however, the civil rights movement was in decline, and most Americans appeared to return to the asocial outlook of the 1950s and early 1960s. The situation comedy, with its trivialization of social issues and barrage of one-liners, became the rage and has remained prominent to the present day. Following the success of a number of all-white shows, there appeared such all-black or black-dominated shows as *The Jeffersons, Good Times, What's Happening, In Living Color,* and *Fresh Prince of Bel Air.* Many African American analysts have widely criticized these shows, suggesting that the actors' style, particularly their use of "black humor," presents the same kind of witless and deceitful stereotypes of blacks found 30 or 40 years earlier on *Amos 'n' Andy.*

An exception has been the *Cosby Show.* No longer in production but still popular in reruns, it features black actors, but it does not display traditional stereotypical black situations—no ghetto, no drugs, an intact family. The variety of struggles and encounters involving Dr. and Mrs. Huxtable and their children are typically American, not African American. Some critics have pointed out that the show does not address poverty and racism, issues of extreme importance to many blacks, but its significance lies elsewhere: It has presented a middle-class black family in nonstereotyped roles, and it has been a resounding success.

The *Cosby Show* is a clear illustration that African Americans can break long-accepted stereotypes and still be successful. Circumstances surrounding the program are instructive, however. Selling his show to NBC, Cosby had the distinct advantage of being a popular, successful entertainer who was dealing with a network that at the time was dead last in the ratings (Staples and Jones, 1985). The circumstances producing the success of the *Cosby Show* are unusual, and thus it is reasonable not to expect a great flood of nonstereotyped black shows. Nonetheless, black entertainers will probably be able to find some opportunities to step outside narrow roles. In recent years, for instance, *The Oprah Winfrey Show* has become very successful, convincing the American public that an intelligent, quick-witted, outgoing black woman can be an effective talk-show host.

Other hopeful signs exist. For the years 1985 and 1986, a pair of researchers examined the three half-hour, prime-time situation comedies that featured an intact African American family. They found a more positive representation of black families than in earlier programs. In particular, it was apparent that the spouses interacted frequently, lovingly, and equally with each other; that the children were treated with respect and taught achievement-oriented values emphasizing the importance of staying in school, keeping out of trouble, and working hard at all one's endeavors; and that family activity was generally without conflict (Merritt and Stroman, 1993).

Like African Americans and Indians, Asian Americans have had stereotyped roles in the visual media. One analysis indicated that in films, "The evil Jap of World War II and the Communist gooks in Korea, China, and Vietnam—faceless, fanatic, maniacal, willing to die because life is not valued—are endlessly recycled with changes in nationality as our foreign policy changes" (Kitano and Daniels, 1988: 176). Less politically explicit, the karate films that became commercially successful in the 1970s provided similar stereotypes. In 1988 ABC television offered a short-lived series titled *Ohara,* which starred Pat Morita, a Japanese American, in the lead role. Ohara was a small, elderly Japanese American behind whose unassuming bearing lurked an endless series of one-line putdowns reminiscent of the pre–World War II Charlie Chan films, along with, of course, the full martial arts package. It was hardly the series to challenge prevailing stereotypes of Asian Americans developed in films.

Since the Mexican War in the 1840s, white Americans have maintained stereotypes of Mexican Americans. The contemptuous term "greaser" appeared at that time, probably because some Mexicans worked to grease wagon axles. The image that Mexicans were lazy, immoral, untrustworthy, stupid, and dirty was well established by the time films started. The visual media sustained the stereotype. In movies Mexicans were often portrayed as bandits. In the case of the famed Pancho Villa, who conducted raids into Texas, violence and criminality were emphasized, but the films neglected to show that white settlers' exploitation of Mexicans motivated the raids. On television Mexican or Mexican American men were generally presented as lazy, fat, carefree, and immoral and women as flirtatious and promiscuous. Media advertising has also contributed to the Chicano stereotype. Frito ads represented Mexicans as criminals (the "Frito Bandito"), and a deodorant ad showed a grubby-looking Mexican bandit with the caption, "If it works for him, it will work for you" (Feagin and Feagin, 1993: 266; Maldonado, 1982: 193).

About two-thirds of Puerto Rican characters on television are criminals (Staples and Jones, 1985: 15). Undoubtedly the best-known entertainment feature involving Puerto Ricans has been *West Side Story*, first a Broadway musical and later a successful film. While one might concede that it presented a moving Romeo and Juliet type of story and appealing music, it supported prevailing stereotypes of Puerto Rican men as violent, vicious gang members who physically intimidate and dominate their girlfriends.

In his book *A Puerto Rican in New York*, Jesus Colon noted that Puerto Ricans are frequently stereotyped by the mass media, which harp on "what is superficial and sentimental, transient and ephemeral, or bizarre and grotesque in Puerto Rican life" (Colon, 1961: 9).

So far discussion in this section has focused on fictional representations. Stereotyping, however, also occurs in the news area. A study based on 4,000 articles from seven major, general-interest newspapers and the three major newsmagazines indicated that most issues were presented from a mainstream, white-male cultural orientation. Exactly what does this mean? For example, articles pertaining to Barbara Jordan's keynote speech at the 1992 Democratic Convention played up the fact that her call to end white and black racism caused elevated emotions among both blacks and whites, but most accounts provided few or no actual quotes from Jordan elaborating on her remarks. The study found many articles about the competition for black votes but little detailed discussion about African American issues, perceptions, and leaders. The researchers concluded that while minorities are receiving more press coverage, the coverage often fails to reveal the key issues related to their lives (Bridge, 1994).

A similar deficiency has occurred with reporting about Hispanic Americans and Asian Americans. For instance, while mainstream media readily report stories about illegal Asian immigration, the fat content of Chinese food, or other issues enforcing stereotypes, they are much less inclined to give effective coverage to issues that Asian Americans consider significant but that don't fit the stereotypes. Because such stereo-

---

Box 8.1   Mass Media and Internal Colonialism

Tenet of Internal Colonialism	Example
1. Colonial labor principle	Blacks' limited participation in newspapers and television
2. Restriction of minorities' activities	Response to the sense of threat created by Mary Rowlandson's book and Indian captivity novels
3. Racial minorities' supposed cultural inferiority	Past and present television representation of stereotyped black, Japanese American, Native American, and Mexican American characters

---

types are so common and often go unchallenged, many Americans, including journalists, are simply unaware of using them. To restrict stereotyping in reporting, news media need to hire diverse minority group members and permit them a significant role in the planning and development of stories involving ethnic groups (Hernandez, 1994a, 1994b).

Majority group members often enjoy stereotypes of racial minorities' cultural inferiority, finding that they make them feel amused and superior. Whether intended or not, the suggestion of cultural inferiority supports a contention discussed in several chapters, especially the family chapter—that racial minorities' personal inadequacies and not prevailing economic, political, and social conditions are responsible for their lack of success. As we have seen, this victim-blaming perspective supports government programs forcing racial minorities to adopt the majority group's cultural standards. Only then do they have a chance of receiving full acceptance and associated rewards within the society. Box 8.1 summarizes major conclusions from this section.

Sometimes minority group members have mounted significant campaigns to change the media use of stereotypes. The following illustration is a case in point.

Dropping Indian Nicknames

When in 1991 and 1992 the Atlanta Braves twice reached the World Series, a now controversial issue came to national attention: Should professional and college sports teams continue to use nicknames and actions that suggest Indian stereotypes?

Tim Giago (1994), the editor/publisher of the weekly newspaper *Indian Country Today*, suggested that a useful measure is to ask if one would use the nickname if the team were just starting out today. The answer would be negative, Giago concluded. Invariably the nicknames and the costumes, implements, and actions associated with them perpetuate internal colonialist standards, denigrating a people and their cultural tradition: Supporters' claims that such actions are "no big deal" and that the whole thing is just "good, clean fun" become highly suspect (Churchill, 1994).

Let's examine the situation a bit more closely. If one attends an Atlanta Braves baseball game or a Kansas City Chiefs football game, the tomahawk chop in which many fans engage suggests the idea of brutal killing—a perpetuation of the centuries-old stereotype that Native Americans are savage and warlike (Marger, 1994: 170). Furthermore, the "smirking faces painted in Day-Glo colors" suggest to Indians that a spiritual experience in which their ancestors engaged represented no more than a Halloween-like masquerade. Finally, the wearing of feathers or feathered headdresses traditionally honored or blessed the wearer, a significance that the sporting context denigrates.

Hold on there, some readers might say. The call to eliminate Indian nicknames establishes a double standard. After all, white groups are sometimes also given nicknames. Consider, for instance, the Pittsburgh Steelers, the Green Bay Packers, and the Dallas Cowboys. The fact is, however, that none of these are ethnic groups, and thus the stereotyping to which racial minorities are subjected does not occur. Well, then what about the Minnesota Vikings, some might contend. It is true that Vikings represent a onetime ethnic group, but Vikings no longer exist while Indians do. Finally, those citing a double standard might point to the Notre Dame Irish. Here, they could triumphantly conclude, the nickname refers to a living ethnic group. Yes, that is true, but one must mention two considerations. First, it was Irish Catholic officials who created the nickname and not hostile or indifferent outsiders. Second, at rallies and sporting events, Notre Dame supporters have maintained a positive, respectable image. For instance, at football games students do not dress up as popes or cardinals, or ridicule Irish characteristics or culture. One can imagine that if students did engage in such actions, school administrators would take quick steps to repress what would be labelled mischievous or even malicious student behavior.

In the latter case, the key issue would be respect. It is disrespectful to have someone dressed like the pope doing somersaults or backflips, or to have Notre Dame spectators take a swig from a huge mug filled with green beer each time their basketball team scores.

Some observers would say that while this discussion might be interesting, it pales in importance compared with the extensive poverty and other significant problems many Native Americans suffer. However, it might be well to appreciate that if racial minorities want to mobilize economically and politically, respect and self-respect are important incentives.

In recent years some outsiders have been starting to appreciate the nickname issue. As long ago as 1972, Stanford University changed the athletic team's name from "Indians" to "the Cardinal." Recently both St. John's (Redmen) and Marquette (Warriors) have eliminated their traditional nicknames (Giago, 1994; Marger, 1994: 170). Those implementing these changes have developed some ability to see the issue of respect through Indians' eyes. Implicitly they appreciate that the linguistic labels that represent a carryover from the internal colonialist past support a destructive, demeaning tradition.

Having analyzed mass media's treatment of racial minorities, we can examine some impacts of that treatment.

Effects of Mass Media on Racial Minorities

We discuss two issues—the impact on racial minorities of stereotypes in the mass media and actions taken by minority groups to offset discrimination in the media.

Impact of Media Stereotypes and Other Distortions on Minority Group Members

One particularly troubling aspect of black stereotyping in the media involves children's TV programming. African American children watch television extensively. A number of studies have suggested that when family income level is held constant, African American children tend to watch more television than their white age-mates. What they see often presents blacks neither extensively nor positively. In children's shows, blacks are represented well below their proportion of the population, constituting about 7 percent of the characters in weekend programming and about 3 percent in after-school shows. Furthermore, the African Americans presented are much more likely than whites to be poor, jobless, or in low-status jobs. Such results certainly justify many black parents' and professionals' concern that limited and stereotyped roles for African Americans on television are likely to promote low self-concepts and negative views toward African Americans in general (Stroman, 1984).

In addition, Henry Taylor and Carol Dozier (1983) suggested that commercial television has developed a fairly new stereotyped black character—the black super-hero. This person is a policeman or other upright citizen, cut very much in the mold of white counterparts, and he tirelessly and often violently enforces order and keeps society safe for the good, law-abiding people of all races. Such programming both legitimates violence when used by law enforcement officers and encourages young African Americans to join the police and pursue the same violent agenda.

Television viewing can produce other distorted impressions. A study of 161 adult African Americans concluded that heavy viewers were more inclined than light viewers to have mistaken impressions that, in real life, racial integration is extensive and most blacks are middle class. The author argued that when exposed to a glut of commercial television, African Americans readily obtain the false sense that an effective confrontation of racism now occurs and that political activism demanding social justice and equality no longer remains necessary (Matabane, 1988).

Sometimes the potential impact of blacks' representation on television is complex. As we noted, the *Cosby Show* has avoided the stereotyped African American characters of the past. Dr. Cliff Huxtable and his family are successful, upper-middle-class people. They are much more successful than most blacks, and as a result the socioeconomic world in which they live and challenges and problems they face are as remote to the majority of African Americans as if the program focused on a white, upper-middle-class family. The Huxtables are, in fact, in most regards like successful whites. It appears that one of the reasons that the program has become so popular is that it never addresses tough issues related to race—in particular, political and economic conditions that have promoted limited opportunities for many blacks since the days of slavery. With these issues unaddressed, the *Cosby Show* and the steady flow of other sitcoms featuring middle-class blacks imply that blacks who are not economically successful are personally responsible for their situation (Gates, 1989). The discussion and debate about the merits of the *Cosby Show* continue (Tucker, 1997).

Commercial television programs featuring black characters seldom provide significant commentary on the issue of racial identity. When characters start to explore this topic, they tend to do it in a highly specific but nonconducive context—for instance, in a comedy situation involving black children in a largely white environment. Seldom does the program examine the issue in depth, and usually it either concludes that it is not productive to pursue the search for black identity or gives viewers little sense of how to go about the search (Peterson-Lewis and Adams, 1990).

Journalists sometimes contribute directly to stereotypes of minorities. *Chicago Tribune* columnist Mike Royko, who in the past had offended such diverse groups as gays, the police, African Americans, women, and Croatian Americans, wrote that the problem with Mexico was simply that Mexicans, who "don't know what the heck they are doing," ran it. Royko continued, "Just name one thing that Mexico has done this century that has been of any genuine use to the rest of this planet. Besides giving us tequila." While Royko technically apologized two days later, it was done sarcastically, with the columnist also pointing out that "[n]ot until Hispanic [radio] broadcasters lifted words and lines out of context did the salsa suddenly hit the fan" (Fitzgerald, 1996: 19). Many Mexican Americans were angered and offended, organizing a boycott of both the *Tribune* and its Spanish-language free weekly, *Exito.*

Not surprisingly, as Table 8.2 indicates, minority group members are often upset by the way mass media cover their group.

Table 8.2   Minority Group Members' Frequency of Being Upset by Mass Media Coverage of their Group

	African Americans	Hispanic Americans	Asian Americans
Local newspapers			
Every day	4%	6%	–
At least once a week	39	21	20%
Less than once a week	31	22	32
Never	20	44	38
No opinion	6	7	10
Local TV news			
Every day	8%	6%	1%
At least once a week	37	27	19
Less than once a week	28	29	35
Never	24	35	43
No opinion	3	3	2
National TV news			
Every day	9%	1%	1%
At least once a week	33	27	18
Less than once a week	30	36	42
Never	23	36	36
No opinion	5	–	3

Note: While members of all three minority groups expressed discontent about media coverage of events or issues involving their group, African Americans were more upset than Hispanic Americans, who in turn were more disturbed than Asian Americans.

Source: Leslie McAneny. "Ethnic Minorities View the Media's View of Them." *Gallup Poll Monthly.* August 1994, pp. 31–41.

Do Your Own Thing

In early 1985 at the University of California at Santa Barbara, there was a symposium on news media coverage of black America. One of the participants was James Cleaver, executive editor of the *Los Angeles Sentinel,* an African American newspaper. Not only are African Americans and other racial minorities underrepresented in the mass media, Cleaver pointed out, but a more important issue involves white and black reporters' presentation of topics about blacks. Unless black reporters have lived and worked in black communities, they are unlikely to be sensitive to urban black residents. Cleaver analyzed a recent story in the *Los Angeles Times,* a major white-owned newspaper. It discussed African Americans' criminal activities in white residential areas. The factual material was accurate, Cleaver conceded. However, he noted that "the manner in which this was presented led the reader to believe that every person in the black community was a criminal. It led people to believe that they could not be safe in the black community" (*Center Magazine,* 1985: 9). To present African Americans positively, Cleaver concluded, African American mass media must continue to exist.

Certainly there is historical precedent for this position. Often African Americans have not been represented effectively in the mass media, nor have they been permitted to participate extensively in them. Their alternative has been to found their own media. In the middle of the nineteenth century, Frederick Douglass's *North Star* condemned slavery, and late in that century, T. Thomas Fortune's *New York Age* blasted African Americans' treatment as second-class citizens. In the twentieth century, African American newspapers in many cities became vehicles operating on behalf of African Americans. During World War I, they encouraged many readers to move to industrial centers for jobs. While supporting the war, African American newspapers urged the complete integration of African Americans into American life. Many of the newspapers prospered, with several having weekly circulations of over 100,000 by 1920 and more than 200,000 20 years later. Large black papers published several editions to serve different sections of the country, and a few were sufficiently prosperous to form chains in various cities.

During the late nineteenth and early twentieth centuries, no black journalist was more celebrated than Ida B. Wells, who dedicated her life to fighting racism. Just recently her remarkable achievements have started to receive public attention, and it seems fitting to summarize them here.

Wells's first public action involving racism occurred when at the age of 22, she sat in the all-white "ladies' car" of a train and refused to move when ordered to do so; she was forcibly removed from the train. Wells's articles about her protest led to her entrance into journalism, and she soon became the editor and co-owner of the *Memphis Free Speech.*

As a journalist Wells condemned the lynching of three black friends whose grocery store had successfully competed against a white-owned store. Lynchings became Wells's chief target, and she believed that the only effective way to convince whites to stop killing blacks was to punish the oppressors economically—to deprive them of black workers. Wells wrote editorials urging blacks to pack up and move to the newly opened Oklahoma Territory, and thousands went. Analyzing sources of white violence toward African Americans, Wells wrote that sometimes there seemed to be an intense attraction between white women and African American men. Whites were infuriated and stormed her newspaper, destroying the presses.

Wells, who was in the North at the time, was forced into exile and threatened with death if she ever returned to the South. First in New York City and then in Chicago, Wells worked as a journalist for African American newspapers in an effort to alleviate violence against African Americans and to promote African Americans' basic rights. Continuing to believe that economic pressure was the most effective means of ending lynching, she travelled to England, which was a major market for southern cotton. She spoke with prominent individuals and lectured to groups, providing detailed information about the torture and killing of southern blacks and seeking to convince the English to boycott southern cotton if lynching continued. As a result of Wells's action, the English applied some pressure on southern businesspeople.

At the age of 60, Wells risked death, returning to the South for the first time in 30 years. Unrecognized by white authorities, she managed to interview 12 black farmers who had been sentenced to death for defending themselves against a white mob. Back in Chicago, Wells wrote a pamphlet describing the case in detail and demanding the men's freedom. Largely because of Wells's effort, the prisoners were released (*Public Broadcasting System,* 1989).

While the largest black newspapers have lost circulation in recent years, there are still substantial numbers of black print media. In 1979 there were over 350 black newspapers, magazines, and bulletins published on a regular weekly, monthly, or quarterly basis. The most recent growth has involved monthly or quarterly magazines such as *Ebony* and *Jet; Tuesday,* a Sunday supplement in many white newspapers; and *Monitor,* a supplement in many African American weeklies. At present there are only two African American newspapers published daily (Franklin and Moss, 1988: 379; Jaynes and Williams, 1989: 171).

Recognizing in 1981 the limited book-publishing opportunities for African Americans, Jawanza Kunjufu started a company called African American Images, which has produced 8 to 10 African American titles a year and has kept all 60 of the company's books in print. In 1986 the company started distributing books to individuals and schools, two years later developing its own multicultural curriculum for kindergarten through grade 12. In 1992 Kunjufu added a bookstore, which carries more than 10,000 titles, 90 percent by African Americans. The store also contains an art gallery with prints by African American artists as well as a section of artifacts from Ghana, Senegal, and Kenya. In 1993 African American Images expanded into black children's books, games, and puzzles. So what started as a small African American publishing house has expanded into a variety of media-related activities (Angel, 1997).

Like African Americans who have created their own mass-media entries, Native American filmmakers now face new opportunities. The Mashantucket Pequots, whose Foxwoods Resort Casino in Ledyard, Connecticut, has been enormously profitable, are starting to subsidize films. Their first venture titled *Naturally Native,* is the story of three Indian sisters' struggle to launch a business selling natural herbal skin and hair-care products.

The movie is the brainchild of Valerie Red-Horse, an actress, screenwriter, and aspiring producer-director, who is half Sioux and half Cherokee. Although Red-Horse appeared in several popular television shows, she has become frustrated by the limited roles for Native Americans, who, she indicated, are often stereotyped as either "savage warriors" or "mystical wise shamans of the earth." Once Red-Horse auditioned to play an Indian woman and was told she simply spoke too well. If the first movie is successful, Red-Horse has another project in mind that the Pequots can subsidize—a television series set at a huge Indian casino like Foxwoods (Rabinovitz, 1997).

Puerto Ricans have also had limited exposure in popular mass media. Newspapers, which have served a prominent role for blacks, have had a less significant impact on Puerto Ricans. In New York City, for example, Spanish-language papers have not been owned by Puerto Ricans and have not focused on their interests and problems. While generally not concentrating on Puerto Ricans, Spanish-language radio and television stations have provided music, news, and entertainment that have helped give Puerto Ricans a sense of being "at home" in a strange land (Fitzpatrick, 1987: 59–60).

Sometimes when minority group individuals control a media event, controversy about it can develop even within that group. In the fall of 1994, as part of its continuing effort to help people better understand the harsh realities of black history, the African American Department at Colonial Willamsburg decided to reenact slave auctions. The Virginia branch of the NAACP received numerous calls, most of which expressed outrage about the upcoming auction, and eventually the NAACP political director decided to organize a protest against the event (Janofsky, 1994).

As one performance with about 2,000 spectators was just about to begin, six demonstrators pushed through the audience and started singing "We Shall Overcome." Costumed employees of Colonial Williamsburg tried to push them back behind the ropes. During the altercation Jack Gravely, the organizer of the protest, shouted that the actors were turning black history into a sideshow. At that point Christy Coleman, a black actress who was to portray a pregnant house slave, grabbed a microphone and with tears running down her cheeks shouted to the protesters, "I want you to judge with honest hearts and honest minds." Two protesters sat down on nearby steps and challenged officials to call the police. They did not, and the show went on. When the "sale" occurred, Ms. Coleman cried and hid her face in her apron. Among those moved was Mr. Gravely, who startled people by retracting his objections. "Pain had a face," he said. "Indignity had a body. Suffering had tears" (*New York Times*, 1994a: A16).

Discussion Questions

1. Do you have any personal observations or information about minority group members' work in the mass media?

2. Can you recall any stereotypic representations of minorities in the mass media? Do you recall how people around you reacted to these representations?

3. Discuss and debate whether all Indian nicknames for sports teams should be eliminated.

4. Give your most compelling example of how stereotyped media representations of minority groups might have been psychologically harmful to the minorities in question.

Sources

Abarry, Abu. 1990. "The African-American Legacy in American Literature." *Journal of Black Studies* 20 (June): 379–398.

Andrews, William L. 1994. "The Black Male in American Literature," pp. 59–68 in Richard G. Majors and Jacob U. Gordon (eds.), *The American Black Male: His Present Status and His Future.* Chicago: Nelson-Hall Publishers.

Angel, Karen. 1997. "Images' Lesson in Diversification." *Publishers Weekly* 244 (August 4): 37–38.

Bridge, Junior. 1994. "Media Mirror: Distorted Relations—Distorted Treatment." *Quill* 82 (April): 16–17.

Butterfield, Fox. 1990. "Boston in Uproar over Murder Case." *New York Times* (January 8): A12.

Center Magazine. 1985. "American Blacks as Seen by the Media: Getting the Story Straight" 16 (January/February): 8–15.

Churchill, Ward. 1994. "Crimes against Humanity," pp. 73–77 in John A. Kromkowski (ed.), *Race and Ethnic Relations 94/95,* 4th ed. Guilford, CT: Dushkin Publishing Group.

Clifton, James A. 1990. "Cultural Fictions." *Society* 27 (May/June): 19–28.

Cohen, Jodi B. 1996. "Race Colors Newsroom Views." *Editor & Publisher* 129 (November 2): 8–9+.

Colon, Jesus. 1961. *A Puerto Rican in New York.* New York: Mainstream Publishers.

Downie, Leonard, Jr., and Donald Graham. 1996. "Race in the Newsroom: an Exchange," pp. 131-136 in Richard C. Monk (ed.), *Taking Sides: Clashing Views on Controversial Issues in Race and Ethnicity,* 2nd ed. Guilford, CT: Dushkin Publishing Group.

Dubin, Steven C. 1987. "Symbolic Slavery: Black Representations in Popular Culture." *Social Problems* 34 (April): 122–140.

Elliott, Stuart. 1997. "Disputes Develop over the Comeback of 'Amos 'n' Andy.'" *New York Times* (August 18): D7.

Fabrikant, Geraldine. 1994. "Slow Gains by Minority Broadcasters." *New York Times* (May 31): D1+.

Feagin, Joe R., and Clairece Booher Feagin. 1993. *Racial & Ethnic Relations,* 5th ed. Englewood Cliffs, NJ: Prentice-Hall.

Fitzgerald, Mark. 1996. "Royko Again Roils a Minority Group." *Editor & Publisher* 129 (March 16): 19.

Fitzgerald, Mark. 1997a. "Retention Deficit." *Editor & Publisher* 130 (August 9): 10–11+.

Fitzgerald, Mark. 1997b. "Minority Hiring Stalls." *Editor & Publisher* 130 (April 26): 39.

Fitzpatrick, Joseph P. 1987. *Puerto Rican Americans: The Meaning of Migration to the Mainland,* 2nd ed. Englewood Cliffs, NJ: Prentice-Hall.

Franklin, John Hope, and Alfred A. Moss, Jr. 1988. *From Slavery to Freedom: A History of Negro Americans,* 6th ed. New York: Alfred A. Knopf.

Gates, Henry Louis, Jr. 1989. "TV's Black World Turns—But Stays Unreal." *New York Times* (November 12): sec. 2, 1+.

Giago, Tim. 1994. "Drop the Chop! Indian Nicknames Just Aren't Right." *New York Times* (March 13): sec. 8, 9.

Greenberg, Bradley S., and Larry Collette. 1997. "The Changing Faces on TV: A Demographic Analysis of Network Television's New Seasons, 1966–1992." *Journal of Broadcasting & Electronic Media* 41 (Winter): 1–13.

Hartmann, Paul, and Charles Husband. 1974. *Racism and the Mass Media*. Totowa, NJ: Rowman & Littlefield.

Hernandez, Debra Gersh. 1994a. "Stereotypes Refuse to Die." *Editor & Publisher* 127 (August 27): 21.

Hernandez, Debra Gersh. 1994b. "The Race Quotient: Unity Panelists See Race Playing a Hand in the News." *Editor & Publisher* 127 (August 20): 12–13.

Humphrey, Ronald, and Howard Schuman. 1984. "The Portrayal of Blacks in Magazine Advertisements: 1950–1982." *Public Opinion Quarterly* 48 (Fall): 551–563.

Janofsky, Michael. 1994. "Mock Auction of Slaves Outrages Some Blacks." *New York Times* (October 8): 7.

Jaynes, Gerald David, and Robin M. Williams, Jr. (eds.). 1989. *A Common Destiny: Blacks and American Society*. Washington, DC: National Academy Press.

Jones, Alex S. 1990. "Bias and Recklessness Are Charged in Boston Reporting of Stuart Slaying." *New York Times* (January 14): A21.

Jones, Margaret. 1990. "Salt of the Earth Books." *Publisher's Weekly* 237 (October 12): 29–30+.

Keller, Bill. 1994. "Nelson Mandela on a Mug? It's the Rage in South Africa." *New York Times* (April 13): A1+.

Kitano, Harry H. L. 1997. *Race Relations*, 5th ed. Upper Saddle River, NJ: Prentice Hall.

Kitano, Harry H. L., and Roger Daniels. 1988. *Asian Americans: Emerging Minorities*. Englewood Cliffs, NJ: Prentice-Hall.

MacDonald, J. Fred. 1983. *Blacks and White TV: Afro-Americans in Television since 1948*. Chicago: Nelson-Hall.

Maldonado, Lionel A. 1982. "Mexican Americans: The Emergence of a Minority," pp. 168–195 in Anthony Gary Dworkin and Rosalind J. Dworkin (eds.), *The Minority Report*, 2nd ed. New York: Holt, Rinehart and Winston.

Marger, Martin N. 1994. *Race and Ethnic Relations: American and Global Perspectives*, 3rd ed. Belmont, CA: Wadsworth Publishing Company.

Matabane, Paula W. 1988. "Television and the Black Audience: Cultivating Moderate Perspectives on Racial Integration." *Journal of Communication* 38 (Autumn): 21–31.

McAneny, Leslie. 1994. "Ethnic Minorities View the Media View of Them." *Gallup Poll Monthly* (August): 31–41.

McCall, Nathan. 1994. *Makes Me Wanna Holler: A Young Black Man in America*. New York: Random House.

Merritt, Bishetta, and Carolyn A. Stroman. 1993. "Black Family Imagery and Interactions on Television." *Journal of Black Studies* 23 (June): 492–499.

New York Times. 1994a. "Tears and Protest at Mock Slave Trial." (October 11): A16.

New York Times. 1994b. "Minority Book Fairs Fill Retailing's Cultural Gap. (March 13): 42.

Peterson-Lewis, Sonja, and Afesa Adams. 1990. "Television's Model of the Quest for African Consciousness: A Comparison with Cross' Empirical Model of Psychological Nigrescence." *Journal of Black Psychology* 16 (Spring): 55–72.

Pierpont, Claudia Roth. 1997. "A Society of One: Zora Neale Hurston, American Contrarian." *New Yorker* 74 (February 7): 80–86+.

Public Broadcasting System. 1989. "Ida B. Wells: A Passion for Justice." (December 19).

Rabinovitz, Jonathan. 1997. "A Tribe's Casino Profits Invested in Indian Film." *New York Times* (September 9): B1+.

Staples, Robert, and Terry Jones. 1985. "Culture, Ideology and Black Television Images." *Black Scholar* 16 (May/June): 10–20.

Stedman, Raymond William. 1982. *Shadows of the Indian: Stereotypes in American Culture.* Norman: University of Oklahoma Press.

Stein, M. L. 1997a. "Criticism from Within." *Editor and Publisher* 130 (June 28): 47+.

Stein, M. L. 1997b. "Seeking Young Hispanic Readers." *Editor & Publisher* 130 (June 7): 11.

Stroman, Carolyn A. 1984. "The Socialization Influence of Television on Black Children." *Journal of Black Studies* 15 (September): 79–100.

Taylor, Henry, and Carol Dozier. 1983. "Television Violence, African-Americans, and Social Control, 1950-1976." *Journal of Black Studies* 14 (December): 107–136.

Tucker, Lauren R. 1997. "Was the Revolution Televised?: Professional Criticism about `The Cosby Show' and the Essentialization of Black Cultural Expression." *Journal of Broadcasting & Electronic Media* 41 (Winter): 90–108.

VanDerBeets, Richard. 1984. *The Indian Captivity Narrative.* Lanham, MD: University Press of America.

Wexler, Diane Patrick. 1997. "Multicultural Book Fairs by BBG." *Publisher's Weekly* 244 (January 13): 17.

CHAPTER 9

South Africa and Brazil: Comparative Contexts of Racism

On May 10, 1994, Nelson Rolihlahla Mandela stood before a crowd of world leaders who had shunned South Africa during its years of racial separatism and in a husky, resolute voice swore the oath to become the tenth leader of South Africa since its union in 1910. Mandela was the first black president, and the first president elected with the participation of blacks.

In his acceptance speech, Mandela spoke about the shared patriotism of all South Africans, their common pain for their country's humiliation before the world, and the national relief at being readmitted to the company of civilized nations. Mandela promised, "Never, never, and never again shall it be that this beautiful land will again experience the oppression of one by another and suffer the indignity of being the skunk of the world" (Keller, 1994c: A1).

A few minutes later, before a crowd of 50,000 ordinary citizens, Mandela held aloft the hand of F. W. de Klerk, the former president and Mandela's chief rival in the recent election. Mandela hailed his predecessor as "one of the greatest reformers, one of the greatest sons of our soil" (Keller, 1994d: A1). This tribute was consistent with a conciliatory pattern black and white leaders had maintained throughout the election process. At the end of a hard-hitting presidential debate a month earlier, Mandela had leaned across the table, grasped de Klerk's hand, and said, "My criticism of Mr. de Klerk should not obscure one fact. We are a shining example of people drawn from different race groups who have a common loyalty, a common love for their common country" (Gevisser, 1994: 626).

The final returns in the election showed that Mandela's African National Congress (ANC) had received over three-fifths of the popular vote—12.3 million votes representing 62.7 percent of the total. Along with the presidency, the ANC won 252 seats in the new parliament, becoming the majority party. The National Party—the former white ruling unit—obtained nearly 4 million votes, representing 20.4 percent of the total and 82 seats in the parliament. The other organization receiving substantial support was the Inkatha Freedom Party, which obtained 10.5 percent of the vote and 43 parliamentary seats (Keller, 1994d: 8).

For this chapter, South Africa provides one comparative case study and Brazil the other. Stepping outside our own cultural boundaries, we can get different perspectives on how racism affects human relations. On the surface, certainly, South Africa, in spite of the recent remarkable developments, provides an example of even more devastating racism than the United States and Brazil, a considerably milder picture. At the end of the discussion, will we have new insights about whether, as we noted in Chapter 1, race is a "persistent category of advantage and privilege"? Let's wait and see.

The South African Case

We begin with a look at the country's history, then discuss current racial policies, and finally, consider its future.

Development of *Apartheid*

At the end of the eighteenth century, four large black groups dominated what would eventually become the Republic of South Africa. Conflict among these groups occurred frequently, including a series of bloody wars in the 1820s known as the *difaqane*. One significant impact of these wars was that many black tribal settlements were disrupted, making it much easier for recently arrived white immigrants to occupy large sections of land unchallenged.

In the 1650s white settlement started with Dutch immigrants brought over by the Dutch East India Company. During the 1820s over 3,000 British citizens arrived in the Cape Colony, and for the rest of the century, thousands of European immigrants settled in that area. Beginning in the late 1830s, about 15,000 primarily Dutch-speaking whites who were dissatisfied with British rule and seeking more land left the Cape Colony and spread into the interior in what became known as "the Great Trek."

When white settlers encountered blacks, they either expelled or conquered them. Conflicts between British and Dutch-speaking settlers (Afrikaners) frequently occurred over land or other natural resources, and eventually the Anglo-Boer War of 1899 produced the British conquest of what had been two independent Boer states. Afrikaners were defeated but not subdued. They produced an Afrikaner version of South African history, widely celebrating its central events, heroes, and martyrs. Much like nineteenth-century white Americans professing "manifest destiny," Afrikaners stressed that theirs was a divine destiny—to lead the way to wealth and prominence in a white supremacist nation (Oberholster, 1988; Thompson, 1990).

British rule was brief. Afrikaners outnumbered the British, and in 1948 their political party—the National Party—won control of the government and maintained it until 1994. Shortly after the 1948 election, the policy of *apartheid* began. **Apartheid,** which means "apart-hood" or segregation, is a government policy involving racial segregation of major facilities—residential areas, hotels, restaurants, buses, work locations, and even staircases, benches, and toilets. *Apartheid* represents the implementation of internal colonialism on a scale never attempted in this country since the days of slavery. To many modern Americans, *apartheid* has become a term suggesting hatred and bigotry, the epitome of racism; yet most of us don't really understand what the policy involves. Let's examine it.

In the 1950s the winds of change were sweeping across Africa, and a host of new nations emerged from what had been former European colonies. Hendrik Verwoerd, the prime minister of South Africa, recognized that in this social climate Great Britain would be unwilling to agree to a longtime South African request that three British territories bordering on South Africa be incorporated by it. Acknowledging Britain's outlook, Verwoerd declared that he would set aside his country's previous position and encourage Great Britain to permit these territories to become independent.

On the surface Verwoerd's decision might have seemed progressive, even humane. Actually, because of the poverty dominating these areas, the proposed course of action—which Britain quickly accepted—simply assured South Africa's legal separation from land and people that represented an economic liability. These black nation-states and other African homelands were largely overcrowded, with no mining, very little manufacturing, and hardly any arable land. Under *apartheid* there were ten of these territories. Four became independent, and the other six, though maintaining some degree of autonomy, remained part of the Republic of South Africa. With the end of *apartheid,* all homelands were reincorporated into South Africa. These areas remain poor.

To survive, many blacks left independent states and impoverished rural homelands within South Africa itself and migrated to South African cities. Often men went alone, living in barracks and leaving their families behind. In addition, blacks frequently settled in the sprawling black communities on the outskirts of cities. In either case, because of *apartheid*'s requirement that races remain residentially separated, they seldom could avoid long commutes to work.

With a surplus of cheap labor available, whites often made it more difficult for blacks to move into the cities. The dominant group used two major techniques. First, since the middle 1960s, the central government deliberately slowed and in some cases even stopped the construction of African housing in cities. Second, black communities were destroyed outright; in several instances, bulldozers flattened shelters and huts housing upwards of 10,000 people (Badsha, 1986: 10–14). It was apparent, in short, that under *apartheid* white leadership harshly applied the internal colonialist principle of restricting racial minorities' activity, including residential location.

Brutal realities dominated racial minorities' lives, and yet during the 1980s the leadership learned to temper its restrictions, allowing some actions that might strike the outside observer as surprising. For instance, authorities relaxed extensive censorship. In the record section of the O.K. Bazaar, a big department store in Cape Town, an American woman heard Stevie Wonder's "Master Blaster," a song celebrating the independence of neighboring Zimbabwe. Among the white elite, there were a host of encounter groups in which the participants, including a few minority group members, discussed and even debated the country's future.

But most apparent softenings of *apartheid* had an underside. At the very moment "Master Blaster" was heard in the O.K. Bazaar, South African undercover units were taking steps to overthrow the black government in Zimbabwe. And while a few members of racial minorities took part in elites' encounter groups, these participants were carefully chosen "responsible" individuals who were considerably less militant than thousands of other possible spokespeople for racial minorities (Lelyveld, 1985: 29–31). Thus, in the 1980s, the South African government permitted some activities that contrasted with the harshness of *apartheid*, but the policy itself remained a daily reality.

The Eve of *Apartheid*'s Fall

We look briefly at prominent South African institutions and then examine the reality of *apartheid* in everyday life. First, though, as a background for this discussion, we briefly examine the size of different racial groups in the last years of *apartheid*.

South Africa's Racial Composition

In 1996 the population of the Republic of South Africa was about 44 million. Of the total, about 13 percent (5.7 million) were white, with nearly twice as many Afrikaners as whites of British descent. The Coloreds, who are of mixed white, black, and sometimes Malay ancestry, accounted for about 9 percent (3.9 million). Asians, who arrived in nineteenth-century South Africa to work on sugar cane planations, comprised about 3 percent (1.3 million). Finally, blacks were the largest group, accounting for 76 percent of the total (33.4 million) (South African Institute of Race Relations, 1996: 8).

A feature of South Africa which has made it unique among African territories located south of the Sahara desert is that for over a century and a half it has contained a relatively large white group that has made the country its homeland and committed itself to maintaining its position of dominance and privilege. Most sub-Saharan African territories were former European colonies, which contained a small resident white contingent, often less than 1 percent of the country's total population. Zimbabwe, formerly Southern Rhodesia and located directly north of South Africa, was once controlled by its white settler class, but the whites stepped down when a black ticket headed by Robert Mugabe won at the polls. Through the 1980s extensive verbal and guerrilla attacks against the South African ruling class originated from Zimbabwe.

As we look at institutional structures in South Africa, we begin to obtain a more detailed sense of how the ruling whites imposed their control on racial minorities.

Racism in South Africa's Major Institutions

In western democracies people grow to adulthood believing that with the inalienable right to vote in free and open elections, they participate in the process of choosing their rulers. In spite of possessing this right, they realize that tyranny can occur; without it, however, tyranny is inevitable.

In 1984 the South African government adopted a new constitution after a two-thirds majority of the white electorate had approved it the previous year. This document made some concessions to the existing policy excluding all minority group members from national elections. Now, along with whites, Coloreds and Indians could choose their own representatives. Each racial group would elect members to its own parliamentary house, which was proportional to its size in the population—thus 4:2:1 for whites, Coloreds, and Indians, respectively (South African Foundation, 1988: 16–17).

Opponents to this "reform" pointed out that with exclusion of blacks, whites' supremacy was assured. But the supporters of the new plan were quick to emphasize that blacks were permitted political participation: They could elect representatives within their own townships. Most blacks did not buy this idea, boycotting all-black elections, which in their eyes could do little to alleviate the crushing oppression produced by *apartheid*. Furthermore, both Coloreds and Indians turned out for elections in small numbers, realizing that with continued white control they inevitably would remain second-class citizens.

Above all, this constitutional reform did not change the economic picture for racial minorities. In 1985 the average monthly earnings for the four racial groups were R418 (418 Rands) for blacks, R561 for Coloreds, R770 for Indians, and R1,561 for whites (South African Foundation, 1988: 18-19). In South Africa an average African wage earner received about 26.7 percent—barely a quarter—of what an average white person made.

This is a pretty grim picture, but it becomes even grimmer when one considers that it does not include the vast number of unemployed South Africans, who are primarily Africans. One can be working and still remain poor, but one is infinitely poorer without any economic resources. South Africa has no accurate figures on unemployment, but it is certain that large numbers of blacks forced out of farms, towns, and villages all over the country and onto the overcrowded reserves have been without any prospect of employment. One indication of the terrible poverty many Africans face is the estimate that in a given year about 50,000 black children die of malnutrition and other related diseases (Badsha, 1986: 7).

A relationship among political power, income, and education exists in all countries. Not surprisingly, whites, who traditionally have had the lion's share of power and income in South Africa, also have had the best educational opportunities. In 1987 the average per capita governmental expenditure for education for whites was R2,160; for Indians it was R1,450; for Coloreds, R818; for blacks it was R368, or about 17 percent of the per capita government expenditure for whites. Inevitably the overall quality of children's educational experience corresponded with the expenditure. For instance, the teacher-pupil ratio for white students was one teacher to every 19 students; for blacks it was one teacher for every 41 students (South African Foundation, 1988: 56–62). Such a situation represents a perpetuation of internal colonialism's colonial labor principle, with racial minorities' limited educational opportunities keeping them restricted to low-paying jobs that primarily benefit the white controllers.

Those with power and wealth are best situated to obtain a high-quality education, and, in turn, superior education helps them maintain their dominance. In South Africa, of course, whites have been traditionally helped in this regard by the *apartheid* system, which, as we see in the following pages, promoted their dominance with a variety of concrete, drastic measures.

Maintenance of *Apartheid* in Everyday Life

For white South Africans, the country has long been a democracy, but for Indians, Coloreds, and most decisively blacks, one could persuasively argue that until 1994 it remained a totalitarian government, even with its constitutional "reforms." Consider the following situations, which show the impact of *apartheid* on racial minorities.

Since Afrikaners took control of the South African government in 1948, there was an effort to limit the migration of blacks to cities and their environs—a clear illustration of internal colonialism's principle of restricting racial minorities' activity. In Cape Town this policy was sufficiently successful that by 1970 black men in the area of that major South African city outnumbered black women by three to one, and in the African township of Langa, where thousands of workers were kept in barracks, the ratio was eleven to one.

Many men driven to the cities because it was the only place to find work felt that living without their families was wrong. One worker, who had brought in his family illegally, complained bitterly, saying that the construction firm that employed him and was about to build a first-class hostel for single men was failing to acknowledge the importance of the family in a country's development. He said, "That is why I am critical of its approach. Because it neglects the very core of nation building" (Badsha, 1986: 42).

This man lived in Crossroads, a squatter settlement outside of Cape Town. Blacks resided illegally in this area for a number of reasons. Some, like the man quoted above, refused to live in single housing provided by their companies, risking the wrath of the law to be with their families. Others had been forced out of the city as the economy expanded and the legal areas for black residence became hopelessly overcrowded. Still others streamed into the area from outlying black areas looking for both jobs and a place to live. During the 1970s thousands of shacks and modest houses were built.

Authorities reacted harshly. The infamous pass law, which required blacks to have passes to enter so-called white areas, was reinstated, employers were threatened with huge fines if they hired "illegal" blacks, and, finally, the flimsy cottages and shacks of about 25,000 people living nearby were destroyed. The word was out that Crossroads would be bulldozed shortly afterwards.

But Crossroads had become a community. Despite the absence of all modern conveniences and effective housing, life was better there than any place else in the vicinity blacks were permitted to reside. Crime rates were low, work was fairly plentiful, and the nutritional status of children was considerably better than that of children living in the countryside.

Eventually, in 1979, the people of Crossroads won a stay of execution from the government, but the situation remained uncertain as officials refused to make a long-term commitment. Then in 1985 there was a battle between stone-throwing young-sters and police that left 22 people dead. In 1985 the government finally declared that Crossroads would remain and be upgraded (Badsha, 1986: 110). The residents of the community had won a substantial victory.

Difficult as it was, life in urban areas tended to be much better than in the homelands and independent territories restricted to blacks under *apartheid.* In the Qwa Qwa reserve, for instance, a government commission reported that by 1920 the area was already overcrowded with 5,000 inhabitants; by 1970 the number had risen to 24,000.

The level of impoverishment is apparent in the following family history. The Serote family arrived in Qwa Qwa from a nearby white-owned farm in 1974. After that, Mr. Serote worked at a variety of jobs, but in 1982 tuberculosis made him too ill to continue. In that same year, Mr. Serote's eldest son obtained a job some distance away in the gold-mining town of Welcom. He too became ill but clung to the job because it was the family's only source of income. The second son was removed from school halfway through that year; he would have gone to work but he was too young to apply for a job as a migrant worker and could find nothing within the territory.

By the middle of the year, the family faced a severe crisis. Mrs. Serote and her youngest daughter were both diagnosed as suffering from pellagra, an extreme form of malnutrition, and a younger child was sent home from school because he was fainting from hunger in class. Drought and exhaustion meant that even the small vegetable garden near the house no longer received care. Begging or borrowing from neighbors was no longer possible, and because of the impersonal system of blacks' relocation, neither Mr. nor Mrs. Serote had relatives in the vicinity. When interviewed, both parents spoke of their anxiety for and guilt about their children, confessing that they had failed as parents. "I cannot sleep at night any longer," said Mrs. Serote, "because my son was so ill when he last came home, but I sent him back to work [in Welcom] because his is the only income we have. I am forced to kill one child in order to feed the others" (Badsha, 1986: 15) Neighbors were "appalled and ashamed" by the horri-ble sight of a family literally starving to death before their eyes while, besieged by their own poverty, they could do little to help.

Blacks are the poorest, most vicitimized racial group in South Africa, but other racial minorities are also poor and exploited by racism. In Durban, for instance, blacks, Indians, Coloreds, and whites once shared neighborhoods, but *apartheid* laws have forced all but whites out of the choice areas, compelling minority group members to move elsewhere. Indians were ordered to leave prime locations close to the Indian Ocean, and in the vacated areas, real estate speculators cashed in on high-rise apart-ments and shopping centers restricted to whites. In the middle 1980s, an irate Indian leader explained, "They don't need their laws anymore! They've done it! Whoever comes into power will not be able to change *this*" (Lelyveld, 1985: 26–27). In this view racial minorities' displacement has been accomplished: *Apartheid* has triumphed for all times.

A study of racial minorities' residential location in South African cities supported this conclusion, indicating that racial segregation has expanded through the twentieth century, with a marked increase since the 1960s when urban segregation laws were most strongly enforced. The highest level of racial segregation has been among blacks, followed by Indians, and then Coloreds. By the early 1990s, racial segregation in housing prevailed. As a result, even with official elimination of *apartheid*, prospects for urban integration are remote (Christopher, 1990).

In South Africa, blacks customarily lived in a police state. The significance of that statement is apparent in the following section.

Being Black in South Africa: Living in a Police State

While racism continues to exist in the United States, its victims often have the opportunity to confront it—with an appeal to the appropriate agency, some type of legal action, or public protest.

In South Africa, few blacks have had such opportunities. Under *apartheid* they knew that they were considered racially inferior and that the best they could expect was the opportunity to make a modest living, and away from work, to be left alone by whites. Often, however, black South Africans have been subjected to the stringent controls internal colonialist theory postulates.

In his autobiography, Mark Mathabane, a black South African who was born in 1960, described the experience of growing up in Alexandra, a black ghetto near Johannesburg. Both then and now, violence has been an intimate part of residents' daily lives.

As internal colonialist theory emphasizes, the white power structure controlled blacks' physical activity, in this case through police action. Once a year in Alexandra "Operation Clean-up Month" was designated, during which black policemen led by white officers would comb the ghetto searching for gangsters, prostitutes, people whose passbooks (which indicated that they were permitted to live and work in the city) were not in order, or families living illegally in the area.

One winter in the middle of the night, the police raided the shack rented by the Mathabane family. Twice they banged at the kitchen door, yelling that if it weren't opened immediately, they would break it down. Five-year-old Mark was sleeping on a piece of cardboard close to the door, and he was so frightened that he urinated, soaking himself and the blanket in which he was wrapped. From the bedroom his mother whispered not to open the door until she and Mark's father had a chance to hide themselves. When Mark opened the door, two tall black policemen in starched brown uniforms rushed into the room and shined a flashlight in his eyes. One kicked the young boy in the side, sending him crashing into a crate in the corner. Mark tried to stand up, but another kick flattened him. "What took you so long to open the bloody door?" the policeman shouted. He was about to kick the boy again when his partner stopped him.

They began searching for Mark's parents. The bedroom door was locked from the inside, and when no one responded to the policemen's demand to open it, they knocked it down.

Looking under the bed, they spotted Mr. Mathabane, who was naked, and ordered him out. "I'm coming, *nkosi* [lord]," Mark's father whimpered. They asked him where his wife was, and he said she was sleeping at the residence where she was employed as a kitchen girl. Apparently the policemen believed him.

One interrogator demanded to see Mr. Mathabane's passbook, quickly noting that several taxes were unpaid and that one entry indicated that Mrs. Mathabane was expected to sleep at home. How could he account for his wife's absence, the policeman asked, and playfully began prodding Mr. Mathabane's penis with his nightstick. Mark's father offered an excuse for his wife.

Why, the policeman continued, did an old man want to remain in the city? Mr. Mathabane, who was only in his 30s but was prematurely aged by an impoverished life, replied that there were no jobs in the reserves.

The policeman said that the statement was wrong—that until recently he had been living in the reserves and that people like his own father continued to lead comfortable, productive lives there. In Alexandra and other black ghetto areas, residents knew that the white leadership preferred black policemen with a rural background. Such recruits resented the more affluent, sophisticated urban blacks and enjoyed acting as cruel instruments of the white power structure.

The policeman summarized the offenses displayed in Mr. Mathabane's passbook and asked whether he could figure out a solution. Looking up for a moment from the floor, Mr. Mathabane forced a smile—not a spontaneous smile, but "a begging smile, a passive acceptance of the policeman's authority. After smiling my father again dropped his eyes to the floor" (Mathabane, 1986: 22). The policeman whispered in Mr. Mathabane's ear, giving him the chance to buy his way out of the predicament with a bribe. But Mark's father had no money, and so he was forced to serve two months of hard labor on a white man's potato farm.

In 1966 the raids increased, and they often occurred in daytime. Children became adept at observing and analyzing police actions and would rush home to warn their parents. But Mark was unable to do so. He wrote:

> That brutal encouter with the police had left indelible scars. The mere sight of police vans now had the power of blanking my mind, making me forget all I had learned, making me rely on my instincts, which invariably told me to flee, to cower, lest I end up face-to-face with a policeman and get flogged. I became a useless sentry. (Mathabane, 1986: 28)

Many black South Africans have grown to maturity with similar experiences. They found that living in *apartheid,* where the brutality of oppressed status was a constant reality, was a continuous nightmare. Such experiences remain a significant part of South Africa's legacy, but change has been occurring.

Recent Developments

Seldom does significant social change occur so quickly as it has in South Africa. Consider events occurring at the time of this book's first edition. Well past the normal deadline for manuscript correction, Alan McClare, the sociology editor, permitted me to slip in a paragraph about a momentous event that had just occurred—the March 1992 referendum of white voters calling for a formal end to *apartheid.* This was an extraordinary event, but what would follow from it? We can now begin to answer the question.

To eliminate *apartheid,* South Africa's leaders needed to open up the political process to all racial groups. This course of action was fraught with danger. White separatists committed to their long-established control of power and privilege might have engaged in sustained violence to sabotage the election. In addition, African groups vying for political dominance might have taken violent measures or simply boycotted the event, undermining its universal legitimacy. In spite of threats from both camps, general cooperation prevailed: In a country where violence has been widespread, the months leading up to the election produced surprisingly limited violence (Keller, 1994e).

The election process involved major governmental efforts to prepare black voters, many of whom were illiterate, to do something they had had been prevented from doing all their lives—to vote. Because of *apartheid,* blacks, representing three-quarters of the potential voters, were often located in the most inaccessible parts of the country. To acquaint these individuals with the voting process, organizers in vans toured both rural and urban areas. On television and radio, different public service messages anticipated specific dangers: that in traditional tribal areas, husbands would try to dictate their wives' choice or that tribal chiefs would require subjects to make a payment for the privilege of voting; that white overseers would confiscate their black workers' identity cards to hinder their voting (Clines, 1994b).

Frequently election organizers ran a mock presidential balloting to acquaint new voters with the process. A week before the election, Mike Tukai was conducting a mock election with mine workers at a company barracks in Cape Province. The men were concerned that their white overseers might punish them, but still they were determined to participate. As the activity began, the "men were instantly wide-eyed as they saw, then took in their hands sample ballots that they treated like holy writ" (Clines, 1994a: A10). Lucas Mlungana, a 50-year-old quarry worker, suggested why they showed this respect. "Whether my life changes depends on who gets elected" (Clines, 1994a: A10), Mlungana explained. He yearned for fast improvement in a life where he had to sleep in a rickety, gloomy barracks 11 months of the year and then journey a long distance to spend a precious month with his wife and children.

After winning nearly two-thirds of the popular vote, the African National Congress had to face the huge challenge of leading the country during the momentous conversion from white rule to racial democracy. At the top of the ANC ticket was Nelson Mandela—in the eyes of both South Africans and outside observers a remarkable leader. But Mandela was vulnerable to age—he was 75 when elected president in 1994—and the possibility of assassination. So were Mandela to die or be incapacitated, who would succeed him?

Immediately below Mandela in the ANC hierarchy were two men, Cyril Ramaphosa and Thabo Mbeki. Ramaphosa, aged 41 in 1994, fought *apartheid* inside South Africa, forming the black National Union of Mineworkers in 1982 and leading it until 1991. Ramaphosa rose rapidly within the ANC, becoming its secretary general, and played a significant role in the negotiations leading up to the election, but he supposedly lacked Mandela's full support. So, after the election, he remained secretary general with an eye to building up the party. Mbeki, son of one of the men imprisoned with Mandela in 1962, had spent 28 of his 51 years in exile, where he frequently negotiated with diplomats to promote the end of *apartheid.* Moderate and aristocratic, Mbeki struck many people as similar to Mandela, whose confidence in him was apparent when Mbeki was made first executive vice president and the leading candidate to succeed the president.

To fill its seats in parliament, the ANC presented a diversified set of candidates. A third were women, and there was a distinct range of ethnic groups, including Zulus, who dominated the rival Inkatha Freedom Party, Indians, and diverse whites, with even a few Afrikaners. Perhaps the party's greatest challenge has been that beneath the surface of its polished leadership, this large organization with its 400 branch offices lacks skilled administrators.

Another problem the party faces has been the maintenance of constituent support. Many of its backers are poor, often unemployed, and radical. In the 1980s the ANC built extensive support among dispossessed blacks by making black residential areas ungovernable: Tactics included strikes; school boycotts; mass refusals to pay rent, mortgages, and utility payments; and killing of such agents of the white rulers as black police officers and councilmen (*Economist,* 1994b; Keller, 1994d: 5). But, to put it mildly, times have changed, and the ANC is now in power while the old white enemies are now considerably less formidable. The party's new challenge has been to maintain its support while promoting significant change that will improve the lives of *apartheid*'s victims.

Before examining some of those challenges, we consider the reasons why in recent years South Africa has undergone such a significant transformation. It is an involved issue requiring analysts to consider a complex set of factors. First, as South Africa became increasingly urbanized and industrialized, the maintenance of *apartheid* was more cumbersome and difficult. With modern mass media providing so much information about whites' luxurious lives, economic inequalities became blatantly and painfully visible. In addition, forced to live in completely segregated areas, black organizers found ample opportunity to mobilize social movements based on their shared oppression. Furthermore, in an era when an increasing number of countries around the globe were democratizing, South Africa stood seriously out of step with all other modern industrial countries.

While these factors undoubtedly have had a significant impact over time, one must consider why the end of *apartheid* occurred just when it did—in the early 1990s. Certainly the barrage of protests both inside and outside the nation played a significant role. These activities encouraged, even forced, foreign governments and companies to restrict or eliminate economic relations with South Africa. The boycotts, in turn, set the groundwork for negotiations between such exiled ANC leaders as Thabo Mbeki and major South African business leaders, who were losing out financially because of economic bans imposed on their country. While details of their discussions are sketchy, it does appear that the ANC leaders made it clear that they were willing to compromise their radical positions on political issues if the white businesspeople would pressure F. W. de Klerk and other top politicians to support the end of *apartheid.* The impact of these business leaders appears to have been heightened by the fact that theirs has been a fairly small group of highly organized individuals—in sharp contrast to the less cohesive, much larger combination of white farmers and small businessmen who represented the core supporters of *apartheid.*

Finally, one should consider a factor that generally makes sociologists somewhat uncomfortable: the contribution of individuals—in this instance, two individuals. Could the fairly bloodless transition to the end of *apartheid* have been accomplished without two quite remarkable individuals—Nelson Mandela and F. W. de Klerk? Appropriately, de Klerk has received much less credit than Mandela; yet as the most prominent white leader, he played a significant role in orchestrating a peaceful transition to the post-*apartheid* state. Since his release from prison in 1990, Mandela has been able to move the process of ending *apartheid* calmly but persistently ahead. Commenting on Mandela, sociologist S. M. Miller declared, "I am not a devotee of the great man in history approach but Mandela's role does not seem foreordained nor that a stand-in could have performed it" (Miller, 1994: 12).

With the formal end of *apartheid,* South Africa still faces many significant race-related problems.

The Challenges in the Years Ahead

Following the national election of spring 1994, two significant events took place. First, *apartheid* was abolished, at least in a formal, legal sense. Second, for the first time in its history, all the major groups within the country engaged in "one bonding action of civil responsibilities." At least for a while, people felt a sense of shared nationhood (Breytenbach, 1994: 6).

After the election, South Africans have needed to confront the effects of the most developed system of internal colonialism in the entire industrial world. A journalist summed up the situation in the following way:

> Mr. Mandela's government will find that 46 years of *apartheid* have bequeathed it a fearsome legacy. A huge economic and social divide separates black from white. A "lost generation" of black children has gone unschooled. Families have been divided through imprisonment and exile. Perhaps the most devastating and intractable problem of all will be that of dealing with the muddled ethnic identities and feuds that *apartheid* has bred: a process that has not only turned black against white but also black against black. (*Economist,* 1994a: 21)

It is hardly surprising that as I prepare the third edition, these words retain the full power that they had three years ago. The problems that were apparent then are equally apparent now. Overseers simply find more particulars available.

One recent development involves the action taken to confront violations of human rights that have occurred over time. At the end of 1995, President Mandela appointed a commission called the Truth and Reconciliation Commission. Headed by Archbishop Desmond Tutu, a winner of the Nobel Peace Prize, the commission's members were charged with determining as fully as possible the causes and extent of human rights violations that occurred between 1960 and the official end of *apartheid;* to grant amnesty to individuals making full disclosure of acts that at the time were associated with political objectives; to permit victims to relate the violations they suffered; to take measures to provide restitution; and to make recommendations to prevent the reoccurrence of such violations in the future. One analyst summed up the commission's task as "[a] large and complex order" (Ash, 1997: 34).

Undoubtedly the most vicious white and black instigators of violent activity have realized that their chances of obtaining amnesty are remote and have not come forward. Some surprises have occurred, however. For instance, three white police officers who killed Steve Biko, a well-known anti-*apartheid* activist, sought amnesty, revealing what they considered the extenuating circumstances leading to his death. Biko, the officers explained, was completely uncooperative from the beginning of his interrogation, and at one point he took a punch at an officer, triggering a wild fight. Daantje Siebert, one of the officers, said in a written statement, "At that point, all three of us grabbed Biko and we took him to one corner of the room and ran with him into the wall" (Daley, 1997a: A1). During the investigation of the case, it became clear that Biko was left naked and shackled and eventually died alone of a brain hemorrhage on the floor of the cell. One of the officers conceded he felt "very badly about these actions" (Daley, 1997a: A5).

Current violence in South Africa is a major national concern. A survey in 1996 found that 41 percent of blacks and 58 percent of whites named crime as the country's most serious problem. The country's murder rate is about six times that of the United States, with about 19,000 individuals, the vast majority of whom were black, killed in 1995—a rate about 4 percent higher than the previous year (*Economist*, 1996: 22). Furthermore, there exists widespread concern that the politically motivated violence between the ANC and the Inkatha Freedom Party that led to 13,000 deaths in the opening five years of the 1990s might return. Killings escalated in 1997 in KwaZulu/Natal Province, where most of those earlier killings had occurred. Veteran observers suggested that some strategically placed white members of both the police and the army have been seeking to promote black-on-black violence (Daley, 1997b).

Long-run efforts to curtail violence in South Africa require policy makers to address the sources of the anger and frustration that promote it: in particular, the poverty and limited opportunity facing the country's huge poor population. In the short term, however, a critical factor must be effective policing.

In May 1994 officials of the new Mandela-headed government announced a reorganization of the South African police beginning with a name change from the South African Police Force to the South African Police Service. While some observers might be skeptical about the significance of a name change, it well might be important in a country where the police have traditionally been a force dedicated exclusively to affluent whites' interests and goals. Thus, while until the early 1990s a police sweep through the mixed-race township of Manenberg in Cape Town would have focused on a search for political dissidents or harassment of local people, in June 1994 it signified an effort to root out the violent gangs that have plagued all the racial groups in this township. Instead of terrorizing local blacks, police were protecting them.

The buzz phrase "community policing" is as prevalent in South Africa as in Los Angeles, New York, Houston, Miami, Chicago, and a host of other American cities. Details on police reorganization have been limited, but some guidelines are apparent. The country's interim constitution declares that within a given locale, reforms will be the result of consultations between police and local leaders, and the new South African Bill of Human Rights protects all citizens from many oppressive acts the police routinely used in the past—such as searches without warrants and detention without trial (Holmes, 1994c).

Another reorganized system of authority in post-*apartheid* South Africa is local government. With a racial democracy in effect, black officials are now elected to positions previously held only by whites. However, as we saw in the discussion of minority politicians in Chapter 4, election is only the beginning of the battle. Consider the case of Port Elizabeth. This industrial city on the Indian Ocean has the country's first black mayor, Nceba Faku, who spent 13 years in prison for recruiting anti-*apartheid* guerrillas. As mayor, Faku has been widely admired for his emphasis on racial conciliation and energetic plans for political reform, but there has literally been a heavy price to pay: Change is going to be expensive, with whites paying higher property taxes and costlier utilities while waiting longer for their potholes to get filled and their leaky sewers repaired. The great cost and need involve the other three racial groups:

By the year 2000, the formerly disenfranchised minority groups are going to have fresh water, electricity, sewers, garbage removal, decent roads, clinics, fire departments, access to libraries, and recreation services—goods and services they were often denied under *apartheid.* A journalist summarizing the policies established by the Faku administration in Port Elizabeth concluded, "It is the first [local government] to confront a blunt reality Mr. Mandela has tended to play down: that whites have a large bill to pay for the past" (Keller, 1994a: 3).

Another political challenge involves the nation's bloated bureaucracy. The pre-*apartheid* government had 18 education departments, which are certain to be trimmed, but such trimming, though it will save money, will meet resistance from the incumbents who lose their jobs. Each of the 10 black homelands created in the name of *apartheid's* separate development had its own bureaucracy of thousands of civil servants, who find themselves without function now that with the official end of *apartheid* the homelands have been reintegrated into the nation. As part of governmental streamlining, the civil servants are supposed to be retrained and relocated, but how to accomplish that task is not yet apparent (*Economist*, 1994b; Keller, 1994b).

Besides the political challenges, the new government faces myriad complicated economic issues. Overall, black family income is approximately one-sixth of white family income. Although there has been a very slight increase in the number of jobs in recent years, the unemployment rate is high—about 20 percent in the formal taxpaying sector—and if one includes individuals who make an informal living, such as by selling brushes or weeding gardens, the overall unemployment rate is perhaps 33 percent. Unlike their counterparts in West Africa, urban dwellers usually cannot fall back on family members living on farms, because in South Africa such rural holdings are white-owned. While an economic black elite has been developing in the areas of government jobs and black business, the vast majority of South African blacks have no access to these opportunities (*Economist*, 1996; *Economist*, 1997). Some of the most prominent members of this group are trade union members, leading many critics to conclude that the labor movement "has no place in business, and that the process will lead to corruption, alienation, and severe conflict of interest" (Gevisser, 1997: 25).

Not only do poor blacks desperately need the financial benefits of an improving economy, but they are understandably impatient for a better life. Consider the legacy of the *apartheid* laws depriving most blacks of land ownership. Not waiting for the new government to supply public housing, landless blacks have initiated a wave of "land invasion" on a variety of public and private spaces in and around various cities. This development has provoked the wrath of multiracial homeowners fearing a decline in housing values. In addition, such action disrupts government plans for a systematic public housing registration where landless people would place their names on waiting lists.

In spite of such problems, these settlements appear quite promising. For instance, in Canana, a recent settlement about 40 miles from Johannesburg, a committee composed of some of the orginal settlers runs the community. Committee members have laid out wide swaths for streets and marked off lots. Newcomers are assigned numbers that are painted on the outside of their corrugated iron shacks so that one day the postal service will be able to deliver mail. Pit latrines are dug near the street to make it easier for authorities when they install sewer lines. Plots of land are set aside for a clinic, stores, churches, and a nursery. A member of the ruling committee indicated that there had been no conflict or violence since the community was established. Another committee member said, "If the government wants to remove us from here, they must build houses where there are services where poor people are satisfied" (Holmes, 1994a: A4).

In the former black homelands, grinding poverty prevails. A portion of Gazankuku, one of the former homelands, contains about 500,000 people crammed into 140 square miles where local blacks have been restricted to wrenching a meager living from agriculturally marginal land. Separated only by a wire fence is the Sabi Sand Game Reserve, where wealthy, generally white tourists sip drinks on shaded verandas and roam about the bush in Land Rovers photographing cheetahs, lions, rhinos, elephants, and other game.

Until the 1994 election, the wealthy white landowners in the reserve saw little reason to pay much attention to their poor neighbors. Now, however, they have become responsive to blacks' recent efforts to develop laundries, auto repair shops, film-developing enterprises, and other businesses that can contribute to the local tourist industry. Such cooperation represents a form of insurance. Otherwise, landowners realize, they face the distinct threat that local blacks will petition the government to force whites to give up their land (Holmes, 1994b).

Prosperous blacks face their own challenges. Moving into previously all-white neighborhoods in a country where until recently segregated housing for blacks was the law, they often encounter coldness, isolation, hostility, suspicion, and even white flight. Although blacks moving into white areas obtain better housing, paved streets, and nights without gunfire, they feel deprived of the camaraderie their poor communities offered. "You miss your people," said Gladness Ncobo, a real estate agent. "Here you are like in jail, like on Robben Island. Here you don't know if your neighbor is alive or dead. Then you see the car drive up, and you know that he's alive. That's not life" (Wilkerson, 1994: A3).

While enormous problems remain, many modern South Africans find themselves facing new and often uplifting tasks. Penny Siopis, a well-known artist, currently struggles with how to present issues of race and gender in her medium, which is a combination of photography and painting. With *apartheid* officially ended, people are now freer to understand who they are. For instance, how should Siopis, who is white, represent whiteness as a positive entity without conveying overtones of traditional racial superiority? *Apartheid*'s removal also opens the door to examining gender issues more thoroughly. It is essential, Siopis argued, for South Africans of all races and both genders to come to grips with the past and who they are now. She said:

> In my own case, for me *not* to take on the issue of "race" would be evasion, and for all the difficulties presented by the questions of representation . . ., the absence of "race" in my work would be politically problematic as it would be aesthetically restrictive. (Coombes, 1997: 129)

Race relations in Brazil offer a contrasting picture.

The Brazilian Case

Since the emancipation of slaves a century ago, Brazil has had the international reputation of being a racial paradise, or at least close to it. In recent decades, however, that image has begun to tarnish. In 1978 and 1979, for instance, Brazil's leading television network, Rede Globo, presented a widely acclaimed series for children adapted from stories written by Monteiro Loboto, a well-known Brazilian author. In 1979 the African country of Angola, which is also Portuguese speaking, decided to show the series. After seven installments, however, Angolan television abruptly cancelled the series, charging that it was racist, depicting blacks only in inferior positions. Most offensive to Angolan viewers was the role of Tia [Aunt] Nastacia, an elderly, black cook whom the Angolans considered a racial caricature. Brazilians were surprised and asked many questions. Were the Angolans justified? How should blacks be represented in the media? (Skidmore, 1985: 15). If this had been an isolated incident, then concern about racism probably would have soon passed. But it was only one illustration of widespread criticism.

In the following pages, we briefly examine the racial history of Brazil, then analyze current racial inequalities and consider future race relations.

History of Brazilian Race Relations

Three groups have predominantly produced the current racial composition of Brazil—European, initially Portuguese, whites; Indians; and African blacks.

In the sixteenth century, Portuguese colonists, primarily men, began immigrating to Brazil. Many of these men fathered numerous children whose descendents are currently found both among whites and racial minorities. Some of these early immigrants became sugar plantation farmers while others, former Jews known as "new Christians," settled in small ports along the sea coast and engaged in skilled trade, skilled labor, and the professions and became moneylenders to the sugar planters, who were often heavily in their debt. In the nineteenth century, immigrants from other European countries began to come to Brazil. At first Germans and Swiss arrived, followed by Italians, Poles, and Spaniards.

To supply laborers for the first sugar plantations, early Portuguese colonists hunted down and enslaved substantial numbers of Indians because each large sugar plantation required about 200 workers. Early settlers had a few black slaves and found them more manageable than Indians since they had been subdued by the slavery system. However, because of wars with Holland during the colony's first two centuries, whites were unable to add appreciably to the number of black slaves. When the wars with Holland finally ended, African slaves replaced Indians in agricultural work; Indians were often used to care for livestock (Smith, 1972: 52–55).

Brazilian working conditions were so harsh that barely 20 percent of slave children survived, and adults often died after a decade of labor. Facing a chronically inadequate supply of slave labor, white Brazilians imported African captives for a longer period of time than their counterparts in other slave-owning countries. Without any territory to which they could flee to be free, Brazilian slaves revolted in large numbers (Abreu, 1996; Barickman, 1996; Marx, 1996).

In 1819 the population of the country was about 3.6 million people, with about 80 percent—2.9 million—blacks or mulattoes (people of mixed race). In contrast, in the United States, the ratio was reversed, with whites forming about 80 percent of the population, and racial minorities—blacks and Indians—comprising the remaining 20 percent. Even in the American South, where blacks were most heavily concentrated, they never represented more than 38 percent of the population.

The different proportions are significant, because, unlike the United States, nineteenth-century Brazil simply did not have enough whites to fill key positions in a commercially expanding country, and so blacks and mulattoes could become skilled tradesmen, cowboys, small food growers, and boatmen (Drimmer, 1979: 102). Out of economic necessity, in short, the colonial labor principle gave slaves a greater range of work opportunities in Brazil than in the United States.

Nonetheless, most slaves remained unskilled agricultural workers. When blacks were freed in 1888, they found few jobs available. At that point they had to compete for agricultural jobs with Indian laborers now willing to work for wages and with a steady stream of European workers better prepared to function in the post-slavery economic system. Many blacks could not find jobs and quickly slipped into terrible poverty (Fernandes, 1969: 1–3). For many Brazilian blacks, that poverty has continued into the present era.

Thus racial minorities in Brazil have historically had diversified economic opportunities. Socially modern Brazilian society gives the impression of being racially liberated. Currently racial intermarriage is common, and explicit racial segregation is both unusual and illegal (Webster and Dwyer, 1988). Historically, racial practice in Brazil has been generally more progressive than in either South Africa or the United States.

But many Brazilians have not been content with such modest claims. Since about 1950 governmental officials and other leading citizens have vocally asserted that Brazil is a racial democracy. They have emphasized two themes—that under no circumstances should people admit that racism occurs in Brazil and that any claim about the existence of racism should be attacked as "un-Brazilian" (Smith, 1972: 59).

In the 1970s such attacks were extensive. For instance, when a major newspaper ran a feature story describing the "black is beautiful" movement in Rio de Janeiro, powerful whites sharply criticized the paper, claiming that publicizing such "un-Brazilian" groups was itself "un-Brazilian." The white elite, in fact, went much further to protect the country's racially democratic image: In particular, prominent faculty members at the University of Sao Paulo were forced to retire. While ideologically varied, these men all were involved in race relations research, where they raised questions members of the white elite found troubling. In addition, the federal government confiscated a modern journal of opinion, *Argumento*, which featured a hard-headed analysis of Brazil's racial situation. But an even more significant action occurred. Government officials decided to omit the topic of race from the census of 1970, thereby preventing researchers' access to a potentially revealing data source. Without this information or any other large studies on race in Brazil, meaningful analysis and discussion of the issue were impossible. Thus supporters of the doctrine of racial democracy temporarily defeated a potential major threat (Skidmore, 1985: 15–17).

By the late 1970s, however, the tone of the times had changed, and as we will see, a major study of race in Brazil produced some important, interesting findings.

Racism in Modern Brazil

A 12-year-old black boy reached through a car window and snatched a woman's necklace. As he fled, four white men grabbed him and started beating his face and ribs. A black woman intervened, and she too was beaten. Eventually the police arrived and carried off the badly bruised boy. In such situations angry crowds often lynch young thieves on the spot.

Currently there are about 36 million Brazilians under 18, with about 60 percent of them needy and about 7 million of them maintaining few or no links with their families (Riding, 1985). The most desperate poor in Brazil—abandoned children; youths who live from muggings, robberies, and other crimes; and families who must remove children from school to perform menial jobs contributing to the family's survival—are overwhelmingly black (Sundiata, 1987: 68).

About 44 percent of Brazil's population is black or mulatto (Christmas, 1988), and many Brazilian minority group members suffer life-threatening poverty. Two factors contribute significantly to making poor racial minorities' situation in Brazil worse than in the United States. One major difference is that since Franklin Roosevelt's New Deal in the 1930s, the American government has been willing to supply a welfare "safety net," albeit an increasingly flimsy one, for the nation's poor while Brazil offers the poor no similar support.

The second major advantage in the United States has been the strength of the black professional class, whose members, unlike blacks and mulattoes in Brazil, have historically been denied full participatory rights in society. As a result American black professionals have developed a race consciousness that has extended concern to all members of their race, even the poorest (Sundiata, 1987: 68). The irony is that in Brazil the relatively open racial situation has tended to discourage a sense of black consciousness, including a systematic concern by affluent blacks for poor members of their race.

The lack of a historically significant black-consciousness movement in Brazil does not imply that blacks have been spared diverse effects of racism. Using data from the large 1976 National Household Sample Research, investigators revealed clear indications that racism in Brazil has occurred and continues to occur.

As in the United States, in Brazil educational attainment is linked to occupational success. About 27 percent of whites reported no schooling or less than a year while the comparable figure for racial minorities was 46 percent. As the amount of education increased, the gap between whites and racial minorities expanded. Thus while 19 percent of whites and 12 percent of minority group members completed five to eight years of school, 11 percent of whites and only 3 percent of racial minorities obtained nine or more years of education. For the five-to-eight-year bracket, whites had a 1.55 greater chance of completion, but at the nine-year-and-more level, their chances were 3.15 times greater.

Income differences were equally distinct. Among racial minorities, 54 percent received the minimum wage or less while a considerably smaller percentage of whites—23 percent—fell into this category. At the affluent end of the income distribution, 24 percent of whites and 15 percent of minority group members had an income two to five times the minimum wage, and 16 percent of whites and 4 percent of minority group individuals received over five times the minimum wage. Overall, whites' income was about twice minority group members'.

For both education and income, the gap between Brazilian racial minorities and whites increases when one evaluates higher status categories. Data on these topics indicate racial inequality, but what needs more analysis is whether racial minorities' inferior job attainments occurred simply because they started from disadvantaged positions, or, in addition, because they encountered racism. Research on social mobility provides clues.

Social mobility is the movement of a person from one social class or status level to another, either upward or downward, with accompanying gains or losses in wealth, power, and prestige. The following analysis of social mobility involves people in three broad occupational levels—manual, nonmanual, and upper; the manual and nonmanual categories are also subdivided.

Among people born into families where the father was employed at the lower-manual level (workers in domestic services, traditional industries, and local trade), only 21 percent of   minority group individuals compared to 38 percent of whites rose to nonmanual positions. Among those coming from the high-manual level (workers in modern industries and unskilled workers in services), 29 percent of minority group members and 41 percent of whites obtained nonmanual occupations. Among those born into the lower-nonmanual level (lower clerical workers and small owners in commerce and services), 64 percent of whites and 53 percent of minority group members achieved positions equal to or higher than their fathers'. In the higher-nonmanual category (high-level clerical workers and small farmers), the proportions were 44 percent for whites and 26 percent for racial minorities. At the upper level (professionals, managers, and big-business owners), 47 percent of whites and 24 percent of minority group individuals stayed in this highest occupational category; or, reversing the focus, one sees that 76 percent of minority group people compared to 53 percent of whites at the upper level were downwardly mobile from their fathers' upper-level occupations.

These data involve situations where racial minorities and whites originated from families with about equal socioeconomic status, and yet whites' upward social mobility or sustained high status was consistently greater than minority group members'. Since no other factors influencing these outcomes are readily apparent, it is hard to avoid concluding that racism plays a significant role.

Occupationally the white leadership seems to subscribe to internal colonialism's governance principle, keeping blacks least represented in the political structure. Whites completely dominate the top governmental positions involving the economy, the military, and education. In 1988 none of the country's 23 state governors was black, and of the 559 members of Congress, only 7 considered themselves black. The only occupational areas where blacks play a prominent role are sports and entertainment (Marger, 1997: 437–438; Schneider, 1996).

Two major processes account for racial inequality in Brazil's occupational structure. First, racial minorities obtain less education, and as a result they enter the labor market with fewer qualifications. Second, racial discrimination affects workers' hiring and promotion. Because of these processes, racial minorities suffer "a cycle of cumulative disadvantage" in their quest for status attainment (Hasenbalg, 1985; Silva, 1985; Telles, 1994).

These are harsh, important facts that might strike some readers as somewhat abstract. If that be the case, the following illustration should help clarify how racial discrimination can occur in Brazil. José (a pseudonym), a well-known black lawyer and legal scholar, tried in 1970 to pass a set of examinations to receive an appointment to the Law Faculty of the University of Bahia. In a competition organized within the university, José received the highest score on the written examination but failed the oral examination, which could be attended only by candidates and their examiners. In the following four years, José continued to fail the oral examination, and while he was reluctant to conclude that racism was involved, he saw no alternative explanation. Then in 1974 the oral examinations were opened to the public. José invited friends and legal colleagues to attend, and this time he not only received the highest score on the written examination but also passed the oral exam(Turner, 1985: 76). He had triumphed, but not without extensive exposure to racist treatment.

Racial differences also exist on basic survival issues. A study indicated that whites outlived minorities (classified as "nonwhites") by 6.7 years in 1980—no more than a modest reduction from the 7.5-year margin in 1950 (Wood and Lovell, 1992).

Besides blacks and mulattoes, Indians also suffer racial oppression in Brazil. In the state of Roraima, the government has failed to take active steps to prevent illegal gold mining and drug smuggling on Indian reserves. In Roraima and the nearby state of Acre, forest Indians' traditional way of life is rapidly disappearing as poor people from the rest of Brazil move in and clear the forests (*Economist,* 1987).

In the fall of 1993, there occurred a celebrated, savage incident in which Indians were victimized in a situation fitting the frustration-aggression theory described in Chapter 2. Since 1990 gold miners have been trying to enter the Yanomamö homeland located near the Venezuelan border. To discourage this illegal activity, Brazilian police raided a mining camp in August 1993, destroying the miners' water pumps, generators, and air strip. Infuriated, the miners struck not at the most logical object of their wrath—the police—but at a more vulnerable group—local Yanomamö. Attacking a nearby village, the miners massacred 20 Yanomamö: They shot the men and then used machetes to slit women's and children's throats. Ten children were killed, with some of them decapitated. Two months later 20 Brazilian miners were charged with the murders and scheduled to stand trial (Brooke, 1993; Chagnon, 1993).

The following situation illustrates some complexities of discrimination against blacks in modern Brazil.

The African Connection: An Uncomfortable Policy

During a major holiday in Rio de Janeiro, ambassadors from Ghana and Nigeria appeared in a street celebration, singing in the Yoruba language and dancing with a well-known Brazilian dance troop. Many onlookers were confused about their identity, and in his column a journalist asked, "Who are these two personalities with complicated names?" (Dzidzienyo, 1985: 135). Why was these African ambassadors' public appearance a distinctly incongruous event in Brazilian society?

Throughout the book we have noted that racial oppression involves imposing restrictive norms on the racial minority, particularly limited access to the prized economic, political, and social rewards within the society.

Suppose, however, that the nation's dominant group—in this case, Brazil's white power structure—wants to establish close, mutually beneficial economic and political relations with groups racially and culturally linked to their own oppressed racial group—in this instance, African nations. Let's consider how Brazil's African connection has developed in the past three decades.

Since the early 1960s, Brazilian leaders have encouraged increased relations between their country and independent African countries. Such connections interest many Brazilian groups, including political leaders seeking to increase the nation's stature through broader political alliances, white businesspeople wanting to develop new markets for their products, and black Brazilian groups trying to establish a variety of political, economic, and cultural ties to citizens in African countries.

During the 1960s the all-white Brazilian leadership acted efficiently to advance the African connection, condemning *apartheid* while maintaining political and economic ties to South Africa; encouraging an increasing number of African leaders to make offical visits to Brazil; and giving repeated affirmations of historical and cultural linkages between Africa and Brazil.

But from the African viewpoint, something critical was usually missing—visible involvement of black Brazilians in the official relations between Brazil and African nations. For instance, many black Africans consider the city of Bahia the place where black culture thrives in Brazil. However, when the *Asantehene,* the monarch of the Ashantis of Ghana, visited Bahia, he was not officially introduced to any black Bahians during his two-day stay. In contrast, in São Paulo his party met a large number of black Brazilians, including federal and state politicians, professionals, journalists, and students. The reason for the difference was that in São Paulo, Adalberto Camargo, a black elected official, played a major role in planning the *Asantehene's* schedule.

Sometimes the African connection produces controversy among black Brazilians. For instance, Abdias do Nascimento, a well-known writer, painter, and activist, criticized black organizations in Bahia for failure to promote black Brazilians' involvement in relations with African officials. Nascimento's critics, in turn, have accused him of being argumentative and anti-white.

At present black Brazilians are minimally involved in their nation's official relations with African countries. While the white political and economic leadership in Brazil would like the involvement to remain modest, many black Brazilians and African officials take an opposing view. How this situation unfolds will affect not only the African connection but also many black Brazilians' political, economic, and social status in their own society.

Future of Brazilian Race Relations

Since the middle 1980s, an upsurge of black consciousness has occurred in Brazil. Groups involved have differed in style and goals but have shared the strongly held belief that the myth of racial democracy has been harmful for blacks and mulattoes and must be destroyed (Turner, 1985). Some observers have suggested that, inspired by the American civil rights movement, Brazilian blacks are about to embark on a period of social activism (*Ebony,* 1997: 36).

Certainly racism thrives in Brazilian society. While internal colonialist policies are toned down in Brazil, whites hold minority groups in check. A larger, related problem is that in this society dire poverty exists for an enormous number of people, primarily members of racial minorities, whose plight results principally from historical racial oppression rather than explicit racist practice today. Elimination of current racist practices would do little to benefit most of them. To significantly change their lives, the government would need to enact drastic economic reforms, beginning with a "safety net" welfare program.

But such a policy is not likely to be forthcoming as the following event illustrates. In 1990 Fernando Collor de Mello was elected president, campaigning as a champion of the "shirtless and shoeless" and an enemy of the "corrupt elite." Once in office, however, his policies reversed these priorities: Brazil's poor racial minorities faced new rounds of layoffs and income cuts while the Collor government protected elites' economic interests (Silverstein, 1990).

Conclusion

The material in this chapter offers distinct contrasts to the American racial picture, and in the end we find ourselves with three quite different situations. In recent years certainly the greatest change has occurred in South Africa; in the near future, that country probably remains the least predictable of the three, with the possibilities ranging from the development of a successful multiracial democracy to a significant political deterioration where violence and chaos dominate. Even though *apartheid* has been officially dismantled, its negative impact in politics, work, housing, education, and the family will persist indefinitely.

In the United States, the mainstream ideology involving race has been changing, showing signs of lessened racism. Survey data suggest that most white Americans don't like to think of themselves as racist and don't wish to assert a sense of racial superiority. Nonetheless, ample evidence of racism exists. One might conclude that the American racial picture is somewhat like Brazil's. In both cases current ideology differs from the present reality of sustained racism.

Furthermore, another parallel between the two societies might be occurring. Earlier we noted that because of more pronounced historical racism in the United States than in Brazil, the black professional class has maintained closer ties to poor blacks than have their affluent counterparts in Brazil. That connection, however, is starting to change. Perhaps 10 to 15 percent of young American blacks are completely removed from any contact with poor people (Clark, 1979), and thus, like successful Brazilian blacks, they are developing an insensitivity to the combined impact of poverty and racism.

What is unique about Brazil is its established ideology of racial democracy, which the elite has strongly supported and even defended. Brazilians making the claim that racism occurs in their country are unpatriotic—un-Brazilian.

In all three countries, notable parallels occur: In each of these societies, minority group members tend to be considerably poorer and more deprived educationally, economically, and politically than whites; in addition, all three societies offer explicit illustrations of recent racial discrimination. Unfortunately, we have found cross-cultural evidence from three very different societies indicating that race continues to be a remarkably persistent category of advantage and privilege.

Discussion Questions

1. Does the end of *apartheid* mean the end of racial oppression in South Africa? Discuss.

2. If you were an elected politician in South Africa, what would be the top two or three items on your agenda? Justify your position.

3. Evaluate whether Brazil is truly a racial democracy.

4. Do you have any information you obtained personally or in conversation about race relations in Brazil and South Africa?

5. Compare the challenges minority groups face in South Africa, Brazil, and the United States. What about majority groups?

Sources

Abreu, Martha. 1996. "Slave Mothers and Freed Children: Emancipation and Female Space in Debates on the 'Free Womb' Law, Rio de Janeiro, 1871." *Journal of Latin American Studies* 28 (October): 567–580.

Ash, Timothy Garton. 1997. "South Africa: True Confessions." *New York Review of Books* 44 (July 17): 33–38.

Badsha, Omar, (ed.). 1986. *South Africa: The Cordoned Heart.* Cape Town, South Africa: Gallery Press.

Barickman, B. J. 1996. "Resistance and Decline: Slave Labour and Sugar Production in the Bahian Reconcavo, 1850–1888." *Journal of Latin American Studies* 28 (October): 581–633.

Breytenbach, Breyten. 1994. "Dog's Bone." *New York Review of Books* 41 (May 26): 3–6.

Brooke, James. 1993. "Miners Kill 20 Indians in the Amazon." *New York Times* (August 20): A10.

Chagnon, Napoleon A. 1993. "Covering Up the Yanomamö Massacre." *New York Times* (October 23): 21.

Christmas, Rachel Jackson. 1988. "In Harmony with Brazil's African Pulse." *New York Times* (November 20): 43.

Christopher, A. J. 1990. "*Apartheid* and Urban Segregation Levels in South Africa." *Urban Studies* 27 (June): 421–440.

Clark, Alisha. 1979. "African-American College Students' Attitudes." *Journal of Black Studies* 10 (July): 243–248.

Clines, Francis X. 1994a. "Enrollment Teams Hunt the Forgotten Corners." *New York Times* (April 21): A10.

Clines, Francis X. 1994b. "South Africa Tries to Prepare Those It Long Denied Ballot." *New York Times* (April 12): A1+.

Coombes, Annie E. 1997. "Gender, 'Race,' Ethnicity in Art Practice in Post-Apartheid South Africa." *Feminist Review* 55 (Spring): 110–129.

Daley, Suzanne. 1997a. "Apartheid Inquiry Is Told Details of Biko Killing." *New York Times* (September 11): A1+.

Daley, Suzanne. 1997b. "Fears of Shadowy Force Return to South Africa." *New York Times* (August 11): A3.

Drimmer, Melvin. 1979. "Neither Black Nor White: Carl Degler's Study of Slavery in Two Societies." *Phylon 40* (March): 94–105.

Dzidzienyo, Anani. 1985. "The African Connection and the Afro-Brazilian Condition," pp. 135–153 in Pierre-Michel Fontaine (ed.), *Race, Class, and Power in Brazil.* University of California, Los Angeles: Center for Afro-American Studies.

Ebony. 1997. "Brazil: The Awakening Giant." 52 (February): 35–36+.

Economist. 1987. "An Amazonian Tragedy." 305 (October 17): 52.

Economist. 1994a. "South Africa's Election: The Second Struggle." (April 23): 21–22+.

Economist. 1994b. "The ANC on the Road to Power." (February 19): 46+.

Economist. 1996. "South Africa: How Wrong Is It Going?" 341 (October 12): 21–23.

Economist. 1997. "Black Can Be Rich." 342 (March 15): 44+.

Fernandes, Florestan. 1969. *The Negro in Brazilian Society.* New York: Columbia University Press.

Gevisser, Mark. 1994. "Race against Hope: Fear Campaign in South Africa." *Nation* 258 (May 9): 624–626.

Gevisser, Mark. 1997. "Ending Economic Apartheid." *Nation* 265 (September 29): 24–26.

Hasenbalg, Carlos A. 1985. "Race and Socioeconomic Inequalities in Brazil," pp. 25–41 in Pierre-Michel Fontaine (ed.), *Race, Class, and Power in Brazil.* University of California, Los Angeles: Center for Afro-American Studies.

Holmes, Steven A. 1994a. "Mandela Is Facing Squatter Challenge." *New York Times* (July 6): A4.

Holmes, Steven A. 1994b. "Trying to Bridge South Africa's Rich-Poor Chasm." *New York Times* (June 29): A4.

Holmes, Steven A. 1994c. "South Africa Tries to Take the Force Out of Police." *New York Times* (June 18): 3.

Keller, Bill. 1994a. "Now the Hard Part in South Africa: Local Taxes." *New York Times* (July 9): 3.

Keller, Bill. 1994b. "Mandela's Inheritance: Bloated Bureaucracy." *New York Times* (May 15): 14.

Keller, Bill. 1994c. "Four Years after Release from Jail, Mandela Assumes Control." *New York Times* (May 11): A1+.

Keller, Bill. 1994d. "Mandela Picks Old Comrades to Fill His New Government." *New York Times* (May 7): 1+.

Keller, Bill. 1994e. "Can South Africa Do It?" *New York Times* (April 24): Sec. 4, 1+.

Lelyveld, Joseph. 1985. *Move Your Shadow: South Africa, Black and White.* New York: Times Books.

Marger, Martin N. 1997. *Race and Ethnic Relations: American and Global Perspectives,* 4th ed. Belmont, CA: Wadsworth Publishing Company.

Marx, Anthony W. 1996. "Race-Making and the Nation-State." *World Politics* 48 (January): 180–208.

Mathabane, Mark. 1986. *Kaffir Boy.* New York: Macmillan.

Miller, S. M. 1994. "Theorizing South Africa." *Footnotes* 22 (Summer): 12.

Oberholster, A. G. 1988. "Evolution of South African Society," pp. 39–58 in H. C. Marais (ed.), *South Africa: Perspective on the Future.* Pinetown, South Africa: Owen Burgess Publishers.

Riding, Alan. 1985. "Brazil's Time Bomb: Poor Children by the Millions." *New York Times* (October 23): 2.

Schneider, Ronald M. 1996. *Brazil: Culture and Politics in a New Industrial Powerhouse.* Boulder, CO: Westview Press.

Silva, Nelson do Valle. 1985. "Updating the Cost of Not Being White in Brazil," pp. 42–55 in Pierre-Michel Fontaine (ed.), *Race, Class, and Power in Brazil.* University of California, Los Angeles: Center for Afro-American Studies.

Silverstein, Ken. 1990. "Collor's 'New Brazil': Shock Treatment for the Poor." *Nation* 251 (November 12): 554–557.

Skidmore, Thomas E. 1985. "Race and Class in Brazil: Historical Perspectives," pp. 11–24 in Pierre-Michel Fontaine (ed.), *Race, Class, and Power in Brazil.* University of California, Los Angeles: Center for Afro-American Studies.

Smith, T. Lynn. 1972. *Brazilian Society*. Albuquerque: University of New Mexico Press.

South African Foundation. 1988. *1988 Information Digest*. Johannesburg: South African Foundation.

South African Institute of Race Relations. 1996. *South African Survey 1995/96*. Johannesburg: SAIRR.

Sundiata, I. K. 1987. "Late Twentieth Century Patterns of Race Relations in Brazil and the United States." *Phylon* 48 (March): 62–76.

Telles, Edward E. 1994. "Industrialization and Racial Inequality in Employment: The Brazilian Example." *American Sociological Review* 59 (February): 46–63.

Thompson, Leonard. 1990. "South Africa: The Fire This Time?" *New York Review of Books* 37 (June 14): 12+.

Turner, J. Michael. 1985. "Brown into Black: Changing Racial Attitudes of Afro-Brazilian University Students," pp. 73–94 in Pierre-Michel Fontaine (ed.), *Race, Class, and Power in Brazil*. University of California, Los Angeles: Center for Afro-American Studies.

Webster, Peggy Lovell, and Jeffrey W. Dwyer. 1988. "The Cost of Being Nonwhite in Brazil." *Sociology and Social Research* 72 (January): 136–138.

Wilkerson, Isabel. 1994. "The Suburbs of South Africa Stay Cold to Blacks." *New York Times* (November 3): A3.

Wood, Charles H., and Peggy A. Lovell. 1992. "Racial Inequality and Child Mortality in Brazil." *Social Forces* 70 (March): 703–724.

CHAPTER **10**

Racism in the Land of Dreams

■ Combatting Racism
  Local Initiatives
■ Conclusion

A t dusk on an April day in 1997, Malik Jones, a young black man, was driving in
East Haven, Connecticut. Officer Robert Flodquist ordered Jones to pull over.
Apparently Jones panicked, made a quick U-turn, and sped onto Interstate 95
toward his home in New Haven. Moments later Flodquist and a high-speed convoy of
East Haven police gave chase. The pursuit ended 10 minutes later with Jones and his
friend Sam Cruz cornered several blocks from Jones's mother's house.

Flodquist rushed from the car, broke the driver's window with his revolver butt,
and ordered Jones to turn off the motor. Terrified, Jones attempted to flee. When
Jones tried to accelerate in reverse, Flodquist fired four shots into his upper body,
killing him. Later Flodquist explained that he was convinced Jones was trying to run
him down.

Jones's death produced a very strong reaction in greater New Haven. Both his
parents were well-educated professionals who were very active locally. In the ensuing
months, they spoke out, calling for a thorough investigation but urging that their son's
death not create racial dissension.

Since the chase crossed town lines, the official investigation was the state's responsibility. As a state attorney conducted his investigation, Mrs. Jones hired her own
lawyer, who issued a statement saying he believed it unlikely that Flodquist would be
charged (Bass, 1997; Shapiro, 1997; Zavadsky, 1997).

The lawyer was correct. On September 22, 1997, State Attorney Michael
Dearington issued a report declaring that under the circumstances Officer Flodquist's
use of deadly force was "reasonable and justified" (Altimari, 1997: A1). Reaction was
sharply divided. While most police and many citizens applauded the decision, others
opposed it. Police Chief Melvin Wearing of New Haven was very critical of
Dearington's report, saying that the evidence made it clear that "Officer Flodquist
used poor judgment, his tactics were improper. We in policing have to know when to
back off" (Griffin, 1997: A1).

Some police officers accused Wearing of giving in to pressure from blacks—that as an African American he was particularly susceptible to such influence. The issue, however, did not simply divide along racial lines. White politicians, including New Haven's mayor and both candidates for governor, spoke out strongly against the report. In the case of the incumbent governor, a conservative Republican, such a stance was particularly surprising.

The day after the state attorney's report became public, the *New Haven Register* contained about 30 letters to the editor, the majority of which supported the report. A number of the letters lashed out at Jones, the Jones family, or local black organizations. Several described Malik Jones, who had several minor drug charges and motor vehicle violations, as a criminal. Edith of East Haven asked, "Where was Mr. and Mrs. Jones when their son was acquiring all this long police record?" Janet of New Haven stated, "Malik Jones lived like a criminal and he died like a criminal, and Officer Flodquist was completely justified in what he did." Gerry of East Haven wondered, "What I'd like to know is where are all these aldermen, NAACP leaders, ministers, priests, police chief, and the governor when every day African American men and boys shoot and kill each other" (*New Haven Register,* 1997: A2).

Certainly these statements leave readers with the impression that their authors, presumably whites, had basically written off Malik Jones, his family, and quite possibly African Americans in general. They saw the police as protecting them and other majority group members, acting in their interest, and as long as that was the case, believed it was not productive to dig too deeply into how they performed their duties. Little or no cultural camouflage for modern racism here: The writers' racism was quite observable.

But others, including some from the nearly all-white suburbs, expressed outrage and sorrow at the shooting. Sue from Guilford suggested that Jones feared for his life—that to stop him Flodquist should have shot the tires, not the man. She added, "Something needs to be done to change what's going on in this world" (*New Haven Register,* 1997: A2).

The rest of this chapter attempts to support her conclusion, at least as far as racism is concerned.

Combatting Racism

Public service announcements, sermons, and classroom lectures often stress that racism is wrong. But the impact of most efforts to condemn racism is limited. The problem is that such efforts do not alter structures supporting racism.

Public officials often either fail to appreciate or simply deny that reality. When a major racial incident occurs in a city or at a college or university, authorities are likely to call meetings, create task forces which issue reports, but make few meaningful changes.

Nor can one hold the mayor of a city or the president of a college or university mainly responsible for failing to eliminate racism. As we have seen throughout this book, racism permeates American society: The steps to restrict it significantly go well beyond the capacities of political or university officials. What needs to be done?

To begin, we must keep the internal colonialist perspective firmly in mind, for two reasons. First, internal colonialism suggests that racism has been relentless and widespread throughout the history of American society. Second, the implication of this conclusion is that measures to eliminate or even restrict racism require major efforts. Inexpensive, painless solutions to racism won't work. In several chapters we have considered some specific courses of action. Now our approach becomes more general, moving beyond specific topic areas.

Stephen Steinberg (1989) contended that an effective policy to eradicate the historical impact of racism must address fundamental problems. The following discussion includes a pair of Steinberg's issues, along with an additional point:

1. There must be a national commitment to eliminating ghettoes. Poverty inherited from the days of slavery and discrimination in housing have produced and maintained ghettoes, and ghetto residence restricts a person's educational and occupational opportunities. Yet on television news and in textbooks, ghettoes are discussed with the same neutrality shown suburbs. That shouldn't be: Ghettoes are among the most stark representations of internal colonialism's emphasis on the restriction of racial minorities' physical movement.

   Steinberg pointed out that to implement such a multi-billion-dollar program effectively, organizers would need to keep a vigilant watch on its activities, making certain that it did not become simply another scandal-ridden opportunity for construction, real estate, and political interests. In addition, it would be essential to enlist the participation of local individuals and groups whose perspective on ghetto dwellers' needs and interests emerges out of daily experience, not from some far removed, possibly misguided, or even racist viewpoint.

   On this topic we should consider one word of caution. A clear distinction exists between eliminating negative aspects of ghetto life and destroying vital, if poor, inner-city communities. Herbert Gans (1962) and Jane Jacobs (1961) produced classic studies stressing that most city planners tend to view poor, urban neighborhoods negatively, simply assuming that they are destructive for their residents and the city at large. As a result their orders are to bulldoze indiscriminately, with the frequent tragic result that vital communities developed over long periods of time are destroyed. Eliminating ghettoes, in short, should not mean destroying vital communities. Before determining appropriate alterations, each area must be carefully examined to assess its strengths and weaknesses.

2. Affirmative action needs continued support and growth; it represents a direct attack on the colonial labor principle. Historically, racial minorities were restricted in education and work, limited to training and jobs that would directly benefit white controllers. Affirmative action programs attempt to address historical wrongs.

   Consider some impressive successes. American Telephone and Telegraph Company, one of the largest private employers in the United States, established an agreement in 1973 with the Equal Employment Opportunities Commission to redress past discriminatory hiring practices. By 1982 the percentage of minority craft workers had increased from 8.4 percent to 14 percent of the work force, and among management the proportion of minority group members had risen from 4.6 percent to 13.1 percent. Between 1962 and 1968, the number of black employees at IBM rose nearly tenfold—from 750 to 7,251—and then in 1980 more than doubled, to 16,546. Under threat of court orders, government agencies have aggressively pursued affirmative action policies, and the results have been decisive. One result has been that since the late 1960s, the number of black police officers has increased by 20,000 (Steinberg, 1989).

In general, research found that between 1966 and 1973, companies forced to establish affirmative action programs because they were doing business with the federal government increased their percentage of black workers more than companies not required to meet affirmative action standards. Between 1974 and 1980, the number of African Americans receiving jobs because of affirmative action increased even more than in the previous seven-year period. In fact, between 1968 and 1991, the number of blacks in the work force grew by 50 percent—a solid advance even considering the expanding black population (Gleckman et al., 1993; Jaynes and Williams, 1989: 316–317; Leonard, 1985). Reviewing investigations on the topic, a team of researchers concluded that "affirmative action seems to have effected educational and occupational gains for women and for racial minorities" (Crosby and Clayton, 1990: 65).

Thus, while affirmative action has lost some of its public support, it remains a policy with some distinctly productive contributions.

3. So far we have covered two major issues addressed by internal colonialism: The first point relates to the restriction of physical activity and the last addresses problems associated with the colonial labor principle. The final issue relates to the tenet declaring minority cultures inferior and the dominant culture superior.

Even specialists on racial issues find themselves contributing to racism. Stephen Steinberg raised this point with his analysis of the term "underclass," which became popular in the early 1980s. The term focuses on individuals' and groups' failures to attain conventional rewards, thus keeping them "under" the established class system. It is a vague term, lumping together diverse ethnic and racial groups and failing to single out specific conditions, especially racism, that have played a crucial role in limiting their opportunities (Steinberg, 1989: 43–44). This term has racist, blaming-the-victim overtones, implying minorities' cultural inferiority; and it is used widely, with even experts on race relations sometimes failing to see that their analysis of racial situations is simplistic.

The previous discussion might seem inconsistent with the book's emphasis on the importance of institutional structures producing racism. Why consider individuals' attitudes? While altering institutional structures producing racism must be the priority, perhaps an individual or group's starting point should be recognition that successful steps must be modest but concrete, located in people's attitudes.

We have been discussing broad goals. But in the short term, isn't it possible to accomplish something tangible at the local level? That is where most people can readily have an impact. Consider a pair of examples.

Local Initiatives

In Oakland, California, an organization called People United for a Better Oakland (PUEBLO), whose members primarily came from poor minority groups, initiated a plan to reframe law enforcement policies in a positive direction. A member of the organization explained:

> Everyone should have the right to walk the streets in safety, feel secure in their own home and be able to go out at night without worrying about being robbed, beaten, raped, or killed. Too many of us, however, have as much fear of the police and other law enforcement agents as we do of bandits and law-breakers. (Anner, 1996: 121)

PUEBLO members were fed up with seeing their local police follow the national trend of simply sending more local people to prison and hiring more officers. So they spent a year organizing support for a different idea. The plan was to divert a portion of the money the police obtained from the confiscation of drug dealers' assets— their homes, cars, cash, and anything else of value. Normally all the funds go to help subsidize police equipment and training. Instead PUEBLO wanted at least some of the funds to go back into their community. After a year-long campaign, PUEBLO was able to get the city government to agree to turn over 15 percent of confiscated assets to community programs that would help fight crime by emphasizing prevention, not arrest and incarceration.

As the money became available, a new board was formed, with two members from PUEBLO sharing responsibility with police officers for determining what organizations should receive the funds. "The partnership is the first of its kind in the nation," *San Francisco Chronicle* reporter Henry Lee wrote, "and represents a major departure in the way police departments around the country use money from asset forfeiture programs" (Anner, 1996: 121). Furthermore, as part of a coalition of community organizations around the country, PUEBLO was able to share its strategy with organizations in other cities facing similar challenges in dealing with crime and the police.

The second situation occurred in an elementary school setting. In the summer of 1992, a mathematics professor known simply as Charles started a project called Mathematics Education, Equity, and Leadership (MEEL). Charles wanted to develop a cadre of teachers who would foster change in their schools through both their teaching and their determined effort to promote equity in their relations with others. For change to take place, Charles believed, teachers would need to use new ways of teaching that would probably prove emotionally and intellectually taxing. This would particularly be the case with mathematics because elementary school teachers' training has been especially weak in this area.

What Charles did was set up a two-week summer institute where elementary school teachers who were bilingual in Spanish and English would not only start understanding mathematics more effectively but learn about it under circumstances promoting equity in relationships.

Consider how the two goals dovetailed during training. In an early session, Charles was discussing the mathematical concept of symmetry, illustrating it with Pueblo pottery designs and pattern blocks. At one point he produced a representation of a rectangle and drew what he said were the only two lines dividing it into symmetrical parts.

Maria, a Mexican American teacher who had participated in the project's organization, listened to the explanation and then asked, "Does it have three?" She demonstrated the line she had in mind, exploring her thoughts on the topic at some length. Then the participants began to examine Maria's hunch, considering whether or not it would divide the rectangle into symmetrical sections.

What makes this situation notable is the fact that Maria had grown up in a cultural setting where women were expected to defer to men, never publicly disagreeing with them. The authors of the article about MEEL wrote:

> [T]his sort of risk-taking is quite unusual in traditional teacher development because it demands that a teacher learner expose her mathematical thinking and learning in a semi-public environment. Teachers . . . are expected to know their subject matter, and admitting that they have questions might cast doubts on their teaching ability. (Peterson and Barnes, 1996: 487)

This simple issue demonstrates the direction in which the MEEL program has been moving. One testimony to its success has been its increasing numbers. The first session had 9 participants, but by 1996 there were 30. Three-quarters of the teachers have been bilingual and two-thirds people of color.

The two projects just discussed demonstrate that there continue to be individuals with ideas and energy to improve race relations and confront racism. That is encouraging, but can we go a step further—consider how to establish some means of generating such ideas?

Where would it make sense to locate such activities? For some time those addressing issues of race and ethnicity have suggested that universities are the most reasonable sites for discussing and proposing solutions to problems in these areas (Sankowski, 1996; Trueba, 1995).

I believe that now is the time for committed colleges and universities to undertake a new approach—to establish themselves as hosts for ongoing study groups that examine and eventually make practical policy proposals about how to address specific issues related to race and ethnicity.

Let's consider several productive steps here:

1. With the support and blessing of its administrative leadership, the college or university convenes a small committee of faculty and administrators who will coordinate the upcoming activity. The members of the committee need to understand that in the ensuing activity they will be hosts and coordinators, *not* the basic decision makers in determining policies. Otherwise they undoubtedly would alienate some participants, making it likely that the eventual proposal would have limited or no community appeal.

2. The university committee's first major task is to decide on a focus issue. It could be something to do with schooling, such as literacy development; recreational programming, such as summer programs for inner-city children; housing, such as a plan for the creation of the most effective low-cost apartment construction; or many other projects. The initial choice of topic is very important, because the future of the entire venture rests on its having some positive

local impact. Above all, the task should involve something important but something where different key community groups should be able to develop policy together without undue dissension.

3. The committee approaches key individuals in the greater community—political figures, businesspeople, specialists on the topic at hand—and asks if they will come to the university perhaps once a month for ongoing discussions about the topic at hand. Again the committee faces difficult decisions about whom to include. The individuals must be local players on the topic at hand; they must be able to work with the other participants; and the university committee must take pains not to overlook people whose absence would detract from the impact of an eventual report. Furthermore, the committee should be fairly small—perhaps 12 to 20 people. A greater number will make lengthy discussion on the topic at hand unwieldy and awkward.

4. After perhaps 10 or 12 monthly meetings, carefully coordinated by the university personnel, the discussion group issues a policy report. Hopefully the group's participants and the quality of the report provide sufficient incentive to lead to some positive, decisive steps.

While this proposal for university activity is unusual, it appears that the unusual is needed: Business as usual is not solving most of our society's race-related issues. This approach could readily yield some positive developments that could help address these formidable problems.

During the meetings, sociologists and others concerned about racism will have a chance to learn firsthand how internal colonialism, the cultural camouflage for modern racism, and other concepts and ideas discussed in this book impact the participants' thoughts and actions.

Conclusion

In the years ahead, Americans will be forced to make tough decisions about race. What programs will most effectively curtail or eliminate the legacy of racism? Throughout this book we have examined the inhumanity of racism. Certainly it is fitting to do everything to be humane—to give all citizens an opportunity to participate fully in the bounty of our great nation.

It has become painfully apparent that a great shadow has spread across our society—fear of the ever-expanding violence of primarily minority citizens who have been denied access to valued opportunities and rewards. No token measures are going to buy them off. If the United States doesn't make a frontal attack on the combined forces of racism and poverty, then those formidable foes are going to grow in strength as will the terror they produce. Reviewing race relations in the 1990s, sociologist Lewis Killian concluded that new taxes and a more equitable distribution of wealth are necessary. He warned that without such measures "the new enemy will be our own underclass" (Killian, 1990: 13).

At the moment American culture is a racist culture. This condition is undeniable, regrettable, but potentially changeable. Collectively Americans should do what those addicted to alcohol or hard drugs are required to do: Look hard and long at themselves and face their problem head on, saying, "We are racist. How can we change this hateful condition?" A heartfelt realization can be a first step toward effective action. And effective action, I'm convinced, is the best way each of us can personally come to grips with this terrible enemy.

Discussion Questions

1. Discuss as concretely as possible your personal feelings about race and racism.
2. Has participation in this course changed those feelings in any way? Explain.
3. How would you propose to attack racism? Consider this issue at both the national and the local levels.

Sources

Altimari, Dave. 1997. "Reasonable and Justified." *New Haven Register* (September 23); A1+.

Anner, John. 1996. "Linking Community Safety with Police Accountability," pp. 119–134 in John Anner (ed.), *Beyond Identity Politics: Emerging Social Justice Movements in Communities of Color.* Boston: South End Press.

Bass, Paul. 1997. "Cops Who Kill." *New Haven Advocate* (May 15): 11+.

Crosby, Faye, and Susan Clayton. 1990. "Affirmative Action and the Issue of Expectancies." *Journal of Social Issues* 46: 61–79.

Gans, Herbert J. 1962. *The Urban Villagers.* New York: Free Press.

Gleckman, Howard, et al. 1993. "Race in the Workplace: Is Affirmative Action Working?" pp. 152–159 in John A. Kromkowski (ed.), *Race and Ethnic Relations 93/94,* 3rd ed. Guilford, CT: Dushkin Publishing Group.

Griffin, Alaine. 1997. "Wearing, DeStefano Rip Decision." *New Haven Register* (September 23): A1+.

Jacobs, Jane. 1961. *The Death and Life of Great American Cities.* New York: Vintage Books.

Jaynes, Gerald David, and Robin M. Williams, Jr. (eds.). 1989. *A Common Destiny: Blacks and American Society.* Washington, DC: National Academy Press.

Killian, Lewis M. 1990. "Race Relations and the Nineties: Where Are the Dreams of the Sixties?" *Social Forces* 69 (September): 1–13.

Leonard, Jonathan. 1985. "The Effectiveness of Equal Employment and Affirmative Action Regulation." Report to the Subcommittee on Civil and Constitutional Rights of the Judiciary Committee, U.S. Congress. Berkeley, CA: School of Business Administration, University of California, Berkeley.

New Haven Register. 1997. "Soundoff." A2.

Peterson, Penelope L., and Carol Barnes. 1996. "Learning Together: The Challenge of Mathematics, Equity, and Leadership." *Phi Delta Kappan* 77 (March): 485–491.

Sankowski, Edward. 1996. "Racism, Human Rights, and Universities." *Social Theory and Practice* 22 (Summer): 225–249.

Shapiro, Bruce. 1997. "When Justice Kills." *Nation* 264 (June 9): 21–23.

Steinberg, Stephen. 1989. "The Underclass: A Case of Color Blindness." *New Politics* 2 (Summer): 42–60.

Trueba, Henry T. 1995. "Race and Ethnicity: The Role of Universities in Healing Multicultural America," pp. 396–406 in Adalberto Aguirre, Jr., and David V. Baker. *Sources: Notable Selections in Race and Ethnicity.* Guilford, CT: Dushkin Publishing Group.

Zavadsky, Susan A. 1997. "City Braces for Decision." *New Haven Register* (September 21): A1+.

Glossary

Apartheid South African government policy involving racial segregation of major facilities—living areas, hotels, restaurants, buses, work locations, and even staircases and toilets.

Authority Power that people generally recognize as rightfully maintained by those who use it.

Caste system A socially legitimated arrangement of groups in which the ranking of the different groups is clearly designated, members' expected behavior is specified, and the movement of individuals from one group to another is prohibited.

Conflict theory A perspective contending that the struggle for power and wealth in society should be the central concern for sociology.

Cultural camouflage for modern racism The current reality in American society, where many majority group members' racist outlooks and behavior are hidden behind an outward appearance of favoring racial equality and are revealed only if race-related fear or opportunity for exploitation promotes their appearance.

Discrimination The behavior by which one group prevents or restricts a minority group's access to scarce resources.

Ethnicity A classification of people into a particular category with distinct cultural or national qualities.

Ethnocentrism The automatic tendency to evaluate other cultures by outsiders' cultural standards, invariably designating any different standards or ways inferior.

Frustration-aggression theory A perspective emphasizing that people blocked from achieving a goal are sometimes unable or unwilling to focus their frustration on the true source, and so they direct the aggression produced by frustration toward an accessible individual or group.

Index of dissimilarity A calculation indicating the proportion of a particular racial group that would need to change residential location in order to achieve racial evenness—a condition in which that racial group's representation throughout a city's census districts would be dispersed proportionate to its overall representation in the city.

Individual racism An action performed by one person or group that produces racial abuse.

Institutional racism Discriminatory racial practices built into such prominent structures as the political, economic, and education systems.

Internal colonialism A theory emphasizing that the control imposed on indigenous racial minorities passes from whites in the home country to whites living within a newly independent nation.

Looking-glass self Individuals' understanding of what sort of person they are based on how they think they appear to others.

Lynching One group's use of mob action to kill a member of an oppressed group, thereby warning members of that oppressed group either to accept an even more lowly status or to forsake any plans to rise above their subordinated position.

Macro level The large-scale structures and activities that exist within societies and between one society and another.

Majority group A category of people within a society who possess distinct physical or cultural characteristics and maintain superior power and resources.

Mass media The instruments of communication that reach a large audience without any personal contact between senders and receivers.

Mentoring A process by which people of higher rank and achievement instruct and guide the intellectual or career development of less experienced individuals outside of classrooms.

Micro level The structure and activities of small groups.

Minority group Any category of people with recognizable racial or ethnic traits that place it in a position of restricted power and inferior status so that its members suffer limited opportunities and rewards.

Normification Behavior that gives the impression that an individual widely considered inferior is trying to deny being different.

Pluralism A theory emphasizing that a dispersion of power exists in government or other structures within American society.

Political incorporation Inclusion of racial minority group members as significant players in political coalitions that contain some whites and successfully challenge established white conservative groups for control over a city's political activity.

Political institution The system of norms and roles that concerns the use and distribution of authority within a given society.

Power The ability of an individual or group to implement wishes or policies, with or without the cooperation of others.

Prejudice A highly negative judgment toward a minority group, focusing on one or more characteristics that are supposedly uniformly shared by all group members.

Race A classification of people into categories falsely claimed to be derived from a distinct set of biological traits.

Racism The belief that actual or alleged differences between different racial groups assert the superiority of one racial group.

Self-fulfilling prophecy An incorrect definition of a situation that comes to pass because people accept the incorrect definition and act on it to make it become true.

Sexism The belief that actual or alleged differences between women and men establish the superiority of men.

Social distance The feeling of separation between individuals and groups.

Social mobility The movement of a person from one social class or status level to another, either upward or downward, with accompanying gains or losses in wealth, power, and prestige.

Stereotype An exaggerated, oversimplified image, maintained by prejudiced people, of the characteristics of the group members against whom they are prejudiced.

Structural-functional theory A perspective suggesting that interacting groups tend to influence and adjust to each other in a fairly stable, conflict-free pattern.

Vicious cycle of poverty A pattern in which parents' minimal income significantly limits children's educational and occupational pursuits, thereby keeping them locked in to the same low economic status.

Index